The Acid Queen

The
Acid Queen

THE PSYCHEDELIC LIFE and COUNTERCULTURE REBELLION
of ROSEMARY WOODRUFF LEARY

Susannah Cahalan

VIKING

VIKING
An imprint of Penguin Random House LLC
1745 Broadway, New York, NY 10019
penguinrandomhouse.com

Frontispiece courtesy of Gary Woodruff.

Grateful acknowledgment is made for permission to reprint the following:

Excerpts from *Psychedelic Refugee* by Rosemary Woodruff Leary
published by Inner Traditions International and Bear & Company,
© 2021. Reprinted by permission of Inner Traditions International
and Bear & Company. www.innertraditions.com.

Excerpt from poem by Georgia Coxe on page 256 used with permission.

Designed by Amanda Dewey

LIBRARY OF CONGRESS CATALOGING-IN-PUBLICATION DATA
Names: Cahalan, Susannah, author.
Title: The acid queen: the psychedelic life and counterculture
rebellion of Rosemary Woodruff Leary / Susannah Cahalan.
Description: [New York] : Viking, [2025] | Includes
bibliographical references and index. |
Identifiers: LCCN 2024043049 (print) | LCCN 2024043050 (ebook) |
ISBN 9780593490051 (hardcover) | ISBN 9780593490068 (ebook)
Subjects: LCSH: Leary, Rosemary Woodruff, 1935-2002. |
Hallucinogenic drugs. | Hallucinogenic drugs—Social
aspects—United States—History—20th century. |
Counterculture—United States—History—20th century. |
Fugitives from justice—United States—Biography.
Classification: LCC HV5822.H25 C34 2025 (print) |
LCC HV5822.H25 (ebook) | DDC 362.29/4—dc23/eng/20241218
LC record available at https://lccn.loc.gov/2024043049
LC ebook record available at https://lccn.loc.gov/2024043050

Printed in the United States of America
1st Printing

The authorized representative in the EU for product safety and compliance is
Penguin Random House Ireland, Morrison Chambers, 32 Nassau Street,
Dublin D02 YH68, Ireland, https://eu-contact.penguin.ie.

For Stephen

We walk a magic carpet which, as we move, unrolls.
Thus the surprises, thus the continuity.

—M. C. RICHARDS, *Centering:*
In Pottery, Poetry, and the Person

Contents

Author's Note

This book relied on an unusually rich trove of sources. Rosemary documented her life in many ways—letters found in personal and public archives, diaries, calendars, notebooks, and several drafts of her memoir, including one published as *Psychedelic Refugee*. My most important source was the Rosemary Woodruff Leary Papers in the New York Public Library (NYPL). In addition, Gary Woodruff supplied me with hundreds of pages of archival documentation—letters, receipts, photographs, writings—that exist outside her archive. I interviewed dozens of people with firsthand knowledge of the events that transpired and consulted Timothy Leary's books, articles, archive (also in the New York Public Library), and biographies. His perspective helps to supplement and augment Rosemary's. When in outright disagreement I defer to Rosemary's version of events.

Preface

They wrote to each other in code.

Timothy Leary, the high priest of acid, had sent her letters every single day he sat in California state prison—sentenced to a near lifetime for a handful of marijuana. THE BRIEF was the escape. LAND DEEDS were the documents needed to skip town. ARIES was the code name for their lawyer who had connected them to political radicals who would help smuggle them out of the country.

During their final meeting, Timothy and Rosemary firmed up the details of his prison escape.

"I can be free," Timothy said.

"On appeal, the lawyers . . ." Rosemary responded, urging patience—even now.

"No," Timothy said. "If you do what I tell you, you can free me."

"My help could amount to human sacrifice."

"Stay here then. And divorce me."

"Divorce you? What about the operation and our child?"

"You can have that in Europe, France, Switzerland, anywhere. Just do what I tell you. It'll be fine."

"Yes, but will I be?"

Her question hung in the air, unanswered. After their meeting, Rosemary bought a blond bouffant wig, orange-pink lipstick, a skirt suit, and stockings. Her new name, Sylvia E. McGaffin, came from a dead baby's birth certificate.

She sent him one last message via telegram, giving the go-ahead, using her fertility surgery as a code word for the prison break.

This was her signature magic trick—making herself disappear.

ROSEMARY WOODRUFF LEARY is everywhere and nowhere. There's a good chance you've seen her face dozens of times without ever registering her existence. In one of the most iconic images of the twentieth century, Yoko Ono and John Lennon sing "Give Peace a Chance" in a hotel room bed in flowing white robes protesting the Vietnam War. If you allow the eye to wander, you will notice—perhaps for the first time—a striking brunette in the foreground. She sits beside the silver-haired Timothy Leary, who smiles wide, clapping, fully consumed by the moment. Unlike her husband, Rosemary stares straight at the camera—at you, the viewer—lips pursed together in a knowing grin, enigmatic and unruffled. She appears to exist outside the scene, commenting on it, an appropriate look for a woman who stood unnoticed on the edge of the world stage.

Her name hit the newspapers in 1965, after her first arrest with the fired Harvard psychologist Timothy Leary, at the Mexico border. The media didn't know what to do with the thirty-year-old, so they dubbed her "the Woodruff woman." When she married Leary in 1967, she became "the perfect love" to her husband; "the former administrative assistant" to the media; and earth goddess—nurturing, sensual, and otherworldly—to his followers. Two years later she remade herself once again into a one-named media heroine—Rosemary, the acid queen—who championed her husband's causes as he languished behind bars. For the sake of her perfect love she became a fugitive forced to face the limits of her freedom and her marriage. Fading into obscurity at the end of her life, she served as a footnote, an afterthought, in order to preserve the legacy of her ex-husband, who changed the world with his still infamous slogan "Turn on, tune in, drop out."

Timothy Leary and his supporters have dictated most of what has been written about Rosemary since. The vast majority of takes liken her to a beautiful accessory, an expensive leather bag that completes an outfit. But the contradictions abound. She was more political than her husband, some have argued, driving him insane enough with jealousy to escape prison and land in the arms of revolutionaries. To others, she was a whore who "hadn't worn a bra in years," as one recent book alleged, merely "the broad in [Leary's] bed," as a male contemporary described her. "As beautiful as she was, she wasn't the brightest star in the sky," another male memoirist wrote. She had two possible parts to play in the Leary saga: advocate or interchangeable woman. As time passed, and fewer people recognized the name Timothy Leary, the world settled on the latter. When Rosemary died in 2002, few people outside the insular psychedelic underground bothered to distinguish her from the four other women in Leary's life.

Consequently, Rosemary offers us an unfamiliar kind of hero's journey. She was the perfect hippie who was a generation older than the baby boomers. She was muse and protégée; worshipper and defier. While she was ambitious, she chose to sublimate her own greatness by shaping a mythology that didn't have room for her in it. She was an escape artist whose primary creation was herself. She was a woman who tasted fame and found it both repulsive and intoxicating and who desperately wanted to be seen while hiding from even her closest friends.

She was a person betrayed who returned to her betrayer, a woman of great integrity who also happened to be a criminal, a fugitive whose bravery helped preserve a key part of American history. Hardly anyone knew—or still knows—the debt owed to the woman behind the so-called psychedelic guru, whom the government viewed as a threat to democracy. The thread of her self-sacrifice entangles itself with the upper echelons of modern American culture and politics, including three U.S. presidents. These are just the flashiest waves in the Rosemary butterfly effect, but there are quieter reverberations across a universe of interconnected figures, some of whom continue to shape our realities, especially for people who use and study mind-altering drugs.

Members of the psychedelic movement, who know of Rosemary's work behind the scenes, call her a pioneer, whose unacknowledged sacrifice helped safeguard an underground movement. Her devotion to psychedelics—despite risk of imprisonment and ostracism—is especially relevant today. A topic that was once verboten is now top of mind for PTSD sufferers, open-minded psychiatrists, and Silicon Valley tech companies that want to patent the experience. To many, psychedelics are medicine—chemicals that can be used to heal or hack the psyche. But Rosemary's perspective, rare in the male-dominated 1960s milieu, illuminates our ongoing attraction to mind-altering chemicals that extends far beyond the clinical. She believed that these substances, which have been in use for thousands of years, provided connection to the great cosmic mysteries.

This ineffability calls us, as it did Rosemary, though fully succumbing to that call requires a level of sacrifice. At almost every pivotal point in her biography, Rosemary ran—from home, from reality, from her husbands, from the law, from her past—and at each step she made herself anew. As Rosemary herself said, "I've lived the same type of life as everyone else, just in more exotic places." Whether this is true or not, who among us cannot, at some point in our lives, relate to the driving desire to bury, or even destroy, the person we once were? Or are.

Rosemary reveals the very human cost of the pursuit of such transcendence. No net will catch us when we choose to leap into the void.

PART ONE

The Stewardess

The thing was, not to go home.

—Joyce Johnson, *Minor Characters*

One

The Genius and the Goddess

He advertised himself as Victor the Magician. An amateur, Verl Woodruff performed sleight of hand card tricks for the Saturday night crowd at his local tavern. Verl's daughter, Rosemary, seven years old, acted as his assistant, handing him props and cheering him on, even when his fingers, out of the habit and tired from his day job working on the levees in St. Louis, failed to enchant his audience.

His show ended with Rosemary jumping on the bar, kicking away the suds, and tap-dancing as the men laughed and cheered. She learned too early how easy it was for her to make men desire her.

"She ought to be in the pictures," they would say.

Verl agreed. He took dozens of photos of Rosemary—in an Easter bonnet, at a swimming hole, in frilly outfits for dance recitals, in gloves and a hat for Christmas at church—curlicued, doe-eyed, adorable. A brown-haired Shirley Temple filled with a fire that he felt compelled to document—a fire that he might have wished he had.

Beginning with her father, Rosemary would devote her life to supporting magic men, a pattern that starts long before her psychedelic origin story.

HER PARENTS RECORDED the name Rose Marie Woodruff on her birth certificate on April 26, 1935, in St. Louis, Missouri, though she would later change the spelling into the two fragrant herbs side by side: Rosemary Woodruff. A perfect combination of images: sweetly herbal, hearty, and healing. Such a small shift—visible but almost inaudible—that signals her lifelong dedication to the art of reinvention.

Like Rosemary's, her mother Ruth Woodruff's given name wasn't her own. Though she came from a family of Hegels, the name on her birth certificate is Madeline Ruth Broker. Her father, a smooth-talking debtor, "couldn't be broker" when she came into the world and, dodging his creditors, gave his daughter a new identity. Ruth, a slight woman with a fondness for fine clothes and costume jewelry—most of which, even the jewelry, she made herself—loved puzzles, the act of making meaning out of the purposely opaque. When she quit her job as a secretary at the Anheuser-Busch factory, she pursued a hobby of cryptology, the study of code breaking, which was a popular pastime in postwar America. Ruth's own code name was "Splinters"—a riff on "Woodruff."

Rosemary was a rambunctious and willful child, especially in those sweaty St. Louis summers. She played ball with the boys, outrunning most of them, jumped in the pool at Carondelet Park with her clothes on, raced in the cornfields after Sunday school with the neighbor kids, and twisted tomatoes off the vine in her mother's garden, letting the juice drip down her chin as her teeth hit flesh. But she also loved to entertain—to please. In addition to nights with her father at the local tavern, she performed as a majorette in a dance troupe during a citywide parade to boost morale during the war and starred in her school plays.

Early on, Rosemary's parents identified in her a young storyteller. They gave her a scrapbook to collect articles she had cut out about U.S. presidents' wives and a toy typewriter with which to compile a neighborhood newsletter. But Rosemary preferred the apocryphal. She spun tales about her family's Native blood and distant relations to Abraham Lincoln. None of this was true.

She was a born mythologizer. "I wanted things to be grander than they were in my little neighborhood, in my little home," Rosemary said.

She stole her mother's copy of *Forever Amber*, a doorstop of eroticism, a book condemned by the Catholic Church and banned by several states for indecency. In it, Amber, a randy orphan in seventeenth-century royal society, takes pleasure in the widest variety of suitors possible, climbing the titled ladder up to the king of England. Amber taught Rosemary that sex could be a fun and powerful tool.

She had her first mystical experience in 1943, the summer after her eighth birthday. One day she was struck—and struck is how it felt—as she was walking alone near her home. She felt a tingling sensation rise up from her spine. The trees crackled with energy. She had plugged herself into the electrical grid, and the whole world flickered in confirmation of her sudden second sight: everyone and everything were connected. It happened for a second, a nanosecond, but that shining moment of divine union would stay with her. It's common for children to report experiencing mystical states before they learn to repress or ignore them. But like many seers, sages, and shamans with similar childhood episodes, Rosemary couldn't forget it. Reality never felt fully real again. Other realms called. She longed to return to that blissful state.

The year after her brother, Gary, was born, in 1947, she became a teenager and lost her place as the center around which her cramped tract home revolved. Her maternal grandmother, Nana, moved into Rosemary's bedroom, displacing the star of the family to the couch, and took over the responsibility of raising the increasingly wayward girl. Nevertheless, Rosemary, already bored by talk of prom and homecoming, dropped out of high school by sixteen.

That same year she met a handsome air force pilot named John Bradley, seven years her senior. The two were so overcome by their mutual passion that they barely noticed the barrage of mosquito bites that covered their sweaty bodies during their nightly meetings by the Mississippi River. She knew even then that sex offered the clearest path out of her stifling home life, though she had to wait a full year to get married as he finished his flight training.

In October of 1952, at age seventeen, Rosemary became Mrs. Bradley. Everyone knew why the two had rushed to the altar. Even her baby brother had heard the rumor that she was already pregnant. She wore a pop of pink tulle under her wedding dress but shook so badly during her walk up the aisle that her father had to prop her up.

John's demons emerged during their honeymoon in Las Vegas. "Beaten when I answered back, swore, or got angry," she wrote. The newlyweds moved to an air force base located in a desert in the eastern part of Washington State. The beatings intensified. She felt marooned in a sea of military wives. "Protective of my budding self," she wrote, she left him before their first anniversary, leaving her wedding rings in the sugar bowl and returning home to her family, where she suffered her first miscarriage.

"His lower blows unmade the baby," she wrote. And that was it. No other scrap of writing exists about this loss.

～

HER NEXT ESCAPE hatch seemed the most unlikely given her circumstances as a teenage divorcée without a high school diploma. And yet off she went, persuading a train porter to let her ride for free all the way to Manhattan, a city bursting with postwar cash. It was 1953. James Dean hadn't yet smoldered in *Rebel Without a Cause*, and a bestselling book of the time was *How to Survive an Atomic Bomb*. To combat the looming terror of nuclear war, women were advised to work in the home and preserve the sanctity of the nuclear family, birthing more babies than at any other time in American history. Rosemary would do the opposite—live as a single woman in search of a career, during a time when some banks refused to provide loans to women without a male countersigner and most credit card use required a man's consent. To Rosemary, New York meant that she could finally be, as she wrote, "the star of my own movie."

She first moved into the Allerton Hotel, a towering Midtown residence for young women, where the only man allowed was the ancient elevator operator. She took on a variety of odd jobs—dog-sitting, selling handbags, and working part-time as a hostess in a cowboy-themed restaurant, greeting guests with a "Howdy" at the door. She even applied for a cab license.

Rosemary honed sophisticated tastes on a tiny budget. Her mother, Ruth, with whom Rosemary maintained steady and intimate contact through handwritten letters, sewed Rosemary clothing on demand— a velvet evening jacket or crepe A-line dresses in multiple hues, cut daringly, well above the knee. She established long-standing preferences: for the woodsy perfume Rain from Kiehl's Pharmacy on the corner of Thirteenth Street and Third Avenue; for fresh papaya juice on Eighty-Sixth Street; for sea bass at an unassuming Cantonese restaurant on West Eleventh Street in the Village. She luxuriated in a bohemian life, as the poet Diane di Prima would later write, of "laughter, the silliness and glee unscrutinized, one's blood running strong and red in one's veins."

Her beauty stood out, even in Manhattan. The cheekbones. The eyes. The regal way she carried herself. The founder of Ford Models, Eileen Ford, stopped her on the street and invited her to take test shots. When the photographer told her that she'd have to lose ten pounds, she headed straight to the kosher deli Ratner's and ordered a pastrami on rye, later bragging that she ate herself out of modeling. She did, however, attend modeling school and landed a variety of gigs—a promotional poster for Coke, a commercial for the at-home permanent "Easy to Wave," a walk-on part on *The Perry Como Show.* The headshot she carried to auditions featured the name Rosemarie Bradley, a new identity built from hybridizing her birth name and her maiden name. The headshot is of an old-fashioned woman from a by-gone era—hair freshly curled and coiffed, her tailored dress cinched at the waist, her face lacquered with red lips and arched eyebrows. Everything about Ms. Bradley exuded a prim innocence. Except for those eyes, which so clearly had experience. Beauty isn't rare, but the warmth, pain, and grace that emanated from her eyes is.

Struggling to book gigs as a model, Rosemary decided to pursue the second sexiest legal job available to her—airline stewardess. The industry was harder to get into than Harvard. You couldn't be married, weigh more than 135 pounds, or have worse than 20/40 vision. Hugh Hefner took several cues from the airlines when training the Bunnies who worked at his Playboy clubs. Male airline executives conducted surprise weigh-ins and handed out addictive amphetamine diet pills by the handful.

Rosemary attended flight training at a stewardess school in Miami, where she learned how to carry herself properly, how to fold a suit jacket and tie a scarf over a summer raincoat, and how to apply makeup in tight spaces. After her graduation, she landed a job at National Airlines and then transferred to El Al, Israel's first airline, known for employing the industry's most beautiful stewardesses. El Al executives tapped Rosemary, who stood out even among her photogenic peers, to pose for the airline's ad campaign in Switzerland. Under her beaming face, framed by a navy garrison cap emblazoned with a Jewish star, read, "Willkommen in Zürich!"

In the off-hours, she read her way through the stacks of the Tenth Street Library, claiming that by the end of her decade in New York she had read every book there. Spines popped out of her bag: the Brontës and time-traveling science fiction stories; the French dramatist Antonin Artaud, whom she never quite understood. She read as she rode the subway, as she sat in traffic on buses, en route to the airport. Her feelings about literature were best described by writer and critic Anatole Broyard: "We didn't simply read books; we became them. We took them into ourselves and made them into our histories. . . . Books were to us what drugs were to young men in the sixties."

Rosemary embodied the trend of intellectualization spreading across cities around the country—"the new consciousness." While the straight world reacted to the shadow of World War II and the threat of nuclear apocalypse by making more babies, the horrors of the prior decade also nurtured a growing counterculture, which was anti-conformist in its quest for meaning. Accelerated by cheap paperbacks and foreign translations, the spread of Eastern philosophy and religion, the popularization of jazz music, and the proliferation of French art-house cinema, a new generation of college-age men—and women—felt compelled to buck against what they saw as an empty system. The Beats, as they were called, chased the divine, not through organized religion, but through art, literature, and drugs.

There were few, if any, positive examples of bohemian rebel women to emulate in the popular culture. So Rosemary conceptualized her newfound freedom through the eyes of male writers. She recognized the double-edged nature of her quest not through the work of Simone de Beauvoir but from Beauvoir's lover, the philosopher Jean-Paul Sartre: "I am condemned to be free." And she found a justification for her self-mythologizing in the writings of Albert Camus: "Don't lies eventually lead to the truth? And don't all my stories, true or false, tend toward the same conclusion?"

Rosemary moved way downtown into a brick brownstone in the East Village right next to Tompkins Square Park to live with the second man she would marry. The accordionist Mat Mathews was born Mathieu Hubert Wijnandts Schwarts in 1924 in The Hague. When he was sixteen, the Nazis invaded the Netherlands. Mat never talked about how many of his Jewish family members he lost during the war, but he suffered recurrent night terrors.

When Mat immigrated to the United States in 1952 at age twenty-eight, he learned how to speak vernacular English in Harlem and took on a persona—aggressive, angry, fearless, and self-aggrandizing, traits that seemed to complement his steely-blue eyes and ash-blond hair. Most people fell into his thrall; he could make you feel special by tolerating you. A colleague described him as the ultimate hipster. Miles Davis loved him because he did not suffer fools and would tell anyone—didn't matter who—to fuck off.

Rosemary accompanied Mat to his gigs, watching him as he smoked a cigar while hugging his accordion, in apparent ecstasy, making it all look easy. He transformed in front of an audience, just like her father. Rosemary admired him from the seats, in her black shift dress, severe black bob, and thick black dancer's stockings. Rosemary was a Beat chick years before Kerouac's *On the Road* or William S. Burroughs's *Naked Lunch* and before followers from all over the country descended on the West Village like locusts in black turtlenecks. But most women weren't artists, writers, or musicians. They catered to men's joys while remaining "girls," who, as Jack Kerouac wrote in 1959, "say nothing and wear black"—the ideal woman of the era's enlightened men.

Like Rosemary's father, Mat could not make a living doing what he loved. While her father worked the railroad and the levees and dreamed of being a magician, Mat begrudgingly cashed paychecks as a studio musician. His apartment, though, became a popular destination for a revolving door of jazz greats—Herbie Mann, Kenny Clarke, Carmen McRae. Mat introduced Rosemary to a whole new milieu you couldn't just walk into as an ingénue from the streets.

Rosemary, out of gratitude and genuine enjoyment, would spend hours assembling spectacular spreads of thinly cut prosciutto, Dutch cheeses, and egg salads. She socialized with the artists and scholars as easily as with "the mad ones," as Kerouac called them, the downtrodden alcoholics and grifters who epitomized the Beat Generation. Rosemary filled the apartment with her charm and goodwill, knowing exactly when to speak and when to stay silent. His friends noticed. "Rosemary was a truly special person," said David Amram, composer and musician who played horns on Mat's 1957 album *Four French Horns Plus Rhythm*. "She was a wonderful woman who made the world a more beautiful place. That was her art. She elevated the world."

Rosemary learned how to get high properly with Mat and his friends. She received an education in not only how to smoke, snort, or inhale but what to expect and in which context to use. She learned to find pleasure in the sensation of her heart beating in her ears when she smoked cannabis in jazz clubs. And how to portion out correct dosing of the hash fudge she baked from Alice B. Toklas's famous 1954 cookbook. Like a growing number of Americans, Rosemary was joining an emerging drug subculture, not for medical or spiritual use, but for pleasure, identification, and belonging.

People's minds were open, their pockets were filled with postwar cash, and flights were cheaper than ever, which gave smugglers ample opportunity. This is the era when the term "junkie" emerged. Aboveground drug use also skyrocketed in the 1950s as part of the golden age of biological psychiatry when pharmaceutical companies fattened into Big Pharma. Amphetamines—used by Americans in unprecedentedly large doses—were also the key intoxicant of the Beat movement. Modern life and postwar trauma caused a slew of ailments, and psychiatry prescribed rainbow-colored pills to cure them. People found relief from their local pharmacist or back-alley drug dealer. Rosemary opted for both: diet pills for the day; marijuana at night.

Rosemary and Mat married in 1955—the same year Rosemary's divorce from John Bradley was finalized—while Mat was touring out west in Ely, Nevada, a tiny mining town on the eastern edge of Highway 50, known as the loneliest road in America. Ely had become a popular spot for UFO sightings, but she noticed only the burned-out bus station, the drunken potato farmer in a stupor at a dirty slot machine, the broke short-order cooks, the whores stalking the bingo parlors—an unfortunate backdrop for nuptials. A justice of the peace married them with two strangers as witnesses, after which Mat and his band had to work two weeks to buy their tickets back to New York.

When she introduced her new husband to her family, who had relocated to Southern California from St. Louis in her absence, they were perplexed. This strange hybrid of Jewish immigrant from the Netherlands who played the accordion and spoke like a jazz musician threw them. Still, Rosemary's father agreed to help Mat learn how to drive until Mat was good enough to circle the block on his own, which he would do in the early hours of the morning wearing only his underwear. She had moved from air force stud to eccentric accordionist, and her family didn't know what to make of it. But Rosemary did. Along with an attraction to talent, she had a need to bury her own greatness in men who in turn recognized this desire and wanted to break her for it.

Mat could be petulant and mean. David Amram watched him

regularly berate and humiliate Rosemary. "He treated her like shit," he said. Mat was also habitually unfaithful—a fact she learned around the time that a handsome composer named Charles Mills started showing up at their apartment, clearly interested in Rosemary. Charles was a prodigy who wrote symphonies with pen and paper—like Mozart—even scrawling out notations on bar napkins. He started showing up at Mat and Rosemary's apartment to share snippets of a symphony he had recorded. While he played the recordings, he would stare at Rosemary. He saw the goddess in her; she saw genius in him. And a reason to leave. Many women of the era remained in abusive relationships, but Rosemary wouldn't. Charles was an exit ramp in the shape of a man.

On the eve of a tour that would take Mat away from the city and his wife, Mat asked David Amram to keep an eye on Rosemary while he was gone. David took his job seriously—plus, he enjoyed being with Rosemary—so he picked her up in his convertible with the top down on a sunny day and took her to Wall Street. She'd never been. And who asked to join them? Charles Mills. Though David knew that Charles had the hots for Rosemary, he didn't think she had the same feelings. Together they stared at the men in beautiful suits with crazed looks in their eyes and laughed: the freaks versus the squares. At some point, David adjusted his rearview mirror and saw Rosemary and Charles in the backseat holding hands.

When Mat returned, Rosemary confessed to him about her dalliance with Charles, which had continued at their apartment after David dropped them off. She told Mat that she was in love with Charles, though even as the words left her lips, she knew it was a lie.

Rosemary moved her belongings into Charles's Lower East Side tenement apartment the next day. That night, she developed a rash and then a fever. When she began vomiting, the thought occurred to her: *What if I've made a mistake?*

She and Mat divorced in 1956. Marriage number two, like marriage number one, had ended within a year. She was only twenty-one years old.

Meanwhile, her lover Charles was possessed by an obsession with the famed Lakota warrior Chief Crazy Horse, the subject of his new symphony. Though there is no evidence Chief Crazy Horse consumed peyote, Charles devoured books about peyote cacti ceremonies of the tribes along the Rio Grande. Taking peyote was a sacred affair involving all-night dancing and drumming, working in service to something greater than the individual—like praying for the sick to be healed.

Despite the U.S. government's attempt to ban and criminalize the plant, peyote landed in the West Village through the world of Antonin Artaud, the same playwright whom Rosemary had once struggled to read. Artaud had visited the Tarahumara people of northern Mexico and attended a peyote ritual. There he took "enough," as one priest told him, "to see God two or three times, for God can never be known." *D'un voyage au pays des Tarahumaras*, published in French in 1947, passed like a lightning bolt through New York's literary avant-garde, inspiring works like Allen Ginsberg's infamous poem "Howl." Aldous Huxley's *The Doors of Perception* followed in 1954, an account of a revelatory experience with synthetic mescaline, one of the psychoactive compounds in peyote. Huxley, who had helped coin the term "psychedelic," adapted from the Greek word for "mind manifesting," extolled mescaline's ability to induce the gravity of the "blessed Not-I" and "the miracle, moment by moment, of naked existence."

"The man who comes back through the Door in the Wall," Huxley wrote, "will never be quite the same as the man who went out."

Tellingly, Rosemary's favorite Huxley work was not *Doors* but his more obscure novel *The Genius and the Goddess*, about a woman married to a Great Man who finds her worth through sex. "I subscribed to 'the genius and the goddess paradigm,'" Rosemary said. "I wanted genius men, and it was part of my heritage to be submerged, like the Jungian view of woman as reflective." Rosemary tried to convince herself that she had found her own Great Man in Charles.

But Charles was an addict. Desperately dependent on alcohol and Benzedrine, an over-the-counter nasal decongestant, Charles would crack open inhalers and swallow the amphetamine-soaked cotton balls whole to keep himself working, and drinking, for days on end. When one of his compositions was performed in Carnegie Hall, a career-defining feat for any composer, he was so blitzed that he wasn't let in.

~

CHARLES WROTE to a Texas nursery called Brown's. For $8, you could get a hundred peyote buttons through the mail. A few weeks later, they arrived. Like many of the other male psychonauts of the era, Charles needed his woman to join him. Of course, she obliged with enthusiasm.

Rosemary gagged on the bitter, metallic chunk as it slid down her throat; she hadn't done a thorough enough job of pounding it down into a paste. A heaviness in her stomach came on first, followed by waves of spasms that laid her out flat on the bathroom floor. As the effects started to come on, and with them a kind of glow, she saw the world as if she were a distant observer.

She scrutinized the low-rent tenement apartment, where she had somehow already been living with Charles for more than a year. She took in the piles of composition books and papers and cigarette butts strewn around the place, the dust and dirt and dinginess, with a stranger's eyes. The decrepit apartment, her madman boyfriend, the drinking, the obsessions, the insanity, the degradation—all wrong. These cacti were meant to be used as sacraments. There was nothing reverential here. Rosemary had not inherited wisdom. There was no chain of knowledge passed down through a shared history. She had not been trained or chosen for this. She was on her own. Peyote made her see what had been right in front of her face: She had to change her life.

She packed her bags the next day.

Two

The Book of Changes

After her breakup with Charles, Rosemary crashed at the Chelsea Hotel, then briefly moved to a fisherman's cottage in South Street Seaport before finally landing in a Greenwich Village town house apartment off Fifth Avenue with a working fireplace. Finally, a room of her own.

She made unapologetic use of that room, fully embracing the sexual revolution. "I have trouble relating to anyone I'm not sleeping with," she said. There was Kenneth Karpe, a jazz promoter consumed with get-rich-quick schemes, a doctor named Vincent, and a rumored dalliance with the baseball legend Joe DiMaggio.

Sometimes she and her best friend, Susan Firestone, a fellow divorcée, attracted the same men. After Susan ended a brief affair with a married lawyer, she introduced him to Rosemary at a party. Perhaps feeling insecure about being compared with Susan, who was a college graduate, Rosemary bragged that she was related to the German philosopher Georg Wilhelm Friedrich Hegel, who shared her mother's maiden name, and jumped into bed with the lawyer that night.

Rosemary's brother, Gary, recalls a vivid encounter during one of Rosemary's visits to the family's new house in California: As he was driving around town after a party, his headlights startled a couple passionately kissing, their bodies slamming against each other. Gary recognized his older friend Don, a James Dean–type cement truck driver whom he idolized. *That's how he does it!* Gary thought. And then the woman turned to face the headlights. He realized he was ogling his sister.

While enjoying the exhilarating tremors of the youthquake, Rosemary also experienced its aftershocks. She obtained an illegal abortion, which she only discussed in a self-reported medical history she wrote two decades later. Two friends remember her describing it as "botched." Otherwise, Rosemary did not mention it. Another revealing absence.

Through a few wives of her jazz musician friends, Rosemary heard about the artist and scientist psychonauts of the nineteenth century, who investigated the potentials of their minds by experimenting with various substances—hashish, cocaine, opium, and nitrous oxide. She read about their direct encounters with the mystical and the characteristics they shared, as outlined by psychologist William James: ineffability, transience, intuitive knowing, and passivity. Waking life was for James "but one special type of consciousness." Rosemary already had learned from her flash of second sight at age eight that there were many others.

She also embraced the legend of Madame Helena Petrovna Blavatsky, a Russian spiritualist who communed with ghosts and cofounded the mystical Theosophical Society. A world traveler, a circus performer, and a noted trickster, Blavatsky introduced an ancient "secret doctrine" that united all mystical belief systems. The Theosophical Society believed in the power of thought—that there are invisible spirit worlds, astral planes, telepathic projections, where energy is exchanged and emotions vibrate at higher or lower frequencies. Rosemary also admired the Belgian-French opera singer and explorer Alexandra David-Néel, who disguised herself as a peasant to become the first Western woman to visit Lhasa, Tibet's "forbidden city." Like Rosemary, David-Néel harbored grand ambitions as a child. "Ever since I was five years old, a tiny precocious child of Paris, I wished to move out of the narrow limits in which, like all children my age, I was then kept," David-Néel wrote.

At the same time, Rosemary discovered an English translation of the *I Ching*, an ancient Chinese divination text that had, in 1950, been reprinted with a new foreword by the Swiss psychoanalyst Carl Jung. The *I Ching*, also called *The Book of Changes*, consists of sixty-four hexagrams based on the results of six throws of coins or yarrow sticks. Each throw corresponds to a broken or solid line. Some of these lines are moving, meaning that they are in the process of trans-forming into their opposite—a broken line into a solid one, or vice versa, resulting in an entirely new hexagram. The book, one of the oldest texts in human history, is a record of a moment in flux—a doc-umentation of the invisible forces of chance and destiny. For Rose-mary, the *I Ching* was indispensable: it was a way to make sense of a situation when she didn't trust her own mind. She threw the coins before almost every single decision to come.

In 1959, Rosemary landed an uncredited role in the naval comedy of errors *Operation Petticoat*. The movie was a hit. Rosemary walked away with a little pocket change and four keepsake photographs, two with the actor Tony Curtis. Rosemary, in her Parisian striped shirt and hair tied back in a kerchief, looks like a wealthy woman on vaca-tion in St. Tropez.

During publicity for *Operation Petticoat*, the superstar Cary Grant, one of the movie's leads, went public for the first time about his use of an experimental mind drug called lysergic acid diethylamide (LSD).

He told a reporter that LSD saved his marriage—shocking his handlers and igniting a burning interest in his audience. Grant became an early proselytizer of LSD's benefits to the masses.

～

LSD WASN'T ILLEGAL—NOT YET. In 1938, the Swiss chemist Albert Hofmann, in search of a novel respiratory and circulatory stimulant for Sandoz Pharmaceuticals, synthesized the chemical LSD-25 from alkaloids found originally in ergot, a grain fungus, which can cause hallucinations and convulsions. Decades later, archaeologists would find traces of ergot in the vessels that held the potions made by priestesses in ancient Greece as part of the Eleusinian Mysteries, ceremonies performed in honor of the Greek goddess of grain, Demeter. Hofmann did not anticipate the full effects of his cold remedy until he accidentally ingested trace amounts of it five years after his discovery. For the next two hours, his world exploded. "Kaleidoscopic, fantastic images surged in on me . . . rearranging and hybridizing themselves in constant flux," he wrote. "The world was as if newly created." The LSD age had begun.

By the middle of the 1950s, American psychiatrists had embraced LSD as another in a slew of new mind-changing medications, along with antipsychotics and antidepressants. Sandoz branded LSD with the clunky name Delysid and marketed it as a psychotomimetic, a drug that mimicked madness. Sandoz sent supplies of LSD to researchers with nearly free rein to decide how to use them. The decade of scientific study that followed revealed that LSD actually provided an experience that seemed to *cure* alcohol dependence, depression, garden-variety neurosis, even homosexuality, which was at the time considered a mental illness. It did not need to be used chronically, like most other psychiatric medications. For some, one time was enough for lifelong change. Psychoanalysts started using the drug as a way for patients to thin their egos and release their subconscious, allowing for childhood or unresolved trauma to emerge. Analysts for women used LSD to treat the epidemic of "frigidity," a diagnosis attached to 40 percent of women during the 1950s, using the drug to thaw their "castrating and unfeeling" natures, as one male psychotherapist wrote. It was much easier to prescribe drugs than to try to figure out what caused the existential crises facing the modern middle-aged housewife.

LSD was also one of the many drugs that the U.S. Army tested as a truth serum as part of the CIA's clandestine MK-ULTRA experiments on humans, which started in secret in 1953. MK-ULTRA dosed military personnel and civilians—often without their knowledge—to see how these drugs "destroy integrity and make indiscreet the most dependable individual," according to one of the few surviving reports. This included pairing high doses of LSD with sleep deprivation and electroshock on unwitting psychiatric patients in Canada; secretly recording dosed male patrons at brothels in San Francisco; and studying LSD as a torture device in detention centers in Japan, Germany, and the Philippines. More subtly, the CIA also provided funding (whether directly known by the recipients or not) to many of the academic and medical institutions studying brainwashing techniques and psychedelics in this era.

Meanwhile, LSD also infiltrated Hollywood via the psychiatrist to the stars Oscar Janiger, who had administered the drug to more than nine hundred people by 1962, including Cary Grant. At this time, LSD was still considered an innocuous, relatively inconsequential drug outside the twined worlds of medicine and Hollywood—a pharmaceutical tool offered to the privileged few who could afford the time and expense (upward of $5,000 a trip, in today's dollars) of eight-hour LSD therapy sessions.

That is, until LSD escaped the lab and jumped off the analyst's couch and into the minds of people like Rosemary and her friend Susan Firestone.

Susan had been the one to suggest that Rosemary try acid. Susan had dabbled with LSD with her boyfriend, the painter Allen Atwell, who tripped at an experimental psychological research center in Millbrook, New York.

To prepare for Rosemary's first time, the two friends had rearranged her apartment, drawing the curtains, lighting candles, and building a fire in the fireplace. A bouquet on the table, placed there for the occasion, was likely inspired by Huxley's musings on flowers during his mescaline trip in *The Doors of Perception*. They cobbled together a shrine made of iconography from Eastern and Western religions that they felt augmented the "set and setting," a term popularized by Susan's boyfriend Allen's friends at the research center in Millbrook.

Rosemary noticed a new saltiness in her mouth. The flames of the candle started flickering in unison with her inhales and exhales. She fixated on her heart beating in her chest, in her ears, and into her fingertips. She became enthralled by a sudden appreciation of how the organs of her body functioned—the tissue clenching and releasing and pulsing. She felt overwhelmed by the world within her body. It was not an entirely pleasant sensation, being this aware. Senses merged. She felt absorbed by all the patterns in her apartment until the concept of intensity seemed *moronic*.

There, in her living room, an overwhelming vision came to her: the Hindu goddess of birth and destruction. Rosemary described what she saw: "Eyes upturned, crescent moons cradling the sun. Armed and militant. Dancing upon lovers, flailing the abyss."

Mother.

Kali.

Generatrix.

A woman who destroys in order to create.

Though unreal, the Kali visitation felt *true*. She had glimpsed the power of her own mind. She described the encounter: "Before my first psychedelic experience, I didn't have the feeling of belonging anywhere, even not in my own body. . . . I always felt I was alien."

She was preparing her mind for something. For what, she didn't yet know. "It was part of my journey back home," she later said, "and it was only the beginning."

By 1964, she had lost her stewardess job, an inevitable outcome for an occupation with mandatory retirement before age thirty-two. Over the years that Rosemary worked in the airline business, six stewardesses had killed themselves after being fired for aging out, one despairing about being "old and useless."

Rosemary, however, did not see herself as useless. Instead, she felt underutilized and bored, tired of her friends, New York City, and the person she had become.

So Rosemary repeated a long-established pattern and put her future in the hands of yet another man who wasn't worthy of it. Allen Eager, a genius like the others, who had mastered the tenor sax and played alongside Charlie Parker and Stan Getz, was even more "wounded than the rest," she wrote. Allen became Rosemary's new project.

Like so many people for whom the difficult comes easily, Allen took it all for granted, redirecting his energies outside music to car racing and carousing. By the time he and Rosemary hooked up, he had drifted into obscurity. He was "the epitome of graceful dissipation," Rosemary wrote. And his preferred kind of dissipation came from intravenous heroin use.

He hung with a fast crowd of "acid gypsies," as she called them, who came over to her house, played her records, destroyed her furniture, and drew on her walls. Allen had also visited the experimental center in Millbrook through his ex-girlfriend, the oil heiress Peggy Hitchcock. Hitchcock had also dated the center's lead researcher, the psychologist Timothy Leary, who, after having been fired from Harvard, continued studying the effects of psychedelics on cohabitation, creativity, and attachment. Allen had joined one experiment conducted in a stone chalet bowling alley, where a group took acid at regular intervals for two weeks. There he had learned the hard lesson of the diminishing returns of upping dosages. Everyone hated one another by its conclusion.

But when Allen invited Rosemary to join him for a weekend to visit the acid commune in the woods, Rosemary said yes.

In January 1965, Rosemary wandered the fifty-plus-room mansion, smoking a joint, in search of a session, in which a dozen or so people dropped acid simultaneously with a guide. She found one and settled in next to a stranger, whom she watched devolve from a man into a baby. As she held him in her arms, he became an ovum in her womb.

Tellingly, the one article Rosemary had clipped out a month after her first visit to Millbrook came from its lone female voice, Lisa Bieberman. The article, "Psychedelics: Who Says You Can't?," published in *The Realist* in February 1965, promoted a responsible, open-borders approach to psychedelics. Bieberman's mission—the true democratization of psychedelic use for all—would stay with Rosemary long after Bieberman grew disenchanted, leaving the movement behind to become a Quaker.

The second time she visited Millbrook, on May 1, 1965, Rosemary packed a bottle of sweet woodruff-infused German wine and a heavily underlined book by the Viennese philosopher Ludwig Wittgenstein. There's something perfectly orchestrated about bringing a text about the limits of communication and perception—key quotation: "What we cannot speak about we must pass over in silence"—to a house dedicated to testing them. She was sending a signal. A book like that was a mating call for a certain type of man. Perhaps she even suspected she'd see that man that night.

Timothy Leary spotted Rosemary as she walked into the estate with a group of friends. She wore tight bell-bottoms and a button-down shirt tied at the waist, exposing a strip of creamy skin. His knees buckled. It wasn't merely her physical beauty but her shoes—her high-top tennis shoes. He had worn the same ones back at Harvard with his tweed suits. When he spotted the Wittgenstein book poking out of her bag, he joked that she was an undercover narc—the Feds had nailed his taste in women. Hook, line, and sinker.

Timothy waited for Rosemary to notice him. She walked over, held up her bottle of sweet wine, and asked if he had an opener. He brought her into Millbrook's cluttered kitchen, past its walk-in freezer, and rifled through drawers until he found a corkscrew.

"You are the kindest man in the world," she said. "I'd like to come back."

"Anytime," Timothy replied. And he meant it—the sooner the better.

But Rosemary didn't take him up on his offer. She had a boy-friend, and despite his clear interest (and hers), she knew that Timothy was married. She didn't need him. Not yet.

Rosemary returned to New York and tried to forget the instant connection she shared with the alluring silver-haired psychologist who was about to throw away his reputation to become the martyred star of the emerging psychedelic movement.

Three

A Real Visionary

Timothy Leary's first glimpse behind the veil occurred spontaneously, without psychedelics, like Rosemary's.

In 1959, while on sabbatical in Spain with his two children, the thirty-eight-year-old recent widower experienced what he called "the death-rebirth experience" after he developed a sexually transmitted disease from a prostitute. His scalp burned. Blisters blossomed on his cheeks. His ankles ballooned and his pus-filled eyes swelled shut. He sent twelve-year-old Susan and ten-year-old Jack away to stay with family friends as he endured these agonies alone in a hotel room. "I died. I let go," he later wrote. "I slowly let every tie to my old life slip away."

Leary awoke the next morning on a chair, wrapped in his Burberry trench coat, still shaking but improved. He wrote three letters: the first, quitting his job as a psychologist at the Kaiser Foundation Hospital back home in California; the second, cashing out his insurance policy; and the third, outlining his new philosophy of consciousness.

Timothy Leary's life as a prophet had begun.

∿

FEW WOULD HAVE SEEN that last turn coming. Born in Massachusetts in 1920, before the invention of sliced bread and car radios, Leary learned to navigate a chaotic household headed, at least nominally, by an alcoholic. Timothy "Tote" Leary, an army dentist, abandoned his family for good when his namesake son was thirteen and Leary, an only child, displaced his rage onto his mother, Abigail. He resented her, he would later say, because of the great burden of her lofty expectations. Abigail wanted her special son to follow the family line and become a priest, like her beloved uncle. She scraped her pennies together to give him the best education possible, and he, in turn, seemed eager to thwart her. Leary would say he sought women who were nothing like his mother, yet he would spend his life shaped by and resentful of the women devoted to him.

In his first and only year at West Point in 1940, Leary was court-martialed for drinking in public. During the interrogation he named the other cadets who had also been drinking. Though he was eventually found not guilty, his peers ostracized him for months. It was a defining moment as an outsider. He would dedicate his psychology career to making sense of the invisible forces that shape an individual—brain, behavior, and, most important, relationships.

Leary left West Point after a year to study psychology at the University of Alabama until he was expelled for spending the night with his girlfriend in the women's dormitory. Now without a deferment, Leary was drafted into World War II, but never fought. The army instead placed him at Deshon Hospital in Pennsylvania as a psychometrician, where he administered psychological tests to veterans. At Deshon, Leary experienced the allure of augmented reality when a raven-haired audio technician named Marianne Busch mistook him for a patient and tested his hearing. Unbeknownst to him, Leary actually had hearing loss, the result of a shot fired too close to his ear during basic training. Marianne fitted him for a hearing aid. The world not only sounded different; it had irrevocably changed. They embarked on a wild affair and married less than a year later.

The Learys had two children—Susan in 1947 and Jack in 1949—and moved to California, where they built their dream house in the redwoods of the Berkeley Hills. Though the house was relatively modest, it had a grand, open feel—modern, future thinking, communal—thanks to its orientation toward the sliding glass doors at the back that looked out on the bay, even to the Golden Gate Bridge on a clear day.

By his early thirties, Leary had received a PhD in clinical psychology at Berkeley and was running a research lab at Kaiser Foundation Hospital, an impressive feat for a man so young. Despite this early success, Leary was, in his own words, becoming "a middle-aged man involved in the middle-aged process of dying." He watched football, drank martinis, grew a paunch, and had affairs. An original mind becoming a cliché.

People called the Learys "the Fitzgeralds"—like the famously toxic literary couple. Their fights were explosive. Marianne, blackout drunk, would wander the neighborhood without shoes. Leary openly dated a colleague, the Kaiser Foundation secretary Mary Della Cioppa, and planned to leave his wife and children for her.

On October 22, 1955, his thirty-fifth birthday, Leary woke up to find a note left on Marianne's pillow: "My darling, I cannot live without your love. I have loved life, but through you. The children will grow up wondering about their mother. I love them so much and please tell them that. Please be good to them. They are so dear."

Leary frantically searched the house until he spotted the closed garage door. He could smell exhaust. When he pried the door open, he found Marianne in the front seat of the car in her nightgown. Six-year-old Jack ran out in his pajamas and saw his mother's limp body. Leary called out for Susan, eight years old, to run to the firehouse to get oxygen. Marianne died on the way to the hospital.

Within months, Leary had married his paramour Mary in a ceremony in Mexico that might or might not have been legit. The marriage ended a year later.

In 1957, he established himself as a serious contributor to personality theory with his highly regarded textbook *Interpersonal Diagnosis of Personality*. In the book, Leary described how identity is formed by relationships and the need for love and power (or their opposites, hate and dependency). Leary laid out his belief that social interactions revolve around game playing: the jail trains the prisoner to behave like a criminal; the sullen introvert teaches others to reject him; the psychiatrist takes on the veneer of authority over the lost patient. He believed that psychiatrists had very little—if any—ability to alter these predetermined roles. The power to adapt or improve landed squarely on the individual. He dedicated the book to Marianne.

The textbook and its resulting four-hour interpersonal assessment, visually depicted as four quadrants, called the Rose of Leary, would be used by employers in health care and government agencies to anticipate how personality types will behave in different social settings.

In the spring of 1959, after his illness-induced "breakthrough breakdown," as he called it, in Spain, out of a job and working on a new book, Leary moved his family to Florence. A chance encounter in Italy with the famed Harvard psychologist David McClelland, an expert in motivation and personality, led to an offer for Timothy to take a lecture position at the university. McClelland would later say he was impressed not only by Leary's work but also his charm. Timothy packed up his children again and moved them to a house in Newton

Centre, enrolled them in school, and bought himself an Ivy League tweed jacket.

The summer after his first year at Harvard in 1960, he traveled to Mexico and found God, the devil, and all of cellular history after eating seven musty magic mushrooms. While ten-year-old Jack chased an iguana, Leary's life shifted course. It "was above all and without question the deepest religious experience of my life," Leary said. "I learned more about psychology in the five hours after taking these mushrooms than in the preceding fifteen years of studying and doing research in psychology."

A more experienced friend suggested that he read *The Doors of Perception*, and like Rosemary he immediately felt drawn through a Door that had always been there, like discovering a new room in a childhood home. "You are never the same after you've had that one flash glimpse down the cellular time tunnel," Leary wrote. "You are never the same after you've had the veil drawn." When he returned to campus, his new aim was to broaden and deepen the human experience by studying psychedelics.

Within a year, Leary launched the Harvard Psilocybin Project. With full support of the department, he recruited a small army of devoted professors and graduate students, notably the ambitious twenty-nine-year-old assistant professor Richard Alpert. A rich kid whose father ran the East Coast railroad system, Alpert, who would later take the name Baba Ram Dass, seemed bred for his fancy position in his tailored suits and black-rimmed glasses. But he couldn't shake his impostor syndrome. He also had a hidden life. Alpert spent his nights in the shadows, cruising for men in parks and public restrooms. That is, until Timothy moved into a repurposed typist's closet next to his corner office on the psychology floor and introduced him to psychedelics. Timothy, a decade older, became Alpert's mentor and surrogate father. "Now here is a man who is a real visionary," Alpert thought.

The third spoke in the Harvard wheel, a graduate student named Ralph Metzner, provided the intellectual rigor. Metzner, born in Germany but educated in Great Britain, earned a reputation as a reliable, learned, and practical sounding board for many of Leary's ambitious ideas. As the writer Eve Babitz, who dated Metzner, wrote, "I cannot believe that either Timothy Leary or Richard Alpert ever got in the way of Ralph Metzner doing the hard part." Metzner's first experience with psychedelics, on a high dose of crystalline psilocybin, brought him nearly to suicide. The hazy hallucinatory lines coalesced into a "deadly mechanical spider's web." The roar of a passing train made him yearn for it to "barrel through the house and kill me." His first call was to Leary, who helped soothe him over the phone. Though it was humbling, Metzner said he never regretted that experience; to the contrary, it helped him realize the importance of providing a framework around which to guide and integrate these altered states. This would remain a lifelong interest.

Out of hubris or fear, Leary avoided LSD. That is, until British LSD evangelizer Michael Hollingshead appeared on Harvard's campus. Hollingshead was a mystery, a charlatan and confidence trickster—worse, maybe. "If you encountered Hollingshead's dark side you were in danger of losing your money, your mind or possibly both," his biographer Andy Roberts wrote. No matter, Hollingshead will forever be memorialized as the man who turned Leary on when he offered a lick from his infamous acid-laced sugar paste–filled mayonnaise jar.

LSD was supercharged compared with psilocybin. Psilocybin is an earthbound trip, while acid shoots you straight into outer space. Leary saw himself as a "pathetic clown, the shallow, corny, twentieth-century American." The world became a literal stage—two-dimensional, flat. He watched his son sitting in front of the television and his daughter spinning her rock 'n' roll records like every other teenager. Humans were nothing but puppets. Leary walked around in a daze for days, fully consumed by the fear that if nothing was real, if it was all for show, then life had no meaning. It would take several more trips for him to discover the amoral comedy buried in nihilism: if nothing really matters, then he might as well have some fun.

A series of now famous experiments commenced. The Harvard Psilocybin Project sent the psychedelics to artists, writers, and jazz musicians in New York City—Jack Kerouac, Dizzy Gillespie, Allen Ginsberg, and William Burroughs—to study the effect on creativity. One recipient of the Harvard researchers' magic pills was the jazz saxophonist Allen Eager, who had just started dating a beautiful, young ex-stewardess named Rosemary Woodruff.

The Concord Prison Experiment, which started in 1961, investigated how psilocybin use altered the behavior of prisoners at a maximum-security penitentiary in Massachusetts. The team tripped with the inmates to test the drug's effects on recidivism. The results were overwhelmingly positive, with return imprisonment rates reportedly cut nearly in half. In 1963 the results of the Good Friday Experiment, which tested psilocybin's ability to induce religious ecstasy, were also published. Two groups, one control and the other receiving psilocybin, attended a Mass on Good Friday at Boston University's Marsh Chapel. Almost every participant who received psilocybin reported profound mystical experiences. Psychedelics, in other words, provide a bridge between secular scientific theory and spirituality.

The majority of the experimentation occurred at Leary's home. Leary, Alpert, Metzner, and about fifty others facilitated drug trips for more than two hundred people. The sessions took place in the supportive "relaxed and natural atmosphere" of Leary's living room with guides, who would almost always trip with their subjects. The guides would ensure that the space contained comforts: "easy chairs, rugs and cushions" and a "wide range of recorded music, books, paintings, and prints," approved lighting, and an array of food and drink options. Some were interviewed as they tripped. The subjects would then integrate their experience by filling out trip reports and questionnaires about their subjective experiences. Graduate students eagerly offered themselves up as guinea pigs.

In Leary's house, the Harvard group developed the concept of set and setting—the project's most important contribution to psychedelic science. Set denoted a person's mindset or baggage coming into the session—personality type, mood, and expectations. Setting described the environment that surrounded the individual, everything from established cultural norms to the other people present to the color of the couch cushions.

Researchers found a clear imbalance of power between guides and the guided. "The nervous system, stripped of all previous learning and identity, is completely open to stimulation (and here is the joy, the discovery, the revelation), but it is also completely vulnerable. Naked suggestibility," Leary later wrote. Guides held almost godlike sway— at least during sessions. "A frown. A gesture. A word . . . and whoom! you are catapulted into unexpected orbit." Boundaries dissolved between observer and participant. At least seven women declared their love for Leary after tripping with him.

Allen Ginsberg wandered around Leary's house naked and tripping. An ex-con from the Concord Prison Experiment lived in Timothy's attic, along with Michael Hollingshead. All the while, Susan and Jack went about their lives as typical teenagers. Sometimes the Leary kids would become unwitting participants in their father's experiments. During one session, a colleague on a high dose of psilocybin pills aggressively crashed Susan's slumber party and refused to leave.

Leary, also drugged, debated whether to intervene. Eventually he came to the painfully obvious conclusion. *"She doesn't want you there,"* he said and forced the adult student out of his teenage daughter's bedroom. At this point his children avoided their father's drugs. "I was afraid I would get high and I would not come back to my normal level of consciousness," Susan said.

Alpert and Leary took on the roles of psychedelic parents to their graduate students. "I took care of the kitchen," Alpert said, "the children, the relations with the administration and the bank statements and the neighbors and the garbage and the dogs and the whole thing that Jewish mothers do. But man, his was the vision." Like a good wife, Alpert handled the day-to-day responsibilities of keeping house, which left Leary unfettered to pursue his research endeavors. Yet, despite Alpert's dedication and Leary's talk of opening minds, he never accepted Alpert's sexuality.

Rumors of Leary's unethical experimental practices hit the Harvard establishment just as infighting erupted inside the greater research community after the Food and Drug Administration introduced stricter regulations around psychedelic studies. Results, many skeptics found, were often not replicable, and positive outcomes seemed directly correlated with the enthusiasm of its researchers.

The same year, in 1962, during the FDA clampdown, *The Harvard Crimson* ran a series of exposés on the Harvard Psilocybin Project, and word reached the pages of national newspapers like the *Boston Herald* and *The New York Times*. By 1963, Alpert was fired for giving out psychedelics to an undergraduate he was trying to seduce, and Leary, who went AWOL from teaching his classes, was not invited back to lecture.

Once freed from the constraints of academia, Leary broadened his message and rejected his earlier interest in using conventional scientific methods to study LSD. He started to promote the widespread use of LSD without the oversight of trained medical professionals—but rather in the living room of all Americans. He advocated for "the right, right now, of thoughtful Americans to change their own consciousness"—a frighteningly difficult notion for mainstream society to wrap their minds around.

To Leary and his brethren, LSD was a tool—more akin to the microscope than medication—that enabled trained users to grasp cellular, molecular, and atomic energy. LSD could make you see the materiality of what physicists, biochemists, neurologists, and biologists were merely theorizing about. As a psychedelic user, you could experience what Leary described as "the long telephone wire of history that goes back two billion years."

Still it wasn't enough just to drop acid and see. Tapping into this knowledge required dedicated practice. You could take LSD for kicks—and Leary advocated this within bounds (he urged people to have at least one experienced guide with you the first time and always in a supportive set and setting)—but the ultimate goal involved the intentional preparation of body and mind to put these chemicals to their greatest use.

The first training center for this type of work opened under the name the International Foundation for Internal Freedom (IFIF) in Zihuatanejo, Mexico, in the summer of 1962. Funded by the heiress Peggy Hitchcock, the IFIF hosted about forty or so people—including Harvard expats, psychiatrists, a rabbi, and a stockbroker—to study spiritual growth and behavioral change through repeat psychedelic use while surrounded by the ocean and the jungle. A year later a dead body, unrelated to the IFIF, washed up on a nearby shore. The Mexican government used the corpse to kick the bewildering group out for "besmirching the name of Mexico." Leary, the leader, was banned from returning to the country.

Back in America that fall, Peggy Hitchcock swooped in and found them a new home on her twin brothers' estate in Millbrook, New York, for $1 a year.

At Millbrook, the group continued their Mexican IFIF work. They practiced communal child rearing and experimented with vegetarianism and gardening, while also studying the liberated mind through ritualized psychedelic use—pleasure offering a route to transcendence. They often tested their theories out on willing subjects in residence. In one, called the Third Floor Experiment, a person would pick a room and sleep with whoever else chose to share their bed. In another experiment, people drew straws and had to spend a week dropping acid alone or with another randomly chosen person. While Leary still pulled heavily from his background in behavioral psychology, the group rebranded as the Castalia Foundation, a name Leary took from the Hermann Hesse novel *The Glass Bead Game*. The new Millbrook philosophy incorporated aspects of neuroscience with Buddhism, Hinduism, and Taoism along with a few dashes from the emerging Human Potential Movement, which centered on self-actualization. "The history of our research on the psychedelic experience is the story of how we learned how to pray," Timothy said.

Communal living arrangements like Millbrook, though closely associated with the hippie movement that hit its stride in 1967, were still unusual in 1963. The estate's two thousand plus acres became a site of mysticism and social experimentation, where scientists, philosophers, and artists could gather to plumb, augment, and challenge the psyche in order to change behavior and transform the self. They believed that this work would reshape the community—and, eventually, the world.

Only whispers from the outside world reached them on their spiritual path: the assassination of JFK, the signing of the Civil Rights Act, the rise of the United States' involvement in the Vietnam War.

It was, as Alpert later said, "a cult turned inward."

In 1964, Leary, Metzner, and Alpert released the seminal *The Psychedelic Experience*. The book, based off the Buddhist text *The Tibetan Book of the Dead*, a text used to guide consciousness through the stages, or bardos, between life and death, provided, for the first time, an instruction manual that could program the psychedelic experience. *The Psychedelic Experience* offered "road maps for new interior territories" that could lead, if used correctly, to ego death. The book continued to popularize the concept of set and setting and shaped a whole generation of emerging psychedelic users, including John Lennon. The book's most famous line—"Whenever in doubt, turn off your mind, relax, float downstream"—appear abridged in the Beatles' "Tomorrow Never Knows." To this day, almost every American dropping a tab has an imprint of what to expect thanks, in part, to this manual.

Leary became the face, the rising celebrity, of the democratized psychedelic movement. He coined memorable slogans, such as "LSD is a strange drug that produces fear in people who don't take it."

Timothy Leary was a man on his way to becoming a myth.

In June 1965, a month after Rosemary's first encounter with Timothy Leary at Millbrook, she attended a gallery opening in downtown Manhattan. She was embarking on her first Saturn return, an event that occurs every twenty-nine years or so, when her sun planet returned to the same degree and sign of her birth. She had dropped a sizable dose of acid a few hours before and felt satisfied and blissful.

Rosemary recognized Timothy's voice from across the gallery, lecturing and bewitching his audience like a sweet-talking snake charmer. She heard the words "audio-olfactory-visual alternations of consciousness," and she smiled, despite herself, at the obtuseness of the phrase. She noted his flat-footed buoyant stride that "emitted ebullience, enthusiasm on upturned toes." Vitality. Verve. Gusto. A delightful and bewitching Irish faerie devil who made each person he encountered feel special. His eyes twinkled—the wise fool—and suddenly you felt you were both laughing at an inside joke. Though he spoke about himself as a visionary prophet, he peppered that talk with acknowledgments of his own absurd chutzpah: "Of course for every hundred men who think they are pioneers, 99 percent are cranks. And I may well be a crank. That's the statistical risk you take in my business."

Over six feet tall and thin, with high cheekbones on a handsome face that projected high IQ, he drew women, even in this small, intimate gallery opening. "I adore holy men," one enamored ex-lover said of him. When he approached and remembered her, Rosemary couldn't help herself. She felt flattered. Out of all the women, he had chosen her. She identified in herself an "early imprint, a sexual glint" from her youth of the attraction she felt for a silver-haired father in her neighborhood with whom she used to play softball. To Rosemary, Timothy was "the first draft of pure oxygen after a trip to the dentist's chair."

Timothy also happened to be staggeringly *interesting*. His mind did backflips while the rest of the world watched and cheered him on. He had a kind of animal magnetism, a hot heat.

And most important, what he was speaking about was not only kinetically exciting and vital; Rosemary knew in her heart that it was also *true*. She had felt it on that first peyote trip that had changed her life; she met it face-to-face when Kali came to her on LSD.

And yet she sensed something underneath her attraction: his vulnerability and irresistible tenderness. She noticed his hearing aid. "It was love and pity at first sight," she said. Her own hook, line, and sinker.

"You remind me of someone I once loved," he told her.

"Let's see." She didn't miss a beat as if reading lines from a Noël Coward play. She pulled out a pocket two-way mirror and held it between them. She angled the mirror to hit the spot where they could see their faces transposed on each other.

"My hair and your smile. My nose and your eyes. What do you see?" she asked.

"Good match," he said, lit a cigarette, and handed it to her.

"Perhaps."

They clinked glasses.

As Wittgenstein wrote, "An entire mythology is stored within our language."

Rosemary would throw herself wholeheartedly into history by jumping into Timothy's arms.

Four

The Match

Rosemary tried to conceal her black eye with makeup, but the bruising refused to be covered. Allen's bad behavior had escalated into physical abuse. He had pawned Rosemary's jewelry to pay off debts to hostile drug dealers. He also cheated and, unlike Mat, didn't have the decency to hide it. His "junkie queen," as Rosemary described one of his lovers, often arrived with drugs. Sometimes, when Allen couldn't pay her, she'd tear up Rosemary's apartment in search of anything of value. Out of options and over her head, Rosemary looked for another escape route before having to take what she considered the last resort, moving to the West Coast to live with her family.

Rosemary enlisted her friend Susan, who sought help from Peggy Hitchcock, the heiress who had dated Allen before Rosemary. "We have this friend, and she has now been living with Allen, and I think he's been abusive," Susan told Peggy.

Peggy was shocked. She had dated Allen for three eventful and sometimes unpleasant years. There were two abortions and a broken engagement—but never physical abuse. Despite herself, Peggy still had a soft spot for Allen, especially because he was the reason she had tried acid. When she had finally called their relationship off for good,

Peggy went into therapy to try to figure out why "I am choosing someone who is a junkie." Her therapist supported her decision to try some mescaline to unlock the answer. A mutual friend connected her with Harvard's Timothy Leary, whom she dated on and off for several years in a "swinging door relationship," which ended when he announced his engagement to model Nena von Schlebrügge, his current wife.

Though Peggy had only met Rosemary at parties, she felt an immediate need to intervene on her behalf. "We should get her out of there and up to Millbrook," Peggy told Susan.

The plan worked even better than Rosemary dared hoped. It just so happened that Timothy Leary was visiting the city and planned to head back upstate that night. Rosemary didn't need convincing. The decision had already been made.

Timothy arrived promptly outside Rosemary's apartment building in a borrowed rusted-out Jeep. In haste, Rosemary grabbed only a few items, not realizing this would be the last time she'd be in her apartment for weeks. Walking to his car, she saw herself as she imagined he did—with her bruised face and untied tennis shoes. She burned with embarrassment.

The broken muffler filled the Jeep with bluish-gray smoke, forcing them to drive with the windows all the way down in the swampy heat of the August night, even on the highways. A constant knocking sound accompanied the roar of the engine. But Timothy had champagne on ice with flutes. Rosemary, sitting in lotus position, refilled his glass as he drove.

"Why didn't you come to Millbrook when I asked you?" Timothy asked, referring to the invitation he made during their first meeting.

"I didn't need rescuing then." Rosemary, a verbal jouster, had a breezy humor and quick turn of phrase—skills Timothy would come to respect and profit from.

"What have you been doing all summer?" he asked.

"Dying by degrees of heat and madness," she quipped.

"I have a theory about death. Would you like to hear it?" He throttled the gas, dive-bombing between cars as they headed out of the city. "Ecstasy comes to everyone at that moment, dying is a merging with the life process. What do you think?"

"I don't know. I really don't believe that death is a way out," she said. "But lately I've found myself wishing this life would cease."

"So have I, many a time."

They didn't yet know how many wounds they shared.

Rosemary prodded him with the question at the forefront of her mind: "How is your lady?" She couldn't ignore Nena von Schlebrügge any more than the rest of the planet could. Her face sold cars and makeup in ads on New York City buses.

"Which one?" he asked.

"You've got more than one?"

"Had, alas, those pleasures are now forbidden."

"Will I find them in the attic behind a secret door?" She owned a well-thumbed copy of *Jane Eyre*.

Boom. Boom. Boom. The one-liners flew back and forth. Timothy realized that in addition to her beauty she could keep up—one-up, in fact. He could barely contain his giddiness.

"Actually, she's with a Tibetan monk," he said, speaking of Nena's new boyfriend and future husband, the Buddhist scholar Robert Thurman. "Of the second I rarely speak."

"And the first?"

"She killed herself on my thirty-fifth birthday."

Rosemary noticed a flickering in his eyes. His first wife's death set forth a path he wouldn't have likely forged without it—a path that led him barreling upstate into the future with Rosemary in this smoked-out, beat-up car.

"Now what would you want to happen at Millbrook?" he asked her.

"Sensual enjoyment and mental excitement."

"What else?"

She examined him. A handsome professor. Absolutely brilliant. Blue eyes twinkling. The energy between them vibrant and exciting, strong hands at the wheel.

"To love. You, I suppose."

In Timothy's retelling, she utters a different phrase.

"I want to fall in love with you."

Similar words—two very different takes.

A NEAR-FULL MOON lit their way through the ornate entryway gates of Millbrook's Hitchcock Estate—a Grimm's portal. They drove through a tunnel of trees, limbs dancing in the wind above them as they bumped over the stone bridge. Timothy told her about Millbrook's original owner, the German immigrant Charles F. Dieterich, who made his riches installing gas lamps around American cities. Timothy liked to say that the "precedent for illumination we took as a good omen." Dieterich named the sprawling estate—the result of combining five different farms—Daheim, German for "at home." He built the main mansion, the "Big House," in 1912, which boasted anywhere from fifty-three to sixty-four rooms, depending on whom you asked. There were also half a dozen or so other buildings on the property, including the stone chalet bowling alley, a tennis house, a Bavarian Baroque gatehouse at the entrance, a multilevel barn, and a gold-leafed-ceiling bungalow that Dieterich built for his son. Dieterich was a rumored Rosicrucian, a spiritual tradition that combined features of alchemy with Christian and Jewish mysticism. Some visitors believed that he had set up gateways all over the property where one could travel in time.

As they drove, Rosemary spied the illuminated windows of the Big House. The four-story Queen Anne Victorian contrasted majestically with the acres of gardens and dark virgin woods. Only when they got closer did she notice the disrepair and decay that somehow managed to add to its grandeur. Rosemary's eyes didn't know where to rest—all angles and asymmetry, pyramidal rooflines, gables and eaves, turrets and towers.

Timothy opened the front door for her like a gentleman. More for her eyes to take in: the carved woodwork that Dieterich had shipped in from German masters, fading tapestries on the wall, ceilings inlaid with wooden panels, a giant bell on the stone terrace, mismatched flourishes—local vintage store finds, harem-style low couches surrounded by pillows, Middle Eastern decor, a bed on the floor under a statue of Ganesh, the space covered in books and records. A place "designed for soft landings," as Timothy would write, where one could "learn how to use psychedelic drugs to create a heaven on earth."

A sign in the hall asked visitors to "kindly check your esteemed ego at the door."

"This is your base as long as you want it," Timothy told Rosemary. With a smile, he led her upstairs to a room in a tower, then turned on his heels and left. No drugs, no sex—subverting expectations, as always.

Rosemary woke up alone in bed the next morning. She recalled the physical sensation of the night before, feeling Timothy in his own bedroom below. Though not on anything stronger than pot and champagne, she had sensed his desire radiating through the floorboards, suspending her in a state of anticipation. She had dreamed of a restless man pacing in a red robe.

Rosemary dressed in matching flowing white cotton drawstring slacks and top and joined Timothy in the foyer to stretch and breathe together. They held hands as they walked the estate, stopping at a lake nestled deep in the dark forest. He told her that he had thrown his wedding band in this lake, in the same spot where a man had drowned. The marriage to Nena was dead, too, he told her, after a disastrous honeymoon in India. As was his relationship with Richard Alpert. Timothy had kicked his friend out of Millbrook before Rosemary's arrival due to Alpert's increasingly debauched behavior and his open affairs with men. Timothy was without a female anchor. He was ready and open for Rosemary to fill the empty seat beside him.

Now, finally, Rosemary and Timothy kissed, succumbing greedily to their longing and disrobing by the waterfall.

That night, they dined with Timothy's friends Flo and Maynard Ferguson, who lived in the three-story stone gatehouse with their four children. Maynard was a well-known big band jazz trumpeter. Rosemary enjoyed Maynard's swagger, but gravitated to Flo, a beautiful, fine-boned creature who carried Sartre's *No Exit*. She was warm and open, witty and intelligent without being too academic, and experienced, too. She was the one who had urged Timothy to take the plunge with her for both of their first trips out of Michael Hollingshead's mayonnaise jar. Rosemary had found a sister.

Later, in Timothy's bedroom, sitting on an open windowsill under the midnight sky, Rosemary thumbed through the draft pages of Timothy's new work in progress, *Psychedelic Prayers*, a book of poetry, designed to ground and orient acid trips, inspired by the *Tao Te Ching*, a twenty-five-hundred-year-old Taoist text. She asked him to explain a few of his poem translations.

"I'll tell you a story," he said and blew out the candle by the bed. They were in the dark now under the full moon. He started to speak, his voice gliding over her body. "Once there were three princes; their father, the king, sent them on a quest. To answer the riddle of what every woman wants would prove which prince was the best."

The power in his voice proved irresistible. Aroused, she could barely follow the words.

"And this is what the witch replied: Complete submission is the answer to a woman's pride."

Their love took quick shape. Their brains synchronized, neurons firing together in total harmony. They moved to the former bowling alley, where Timothy read aloud from *The Psychedelic Experience* as they catapulted off into space. "I looked at you and both of us were surrounded by fields of energy. We kissed and held each other. Something clicked inaudibly. . . . The cosmic union," he later wrote.

She felt it, too. "A couple now. I would not be leaving for California anytime soon," she wrote.

That next morning after making love at dawn, the new couple dragged buckets of paint to the second-story porch roof and painted eight-foot-high interlocking triangles on the red brick chimney— ancient geometry of sexual fusion.

There had been many women in Timothy's life before, but Rosemary felt certain that Millbrook was *her* home now.

❧

THEIR BRIEF INTIMACY was interrupted that full-moon weekend when a group of paying guests arrived for a seminar.

Acid had become harder to buy since the early days of open access at Harvard as the FDA instituted new research protocols, which culled the number of authorized research projects in America from hundreds to seventeen before Timothy had even left Harvard in 1963. They couldn't just order up thousands of doses from Sandoz anymore, because it had lowered the spigot of distribution to a trickle. In less than a year, Sandoz would deliver, in an armored car, its remaining stockpile of LSD to the National Institute of Mental Health. Now Timothy and company relied almost exclusively on Hollingshead's connections and underground chemists. To make matters worse, the group lacked regular access to capital and were thousands of dollars in debt. Timothy, as the group's leader, decided to monetize his notoriety by inviting rich New Yorkers to spend a summer weekend at Millbrook for $75 ($700 today) to transcend reality *without* the aid of drugs.

Twenty or so visitors were greeted at the door of the Big House by a young woman who handed them the first of a series of notes:

> *Welcome to an*
> *EXPERIENTIAL WEEKEND*
> *Your weekend in Millbrook has been planned to provide a series of novel and consciousness-expanding experiences.*
> *The first step in the process of going beyond your routine and familiar patterns is a period of*
> *ABSOLUTE SILENCE*
> *Shortly after your arrival at Castalia you will be given further instructions. Please do not engage in conversation of any kind until the breaking of the silence is publically announced.*
> *For now—*
>   *LOOK*
>   *LISTEN (to the non-verbal energy*
>   *around you)*
>   *EXPERIENCE DIRECTLY*

In their rooms, they found MESSAGE #2: silence, again ("One of the oldest methods of getting high," Timothy said) and instructions to turn off the light, spend twenty minutes directing their gaze at a lit candle, and continue meditating until they were ready to take on MESSAGE #3, which outlined "the game" of the weekend. Social roles were now discarded, bedsheets replaced clothing, and chores were assigned. Some would cook dinner. Others would clean toilets. During the weekend, at any odd hour, a bell would ring, prompting everyone to run to their journals and record themselves: Where are you? What societal charade were you maintaining? They dyed the scrambled eggs green and the milk black to destabilize. Few people ate. Some of the tasks were taken seriously and incorporated into day-to-day life; others were dreamed up by the Millbrook group only for the rich visitors, who didn't realize they weren't in on the joke.

The weekend included psychedelic theater of dance, music, and light shows meant to mimic a guided trip and induce visions like the ones experienced under the influence. Guests would walk in the woods, as the Castalia Foundation pamphlet suggested, engaging in "silent experiment of looking" by taking in the "sensuous impact of the grass, and the trees, and the animals."

This weekend's lectures centered on the Russian Armenian spiritual teacher (and noted fabulist) George Gurdjieff. "A modern man lives in sleep, in sleep is born, and in sleep he dies," Gurdjieff wrote. He endeavored to awaken his followers using deprivation of basic needs like food and sleep coupled with extreme bouts of physical exertion—Sisyphean tasks like cutting a lawn with a pair of scissors. Timothy expressed a similar belief in humanity's stupor, writing, "We live as sleeping robots, cut off from life, from our own brains, and from each other."

Rosemary wasn't one of the paying visitors, so she became an actor when a Canadian Broadcasting Corporation TV crew arrived (as they often did those days) to record a segment, later called "The LSD Crisis," a title that represents an early but already emerging backlash.

The footage opens with an interview with Timothy outside near a garden. Timothy was careful and thoughtful in his responses. He counseled restraint. "Don't take LSD unless you are very well prepared to go out of your mind," he told the interviewer. "Don't take it unless you have someone very experienced with you to guide you through it, and don't take it unless you are ready to have your perspective on your self, on your life, dramatically changed. Because you are going to be a different person."

The segment then moved to a group in the drawing room. Speakers played Indian music overlaid with Timothy's voice reading from *The Psychedelic Experience*. As the camera panned around the room, it briefly stopped on Rosemary's face, revealing the bruised left eye that she quickly tried to cover with her auburn hair.

"The human brain receives several billion signals a minute," Timothy said in his sweetly sibilant, hypnotic voice clipped with a touch of New England. "This waking up entices you. . . . This is a form of magic."

In a third segment, Timothy continued his lecture outside on the porch about the "joyous slippery union" of sex. "Molecules, cells, germs, tissues, all higher forms, sliding together in the polar embrace . . . The two-billion-year chain of life is simply the endless dance of couples coupling in fierce ecstasy."

Rosemary, eyes covered by sunglasses and wearing a sweater over cigarette pants, like a psychedelic Holly Golightly, sat a bit removed from the group and watched the scene unfold.

After the cameras stopped rolling, Rosemary questioned him about a few of the statements he made.

"You have to lose your mind to use your head," Timothy had said.

"How often do you coin such . . ." Rosemary asked, reaching for a way to describe such sensationalized slogans.

Tim shot her a look.

Later that night, the group sat in a circle on a rug listening to music as swirling images projected around them. Tim guided the room with a prompt: *Imagine yourself on a spaceship in the middle of outer space; oxygen is depleting fast. You have only five minutes to live. What message would you send home?*

A talking stick passed around the circle. Some joked, others spoke of their family and friends, some confessed long-hidden sins. When the stick stopped at Timothy, he took a deep breath, ready to launch into a practiced sermon, when the fuses blew.

"We need some light here," Timothy said testily. This wasn't an intentional bit.

Rosemary noticed Timothy's irritation. On wobbly legs (even though the paying guests weren't allowed to indulge, those in residence, or invited there, took surreptitious hits from the acid-laced wine in the Millbrook study), she navigated the room and sat down next to Timothy on the side of his bad ear.

"Did you bring a candle?" he asked her.

"No," she said and reached in her pocket, "but here's a match."

Five

The Apprentice

Rosemary and Timothy grew to love each other in that brief five-month span when the overgrown vibrancy of late summer 1965 withered into the early days of winter—"a space between wars," as she called that period. After Timothy paused the weekend workshops, most of the estate's characters departed for more raucous shores in India or California, leaving Rosemary and Timothy more or less alone to settle into an easy rhythm of domestic bliss. She let her hair grow long and sewed her own clothing, wearing smock dresses cut from fabric she found in the communal clothing heap. She made items for Timothy, too, and helped style him during his appearances, replacing tweeds with breezy unbuttoned linen shirts, if he wore a shirt at all.

Chores took up most of her days. She rode the lawn mower, trimmed the apple trees, gathered wood for the fire, and cooked up the meals, feeling purposeful and engaged with the world around her, each night sinking into the deep restorative sleep of the truly active.

Wandering the property alone, sometimes naked if she felt like it, she would howl at the moon with the estate's dogs, Fang and Obie. "There was always the possibility of finding a lost cabin in the woods, a lost place. It was so full of magic," she said. She was Eve before the apple. "Nature girl," she called herself. She felt free and safe and *alive*. She communed with the old-growth trees and received the vibrations of the cornfields. She looked younger now than when she had arrived with that black eye, as if all that time in Timothy's bed had shaved years off. She felt like a teenager in love.

"My life is serene and quiet," she wrote to her mother. And filled with genuine passion. "You are incapable of awkwardness," Timothy wrote to Rosemary, describing how graceful she looked, even on the toilet. In the din of a crowded local restaurant, he told her, "I am so proud to be seen with you."

The greater Millbrook community respected Timothy, calling him "doctor"; even as a former professor, the Ivy League pedigree still carried weight. Timothy and Rosemary would walk down Main Street, past the library, post office, haberdashery, and hardware store on their way to pick up *The New York Times* at the Corner News Store, where the owner, John Kading, treated Timothy like visiting royalty. "I didn't think he was crazy, I thought he was working on something, like Einstein," Kading said.

The starry-eyed couple whispered about starting a whole new life of white picket fences and babies. Timothy could find someone else to run the movement. Somewhere a photo exists of Rosemary ironing clothes while Timothy sits at the piano playing "Let's Fall in Love." These were "still the moments I remember best. The quiet ones. Walking in tandem in Millbrook and having a dinner by the fire," she said.

"What a wonderful mother you will be," Timothy would say. "What beautiful children we will have together."

～

DESPITE HIS RENEGADE REPUTATION, Timothy, who had just turned forty-five, held many of the old-fashioned beliefs typical of his generation. "He was very autocratic, quite old-fashioned in his attitude to women. He expected that he stretched out his hand, someone would be there to put a glass in it. . . . He wanted to be married in a true mashed potato, pork chop, dinner on the table kind of way," Rosemary said. Their arrangement appealed to her, too. Though she was fifteen years younger than Timothy, she was still a generation older than many of the second-wave feminists. Rosemary found joy in taking over the duties of mother/wife/goddess to not only Timothy but also his sixteen-year-old son, Jack, who lived at Millbrook, attended high school in the community, and had already dipped his finger in the infamous LSD-laced mayonnaise jar before she had arrived. As she worked her magic in the kitchen, Jack finished his homework and joined the couple for dinner by the fire. She adored the boy, calling him her "handsome prince." He reciprocated. "She was about the sanest and kindest of the hundreds of people who came to and through Millbrook," Jack said. He told a biographer that he "thought more of her as my mother than Timothy as my father." Susan, now eighteen years old, attended a boarding school nearby and hadn't yet met the new woman in her beloved father's life.

Rosemary could barely believe the estate's library. Books on tarot, astrology, ancient Greek and Roman myths, and philosophy called to her. Many of the titles were published by the Bollingen Foundation, a group founded by Peggy Hitchcock's family and named after the psychoanalyst Carl Jung's country home in Switzerland. She devoured as many books as the hours would allow. Timothy called her his "bookworm. My Wittgenstein schoolteacher."

"She was the best-read person I ever knew," he wrote.

Rosemary compared their astrological charts and found "unbelievable alchemy" between her sun in Taurus and his in Libra, their shared moons in Aquarius and ascendants in Sagittarius. "You both need to contribute to this relationship on an equal basis," read one interpretation of their compatibility. "You need to feel free with one another." She shared a reverence for astrology with Jung, who wrote to his mentor Sigmund Freud in 1911, "I dare say that we shall one day discover in astrology a good deal of knowledge that has been intuitively projected into the heavens."

Timothy didn't wear a watch. And for now, that kind of immersion in the moment based on the Taoist philosophy that "things can't be made to happen" felt like a warm embrace. To have his attentions, his buoyant optimism, all to herself was divine. Rosemary attempted to put in words what it was like to be seduced by Timothy. "He was so graceful and so likable," she wrote. "He reshaped the world according to his momentary vision, which surrounded me like a bower, all flowers and laughing children."

She felt flattered by the affirmation of her own intellect—his assumptions that she had the knowledge to appreciate his insights, catch his jokes, and smirk at his wit. She did not feel that he thought of himself as superior to her because she had never graduated from high school. "I felt clever, graceful, chosen," she wrote. "That I'd met my match."

She wrote ecstatically to her mother. "I am living on a beautiful estate with friends and I have never before enjoyed my life as much as I do now." They laughed so much in those days. Rosemary's one-liners, which seemed to incense the men she had loved before, thrilled him. He loved how surprised she seemed when he laughed. "You are the funniest girl in the world," he wrote to her in a letter.

Their sex was richer, too. He resisted orgasm, and they would spend hours in bed together celebrating each other's bodies based on the ancient Hindu and Buddhist sexual practice called tantra. A "polyphase orgasm," he believed, could alter your consciousness in a way similar to psychedelics—sexual ecstasy as a way to harness and project a new potency. They created their own love mudras together, yogic hand gestures meant to harness or empower. Timothy would later write that he based his sex tantra poem in *Psychedelic Prayers* on the time when he and Rosemary disappeared from a group to have sex outside:

> Can you, murmuring
> Lose all . . .
> Fusing

ROSEMARY WAS NOT "turned on," as in introduced to LSD, by Timothy, but he became her guide for their weekly sessions with acid—a kind of acidhead Pygmalion who would shape her as his hunk of marble with the lessons he learned from three hundred or so trips. Crucially, Timothy gave her a container for the ecstatic. She had learned during her first peyote experience that it was not fulfilling to do it on a whim without knowledge. Allen Eager and the acid gypsies were wandering around in the dark, addicts looking for more oblivion. But Rosemary was different. She was looking for a vocation.

She learned that LSD was not merely a vehicle for spiritual transcendence but a key evolutionary touchstone for humanity as one of the most important discoveries of the century, up there with the creation of the atomic bomb. For the first time in human history, Timothy told Rosemary, humans were harnessing the power of their nervous systems. You could commune with your cells, ride your DNA back in time to the one-celled creatures in the primordial soup, travel to different dimensions, and jet forth into the supersonic future.

So many people struggle to find the words to communicate these discoveries, but Timothy somehow managed to grow more clear-eyed, even self-possessed, when high. "He had that glorious thing that so many acid-takers wish they could have and that is to be able to do what they want with the drug; he was in absolute control," a friend said.

Rosemary described life under his tutelage: "We were playing with Buddhism, Hinduism. We looked for revelations." He showed her the beauty of insignificance. "The fact of the matter is that all apparent forms of matter and body are momentary clusters of energy. We are little more than flickers on a multidimensional television screen," he wrote in *The Psychedelic Experience*. "This realization directly experienced can be delightful. You suddenly wake up from the delusion of separate form and hook up to the cosmic dance." But he was also wise enough to warn her about the horror embedded in this knowledge. "The terror comes with the discovery of transience. Nothing is fixed, no form solid. . . . Distrust."

Rosemary proved to be a bright and willing apprentice. She learned how to prepare her body with clean food and meditation. They started a daily hatha yoga practice, thanks to Aldous Huxley's recommendation that Timothy read Mircea Eliade's book *Yoga*—which described the act of "integration or union"—that could, along with acid, help achieve the godhead.

With a mind slowed and receptive, revelations, messages from another realm, could be spotted everywhere. Stray birdsong at the right moment, the burst of a lightbulb, the crackling of a flame on the fire, something lost and found, it all had meaning. Self and universe had collided. This state of being, as understood by Jung's theory of synchronicity, represented an embracing of the wisdom of the unconscious. It could make you feel connected, superior, or even paranoid and psychotic, depending on your disposition and environment. Rosemary experienced all of these states, though the dominant feeling was of true belief.

All of this training helped make Rosemary into the queen of "setting"; her warm and comforting demeanor grounded those in the throes of even the most challenging trips. She was a natural high priestess, a position she had learned as the perfect host back in New York with her second husband. She intuitively sensed what grounding foods to make, what kinds of bright but comforting colors to drape in cloth around the room, and where to place the candles. She knew what to say when things went sideways and when to stay silent when someone needed to traverse their visions alone.

There were few known female psychonauts to follow for this type of training. She had not heard about the séances of Nganasan female shamans of Siberia or the thousands of years of sacred mushroom ceremony passed down by the *curandera*, or medicine women, of Oaxaca. Even the most famous *curandera*, María Sabina, who introduced her *psilocybe* mushrooms, *niños santos*, or "saint children," to a Western bank executive (and thereby the rest of the Northern Hemisphere), didn't appear by name in *Life* magazine's 1957 article "Seeking the Magic Mushroom." Women were confidantes, calming tethers for the men to embark on frightening journeys into the psychic unknown, and they often wrote themselves out of psychedelic history due to fear of stigma and reproach. Thus, their names rarely made the record.

Rosemary, however, logged her trips—often in handwriting too blasted out to be legible—for posterity: "My new game should be easy. Love, warmth, comfort. My mind cannot be caught by the death fantasy. It is still there but faint, obscured by good feeling." This theme of suicidality, not merely death and rebirth, but obliteration of herself, reoccurs. But her dark musings end with a list, as if interrupted mid-thought: "roast pork and carrots, fennel—thyme, fresh asparagus with hollandaise, and a green, green garlic salad." Even while gazing into the abyss, Rosemary thought of feeding her lover.

"I aspire to be a radical intuitor," she wrote, a person who valued learning over wealth, even food. She felt that Timothy had invited her into a "bubble of specialness." And Rosemary bought into her own exceptionalism, during a time when her alternatives out there in the real world, where she was a high school dropout, fleeing yet another abusive relationship with a man addicted to heroin, were limited. She and Timothy sought liberation or moksha, "release from the finitude that restricts us from limitless being, consciousness, and bliss," the religion scholar and Harvard Psilocybin Project researcher Huston Smith wrote. Together, they strove to slough off the ego, destroy it even—much like the Buddhist's idea of transcendence—while still honoring the body's hedonic need for pleasure. They considered themselves to be like the Buddhists' "Awakened Ones" and Gurdjieff's chosen few with open eyes—those who had truly shaken off the slumber that stifled humankind. It sounds self-aggrandizing, and it was, but it was also pure. Rosemary truly believed.

Rosemary summed up the goal of all this internal work on a piece of scrap paper: "The sense of not existing—it wasn't about LSD changing the world—it was about work to change oneself into a god-intoxicated being." God was inside her, was her, was everywhere. Timothy honored the god inside Rosemary, just as she honored the god inside him, and so the guru/follower relationship didn't flow one way.

"Rosemary—sophisticated, worldly—continually joked me out of the trap of YMCA Hinduism, the goal of which was to become a Holy Man, a prospect she found too amusing for words," Timothy wrote in *Flashbacks*. Rosemary provided a rare quality of authenticity, which was an antidote to Timothy's professorial self-seriousness. She had spent hours in smoky bars with dangerous men. She knew about poverty, about suffering. And because she knew so much more than he did about real life, she felt comfortable poking holes in his inflated ego, pulling him, in a slightly reduced but far more palatable form, back down to earth. She adored him most when he embraced his innate silliness, like the time he discovered a straw hat and a cane in an abandoned trunk. Immediately he started "doing an elegant 'Shuffle Off to Buffalo.' He was a song-and-dance man, and he knew it." The most important part was that she knew it, too.

Rosemary had so much to teach Timothy. "He had a deliberate naivete, he wanted to be taught, to be instructed," she said. She shared with him her love of science fiction—especially the *Lord of the Rings* series and *The Three Stigmata of Palmer Eldritch* by Philip K. Dick—which Timothy later called "a profound contribution to my education." Reading Rosemary's books together altered the content of their psychedelic visions and would inspire Timothy Leary's futurist philosophies—and some of his most out-there beliefs. "Through Rosemary I learned a critically important lesson: that the psychedelic experience could not only illuminate the theological concepts of the past but, more important, could map new visions."

As a break from all this vision mapping, Rosemary periodically invited Timothy back into her old life in New York City. Over steak and scotch at Rolfe's Chop House in the Financial District, where she had once gawked at the businessmen and held Charles's hand in the back of David Amram's car, Rosemary, so open now thanks to months of habitual acid use, unveiled herself.

"You told me the story of your life," Timothy said of their dinner.

Did she speak about the backflips and tap dancing at the local bar with her father or about her brief time in Hollywood, where she had played an extra in *Operation Petticoat*? Did she tell him about her second husband, how proud it made her to watch him caress the button accordion, how she had caught him cheating, how his betrayal had led her to seek out the erratic warmth of an alcoholic composer? Did she even mention her first husband? Not likely. She told few people about him—protecting herself even in this state of radical receptivity.

Whatever she relayed over dinner, Timothy listened without judgment. She felt that he truly *heard* her. His twinkling eyes danced around her face, urging her to make light of the suffering and to make humor out of the pain. "When all the tales I cared to tell were told, the past was banished," she wrote.

He gave her a new way to frame the men from her past. They all—especially Charles and Allen—were holy men in search of something more meaningful than this reality. But they were looking in the wrong places. They used heroin and alcohol as "escape tickets" to envelop themselves in the "warm soft cocoon of nothingness." They had chosen the wrong Door; she had chosen the right one.

That night he asked her to marry him. She said yes, but told him to keep it to themselves until his divorce from Nena was finalized. There was no mention of Allen Eager.

⁓

RALPH METZNER moved into Rosemary's old apartment while Rosemary embraced her new role as right-hand woman. His cerebral, even aloof quality notwithstanding, Metzner loved women. He even invited his mother to move into Millbrook during its early heyday. She joined him in the Big House, dropping acid for the first and last time at age fifty-eight. He was married to Susan Homer when he first moved to Millbrook, though both admitted that, given the context, it was nearly impossible to maintain any form of typical monogamy. Susan slept with Timothy; Metzner bedded a variety of women, including one with whom he'd have a child out of wedlock. "I don't really count it as a marriage," Susan later said, "perhaps a legalized affair?"

Metzner felt an immediate attraction to Rosemary, describing the change of scenery at Millbrook that he attributed to her: "The Millbrook community flowered again with music, meditation, laughter, creativity, happy children, and remarkable people."

She sat at the head of the table on Thanksgiving next to Timothy, serving thirty guests an elaborate meal of two turkeys, a ham, and a haunch of venison. That day they played a game of baseball, and she envisioned herself before her breasts grew in, rounding the bases at a field near her childhood home, when she felt she could run as fast as lightning. She had rediscovered that version of herself, the girl who would dance outside and wash her hair in thunderstorms as her mother called for her to come in for dinner.

Images from her youth returned to her, especially during her trips. The dank, hallucinatory quality of those Missouri summers, pulling tomatoes from the vines that surrounded her house, kissing boys by the mosquito-infested lake by her school, running through patches of poison ivy and never getting a rash.

Her life entered into a continuous loop—all happening at once, the portal of Millbrook combining all these versions of herself. No matter how bad it got down the road, these moments of divine grace would stay with her.

The superficiality of her life before became impossible.

PART TWO

The Assistant

Six

Morning Glory Seeds

A few days before Christmas, Rosemary and Timothy, a couple now for five months that felt to him like "several thousand years in many forms," decided to pack up their Ford station wagon, board up the Big House, and escape from Millbrook's snowcapped pine trees for their first vacation as a family.

They planned to spend a few months on the southeastern coast of Mexico, the Yucatán, where Timothy would finish a memoir in progress. Rosemary would use the time to bond with Susan and Jack, who, along with the family friend Charles Jaeger, joined them on the trip. In a letter to her mother, Rosemary detailed their loose plans: "I don't know exactly where I'll be at Xmas, but my thoughts and love will be with you." Her parents received these vague letters with consternation. They worried, her brother said, that she was a lost soul.

Rosemary sat in the front of the loaded station wagon bursting with scuba gear, sacks of brown bread flour, books, a typewriter, and luggage for five people, keeping sixteen-year-old Jack company as he drove, joining him in sing-alongs to the radio.

Rosemary had brought the weed, purchased from a friend in New York, and hid it inside her sewing basket. Every few hours, she'd move aside embroidery thread and pieces of fabric to find her egg-shaped silver snuff box. Rolling a joint on her lap while Jack drove, she'd sometimes forget to pick up the seeds that had dropped to the car floor.

Jack embraced Rosemary as a friendly maternal figure, but Susan merely tolerated her. The trouble between them had started in New York, a month before the trip, when Susan, on break from boarding school, joined her father to help pack Rosemary's belongings for her to move into Millbrook. In Rosemary's Fifth Avenue apartment, the three placed Rosemary's phone books and jazz recordings into boxes, folded up antique Oriental rugs, and wrapped her paintings in newspaper until Timothy stopped and gazed at Rosemary. He then put his arm around Rosemary's waist and gestured to his daughter.

"Who does Rosemary remind you of?" he asked.

Rosemary felt Susan's eyes appraising her, as if seeing her for the first time.

"Who?" Her voice was ice cold.

"Marianne."

Susan was eight when Marianne died, and she never forgave her mother for abandoning her. With one word, Timothy had identified his new girlfriend as his daughter's nemesis. Susan and Rosemary's relationship would never recover.

Susan had once been a bright and adventurous child. She had learned to tie her shoes before the others, climbed higher in the trees, and loved to dance. Now she barely looked as if she had aged, but her piercing blue eyes—her father's eyes—seemed blank. Despite all that she had experienced—the suicide of her mother, relocations and re-marriages, the introduction of drugs into her daily life as an adolescent in Cambridge, among other traumas, big and small, that we'll never know—she retained an aura of genial innocence. At least with anyone who didn't threaten to take her father's love from her.

To curry favor with Susan, Rosemary had offered her the spot in the way, way back, with Timothy, where they had lowered the row of backward-facing seats to make room for a mattress and a paisley throw. Rosemary intuited that Susan preferred to be as physically close to her father as possible; she often sat at Timothy's knee or even in his lap. Cruel men at Millbrook would joke that she wanted to sleep with him. It seems kinder (and more likely) to acknowledge that she needed a source of love in a world of chaos.

On December 22, 1965, they arrived in Laredo, Texas, a sun-bleached border town on the Rio Grande filled with church spires and adobe houses. They crossed the International Bridge and arrived at the Mexican Immigration building. Timothy went in alone. Getting through this checkpoint would require a little maneuvering, since Timothy had been officially banned from Mexico by the country's government two years earlier thanks to the drama surrounding their research center.

Timothy returned to the car with bad news: He had been recognized by the same policeman who had revoked his visa and deported him in 1963. Timothy was *"prohibido,"* the officer said. For a bunch of people who believed that the universe spoke to them in synchronicities, they were ignoring some key messages.

Rosemary, who had moved to the backseat while Timothy drove, urged him to spend the night in Nuevo Laredo, a free zone that didn't require tourist visas, so as not to pass through customs back into America. Marijuana possession, effectively illegal at the federal level since the 1930s, came with stiffer penalties now. The United States was in the process of shoring up its anti-drug presence at the border in Mexico, focusing mainly on the smuggling of heroin, while welcoming a bonus uptick in marijuana arrests.

Timothy either ignored or didn't hear her because of his bad ear. He kept driving until they were a few hundred yards away from customs.

"Have you ever been in the situation where you feel all the gears shift?" Rosemary would later say. "When everything changes? I felt that so strongly. It just changed everything. All the potential and the possibility for the type of life we were going to lead together ended right then and there."

She rifled through the car, frantically moving aside clothing, sacks of flour, and food until she got her hands on her sewing kit and removed the egg-shaped container. Boxed in by their belongings, she couldn't reach to open the window.

She called out to Charles, who was too scared to move.

"Jackie, shake this out the window!" Rosemary said, handing the egg up to the front seat.

"All the grass out of the car—right?" Timothy asked, only now noticing what was happening. Too late for Jack to open the window and dump it out, Susan grabbed the egg from her brother and hid it in her underwear just as an American customs agent approached. Charles's long hair apparently made the agent curious enough to search the car. He immediately spotted Rosemary's haphazardly discarded marijuana seeds on the passenger-side floor. This is the official story at least. Perhaps the agent had eagle eyes. Perhaps the Mexican officer who had recognized Timothy tipped off American customs. Perhaps it was, as Rosemary believed, all a setup that started with tapped phone lines back at Millbrook.

Nonetheless: "Everyone out," the agent ordered.

Hundreds of cars slowed down to rubberneck as agents swarmed the station wagon, tearing it apart. They confiscated the brown bread flour. Then, at the station in Laredo, they strip-searched the group. Susan disrobed in front of a female agent, who found the silver egg stuffed in her underwear. It contained a few partially smoked joints, a palmful of weak weed, and a few of Rosemary's legal weight loss pills. Timothy said the box was his, but the charges also stuck to Susan, eighteen years old, a legal adult. The next morning, the judge set bail at $10,000 for Timothy, $2,500 for Susan and Jack, and $5,000 for Charles Jaeger and Rosemary.

Unable to make bail, Timothy and Rosemary spent their first Christmas Eve together in separate cells. Rosemary shared her cell with Susan. It wasn't a happy cohabitation.

Susan would later tell her father that their arrests were Rosemary's fault—her karma.

～

THEY RAISED BAIL with help from friends on Christmas Day and headed back to Millbrook. A national media frenzy commenced over the ex–Harvard professor arrested for drugs with his children—especially since the weed was discovered in, of all places, his daughter's underwear. Timothy, who had never been arrested, admitted to the *New York Herald Tribune* that he regularly smoked marijuana. "You can't study consciousness unless you do," he said.

The group tried to resume their lives as a trial date loomed—Susan to boarding school, Jack to Millbrook High School, and Timothy and Rosemary to New York to raise money for the Timothy Leary Defense Fund. The actor Peter Fonda, the poet Kenneth Koch, the biochemist Robert S. de Ropp, and the critic Susan Sontag were among the donors.

The federal Laredo indictments came down in February. The government declined to pursue the case against Rosemary, Charles, and Jack, but not Susan and Timothy, who faced three felony counts each for smuggling marijuana, transporting marijuana, and, most curiously, the failure to pay a "marijuana tax," a Catch-22 law that required people to declare and pay a fee on contraband. Timothy's lawyers advised him to plead guilty, but Timothy seized it as an opportunity to test his new theories on the grand stage.

His defense hinged on two assertions. He argued that as a serious scientist his job entailed experimenting with chemicals and drugs—and that pot should not be classified as a narcotic. To this end, several prominent Harvard and MIT professors backed him. At the same time, he said that his religious beliefs as a Hindu gave him the constitutional right to use marijuana. A Hindu monk testified on his behalf. Timothy adapted his argument from the Native American Church, which had, in 1964, successfully convinced the California Supreme Court that peyote use was a religious rite.

When the trial began, Rosemary stayed in Millbrook, scanning newspapers and awaiting Tim's calls for details. She wasn't the children's mother or the professor's wife; instead, when the media mentioned her role in the arrest, they called her his "assistant." Her presence would likely have confused the jury—or made them even less inclined to sympathy—this older man and this unidentified beautiful, younger woman smoking weed in the car with his children.

During one phone call, Timothy asked Rosemary if he could name her as his marijuana supplier. She agreed as long as she didn't have to name her dealer. When Assistant U.S. Attorney Morton Sussman asked who supplied the pot, the court reported Timothy's response: "Rose Mary Woodruff."

The jury handed down a guilty verdict in less than an hour. Instead of receiving a slap on the wrist, however, as he might have had he pleaded guilty from the start, on March 11, 1966, Timothy was sentenced to a combined thirty years in prison and a $30,000 fine. The vast majority of newspaper editorials, despite the outrage over the presence of his children, agreed that the excessively punitive sentence did not fit the crime. A letter to the editor at *The New York Times* noted that Timothy's prison time exceeded that of the three men sentenced on the same day for the murder of Malcolm X.

Back at Millbrook, Rosemary took a phone call. It wasn't from Timothy but from a reporter who shared the news of his jail sentence.

"Patently absurd," Rosemary told him.

Judge Ben Connally allowed Timothy, who posed no flight risk, to post bail while awaiting appeal. Free from prison and confident about his appeal case, Timothy embraced his moment. "I no longer regretted being an outcast. I was beginning to enjoy the fray," he wrote of the trial. Rosemary witnessed the shift. "He seemed to thrive on the media response, the urgent need for funds and lawyers, the threat of trial and prison, the myth of the tragic hero, a sweet dream of oppression," Rosemary wrote. She added, "It was his movie. . . . The threat of the cross exhilarated him."

But the casualty of the fight would be his daughter, Susan, who was convicted following the U.S. commissioner Jacob Hornberger's decision to throw out her guilty plea and undergo a nonjury trial. Timothy's life would never be the same, but Susan's had barely begun. Before she even graduated from high school, Susan's name had already been dragged through the papers as a drug abuser. Showing her youthful modesty, when asked by a *McCall's* reporter where she hid the drugs, Susan hesitated and smiled shyly before responding, "In my panties." Despite lip service to "games," "patterns," and "insights" of psychedelics, Susan didn't share her father's enthusiasm. A bad trip nearly put her off acid, and since then she'd preferred marijuana.

Susan's mental health deteriorated precipitously after her arrest. She struggled to finish her senior year at boarding school. Her grades slipped, and administrators threatened to send her to summer school. She even resorted to eating food—including frozen raw meat—that she left to chill out on the windowsill of her dorm room in order to avoid dining with her peers in the cafeteria.

Timothy would later admit that he was "slow to realize how much she suffered by what she felt to be a public disgrace." Richard Alpert pointed out at the time what may seem obvious now. "Tim wanted to make this the 'case of cases.' But you don't make the 'case of cases' when your pot is found in your girl's underwear."

When the *McCall's* magazine profiler asked about day-to-day life following her arrest, Susan responded, "Things don't matter, really."

FALLOUT FROM HIS ARREST and attendant trial publicity came from the locals in quiet Millbrook. Residents bristled at the sordid reputation their hamlet was earning. At this point, the greater Millbrook community feared the sex more than the drugs. Orgies. Stag films. Underage girls. Allen Ginsberg with his wild hair and unkempt beard wearing robes in the street. A woman, a presumed visitor to Millbrook, who showed up downtown and shopped, wearing a fur coat and heels—with nothing underneath.

The *Poughkeepsie Journal* devoted wall-to-wall coverage to the estate. A resident historian penned an op-ed for the local newspaper, arguing that the drug addicts would pillage and rape the community. The president of Bennett College, a prestigious all-girls school five minutes from the estate, threatened to expel any student who visited.

The community gave the DA a directive: Get rid of Timothy.

Rosemary noticed unmarked black cars driving the unpaved roads. The owner of the plumbing shop in town confided that agents had asked to borrow uniforms from him to gain access to the house. Timothy, who was still the estate's leader even after the arrest, warned visitors about the threat of random car searches. They played the game "How many miles before we're stopped?" They locked the gates and required invitations after hearing about rumored undercover narcs. Tickets for varied small infractions piled up by the dozens. The barrel-chested sheriff, Lawrence Quinlan, with his ten-gallon hat and overcoat, started to make random stops at the property. Rosemary and Timothy loved to point out that Quinlan, who was notorious for shaving the hair off young men he arrested, shared his last name with the corrupt cop in Orson Welles's *Touch of Evil*.

"It was like society was coming apart," Quinlan told a reporter. There was a roiling. Something had to happen.

ON SATURDAY, APRIL 16, Rosemary planted an early garden of morning glories—appropriate, since the new rumored way to get high was to munch on a handful of these seeds—a pop of bright trumpets around the fence that lined the property.

Thirty people filled the Big House. Peggy Hitchcock arrived with gourmet treats and easy humor, leaving before the end of the night. Other regular couples stayed over, including Eve Babitz and Ralph Metzner and Flo and Maynard Ferguson. There were the irregulars, too. A dry goods manufacturer and a young secretary, and the columnist Marya Mannes, who was working on the *McCall's* profile of Susan.

The group, most of them sober, ended the day by watching a movie in Timothy's bedroom. Cops, spying through binoculars into the bedroom window from the woods outside, assumed that an orgy was about to unfold. To their disappointment, it was something stranger. "You'll never guess what them hippies are watching. A waterfall!" a cop said.

"A what?" another asked.

"A waterfall for crissake! It's just a movie of a goddamn waterfall! It goes on and on and nothing ever happens but the water."

After the movie ended, Timothy's son, Jack, knocked on the door, according to Timothy's recollection, and offered his father and Rosemary a vial of DMT, the hallucinogen *N,N*-Dimethyltryptamine.

Due to its force and short duration, Timothy would christen DMT "the nuclear bomb of the psychedelic family."

Rosemary mixed the yellow crystals with mint leaves to reduce the harshness of the burnt-plastic taste. The fumes built up in the glass pipe. They inhaled clouds of thick white smoke for as long as they could until it escaped in a plume. Rosemary and Timothy slumped in bed as Jack sprawled out on the floor.

An indeterminate amount of time passed—a trip to infinity on DMT could last only ten minutes—before they heard the sound of boots on the floor. Jack left the room and peered over the banister.

"There are a bunch of hunters. Men with guns down there," Jack said.

The beaded curtain separating the dressing room from the bedroom parted. At least ten policemen burst through the room.

First inside was a young, ambitious assistant district attorney named G. Gordon Liddy. Liddy had moved to Millbrook only a few months earlier and had bigfooted himself into participating in the raid. On his way to the raid through the Millbrook woods, Liddy had stumbled, nearly face-planting, over a root with his gun outstretched, like a real life Elmer Fudd.

Rosemary maneuvered her foot over the pipe and vial in bed. Timothy called this her "Wonder Woman reflex." She positioned the blanket over her legs. The police read it as a show of modesty.

"Don't move," said one.

Another turned to Timothy. "On your feet." Timothy grinned as he stood. He wasn't wearing any pants.

"Hands up," said Liddy. "I have a warrant to search the premises." As they shined a spotlight on Rosemary in bed, the men ordered the nearly naked Timothy out of the room. They had no experience with DMT, so they couldn't have placed the smell. Just a family getting together one last time before tucking in for the night—albeit with the father nude from the waist down.

Liddy and Timothy both wrote in their memoirs that Rosemary wore a "diaphanous gown" that left little to the imagination. But Rosemary recalls differently. Instead, she writes, she wore a flannel dress with elastic wrists—the kind a child would wear on Christmas morning—that her mother had sewn for the cold winters in upstate New York. Sometimes you see what you hope to see and remember what you want to remember.

Rosemary shielded her eyes from the light and asked the nervous trooper to move it out of her direct sight line. As he adjusted the light and turned his gaze away from Rosemary, she wiggled her toes under the blanket until she grasped the glass pipe, moving it more fully under her body.

The men turned out drawers, stuck fingers into her fancy face creams, and rifled through Rosemary's clothes, bagging her birth control pills and aspirins as evidence. When an officer inspected a brass urn with peat moss, Rosemary had an idea. "Don't touch my plant!" she exclaimed. "It's a sacrament."

Liddy burrowed through the container and found ground vegetal matter that he believed was marijuana. Days later they would realize that the urn contained only peat moss and an ordinary houseplant. Meanwhile, the cops never found the DMT or the pipe because they never searched the bed. Classic misdirection—a trick Rosemary had learned from her father.

The police tore through the rest of the Big House. They gathered family photographs, books (*The Agony and the Ecstasy*, a 1961 novel by Irving Stone about the painter Michelangelo among them), and bottles of wine, wrecking the place as they searched and taking pictures to make it appear that they lived more squalidly than they did. The cops searched the women, making them strip down to their underwear so that they could hunt for track marks on their inner thighs. Acting on a tip that the house staged stag films, they confiscated every picture in Jack's darkroom, only later realizing that the photographs were for a high schooler's class project.

The bust was a bust.

That night, however, the cops still believed that they had made the raid of the century. Sheriff Quinlan placed a laughing Timothy, who was arrested for operating a home where drugs were used, into an unmarked Pontiac. Rosemary watched the black car leave and changed out of her nightgown. She then shuffled through the papers in Timothy's office until she found an address book, grabbed a pocketful of change, and, since the cops had cut the phone lines, asked someone to drive her to a twenty-four-hour diner so that she could use its phone. But the policemen who had raided her house beat her there, and she walked in to find them laughing and recounting the night over coffee and apple pie. She headed back into the night, returning hours later when the diner had emptied. She slipped into the back room to make two phone calls: to Peggy Hitchcock's brother Billy and to the Timothy Leary Defense Fund lawyer in New York.

She returned to Millbrook in the early hours of the morning to find that the policemen's heavy boots had trampled her morning glory garden. Her hopes for spring flattened before they had even sprouted.

Seven

The Woodruff Woman

The Poughkeepsie lawyer Noel Tepper was nervous to meet the mad professor. Tepper had read the articles about Timothy Leary in the *Poughkeepsie Journal*, including the most recent front-page news about his arrest during the raid two days prior. A local longhair "carpetbagger" (as he called himself), whom the conservative powers in Poughkeepsie labeled a radical due to his left-leaning clientele, Tepper knew enough from his three years practicing law in Poughkeepsie to be skeptical of what the papers reported as fact.

As Tepper crossed the Millbrook estate's gatehouse wearing his signature three-piece suit, he couldn't shake the feeling that he was impersonating a lawyer—a bout of impostor syndrome by a young professional who harbored a secret desire to give up the law and write novels. As he drove, he averted his eyes from the clusters of the barely dressed. "The men looked emaciated and the women looked beautiful," he recalled.

When he arrived at the grand Big House, he noticed that the walls needed paint and the grass needed mowing. There were priceless antiques next to hand-sewn mandalas with mattresses strewn about. Upstairs, Tepper encountered a group in flowing robes who sat in lotus position around Timothy, a flower tucked behind his ear.

Tepper was struck by Timothy's gravitational force; everyone felt pulled into his orbit. As Timothy stood up to greet him, Tepper noticed the ease and fluidity of his movements, like a masterful long-distance swimmer barely breaking the water. He was a pleasure to watch.

"Are you Mr. Tepper?" Timothy asked. His voice was surprisingly soft. "I'm Timothy Leary." Tepper extended his hand for a shake, but Timothy placed his hands together in prayer and brought them to his forehead. Namaste. The pageantry burst the spell. Suddenly Tepper felt self-conscious again.

"You wanted to talk to me?" Timothy asked. Fresh off his second arrest, Timothy had realized that he needed local counsel in addition to his high-powered New York City lawyers working on his Laredo appeal. Since Tepper had represented an anti–Vietnam War group and the folk singer Pete Seeger, he seemed to be the perfect candidate.

"Yes, but not here," Tepper said. "We have to be somewhere private."

On the landing, Tepper watched as Timothy bent down, took a tissue out of his pocket, and picked up a pile of dog excrement on the floor. It was a mundane gesture, but a pointed one, meant to show Tepper that Timothy wasn't just a figurehead. He did the dirty work.

Timothy waved him past the worn easy chairs to an open window across the room. "Okay, follow me," he said, opening the window and jumping out. Tepper stood there in a state of shock. He had heard the stories of people being so high that they believed they could fly. Did his new client just kill himself?

Tepper peered out of the window and found Timothy sitting cross-legged on a dirty mattress on the tin roof over the second floor. Timothy beckoned him and Tepper gingerly stepped out onto the roof, praying that his tight suit pants wouldn't rip.

Timothy could sense Tepper's apprehension and was good at appeasing it. He maintained direct eye contact as he spoke about the importance of LSD to humanity in general—how it could end racism and wars. Though Tepper wasn't into drugs, this kind of belief system was something he could get behind. As Timothy lectured, Tepper even admired his teeth—well shaped and lovely. He felt strange being so taken with another man's teeth, but there it was.

They had barely discussed any of Timothy's pressing legal matters by the time their conversation came to its natural end and Timothy walked Tepper back down the magnificent staircase to the front door. Tepper had passed the test. He was hip, open, and, perhaps most important, willing to let Timothy lead. From that point on, Tepper visited the estate nearly every Wednesday, acting as in-house counsel for Millbrook residents.

Rosemary hired Tepper next. Two weeks after the raid, she received a summons to appear before a grand jury, as the state's chief witness in another ongoing investigation into rumors that Timothy gave drugs to minors. Prosecutors couldn't bring in Timothy because their primary weapon to compel testimony was to immunize, and the community wanted the professor in handcuffs. Local outrage plus national reports of LSD's dangers, including that of a five-year-old convulsing after eating her uncle's acid-laced sugar cube, *Time* magazine's article on the "epidemic of acid heads," and stories about teenagers jumping out of windows thinking they could fly, galvanized the prosecution.

Rosemary's first reaction was to flee. But Tepper explained that she had no choice but to stay and appear before the grand jury. Evading a grand jury summons carried a five-year prison sentence. Since she wasn't Timothy's wife (worse, he was still married to another woman), she didn't have spousal privilege, so they had to devise a case for her refusal to cooperate. Together, they drafted a plan: Rosemary would plead the Fifth, citing her religion—LSD was a sacrament, and she could not speak out about its use in any way that would harm Timothy, her religious leader—as a reason for her to be released from the grand jury.

Timothy was excited about getting to test his philosophies again in a court of law just as he was fine-tuning his Laredo appeal. "Don't you realize this is the first test of LSD in the courts?" he said to Rosemary and Tepper over lunch at a restaurant near the Dutchess County courthouse. "Beginning right here in Poughkeepsie we could change the world. Our grandchildren will be proud of you."

But in a quiet moment away from Timothy, Rosemary turned to Tepper and said, "Don't feel bad if we lose." Both Rosemary and Tepper knew that the chance of convincing the court was nearly impossible. Her case was a Hail Mary, about as "effective as a pagan defense would have been in Salem," she wrote later. She especially disliked having to characterize Timothy as her guru. "I didn't like my role," she wrote. "I wanted genius and domesticity, cerebral excitement and serenity. I wanted to be a freedom fighter and a peacemaker, to destroy injustice and pacify. I needed the appreciation of my lover and the privacy of a cloister; to be lustful, ever pregnant yet a very nun for solitude and habit. But this part called for a hypnotized convert, the potential victim of a mad scientist; white gloves and a pillbox hat, a serious expression and modest demeanor. I was a lover, not a devotee."

Still, she decided to move forward with the argument even though she faced genuine danger to her freedom in refusing to testify. "She understood what was going on, and she understood her risk, going to jail," Tepper said. "She understood the dynamics. That she was going to take the heat."

On the first day of her appearance before the grand jury, Rosemary dressed primly. She looked more like a Kennedy wife than a hippie, with her hair flipped under, her manicured nails, and her pristine off-white, two-piece jacket and skirt suit.

Tepper held out hope that Judge Raymond Baratta, a first-generation Italian American with an oddball reputation in Poughkeepsie's political boys' club, would be lenient. Judge Baratta dressed like a cast member in *Guys and Dolls*, belted out Christmas tunes on the piano during holiday parties, and believed, as he told Tepper, that "criminals had a right to live, too." Out of all the judges, Tepper thought they had the best chance with Baratta.

In the closed courtroom, Rosemary pleaded the Fifth, citing self-incrimination. Tepper had prepared her for what was to come. Assistant District Attorney Albert Rosenblatt then offered her immunity from implicating herself in crimes at the estate, which removed the ability to self-incriminate. There was now no legal basis to refuse the court's questions. But she still wouldn't testify.

Judge Baratta released the grand jury and scheduled a follow-up secondary hearing concerning her refusal. Now in open session, Baratta interrogated Rosemary about her religious practices. She spoke of mantras and mandalas and mudras, inner knowledge, meditation, biblical texts, Huxley's *The Doors of Perception*, Timothy's own *Psychedelic Experience*, and *The Gospel of Sri Ramakrishna*.

"What is the name of this religion that you're talking about if it has a name?" Judge Baratta asked.

"Well, we have yet to name it," Rosemary responded.

"It doesn't have a name?"

"One of the most basic tenets is the sacredness of the relationship between pupil and guru," she said.

"That's a Hindu word? Indian?" the judge asked.

"Yes."

"Who or whom would be considered your guru?"

"I consider Dr. Leary as such," she said.

The judge was having fun now, asking her what she would or wouldn't divulge about her "guru"—what about adultery? Or murder?

She had answers: She couldn't conceive of a situation in which her guru would commit murder; it was against their religion. Regarding adultery, a clear shiv directed at Rosemary since Timothy's divorce was not finalized, she remained unruffled.

"I refuse to testify about the private life or actions of anyone."

The judge liked this exchange.

"Are you a college graduate?" he asked Rosemary.

"No, I'm not."

Judge Baratta turned to the prosecution. "She appears to be a very intelligent young lady."

Still, Judge Baratta found her in contempt of court and sentenced her to thirty days in jail, rejecting Timothy's implicit argument about psychedelics as sacraments.

The local papers ran several pieces on the hearing, referring to Rosemary, who was branded an adulteress and a drug user, as "the Woodruff woman."

ROSEMARY'S NEW HOME was the city-block-long brick Dutchess County Jail, one of the most notorious in the state of New York. The jail was in frequent violation of health and safety standards—people dying in custody and a pregnant woman ignored as she miscarried on the floor.

The matron established Rosemary's schedule as the only sentenced prisoner among the rest of the women awaiting trial. She would wake at six on her sagging green mattress and perform daily chores: serving the other prisoners coffee and doughnuts, collecting the trays, washing the dishes, sweeping the cells and hallways, waxing the floors every other day, and washing the windows every Tuesday and Friday. She cleaned the office of Sheriff Quinlan, the man who had frog-marched her boyfriend out of their home, as the matron watched, those ever-present keys clacking. Rosemary coped by embracing the routine, and she was used to the steady grind of keeping house from the prior half year at Millbrook.

The lights stayed on. The jail had banned bobby pins and utensils other than spoons. The only reading materials available were a Gideon Bible and *Reader's Digest*, so friends filled her room with her favorite books. Residents sent letters filled with well wishes, gifts, and stories of the newborn goat at Millbrook. Ralph Metzner and Eve Babitz sent her a note of support with a promising *I Ching* throw: "Darkening of the light." Babitz wrote, "So dearest Rosemary, though your light is temporarily imprisoned in the dark, good fortune and peace lie ahead. . . . Peace is coming, says Mr. Ching."

Rosemary wrote her notes with a Maybelline brown eyeliner on the back of a copy of *The Gospel of Sri Ramakrishna*, which she hid under her mattress. Her breasts swelled, as if she were pregnant, but she knew that she wasn't. This had happened to her in high-stress times, her body's hormones surging. For a woman so practiced in escape, the confinement made her panic. Every night when the door clanked shut, the dread nearly suffocated her.

Tepper expected the other inmates to shun Rosemary, but found, instead, that they rallied behind her. A pregnant fifteen-year-old arrested for stealing drugs tried to copy Rosemary's yoga poses. Another woman sang hymns and read passages aloud from Ecclesiastes and Revelation. Even the night matron who worked the graveyard shift was kind—often waking her up sweetly with something inspiring like "Hang in there." The head matron pulled Tepper aside to privately denounce what her employers had done to Rosemary; she felt that the court should admire a woman who had stood by her man.

Yet Timothy hadn't visited, claiming he was too consumed with preparations for an impending subcommittee meeting on marijuana and LSD in Washington, D.C. The televised hearing would be a disaster. Looking nervous and deferential, Timothy never mentioned his religion, but was instead bulldozed by Senator Ted Kennedy into admitting the dangers of psychedelic use without oversight and agreeing that greater regulations should be instituted. The Associated Press covered the hearing with the lede "A pioneer experimenter . . . acknowledged today that the drug was out of control." To figure out how to spin future news narratives, Timothy met with the famed media theorist Marshall McLuhan, who counseled him to drop the grave pose of a scholar scientist and sell psychedelics to the masses with a slogan and a big smile—the way a Madison Avenue ad exec would sell a Pepsi. Timothy took this advice to heart.

"The days speed on," Timothy wrote to Rosemary. "You will be home soon."

He sent her a copy of *The Lord of the Rings*. She licked every page, expecting a gift of transcendence on at least one of them. Nothing. "I'm tired of playing this character in search of myth," she wrote. "No more lyricism from the prison cells."

The first friend to visit was her "priest" Fred Swain, a former World War II air force officer turned Hindu monk, who had introduced Timothy to Hinduism back in Boston. Swain told her that the Millbrook residents nightly meditated around a shrine that they had made for her, with her picture at the center surrounded by candles, incense, and a copper pot filled with bloomed daffodils. They appreciated what Rosemary was doing for Timothy—for all of them, really. She wasn't just protecting Millbrook from prosecution; she was standing firm on principle to defend their way of life.

Halfway through her sentence, the press photographed Rosemary on her way to the bail hearing. She is dressed for the hearing like a teenager on her way to a sock hop in the 1950s, a crisp white shirt, her hair pinned back and flipped out at the bottom. She walked arm in arm with another arrested criminal, an elderly woman who faced charges for shoplifting and wore a pillbox hat and an overcoat thrown over a housedress. You couldn't tell from the angle of the photograph that the women were handcuffed together by the wrists. They appeared intimate, even protective of each other—the older woman staring ahead with her chin up and her lips pursed, her fists balled up as if ready to defend them both, and Rosemary with her body angled in front of the woman as if to shield her from the cameras.

Timothy arrived with the press. He kissed her, or rather, he allowed her to kiss him on the cheek. A chaste, unsatisfying kiss as the photographers snapped their pictures. "Meditate and you'll feel me," he said.

Her mind wandered to the pimps she used to see outside the Women's House of Detention in Manhattan. Even they showed up for their girls.

⁓

THE COURT CAME for her on Tuesday, June 21, 1966, her twenty-fifth day of incarceration, not to release her, but to hand her another grand jury summons.

At 10:30 a.m., Rosemary headed straight to the grand jury room, dressed conservatively in a tan skirt and a white sleeveless blouse with matching gloves. She expected that the DA would drop their subpoena. They didn't. Now she faced twenty-five days of prison time for *each* unanswered question. At that rate, she could spend years inside.

Timothy, Jack, and other Millbrook residents gathered outside the courtroom holding armloads of handpicked flowers, expecting to greet Rosemary after her release. Instead, Timothy read a statement from Rosemary to the assembled press: "I've lost twenty-five days of my life. Although I am not a criminal, I've spent the last three weeks in jail. I think it is important that before you complete serving on the grand jury that you visit the Dutchess County Jail and speak to the inmates and see what we do to people in the name of protecting society."

Timothy embraced her during a break from the proceedings. In a rare display of anguish, Rosemary twisted her dainty white gloves in her hand. Her makeup had run and her red-rimmed eyes were bleary with tears. She explained the situation: She faced more prison time for not cooperating. They had broken her. The one upside was that "it looks like I can go home today."

"Courage," the press heard Timothy say to her.

She collected herself before walking out into the scrum of waiting reporters. Moments later, photographers captured Rosemary laughing with her head thrown back and sunglasses on, glamorous and free, holding the stack of books that had kept her company during her time behind bars, as she walked out of the courthouse and into a waiting car with Timothy.

Meanwhile, the grand jury reconvened in her absence as her stunned lawyer realized that his client had skipped out on the remaining portion of the hearing.

"Miss Rosemary Woodruff?" the district attorney said. "Miss Woodruff?" He repeated the name three more times before realizing that Rosemary had left. A fugitive now.

On the drive back to the estate, Rosemary kept imagining that she heard police sirens. But once they passed the gatehouse, that magical sensation returned, and she calmed. She noted the changes to the property in her absence—the lush greenness, the redolent smell of early summer, the fields full of wildflowers. They went directly to the woods.

Rosemary and Timothy immediately started making love. "I tried to talk of jail; he wanted to show me a tantric pose. I was pale from

lack of sun; his body was golden brown. I was fearful, he was confident." For the first time the power of their lovemaking skewed in his
direction. She had always been the more sensual one, the fearless one.
Jail had stripped her of this power.

She stopped him and confessed that she'd absconded. "Look, I
didn't have permission to leave today. I just wanted to be with you,"
she said.

He was angry. "You didn't learn anything in jail, then?"

"I learned how to clean a jailhouse," she said, annoyed.

"They probably have a warrant out now," he said and stormed off
to call Tepper.

Rosemary disappeared farther into the woods, running through
the patches of poison ivy to which she was immune. Just a little more
time for herself before she'd have to go back to the courtroom.

The proceedings continued three days later. The DA interrogated
Rosemary on her sex life, religious convictions, and drug use. Whatever Rosemary said, or didn't say, persuaded the grand jury to decline
to move forward with an indictment, keeping Timothy and the Millbrook residents safe from prosecution, at least temporarily. Despite
the courageousness of her act, Rosemary's contempt case received little attention outside Poughkeepsie.

Two months later, in the September issue of *Playboy*, Rosemary
read an interview that Timothy had conducted while she languished
in jail. In it, he spoke about the lessons learned from 311 trips and
about the acceleration of the nervous system and cellular changes in
the brain after taking acid. In this interview, Timothy uses the phrase
"Turn on, tune in, drop out," a motto that would reach critical mass
the following year in San Francisco at the Human Be-In.

But for Rosemary the most noteworthy parts of his wide-ranging
interview involve sex and LSD. Touch becomes "electric and erotic"
and generates "genital energy," he said. "There is no question that

LSD is the most powerful aphrodisiac ever discovered by man." And later: "In a carefully prepared, loving LSD session, a woman will inevitably have several hundred orgasms."

Rosemary wondered what woman in the world would back that statement.

She felt affronted by his embellishments and the effect they would have on readers. Rosemary had too much respect and awe—awe in that overwhelming, sometimes even terrible sense of the word—to proselytize so widely and in such a sensationalized way. The power Timothy wielded reminded her of Frodo's golden ring in *The Lord of the Rings*. "The idea of turning others on was repugnant to me—the responsibility!" she wrote. Rosemary had worked for months consuming LSD in the most opportune settings with a guide, learning how to do it responsibly. To think that these drugs would be handed out freely, with absolutely zero oversight or set and setting training, ran counter to her respect for the shadow side of these substances—the dark alleyways and subterranean cellars that could level a person for months if not years. How could Timothy promise neurological enlightenment and oceanic orgasms without also warning of what Carl Jung described in 1954 as the price of the "'pure gifts of the Gods.' You pay very dearly for them." Evangelizers like Timothy behaved like sorcerers' apprentices who had learned "how to call the ghosts but did not know how to get rid of them again."

Rosemary paused at the paragraph mentioning a session with his wife, Nena. "I opened my eyes and looked into the eyes of my wife and was pulled into the deep blue pools of her being, floating softly in the center of her mind." The line—about the blue eyes of his famous model wife, from whom he was still not divorced—pained her. When the interviewer asked him about the rumor that he could—and sometimes did—have two or three women in his bed every night, Leary was evasive. "Any charismatic person who is conscious of his own mythic potency awakens this basic hunger in women," he said. But he added that sleeping around was a "very low-level concept."

She wished he would have said something about the religion she had fought so hard for in that grand jury room. She wished that he would have mentioned her at all. In the ten pages *Playboy* devoted to the interview, there is not one reference to Rosemary.

Noel Tepper filed an appeal on the contempt charge. Rosemary felt her jail time had been excessive, unfair, an abuse of power that she wanted rectified, even though she had already served time. The American Civil Liberties Union got behind "the Woodruff appeal," as the ACLU called it, though after two years of paper shuffling, the courts unanimously upheld the conviction. She had fought for her integrity and lost, but she'd fought nonetheless.

Eight

Death of the Mind

After the dustup of the prior year—two arrests, a raid, Rosemary's contempt case, an ongoing appeal, consistent threats from the Millbrook locals—the lawyer Noel Tepper floated the idea of incorporating their acid research collective into a state-recognized religion, following in the footsteps of the Native American Church, which had started incorporating state by state in 1918. Tepper found the process far smoother than he had anticipated, and later in 1966, Timothy's church, named the League for Spiritual Discovery (LSD), achieved tax-free status.

Timothy announced the League at a press conference on September 20, 1966, at the New York Advertising Club. "Like every great religion of the past," he said, "we seek to find the divinity within and to express this revelation in a life of glorification and worship of God." He outlined their commandments: League members, who each received a special beaded "LSD" amulet necklace (a kind of insider status symbol akin to a members-only jacket), would "turn on" once a week with LSD and once a day with marijuana while promising never to "alter the consciousness of thy fellow man" and never preventing "thy fellow man from altering his own consciousness." They planned,

Timothy said, to secede from the Union, print their own money, and eat off their own land. "Our aim, like the aims of any religious group just beginning, is to transform American society."

Timothy's foot was fully off the brake. He was now advocating for the widest possible LSD use—like a true missionary. Timothy "peddled LSD as a chemically synthesized fountain of youth, as satori, the ten sefirot, and an infinite orgasm wrapped up in an easy to swallow tablet," observed one writer.

In addition to establishing tax-free status and a religious doctrine, Timothy launched his "Celebrations," psychedelic theater shows, held once a week—like a Sunday visit to church—at the packed Village Theater in Manhattan for $3 a seat.

Opening night on September 20, 1966, was the first of many sold-out performances with all 2,830 seats filled. A mob of young intellectuals jostled for extra tickets under the marquee that read,

DR. TIMOTHY LEARY
The Death Of The Mind

It had taken six months—a process that started while Rosemary sat in jail—to find a space willing to take the show on, even with Billy Hitchcock's financial backing, until they landed on the Village Theater, next door to Rosemary's favorite kosher deli, Ratner's. Rosemary had visited when it was still called the Commodore, a five-story red-brick vaudeville theater. The nondescript exterior belied an Art Deco extravaganza inside with gilded ceilings and a grand stage encircled by a byzantine proscenium arch that looked like a pulpit in an ornate Roman Catholic Church.

A sitar player greeted the audience as a projector beamed up kaleidoscopes of ink blotches blurring together, "like far outlines of a dream," as Rosemary wrote, a technique inspired by the West Coast's acid tests thrown by the writer Ken Kesey and his band of Merry Pranksters. These parties celebrated a no-holds-barred, "get weird" style of getting high (as compared with Timothy's psychological/ceremonial approach). Still, the desire to connect with like-minded people and lose your bearings drew people from both coasts.

As the master of ceremonies, Timothy greeted the audience barefoot in a collarless white blouse and white pants, sat on a daybed situated stage right under the moody lighting, and opened with a sermon: "Let us pray. We pray for the courage and the clarity, clarity to share with you our revelation. We pray that the energy released will be used for the benefit of mankind and not for our personal gain or psychological enhancement. We pray that your minds may open like flowers and receive the message that was sent in love."

Then he launched into the object of the night's celebration: Hermann Hesse's 1927 novel, *Steppenwolf*. Ralph Metzner, whom Timothy had once nearly dismissed as "too academic, too dainty British, too bookish, too Ivory Tower" to research psychedelics, played Harry Haller, a man transmuted from repressed neurotic into Steppenwolf, or "the free, the savage, the untamable, the dangerous and strong," as Hesse wrote. Over the course of the book, Haller indulges in three-somes, opium binges, and even murder, providing a bizarre foundation for a new religion, even one that revolved around the ritualized use of acid. Rosemary appeared onstage as Hermine, all sex and carnality, wearing an overstuffed bra to amplify her silhouette, breasts jutting out aggressively in shadow on the screen behind her, and introduced Haller to the strange new world of the Magic Theater: "Entrance for madmen only, cost—your mind."

At the climax of Haller's evolution, Metzner as Haller grabbed Rosemary as Hermine and mimed wrapping his hands around her throat, choking her to death. Rosemary flailed cartoonishly—the Jungian female shadow, or anima, fully submerged—acting out the self-obliterating love she described desiring while reading Huxley's *The Genius and the Goddess.*

After her onstage death, Rosemary enjoyed the show as an audience member. "The special effects were fantastic. It really preceded Stanley Kubrick's *2001*," she wrote in earnest. Timothy, her "mental hero," stood "alone on the stage and declared what I too had fervently come to believe as basic to human rights, that what or whom one chose to put in one's body was one's own business and not the government's."

The ceremony ended, and Timothy let the audience go with a flourish: "After death and rebirth comes a period of entry. You will go out now. It must be gentle. Slowly, slowly." Many walked out hand in hand without speaking, totally agog.

To Timothy, the show represented "a mind-loss experience . . . a drug-induced loss of self, a journey to the inner world." Some, not currently under the influence, like the critic Diana Trilling, panned the show as pat and incomprehensible. The dominant reaction, however, was positive. The theater world called it "the biggest off-Broadway event in many seasons."

The "Celebrations" continued for nine weeks every Tuesday night. From *Steppenwolf*, they moved to Jesus Christ, a show that Rosemary directed, and then to the Buddha. During a publicity shot for their Jesus show, Timothy tried to persuade Rosemary to wrap her legs around him as he hung from a handmade wooden cross, but as if enacting the metaphor of the tension between fame and family, it "could not hold the two of us," she wrote.

She attended every performance—so attuned to his voice that she noticed each missed cue and drew her breaths in tandem with his as he delivered his lines. She scanned the audience for any dangers, gauging the reaction to his words and letting him know what had worked and what had failed to captivate. She supported the show and her man in myriad unacknowledged ways, even sewing loose buttons on his costumes.

One day as she was handing out flyers for the show on the street, a woman warned her, "He's the devil, the devil. You should beware of false prophets."

Rosemary laughed off people like this who would never know what it felt like to be so *attuned*. "We were off-Broadway hits, lecture tour triumphs, sure of ourselves, glowing, in love, a hypnotized hypnotist and his assistant," she wrote. Timothy recalled the experience of working with Rosemary: "Standing on stage at Celebrations. Reciting our poetry and hearing your soft voice echoing back. What beauty our love created for the world."

After the show she would put her arms around him and lead him away from his followers to Ratner's. Then they'd drive back to Millbrook, sharing a bottle of champagne, like the first time.

～⌒～

DRAWN BY THE PUBLICITY since their arrests, trial, and grand jury proceedings, greater numbers of visitors came to Millbrook. Rosemary described the new League for Spiritual Discovery members as "city guerillas, urban warriors, priestesses, pirates, protestors, utopian visionaries, mystical enchanters, revolutionaries. Outlaws, hoping to be acquitted, absolved, vindicated, pardoned, excused, forgiven, purged, released, discharged, dismissed, liberated, let go, set free." The residents composted, avoided animal products, grew their own organic vegetables, a novelty at the time, and ate mostly brown rice—a diet, championed by Rosemary in particular, with roots in Zen Buddhism that applied yin and yang principles to food. (Though Eve Babitz also recalled that crates of Velveeta cheese dotted the property alongside cartons of Pall Mall menthols.) A woman named Bhavani, a Hindu convert, ensured that Timothy remained on the spiritual path; Betsy and Bob Ross, siblings, farmed and tended to the new baby goat; Diane di Prima, the famous redheaded Beat poet, arrived with her husband and daughter; Art Kleps, a verbose and charming psychologist who had inspired Timothy when he started his own absurdist acid religion, the Neo-American Church, moved in, drank routinely to excess, and named himself the "chief Boo-Hoo"; the attractive Jean McCreedy, a divorcée with two young sons, fled a middle-class life as a secretary in Washington, D.C., to live in Millbrook, only to do similar work in stranger settings as Timothy's personal secretary. Jean and the other residents, including Susan Leary, who returned to Millbrook on breaks from school, responded to the growing pile of fan mail, embracing their roles as emissaries of mass drug education:

"I'm writing a term paper . . ."

"How do I join your religion?"

"Dear Dr. Leary I would like to turn on the town of Toledo."

In the kitchen, the heart of the Big House, strangers searched the cupboards or boiled water or, for those not following the diet, fried up bacon at all hours. Children jumped on the trampoline set up outside on the porch. Women, most a generation younger than Rosemary, sauntered by in bikinis or with their tops off, perky breasts bouncing as they headed to the waterfall. Most hailed from the White upper-middle class—children given enough rope to feel comfortable throwing away all the bourgeois trappings that their parents had worked so hard to attain.

As always, Timothy danced in the eye of the hurricane, holding court with his shirt off on the porch in between puffs of his cigarettes. Though he publicly called himself priest and prophet, he warned others about falling for power trips and gurus. Yet when he told his acolytes to remove all the pavement on the property, they jumped to break up the gravel. When he asked them to gather all the metal in the house and bury it, they acted without question.

Still, "it was truly beautiful. Truly communal," said the light show artist Rudi Stern, also in residence, who helped design the psychedelic theater shows. "Charlie Mingus playing piano in the living room. Marshall McLuhan would be there for breakfast. The Beatles were on the telephone." Tripping together intensified, even synchronized, their visions. Groups reported receiving collective prophecies, as the Aztecs once did. Someone would ask a question in their mind, and the person next to them would receive the answer. There was a shared dedication to cognitive openness—magic and cohesion. It felt at times like being stranded together on the most exciting desert island with more than enough food and all your favorite records.

The world clamored for more Timothy Leary. He was in high demand as a lecturer, a provocateur, a (fairly) respectable guest on talk shows to explain the behaviors of the youth generation, a reliable source for a perfect sound bite. He embodied the many flavors of the new counterculture: the youthful (but not young) rebel, eccentric professor, jailed prophet, and psychedelic superstar. But fame doesn't equal money. Millbrook required funds. As popular as the "Celebrations" were, accounts still bled red; someone needed to pay for the unending rolls of toilet paper, heat, food, electricity, and even medical bills.

Luckily, there was money in academia. Timothy charged at least $1,000 per one-hour college lecture (almost $10,000 today) and performed his "Celebrations," traveling with Rosemary and half a ton of equipment. In 1967, the year Timothy entertained vast swaths of college students around the country, more than 85 percent of freshmen had listed "developing a meaningful philosophy of life" as a "very important" or "essential" personal life goal.

This meaning, Timothy argued, would not be found in the classroom. Dressed in his guru garments (handpicked and sewn by Rosemary) and donning his megawatt smile, Timothy told the students that politicking and education were pointless—even detrimental. It was an exercise in collective insanity to try to change institutions from within. He was fond of peppering his lectures with provocative quips like, "People should not be allowed to talk politics, except on all fours." Despite the cynical rhetoric, the kids of the New Left, a student-driven protest movement that endorsed freedom of speech, civil rights, and the end to the Vietnam war, connected Leary's higher consciousness philosophy with their own raised political consciousness—whether or not the two were truly aligned. Soon they would learn that Leary held few things sacrosanct and his irreverence was the true source of his power. As an endorser of Timothy's philosophies, you had to stay agile, reminding yourself that Timothy said almost everything with a wink. As he would later say, "You are only as young as the last time you changed your mind."

Life under Timothy meant struggling with the dissonance between perception and reality. Everyone understood that the Big House belonged to Timothy—and by extension to Rosemary. To hammer this in, Timothy would round the house, like the lord of the manor, popping into rooms unannounced, interrupting lovers mid-action, smiling as he closed the door. But no one dared to do the same to Rosemary and Timothy, whose bedroom on the third floor remained off-limits to most visitors.

Rosemary, so accustomed to her place in the audience, treasured her newfound sway. She situated herself as Timothy's first lieutenant, upholding his ideals and embodying his philosophies. She became the queen of set and setting, applying her hostessing touches that she learned during her second marriage. She tidied up trip locations and properly beautified them with bright, engaging colors and prints; she cooked healthy meals, patted out rice cakes, and served green tea before and during the rituals; she even sewed special costumes to wear. She embodied the turned-on, tuned-in, and dropped-out aspiration—a sublimely gorgeous, blissed-out model of earthly transcendence.

On their bed beneath a round stained-glass window, Rosemary and Timothy spent hours writing, propped up by pillows, cigarettes between their stained fingers. Under those covers, Timothy embarked on work that culminated in the publication, two years later, of his most successful books, *The Politics of Ecstasy* and *High Priest*. In addition, he finished a treatise called *Start Your Own Religion*, planned his lectures, and prepped for weekly TV and radio interviews. Rosemary offered her highly honed bullshit detector and her knack for finding the quickest route to the simplest and most memorable lines.

They were revered for the depth and passion of their sex life almost as much as for their contributions to drug culture. As the brief hanger-on and former Harvard colleague Charles Slack put it, "No romance had ever had more claims made for it, ecstatic, spiritual or orgasmic. It was the shining hope of love, with dope for the whole love generation of the sexual revolution. If Mom and Dad would only turn on and fuck like Tim and Rosemary, there would be less hate in the world."

As Timothy embraced his role as the counterculture's wise father figure, he further abdicated his role as parent. While Susan attended her freshman year at the University of Wisconsin, Jack was left to his own devices at Millbrook High. Since no one made sure he ate regular meals, and he was often too high to feed himself properly, he lived on Grape Nuts and peanut butter sandwiches. When he made it to school, he was often so hungry and exhausted that he could barely read the blackboard. He was labeled a pariah, and school administrators did little to intervene.

Timothy was "totally inept at being a father to me and Susan," Jack later told the biographer Robert Greenfield. "Actually, he would sometimes moan about us as the millstones around his neck. That's a direct quote."

Timothy and Rosemary, as the king and queen, exhibited a form of psychedelic "spiritual narcissism," a psychological state described by the Tibetan Buddhist meditation master Chögyam Trungpa as an "ego-centered version of spirituality." At a party at Millbrook, Timothy and Rosemary, deep in an acid trance, believed that they transmogrified into Jesus and Mary. Timothy lay prone on the floor, his arms outstretched as if nailed to a cross, while Rosemary wept over his body. The guests stepped over the lovers and rolled their eyes. Quoting "the wickedest man in the world" Aleister Crowley, who was a noted heroin, cocaine, and peyote user, Rosemary felt "infinitely superior to anything we might happen to meet." The goal was "ego death," but the outcome, at least in this messianic stage of their drug journey, was a combination of snobbery and expansiveness—an ego *inflation*. Rosemary and Timothy (and many others like them) thus dismissed people who weren't as "enlightened," as in those who hadn't done enough work with psychedelics. They expressed an imperiousness while devoting their lives, like missionaries, to sharing their special knowledge with the huddled masses who were inferior in mind, body, and consciousness.

Nina Graboi, an older visitor to the estate, described Rosemary, as the others did, as "unearthly" and "radiant." During Graboi's visit, a group gathered around Rosemary after she underwent a solo twelve-hour trip in the meditation house. Surrounded by eager followers, Rosemary recounted her vision to the rapt crowd: Animals and plants had communicated without voices and affirmed the house's decision to pursue a vegetarian diet. "Don't let your people harm us," they had told her. The group listened, as rapt as a Christian witnessing a visitation by a saint.

The Timothy and Rosemary epic love story was, Rosemary would write later, a folie à deux. A shared delusion.

NINA WAS MORE THAN just an admiring visitor; she also was an early witness to the dark side of this shared delusion.

Nina ran daily meditation sessions at the Center, an outpost for the League for Spiritual Discovery in Manhattan on Hudson Street, open twenty-four hours a day for spiritual exercises. An Indian tabla played from a cheap record player. Everyone sat on the floor because they had no money for furniture. Still, the place was robbed several times.

Nina was born Gusti at the tail end of World War I in 1918 just outside Leopoldstadt, the Jewish quarter in Vienna. By twenty years old, she had fled the Nazis in four countries with her husband and eventually found safe passage to America, leaving her family behind forever in Europe. Nina and her husband wasted no time assimilating to the 1950s American dream. They started a business in children's toys and clothing, moved to Long Island, raised two children, threw money at her theater hobby, and settled into their perfect upper-middle-class existence—glamorous clothes and vacations to Florida—until a gnawing sensation of *is that all there is?* entered stage left.

Like Rosemary, Nina started reading books on Eastern religions and the esoteric and studied supernatural research emerging from Duke University on subjects like telepathy, telekinesis, and astral travel. Her soul-searching led her to attend a meeting on the metaphysical, where she first laid eyes on Timothy. She fell in his thrall.

"I cannot now remember one thing he said," she wrote in her memoir *One Foot in the Future*. "For the few minutes I faced him, he gave me his undivided attention, while his eyes held my gaze."

She embarked on her first psychedelic experience in 1966 at age forty-seven taking DET, a milder derivative of DMT, with Ralph Metzner. When she did, Hitler appeared. "He smells of glue and I see that he is a puppet. Glue oozes from his joints," she wrote. She began to laugh, and despite enduring that horrific image, she became a die-hard advocate. Her "familiar reality had cracked," and she moved to her Manhattan studio full time, leaving behind her husband and fourteen-room mansion in Long Island. After that trip, the Millbrook community embraced Nina, and she often entertained Timothy and League guests in her apartment.

It was at one such party that she first witnessed a fight between the high priest and his perfect love. Nina knew that Timothy's temperament ran hot and cold. He could be warm and charismatic and then cruel. His contempt had landed on Nina in the past, but she'd never seen it directed at his queen. Timothy sat on a couch between Rosemary and Susan Leary, who was home from college. The two women had the same vacant and weary expressions, while Timothy, more animated than even his typical high-octane energy, poured glasses of champagne from the two bottles he had brought, and spoke almost nonstop. As Timothy held court, Nina observed Rosemary. "I saw her attempt a wan smile from time to time, but the drawn look did not leave her face."

Since the Laredo arrest, Rosemary had become the focus of Susan Leary's unyielding hatred after Timothy deputized Rosemary to act as his daughter's primary caregiver. Susan called Rosemary an "evil woman"—"frigid and barren," words that cut deep—who set out to "destroy everything she could lay her spells on." To emphasize the point, Susan played Donovan's hit song "Season of the Witch" for hours, the rumbling of the deep bass line resonating through the house.

Nina felt the vibe lift, however, once Allen Ginsberg, Richard Alpert, the Indian spiritual teacher Sri Shyamji Bhatnagar, and his new disciple, John Schewel, arrived. John, an acting student at NYU, had the face of Bob Dylan, the body of a basketball star, and the confidence of a man twice his age. Born into money (his father was a successful lawyer, his grandfather owned a chain of office supply stores, and his aunt married into a politically connected family), John grew up in Miami Beach, an oasis of midcentury wealth, and spent his free time wandering the newly built rooms of the iconic crescent-shaped Fontainebleau Hotel on Millionaire's Row. There he observed stars like Frank Sinatra and Sammy Davis Jr. and other men who weren't stars but possessed their same command—men who had clear power over their domain. John was a sponge. He soaked all that swagger in. His family expected him to pursue the law or politics, but John knew early that he would dedicate his life to the exploration and the journey, not to the destination.

The crack in John's Door occurred early, in middle school, long before he had tried psychedelics, just like Rosemary and Timothy. It happened onstage when he played Willy Loman in *Death of a Salesman*. During a particularly salient line of a monologue, John took a beat and watched as the audience held its collective breath and leaned forward in anticipation of his next line. For that brief moment he commanded the room. There was magic in this silence—an "invocation," as he called it—the ability to manipulate reality.

John, a highly intuitive young man, sensed a feeling of predetermination about the party. And as he adjusted to the big names in the room, he felt his attention shift and noticed the beautiful, somber woman sitting silently on the couch. He could feel her notice him, too. "More than attraction at the central level or an emotional level or even an intellectual level," he said. "It was more like being familiar. We were familiar."

Meanwhile, Timothy kept drinking and talking. After he had finished the two bottles of champagne, he said something inaudible but clearly nasty.

Rosemary left the room. Nina followed.

"What's going on?" Nina asked.

Rosemary broke down. "He wanted me to bring his phonograph

to the Center, but I know how much he'd miss it," she said, sobbing. "He'd be mad at me tomorrow if I'd brought it." These were the kinds of fights that occurred between them, the petty nonsense that would bloom into something hideous. A few months prior at Millbrook, after a visit from Timothy's wife—his divorce was still not finalized—Timothy had lashed out at Rosemary over a minor infraction. "It would be easier to go back with her," he said, meaning Nena, his wife.

When Nina heard the reason for Timothy's temper tantrum, she couldn't help but laugh. "What a dilemma! Part of him wants to give everything away and another part wants to keep it, so he makes you the scapegoat!"

Rosemary found that funny, too. She returned to the room in good spirits, which agitated Timothy.

As dawn broke, Timothy still didn't want to leave, so Rosemary and Susan waited by the elevator as Sri Shyamji Bhatnagar and John said their goodbyes and joined them in the hall. Nina couldn't have known it—and might not have even realized years later when she wrote about it in her memoir—but this image, of Rosemary standing in a shadowy corridor, deciding whether to leave or stay, would become a recurrent theme, an echo from the future that felt like something Nina would have read in her esoteric books.

And John saw it, too. "From the first time I ever saw Rosemary at the party," he said, "we never talked, but I knew that there was something of destiny about her and myself."

⁓

Cars arrived to shuttle Rosemary and Timothy from interview to airport to interview. Sometimes Rosemary forgot what city she was in. When they were deplaning in Pocatello during a trip to Idaho State University, an unexpected group of cameramen met them on the tarmac. She watched Timothy transform from a tired middle-aged man with stubble and unbrushed teeth into "a star whose essence was the certainty that he could charm anyone." It reminded her of watching the actor Gary Cooper interact with strangers at the Manhattan restaurant Toots Shor's, how he seemed "to have thicker skin, poreless, inches deep as though carved from something other than flesh and shining from within," she wrote. Timothy had this skin.

He lived to serve his audience—an hour of meditation before the show, followed by a required meet and greet after it, where admirers plied him with drugs and alcohol. He shared his radiance with the world, leaving less of it for Rosemary. She rarely got him alone. She held his coat and gathered his items, collecting gifts from rabid fans— messages, flowers, and weed—and preserved the stray papers and ephemera to add to his growing archive. Rosemary became the enforcer, the protector of her special human, standing guard in the cloakroom or by the entryway to the greenroom backstage. When two unwanted young male guests, each more than six feet tall, muscled their way backstage, Rosemary asked them to leave "politely but oh so strongly," one of the men recalled in a follow-up fan letter to her. She noticed the exits and planned for emergencies.

Still, they maintained their deep cognitive merging—engaging in an almost telepathic ability to know what the other felt or thought, especially in crowds. "Our confidentiality was public, unspoken," she wrote. They fueled the endless days of touring with small doses of LSD that made everything "amusing or weird by glances and a quick smile." Rosemary turned on whenever Timothy did, and he liked to drop acid before every performance. High in the control booth, she would chant along and echo back his words to him.

"Can you float through the universe of your body and not lose your way?" Timothy asked the crowd.

That was the question, wasn't it?

Nine

The Robot

Timothy's celebrity hit a West Coast crescendo at the Human Be-In on January 14, 1967, in San Francisco, a protest against California's new law outlawing LSD. The local underground paper *The Oracle* had billed it as a "gathering of the tribes"—or the two primary factions of the youth generation, the heads, Timothy's acolytes, versus the fists, those who formed political parties to fight the power. Though these two groups often diverged in their interests (super-high people rarely found the energy to march or protest or canvass for candidates), twenty thousand of them danced the day away in the sunshine together in Golden Gate Park.

Dennis Hopper stood in the crowd taking pictures with his Nikon camera. Gary Snyder blew a horn to mark the beginning. Allen Ginsberg took the stage in a flowing white robe playing finger cymbals. Timothy, dressed in white with flowers behind his ears to cover his hearing aid, delivered the line that would echo across the culture, just as it echoed across the crowded park.

"Turn on . . . Tune in . . . Drop out," he said, enunciating each word and repeating the phrase. "Drop out of high school, drop out of college, drop out of graduate school, drop out of junior executive, drop out of senior executive."

The speech ushered in yet another moral panic. Now parents and lawmakers worried about a trend called the "dropout effect," the aftermath of taking too much LSD that led to "permanent dropouts from society, abjuring family, friends and productive activity, and embracing instead a hallucinogen-oriented, solipsistic, unproductive existence," according to one psychiatrist. *The Saturday Evening Post* warned that "if you take LSD even once, your child may be born malformed or retarded," quoting from a soon-to-be-retracted article on chromosome abnormalities in LSD users published in *Science*. The panic not only led to further steps toward harsher drug laws and sentencing guidelines but also stymied research efforts. Fewer doctors now wanted to research the substances—and, if they did, were taken less seriously by their peers—at the same time that test subjects became less likely to sign on to be studied.

It is telling that Rosemary didn't accompany Timothy to this legendary event, preferring instead to remain at his home in the Berkeley Hills. Rosemary had grown weary of his fame and suspicious of some of his followers. And insecure about her place in the new hierarchy. "Some sense of vulnerability, perhaps, or not looking my best and not wanting to face the huge crowd at Golden Gate Bridge Park . . . It was peaceful in the house. I loved being alone there an entire day." While Timothy chased the bright lights of controversy and fame, Rosemary's priorities had shifted: She wanted to settle down, start a family, and move away from the chaos—an early fracture between them that would only widen over time.

Rosemary and Timothy rejoined the scene when the tour traveled farther south to Los Angeles. They attended parties at a famous producer's house in the Hollywood Hills, where Rosemary, wearing too-tight couture borrowed from Flo Ferguson, told Dennis Hopper and

Peter Fonda, who shared snippets from their *Easy Rider* script in progress, that they should change their ending. (They didn't. It ended with the main characters' double murder. "We blew it" is the memorable concluding line meant to sound the death knell of 1960s positivity.)

They visited Aldous Huxley's widow, Laura, and dined at Otto Preminger's house with Helen Gurley Brown, the editor in chief of *Cosmopolitan*, the actress Carol Channing, and the feminist icon Gloria Steinem. Rosemary remained silent, observing Steinem in her miniskirt flirting with Timothy.

They were among the beautiful people.

Timothy performed his "Illumination of the Buddha" show as an opener for the Grateful Dead at the Santa Monica Civic Auditorium. The SoCal crowd, high on white lightning acid made by the underground chemist and Grateful Dead audio engineer, Owsley Stanley, lobbed tabs of LSD, capsules of mescaline, and packets full of hashish onstage. A lone old lady threw eggs at Timothy as he spoke.

Backstage, Rosemary met the infamous chemist as Timothy lectured. "Are you sure you guys get high?" Owsley asked snidely. Owsley and his girlfriend, the chemist Melissa Cargill, a descendant of one of the wealthiest families in America, had been making their own top-shelf, highly potent acid in tablet, dropper, and capsule form in a variety of basement labs across the country since 1965. People like Owsley wanted to transgress. To get weird. Owsley's sardonic reaction to Timothy was an early indicator of the shifting tides of the counterculture receding further to the extremes as the decade neared its ending.

A chance encounter backstage would be the night's most fateful. A short, bearded man with indigo eyes, wearing embroidered handspun clothing, smelling of incense and ocean, introduced himself as John Griggs. Timothy's League for Spiritual Discovery had inspired

Griggs and his followers—a unique blend of surfer dudes, proselytiz-ers of the gospel of LSD, and hard-core drug traffickers—to start their own acid religion, which they called the Brotherhood of Eter-nal Love.

Rosemary was immediately taken with John, viewing him as a fellow magic man, another hippie messiah. Griggs dazzled Timothy, too, who wrote about him, "Although unschooled and unlettered, he was an impressive person. He had this charisma, energy, that sparkle in his eye."

Griggs, once a small-time local crook, a man quick to whip out his fists, had robbed a Hollywood producer of his stash of LSD, par-took of it, and never recovered. He ran home, high as hell, to share "the divinity flowing within him" with his homemaker wife, Carol Griggs. She tried it, too. And understood. The Brotherhood religion took off from there.

Griggs, whom others called the Mystic, handed them a satchel filled with Owsley's white lightning tabs and hashish that kept them sky-high for weeks.

Meanwhile, Rosemary's parents gawked from the audience at the new man in their daughter's life. They had seen Timothy on their television sets but never before in person.

"What did you think of the show?" Rosemary asked.

"Ro we don't like the smell of incense, but Tim certainly is a fine speaker," Ruth said.

Timothy and Rosemary stayed at the Woodruff family's tract house in the Los Angeles suburbs. Her brother, Gary, a jock who was uninterested in altered consciousness or drug culture hadn't spent any significant time with his sister since she had left for New York a de-cade earlier. Now she had arrived with this famous older man who advocated for drugs. Only when Timothy tagged along to watch Gary ref a local basketball game did he understand. During a break in the game, Gary looked up to the stands to find a group of young men gathered around his sister's boyfriend. Timothy, Gary realized, was a star.

Despite his notoriety, Rosemary's family embraced Timothy. They could relate to him far better than they could the stern Dutch jazz musician who had driven the family car around town in his underwear. Rosemary's grandmother, Nana, in particular hovered over Timothy, feeding and caffeinating him. Timothy, meanwhile, charmed her father, Verl, with talk of carburetors and diesel engines. The magus entrancing the magician.

The family didn't realize how high Rosemary and Timothy were. At one point, Timothy sat on the couch watching a sitcom as the real-life Woodruff family played out the same scene on the TV. When Gary marched in, the young son on the sitcom did the same. When the neighbor came with a pie, so did the fictional neighbor.

"Unbelievable!" Timothy said. "Do you believe this is happening?"

"I could see what he meant, the family comedy," Rosemary wrote, "the tiny tract house that contained them, the love that held them together, while outside freeways roared past glittering supermarkets."

Their tidy suburban existence was just as alien to Timothy and Rosemary as the high priest and priestess's life was to the Woodruffs.

AFTER NEARLY A MONTH on tour, Rosemary and Timothy returned to Millbrook. A hand-drawn, two-story carnival barker's face with oversized earrings painted on the Big House greeted them. This face did not bring happy tidings. The Millbrook magic had faded in Timothy and Rosemary's absence. "It was a drab reality after Hollywood," Rosemary wrote in her diary. Communal life had taken a toll. People filtered in and out on their own path in search of—what? For some, Millbrook offered refuge, for others an opportunity for experimentation, and for others a place to party. It was a site of religious awakening and rank defilement. Big jugs of red wine sat beneath statues of Buddha. "We were saddled with enormous numbers of people all coming through seeking something, wanting something, needing, using, trashing," Rosemary later said.

Drama abounded. Peggy Hitchcock and her brothers rarely came around anymore. Fifty people and three different religious organizations clashed on the grounds—the Sri Ram Ashram, Art Kleps's Neo-American Church, and Timothy's League members. The Sri Ram Ashram's leader, Bill Haines, had, as Rosemary described him, "a barroom brawler's face . . . the mean bleared features of a mean and angry man. His shouts shook the halls. His saving grace was his outrageous humor and intelligence." Haines brought alpha dog energy that attempted—and often succeeded—in eclipsing Timothy's. "There was something nasty in the feeling of the place, something furtive, sarcastic, and hostile," Rosemary wrote. "The house looked ravaged, raided. Rumors were rife, plots were being hatched, knives sharpened, a king about to be dethroned."

The kitchen filled with signs, KEEP OUT or DO DISHES or DON'T EAT or NO LEFTOVERS, so Rosemary asked the League to build her a second kitchen on the third floor by her room. Unfamiliar voices in heated arguments haunted the place. Dropping acid together did nothing to unite the groups. "Their sessions became a battle of personalities and ego clashing," Jean McCreedy said. Few people disparaged Timothy to his face but did so happily to Rosemary.

The vibe toxified further. The League decided to move out of the Big House and into the woods, setting up camps to live out the summer underneath disintegrating and moldy plastic tarps. When the photographer Alvis Upitis, still a college student, visited the Millbrook estate in the summer of 1967, he remembered batting away feelings of disgust as he took in the group's overall lack of hygiene.

Children sat on sagging dirty diapers. The campsite was a mess. They hadn't built the teepees properly. Foundations were waterlogged. Most of these people did nothing, and it seemed exhausting. Alvis noticed the boxes of cigarettes and the jugs of wine scattered around the property. People were fucked up all the time—and not just on the sacrament but on booze and boredom. They did little meditation or yoga.

Several League members noticed that although Timothy pushed the virtues of outdoor living, he and Rosemary maintained their third-floor bedroom compound and often retired there to sleep or work if it rained. Alvis photographed Rosemary and Timothy there. In one shot, he captured Rosemary sitting beside Timothy, pen in hand, editing his forthcoming lecture. It's one of the few images that documents Rosemary's behind-the-scenes role in Timothy's work. Gorgeous, as always, Rosemary appeared older in these shots, worn down, her cheekbones more pronounced, and a new weariness settling in around the eyes. Alvis wondered how a woman like this ended up here.

Rosemary's status had diminished since their return from the West Coast. Timothy left her alone more often than not now, traveling on lecture tours without her. Timothy, ever the psychologist, delighted in hierarchical rankings. He made lists of the League members and residents, ordering them by importance within categories: How many years of education? How many years of religious practice? In almost every category, Timothy came out on top and Rosemary fell short: no college degree; one year of religious devotion.

Rosemary spent her days making coffee, reading books, and cleaning—sweeping the stairs, cataloging Timothy's recorded interviews, washing last week's dishes, cleaning up mice droppings, smoking hash, doing yoga, recording her trip sessions, picking blackberries, sorting the wash, and making the bed. When he was home, she fixed his coffee every morning and offered herself to him every night. She was a sexually available Sisyphus battling the day-to-day demands of maintaining a millionaire's estate.

She found herself matching her breath to Timothy's while he slept. She missed those exchanges on the road—a dart of the eye that would communicate his deeper thoughts, the oneness of having taken a secret dose, a deep neurophysiological bond in front of throngs of his admirers. That flame had since been extinguished. "I could not think of a life without him and could barely stand the life we had together," she wrote in her diary. Editing lost its luster. She started resenting Timothy's fondness for hyperbole and for "paraphrasing," passing off other people's insights as his own. She urged him to use greater precision in his language, but he bristled in the face of any perceived criticism and often threw her lack of education in her face. "He would not stand for my comments or objections, which for the most part concerned the flattery he poured onto others or himself. I resented the intensity he reserved for himself or for visitors but denied to me," she wrote. Eventually, she refused to read his work; instead, she rifled through his scattered notes in an attempt to glean some insight into his state of mind. In her self-possessed moments, she acknowledged her desire to be totally consumed by another person—just as she had with Mat, Charles, and Allen before Timothy. "To think only of him meant that I could avoid the inner emptiness."

She started taking long, luxurious walks with John Schewel, the handsome young college student from Nina Graboi's party, who had joined the League as a guide. Rosemary appreciated that John focused *on her*—not her in relation to her boyfriend. They walked and talked, discovering abandoned railroad tracks that led to a quarry—as chaste as brother and sister.

In June, when Timothy hadn't called for several weeks, she pleaded with herself not to take it too far, to act cool and confident, and, more than anything else, to be *pleasing* so that he'd come back. Though

Timothy's divorce to Nena was finalized in the spring of 1967, they no longer discussed wedding plans. Still, she held out hope that he would make good on his promise to marry her.

That step seemed less likely these days as they fought more often than not. Even their reconciliations were disappointing, involving champagne and unfulfilling sex. As supposed stand-ins for the counterculture's new great sexual awakening, Rosemary felt shortchanged by the quick appeasement of his desire, leaving her less than satisfied. "Every night he loved me with the hurried obligatory before-I-go-to-sleep bucking fuck of an elderly careless man who in his mind is young and innocent and fucking the bejesus out of me . . . no thousand orgasms, no body electric," she wrote. Timothy, defensively, complained to friends that Rosemary "wanted to be fucked all the time." He told her that she was "impossible to live with."

Timothy's disparagement of Rosemary gave tacit approval for the others to pounce. Art Kleps referred to her as "the broad in his bed" and resented Tim's insistence that his followers view Rosemary as "a virtually celestial being." Another resident wondered why they had paired up in the first place. "Rosemary, beautiful as she was, wasn't the brightest star in the sky, and took all the League gobbledygook at face value, which could leave Tim exasperated. . . . She was determined to be the power behind the Throne of Psychedelia."

Rosemary felt equal to Timothy only when tripping. And he refused to trip with her in any regular intervals now—a way of withholding intimacy, their shared glimpse into what she called "the harmony of things." In public, Timothy painted himself as monogamous, which he described in *Playboy* as "neurological and cellular fidelity." But Rosemary's diary paints a different story. He took other women on tour with him in her place. He didn't even try to hide it. And why should he? He was the acid love guru. She imagined the man she could bring into her bed—someone who would never return, whose face she'd never have to see again. That man didn't exist here. Not in Timothy's world.

"What relationship?" he had actually said that when she pressed him on theirs.

"Please, God," she wrote, "let me be free of this pain of loving."

⁓

NINA GRABOI ACKNOWLEDGED the double bind of the many women in residence who strove to behave as freely and openly as the men but faced inevitable double standards. "It was a paradise to some, hell to others, and it always changed, never presented the same face twice," Nina wrote. You could sleep with whomever you wanted, but you'd still be expected to make dinner. Women kept the place running—balancing the checkbooks, cleaning and caring for the people who cracked, making sure the fridge was stocked and the fire stoked. Most Millbrook women understood that talk of "neurological revolution" tended to halt in the face of one simple question: "Who's going to do the dishes?" Peggy Hitchcock remembers this as the curdling of what she called Timothy's "messianic phase." The feeling of "'Oh, I can change the world,'" she said. "But then you realize, 'Wait a minute. You're dealing with human nature here. It's not going to be that simple.'"

Ruth Denison, who would become a well-respected Buddhist teacher and lead America's first all-women Buddhist meditation retreat, described how certain women, young and beautiful, often got away with doing less at Millbrook. Ruth baked bread, cleaned up after the growing number of cats in the house, and acted as den mother to the varied freak-outs and bad trips. "I was always the kind of homemaker," she said.

Diane di Prima, a published poet, sexually fluid and as controversial as the more famous men in her orbit, still found herself saddled with work while the men played touch football and expected their next round of drinks and food to magically appear. When one of the male residents promised to handle the Thanksgiving turkey, she was barely ruffled when he pawned the task off on her. "The light came in, and faded, and I was still in the kitchen," she wrote. "A familiar feeling." Women had two viable roles: sex object and housekeeper.

Suzie Blue, one of the few Black women in residence, whose age was not disclosed but was likely still a child herself, nannied the children, fending off the advances from much older men. Nina Graboi documented a scene she observed in the kitchen, where a drunk visitor verbally and sexually harassed Suzie. "I bet you can suck good," he said, among other unprintable statements. As Suzie raised her hand to slap him, he punched the teenager in the eye. Suzie brushed off the encounter the next day—insisting that the blood on her face was merely a popped pimple—and Graboi interpreted her own horrified response as regressive. Suzie was enlightened because she had turned the other cheek. Millbrook's mind games created a toxic fun house. All those mutable lines and changing mores created a deep well of self-doubt.

Children as young as nine were given acid mixed with apple cider by adult guides who weren't their parents. Diane di Prima's daughter Jeanne, who did acid with her mother prior to moving to Millbrook at age eight, recalled that after one bad trip, where she imagined that the tree branches were "lances and they were piercing my body," she refused to take any more. Instead of backing off, some adults started dosing her against her knowledge. This happened more than fifty times. "No one ever said, 'Oh, you mean it's doing something bad to Jeannie?'" she told the biographer Robert Greenfield. "After some point, you listen to a kid."

Though Rosemary insisted that Jack and Susan "learned to adapt to communal life" and "survived with various degrees of equanimity," she was either willfully ignorant or actively repressing what was really happening. Jack had followed the advice laid out by his father and dropped out of high school, spending hours in his tower room playing the Doors' "The End"—the key lyric references patricide—and blasting out his mind with higher and higher doses of LSD, DMT, and STP, a.k.a. 2,5-dimethoxy-4-methylamphetamine, a hallucinogen that could last upward of twenty-four hours and was described as "hellish" because it could make you feel imprisoned in your body.

Susan also lived at Millbrook full time after dropping out of college. Though she likened Millbrook to "living in a church of jolly people," she had already attempted suicide. One former resident of Millbrook dated Susan, despite her "reputation as a pincushion," to secure a "strategic advantage of father-in-law Tim." He wrote about their first and only sexual encounter, how she immediately pulled him on top of her and "proceeded to lie there while I did my number." He described her dissociation, without using that word, her blank response that he cruelly likened to "making love to a corpse." The high priest might have been off-limits, but his daughter was open season.

Despite Timothy's neglect of his children, Rosemary held on to the belief, one shared by many unhappy couples, that adding a new life to their partnership would secure their bond. But Rosemary hadn't conceived after more than a year of trying. She visited a local doctor and tried fertility diets and herbal remedies, arranging their trysts around moon cycles, but she menstruated every month. The summer that Alvis visited, the cramps descended, causing uterine pain so severe that only her mother's voice across the country could soothe her.

She dreamed of Timothy, and her dreams, like her *I Ching* throws, carried great significance in her waking life. In one, she and Timothy stood on a bridge hand in hand. Together, they leaped off. In the water, they lost contact, and she reached for him in the dark murk. First his hands brushed her waist and he pulled her to his body. She felt relief as they gazed into each other's eyes. Bubbles formed around his mouth: He was trying to communicate something to her. But then, she wrote in her diary, "I felt his hand on my head then pressure on my shoulder as he sped to the surface, his parting touch was his foot on my head pushing me deeper." Rosemary's subconscious screamed out for her to pay attention to the price of this sublimation.

Feeling more secure one summer night when Timothy returned home, viewing him once again as the magician she had fallen for in that Jeep driving up from New York City, she prepared a meal in the outdoor camp's cooking pit as she listened to Timothy's conversation with the other League members.

"No one is real until they have children."

She stopped cooking and moved closer to his voice. She heard other names of various childless women that Timothy presented as examples. And then "Rosemary." The rest of the conversation faded away. "Why name me?" The force of the realization hit her in the sternum. "I wasn't real, am not really real, do not exist, cannot be until I carry his seed. And I can't. Because I'm not real. My tears, laughter, depressions, enthusiasms don't exist. He ejaculates into a void . . . infertile, fallow me."

The other Millbrook residents passed her in the halls without acknowledging her or lobbed terrible epithets at her—or so she imagined. Maybe she was already dead. Maybe these words existed only in her head.

She found it harder and harder to put her finger on the here and now as the miasma of the pain of living in this hostile—or, worse, cosmically indifferent—environment overwhelmed her senses. She took higher and higher doses of acid to escape that vast, empty, uncanny feeling. So destabilized she could no longer discern what was her *self* in relation to the rest of the world. Was she alive? Did she exist? Convinced that she was a man-made robot, Rosemary searched her body for a manufacturer's imprint.

She was without foundation, outside the magic circle that Timothy as her guide once built around her. She had shed her defenses and now she was too open—vulnerable to attack. It was a vicious cycle. She kept upping her doses in search of that ecstatic feeling until she descended into what she called an acid overdose—a period of psychotic depersonalization.

She outlined her possible next steps:

> **Plan A:** "be still, wait it out, hope it will pass."
>
> **Plan B:** run off to her friend Susan's apartment back in New York.
>
> **Plan C:** return to California, to her parents' home.

Finally, she could go "somewhere in the woods."

She packed her bags and drafted a letter to Timothy: "Pray for me. I pray for you. I'm real. Hope you are too." After moving in and out of several of the estate's buildings, Rosemary spent August, during the height of the Summer of Love, living alone in the woods in a small pump house on the Millbrook estate, continuing her daily acid trips. Another escape in order to find herself.

"Day One: This is the beginning of the exorcism of unrequited love."

She wrote about killing herself on the property. She knew of places where no one would find her. She fantasized about digging her own grave, deep in the woods, her bones buried where bucks dropped their antlers. But then she thought about her beloved dogs—the only real company she kept—her *grinning skull* in the jaws of their mouths.

She wrote the concluding line of a poem: "Love / It's a mad magician."

Jack Leary built her a shelf, set up a small camping stove, and helped her drag a bed inside. A visitor to the estate described chancing upon Rosemary at the pump house, wild-eyed and tending a fire on her knees. She looked as unhinged as she felt. "I wanted to be a person again."

She had few visitors other than Jack and the dogs. She took solace in the solitude. The pump house stood next to a defunct Christmas tree garden—a moneymaking gambit long forgotten with stooped and bent trees that surrounded her shelter. "I was alone in all that vastness, learning which way the wind would blow, listening for the screech owl or the deer. They'd scratch their antlers on the tree bark, the sound of tearing silk." The moths danced around her candle flame. She remembered what fellow Millbrookians had told her about the bears on the estate. During one of her walks, she smelled "the febrile breath of damp fur . . . heavy, fear inspiring, actually."

She turned back on the path. There were dangers here, whether she could smell them or not.

Rosemary returned to the Big House to find it overrun with cameramen shooting a psychedelic western. Timothy was dressed as a cowboy. The teepees were painted Day-Glo. There was no part for Rosemary, so she packed her bags again, this time at age thirty-two to visit California and return to a family she had escaped at seventeen.

Ten

The Seagulls

A few weeks later, Timothy called Rosemary at her parents' house with Millbrook news. Venereal disease rates had skyrocketed in Dutchess County, and residents blamed the surge on Millbrook. The producers of his psychedelic western in production were fighting. When Rosemary added her own complaints about living back home, Timothy suggested that she stay at his Berkeley Hills home with Ralph Metzner, who was living there in Timothy's absence.

She considered Timothy's offer. Was Timothy also giving her tacit approval to move on with someone new? She wrote in her diary, "Perhaps I'll make love to Ralph."

And that's exactly what she did.

By Halloween, Rosemary had moved into Timothy's two-story bungalow, where she had stayed during the Be-In—the place where his first wife had died by suicide. Timothy's touches were still everywhere—Danish furniture, Indian textiles, Buddha statues, and pictures of Jack and Susan as children. She paged through family photo albums, giving special care to the photos of Timothy as a new father. She still wanted that for them.

Ralph took Rosemary to a party in Sausalito, where they drank the acid-spiked punch and listened to a mutual friend gossip about Timothy's reconciliation with Peggy Hitchcock.

"Wasn't that great news?" the woman asked Rosemary.

Rosemary slept with Ralph for the first time that night.

She had initially dismissed him as solemn—even dour—a clipboard wielder, as she called him. But she had misread him. Ralph's emotional displays might have been rare, but they were often more genuine than those of his Harvard colleagues, especially Timothy, whose openness was spread widely, but often withheld from those he loved most.

Ralph also happened to be a phenomenal lover.

"So tender, so sweet, so gentle, so kind, so loving, so passionate, so strong, so lasting, so caring, so real, so true, so right, so deep, so beautiful, so good," she wrote. "Just like me." Metzner referred to her, later, as a "tantric love goddess," so the feeling was mutual.

Their reveries were interrupted, however, when Jack, who was also crashing at his father's house, found his father's best friend and girlfriend in bed together and tried to punch his hand through the sliding glass door with views of the bay. Nothing was going to be simple about this romance.

This did not stop the lovers from embarking on a true love affair. She pictured her life with Ralph, a clinical psychologist who still practiced and held an academic appointment. He was kind and true— different from the others. She could be happy with a man like this.

Together, they tried a new drug, MDA, 3,4-methylenedioxyamphetamine, which everyone called the love drug. The drug first hit with a body high. She felt a surge of ecstatic, clear-eyed energy, unlike the full letting go of the acid experience, confident in the here and now and more comfortable in her skin. Her whole body pulsed in anticipation. The electricity that ran from her to him, connecting them, took her breath away.

Metzner used MDA to great effect in his own psychotherapy sessions, noting that the drug created "a shift in perspective, a reframing of a belief that may be healing and have spiritual implications," often linked with psychological insight. Metzner described this process as an "opening of the heart's center," or the fourth chakra, called *anahata*, associated with balance and serenity. Instead of psychedelics, he called drugs like MDA and, later, MDMA (or ecstasy) empathogens.

As waves of tingling euphoria coursed through their intertwined bodies, they came to the same conclusion at the same time: "We were in love."

The couple called Timothy in Millbrook to tell him the news and to get his blessing. He wished them happiness.

BUT, OF COURSE, that wasn't the end of it. Now that Timothy couldn't have Rosemary, he wanted her more than ever. Part of his change of heart came about because of Peggy Hitchcock's decision to call off their affair after witnessing a simple but telling interaction between Timothy and his daughter. Susan had knocked on his door, in evident need of support and comfort, and Timothy had icily brushed her off. Peggy found the dismissal disturbing enough to break up with him. Peggy expressed something that Rosemary could never fully face: that there was no future with a man who could treat his child this poorly.

Nevertheless, buoyed by a new determination to win back Rosemary's heart, Timothy boarded a flight to California and showed up unannounced at his own house. He invited Rosemary to join him for a walk and made his case. Drawn and disheveled, Timothy told her that he would never be happy with anyone else. He launched into his speech. *She* couldn't be happy either, without him. He promised her a quieter life: that he would close Millbrook, that they would find a house for just the two of them, that they would live by the sea—Cape

Cod, as she had once suggested—and that they would raise a family. A simpler life. And then he proposed.

"I want you to come to Laguna with me tonight. We will be married there with your parents present," he said, finally offering the concrete marriage proposal that she had dreamed of for years. They shared an eternal love, he said. She lived in the center of his mandala. That he had "never been unfaithful in thought, word or deed"—a lie, though she had no doubt he felt that this was true. In this life and thousands of lives before, they were meant for each other "and will always be."

Rosemary took it all in. She believed in their eternal love, too. But in *this* life the relationship felt wrong. In this life it *didn't work*. His remonstrations came too late. The chances had come and gone. She explained to Timothy that Ralph could actually be good for her—could fulfill her.

"I need to be a mother," she said.

"We'll have a baby, I promise you," Timothy said.

"I don't believe you."

Though Timothy left that same day to return to Millbrook without Rosemary, he still didn't believe he had lost her for good. "I knew you were trapped in the wrong role and even in my despair, wondered, how will we get us out of this?"

Rosemary returned to Ralph, ready to give herself fully to him. But he was quieter now, uncomfortable. She began to doubt her own senses. Did she love Ralph? The two decided to take MDA again and see where the love drug took them this time.

As the good feelings slid through her body, Ralph glowed with youthfulness. Rosemary envisioned him as a camp scout. They clasped hands and floated on the bed.

"Let's not struggle," she heard Ralph say.

As the drug hit harder, Metzner confessed his concerns about betraying Timothy, a man whom he loved and adored—the person who had turned him on. Rosemary suddenly felt sick. Her head throbbed and her stomach spasmed. She had a fever, and her skin was hot to the touch. Her heart pounded in her ears and her jaw clenched. It reminded her of the painful stomachache she had after leaving her second husband for the mad composer Charles Mills. As she writhed around in pain, she also recalled the peyote session and the epiphany that had come with it: *I had to change my life*. She began to see the relational patterns swirling before her:

> Where had my earlier confidence and conviction come from? Mated to T, mated to him. How had I left Mat? Made love to another man.
> Brad beat me . . . I ran
> Mat was unfaithful . . . I ran
> Charles drank too much . . . I ran . . .
> I wouldn't run this time. I would love him, and he would love me, and we'd live happily ever after.

But with which man?

Still nauseated the next day, Rosemary recovered as Ralph left to work at Mendocino State Hospital. Feeling conflicted in the light of day, she struggled to understand her own mind. "Ralph's youth to Timothy's age. His affection and liking for all parts of my body," she wrote. She parsed out the reasons for embarking on the affair. "My belief that love was necessary for my survival," she wrote. "The need to teach [Timothy] a lesson, perhaps? None of these reasons are sufficient."

Like at every other impasse, Rosemary consulted the *I Ching* to wrest a little control back from the fates and reveal to her the parts of her mind she couldn't—or wouldn't—see. The *I Ching* endowed her with the belief that whichever way forward, things were meant to be.

Her hexagram: number 45, "Ts'ui / Gathering Together [Massing]"
The judgment:

GATHERING TOGETHER. Success.
The King approaches his temple.
It furthers one to see the great man.
This brings success. Perseverance furthers.
To bring great offerings creates good fortune.
It furthers one to undertake something.

She knew the identity of her great man. She called Timothy. She was ready to go home.

～

THE FIRST OF THREE wedding ceremonies occurred in Joshua Tree on November 11, 1967, under two yucca trees facing east, as the sun rose purplish pink in the impossibly blue sky. The actor Ted Markland filmed the occasion on camera as fifty or so of their new Hollywood friends (but not Jack, Susan, or Ralph) witnessed the exchange of informal vows:

"I marry you."

"I marry you."

One might be tempted to call this the perfect wedding location. It wasn't. The sun scorched the earth. The mescaline, a wedding favor handed out to the guests, was too strong for the setting and the altitude. "The wedding march was a symphony of retches and curses," Rosemary wrote.

The second ceremony, a quieter affair, followed a few days later at Timothy's home. Family and friends, once again, were not present to witness the Indian fakir anoint Rosemary and Timothy as he guided them through the marriage rites. "He directed Tim to place a line of red powder on the center part of my hair and a red dot between my eyes. Tim's hand shook and a cascade of powdered rouge covered my head. I looked like the victim of a scalping," Rosemary wrote.

News of another Millbrook raid—after the judge had dropped the earlier case against Timothy—cut their California celebrations short. An undercover agent had provided enough intel for the Poughkeepsie court to order another search warrant. This time they actually found illegal drugs. Rosemary and Timothy returned on December 11 so that Timothy could surrender to the Dutchess County Sheriff's Office. In genial humor, despite the circumstances, Timothy wished the cops a "Merry Christmas" as they fingerprinted him.

Never one to waste time, Timothy applied for a legal marriage license with Rosemary at the courthouse. The town clerk, Joseph Setaro, sat at his wooden desk, diligently filling out the paperwork as a local *Poughkeepsie Journal* photographer captured the scene: Timothy in his button-down trench, orange turtleneck, and suede loafers and Rosemary, one leg bent, posing like the model she once was, hair straight and center parted, daintily holding her bag, beaming out a smile that could sell Ovaltine. A wife now.

Timothy and Rosemary filled out their marriage license applications. Timothy wrote that this would be his third marriage; Rosemary wrote that it would be her second, leaving off her first to John Bradley. Timothy listed his occupation as "priest"; Rosemary listed hers not as "assistant" but as "writer," a fleeting acknowledgment of the new role she had created for herself. No longer mere muse, she was now coauthor. As they signed their names, the local radio station WHVW aired news of Timothy's arrest. The world revolved around them; it wasn't paranoid ideation.

The next day they held their biggest wedding ceremony yet in Billy Hitchcock's enclave on the estate, called the bungalow, a cute name for a wildly impressive manor with marble floors, two regulation-sized tennis courts, a near-Olympic-sized swimming pool, and animal hides on the wall. Rosemary and Timothy covered the room in flowers and let the scrum of reporters they'd invited believe that they lived in luxury, presenting the fantasy of the mad professor and his goddess bride. Susan refused to give her blessing and skipped town during the ceremony. No one mentioned the raid, which had resulted in the arrest of the groom, the groom's son, Jack, and the wedding officiant, Bill Haines, the often-antagonistic leader of the estate's ashram. Jack, shorn of his pageboy hair by Sheriff Quinlan's deputies after his arrest, served drinks from the bungalow's well-stocked mahogany bar.

Rosemary wore a white sari bordered in gold, her auburn hair flowing around a necklace made of amulets. She lined her doe eyes in kohl and drew a red lotus flower on her third eye, her sixth chakra, the seat of untapped wisdom. Even in photographs her energy radiates outward. No bride had ever been more beatific, nor had any bride been higher, thanks to giant tablets of THC, a wedding gift from writer Alan Watts. Timothy, dashing, too, wore white—white shirt, white pants trimmed in blue and gold embroidery, with a garland of white flowers around his neck. He appeared blissful—no Marshall McLuhan–trained media megawatt smile. Sincere happiness.

In an image shared widely in newspapers around the country, including the front page of the *New York Post* under the headline HONEYMOONERS, next to an article on dirty narcotics agents and a third on the increase of American deaths in Vietnam, Rosemary and Timothy sat on an ornate leopard-print couch surrounded by the soft light of candles. Their combined force photographed beautifully. He appears cerebral, content, and paternal; she manifests the Hindu mother goddess Parvati, emanating the soft power of traditional femininity. Her magnificence recontextualized his zaniness.

Moving forward, Timothy would rarely do his publicity tours alone. From this day on, he seemed to appreciate Rosemary as an asset—a newly unearthed precious stone. He subsequently afforded her the respect and gratitude one would a rare jewel. He seemed to understand her power now.

The wedding ceremony, a zenith so far in terms of optics, coincided with the last public gasp of the Hitchcock Estate. After the wedding Rosemary and Timothy skipped town for California to dodge yet another raid headed up by Sheriff Quinlan. After the third raid, Billy Hitchcock lost his patience and ordered everyone off the property. Timothy stood in solidarity with the other Millbrook residents, who wanted to stay, until the couple's belongings—including Rosemary's jazz records and antiques from her New York days—disappeared into Diane di Prima's husband's van, leaving them with only Timothy's filing cabinets and some dirty mattresses. Angry over his lost stuff, Timothy switched sides and supported Hitchcock. Haines and another resident felt betrayed by the shift in his loyalties. Many blamed Rosemary for his flip-flopping.

People dispersed with handfuls of cash, payoffs by Billy Hitchcock. The more obstinate of the bunch moved into the woods until the Millbrook police ran them off the property. The experiment had ended. The League disbanded. LEARY RETIREMENT THRILLS MILLBROOK, read one headline in the *Poughkeepsie Journal*. A year later a Dutchess County Boy Scout troop would operate out of Millbrook, renaming it Sherwood Forest.

"I still count those sixty-four rooms in my sleep," Rosemary said.

DURING THEIR HONEYMOON in Laguna Beach, Timothy invited reporters to join the couple by the ocean to announce that he would be retiring as a public figure. With his hair curling at the collar of his button-down shirt, he looked like a professor on vacation in Martha's

Vineyard, while Rosemary in her white linen shift dress and perfectly straightened hair became the quintessential WASP wife.

Rosemary stared off at the seagulls flying overhead as Timothy spoke. She wasn't the assistant any longer, nor "the Woodruff woman," but Wife. The reporters directed questions to her now—about her thoughts on the hippies in Laguna, about their plans, about what *they* were working on. "A book," she told them.

What's it like in California? they asked her.

"It's not at all like my world used to be—but I wouldn't go back for anything. Now there is beauty and love everywhere."

As Timothy continued to speak, Rosemary grabbed some food scraps to share with the gulls.

"If you study history," Timothy said, "you know that once you are committed to the messiah game there are certain moves—like in chess—that you have to make. You know you are going to have trouble with the establishment."

Timothy repeated his promise to Rosemary in front of the cameras: "I am now dropping out of public life . . . all I need I can get from lecturing."

Hearing these words at a press conference showed her what she already understood to be true: Timothy's first love was the spotlight. It always would be.

"Marriage hadn't changed anything," she wrote.

But, of course, it had.

Despite his promises to retire—*The Pittsburgh Press* covered the news of their nuptials with the headline DR. LEARY MARRIES, ABANDONS HIPPIES—the year after Rosemary and Timothy's marriage was a high-water mark of the couple's notoriety, when Timothy could, as one friend wrote, "sneeze and make headlines."

Timothy released two of his most famous books in this period, which he had worked on in bed at Millbrook with Rosemary by his side. First came *The Politics of Ecstasy*, a compilation of his best published writings to date. Rosemary's one-sentence foreword read, "Timothy Leary is the sanest, funniest, wisest man I've ever met." She also added many of the chapter titles, including a new headline—SHE COMES IN COLORS—for the interview with *Playboy* that had so roiled her after her time in jail. In it, they replaced all reference to Leary's ex-wife Nena with Rosemary, even swapping Nena's blue eyes for Rosemary's brown ones—rewriting the myth as it unfolded. *High Priest*, a chronicle of his psychedelic life in sixteen trips since his first in Mexico in 1960, followed. Reviewers considered it the best of his oeuvre. They gave it raves and took it (somewhat) seriously as a work of nonfiction. Her flourishes are everywhere—the *Lord of the Rings* quotations and John Dos Passos (one of her favorite modern authors) inspired use of newspaper headlines as chapter titles. The *Berkeley Barb* called it a literary masterpiece.

Rosemary now joined him on every leg of the tours, sat beside him onstage, or watched him banter from behind the scenes. She waited for him in the greenroom during a now infamous exchange on *The Dick Cavett Show*, where Cavett famously told Timothy, "I think you're full of crap." Timothy appeared in walk-on roles in the movies *Skidoo* and *Alice's Restaurant* and visited the set of *I Love You, Alice B. Toklas* with Rosemary in tow, prompting the columnist Dorothy Manners to quip, "He must have been nervous about this trip—brought his wife along to watch from the sidelines." Ralph Metzner watched his former mentor, near comatose on a massive dose of LSD, as he lectured a crowd of two thousand people at Syracuse University, sitting next to Rosemary, his former lover, onstage. "He kept looking at Rosemary for assurance," Metzner said.

When a woman ran onstage naked during a talk at Martin Luther

King Jr. High School in Berkeley and Timothy seemed to enjoy flirting a bit too much with her, someone called out, "Where's Rosemary?"

The room went wild.

The wider world now acknowledged the strength of their bond. Her "strong influence on her lover became more visible each day," wrote the biographer John Bryan. "Tim and Rosemary as a dyad," the psychologist Charles Slack wrote. Rosemary "cleaned his hash pipe and never left his side." A friend, identified as Ed the Clown, who lived with them in Berkeley, commented, "Rosemary and Tim just seem to fit together. Not only doing the frug at dance halls or with all the celebrities but during the day and in the morning when everybody has gone home. Tim out on the sun deck doing his yoga and Rosemary cleaning up the place after the freak-out or washing up at the kitchen sink."

Her life had once been reactive—running from one failed relationship to the next in order to survive. Today she was making the firm decision to stay and take on all the triumphs and dangers that accompanied standing still.

She had loved this complicated man for two years—went to jail in Laredo and Poughkeepsie for him, faced down a judge and prosecution to protect him, sailed into infinity with him, and descended into hell because of him. Now she would become a central part of his magic act.

The seagulls flew overhead and the camera bulbs flashed.

Rosemary was now the Acid Queen.

PART THREE

The Acid Queen

Eleven

Blinded by the Sun

The acid backlash began in 1966, but by 1968 it had bubbled over into a panic. The reports were the stuff of nightmares. There were at least four deaths in 1966 attributed to people jumping out of windows while tripping and dozens of less-credible stories of similar fates reported in the media. (This was enough of a phenomenon for Leary to comment on it: "One should never take LSD in an apartment on the third floor in New York. There are too many windows.") The journalist J. Anthony Lukas wrote a blockbuster piece for *The New York Times* on a wealthy Connecticut teenager named Linda Rae Fitzpatrick who had turned on to acid, Ginsberg's poetry, and sex magic before she was murdered, her body discovered in a basement boiler room in the East Village. A former medical student stabbed his mother-in-law to death and after told police, "Man I've been flying on acid for three days. Did I kill my wife?"; a Canadian college student fell into a viaduct while high; another, more outrageous headline in *The New York Times* read 6 YOUTHS ON LSD "TRIP," BLINDED BY SUN.

The papers no longer distinguished between lab LSD and black-market LSD, which was rumored to contain impurities—including strychnine, a rat poison, to make the LSD adhere to blotters, and amphetamines, which can induce manic psychosis associated with truly awful trips. Straight America feared acid as a new form of bio-warfare that if dropped in the water supply would, as one book alleged, "produce a psychosis of the population that would last long enough for enemy troops to take over" (which also happened to be the kind of psychedelic bioweapon that our own government was secretly trying to create).

To many Americans, the psychosis had already hit the streets in the form of youth politics. And this political roiling could be traced back, at least in part, to Timothy, whose novel talk of neurochemical mind revolution (long before psychopharmacology entered the popular lexicon with phrases like "dopamine levels" and "reuptake inhibitors") and waking up to the plastic world made sense in the Vietnam War era. The energy of the protest movement "was first set in motion by Tim Leary's one madman trip. That's why the pigs hate him so much," the New Left writer Stew Albert wrote.

Meanwhile, Lyndon Johnson upped the number of U.S. troops to nearly half a million, resulting in the bloodiest and most expensive year of the war, with three hundred U.S. soldiers dying in Vietnam on average every week of 1968. Rosemary understood the toll on those young enough to be drafted far better than her husband, who was old enough to be their father, because her brother, Gary, had recently been called up to fight.

At the time, Gary essentially shrugged. He had graduated from high school and deferred going to college, to focus his youthful energies instead on drinking with friends, trying to persuade his high school sweetheart to sleep with him, eating weed brownies, listening to Janis Joplin, and bodysurfing under the California sun. He turned down Rosemary's invitation to join their religion as a way to dodge the draft as a conscientious objector. "They'll make me a truck driver or a cook or something like that," he thought. Instead, he became an E-5 sergeant in charge of a platoon of men with the First Air Cavalry, spending a year in the jungle drawing peace signs on his combat boots. With Gary's future uncertain, Rosemary pushed Timothy to put aside his apolitical dance and speak out directly against the war.

But it was too late. The politically attuned noted the absurdity of a middle-aged man speaking as an emissary of the youth generation.

"Don't vote," Timothy would say to the young men facing the possibility of combat. "Don't politic. Don't petition. You can't do anything about America politically."

It sounded so out of touch.

By the spring of 1968, in the wake of the assassinations of Martin Luther King Jr. and Senator Robert F. Kennedy two months apart, Timothy's dismissal of political action as "game playing" and his advice for young Americans to avoid the polls and drop out sounded more suicidal than reactionary. Timothy's "turn on, tune in, drop out" philosophy, as diffuse as it was, provided permission for a lost group of young men to continue drifting, putting them at greater draft risk. Abbie Hoffman, a cofounder of the Youth International Party (Yippie, for short), gonzo radicals who nominated an actual pig for president and tried to use "psychic energy" to levitate the Pentagon, summed up the rage directed at Timothy. "Your peace-and-love bullshit is leading youth down the garden path of fascism," Hoffman said. "You're creating a group of blissed-out pansies ripe for annihilation."

Timothy was scheduled to appear at the now infamous Democratic National Convention in August 1968. As the various factions of the New Left discussed strategy, Timothy suggested naked love-ins. But two weeks before the convention, he pulled out. By August, when television cameras captured National Guardsmen bashing in heads and tear-gassing young antiwar protesters, neither Timothy nor Rosemary could be found. Timothy was, as one writer put it, a "well-fed Brahmin prince who lectures his starving subjects on the karmic values of hunger while stuffing down a ten-course dinner."

Not that the government viewed him—or the drugs they associated with him—that way. In his State of the Union in January 1968, Johnson proposed a new Drug Control Act with stricter penalties "for those who traffic in LSD and other dangerous drugs." He called for a 30 percent increase in the number of federal drug and narcotics officers and a hundred new assistant U.S. attorneys to help prosecute drug offenders as a response to the drastic increase in violent crime occurring across the country. "The time has come to stop the sale of slavery to the young," Johnson said. The most flagrant enslaver of the youth—the one appearing on TV talk shows and quoted in endless numbers of articles—was, of course, Timothy Leary.

The Republican candidate Richard Milhous Nixon took this position and ran on it, campaigning as a law-and-order president. Drugs destroyed families, undermined the country's moral fiber, drove an increase in youth crime, and generally fomented lawlessness and anarchy. And Nixon had a plan. He would target the pushers and the dealers. In Nixon's eyes, Timothy was a leader of the fifth column: an enemy of the state.

Timothy acknowledged the threat that Nixon posed. If Nixon won, "then I would be in a lot of trouble," he wrote. "When the purge came, it would certainly focus on drugs because control of American consciousness was and still is the issue."

Counterintuitively, he ratcheted up his rhetoric, and Rosemary, "besotted, applauded with the rest," she wrote, "though I often regretted his need to be such an ass." From her front row seat, Rosemary observed him now with a more critical eye. Once she saw the self-serving insincerity in his act, it was hard to unsee. It was becoming harder to distinguish what of Timothy was authentic and what was only for show. "I was with him now as a silent witness to what he was becoming," she wrote.

He called himself "the wisest man of the twentieth century" and told a reporter for the Long Beach *Press-Telegram* that he had chemists who could release LSD into cities as experiments. "One million doses were released recently in the Haight-Ashbury district in San Francisco—the most ever released in one place at one time so far, but there are men who can release up to ten million doses at a time."

Though Timothy spoke in hyperbole, his threat wasn't exactly far-fetched. LSD was relatively easy for creative chemists to hack—and in mind-bogglingly large quantities. The infamous underground chemist Owsley Stanley later estimated that between 1965 and 1967 he and Melissa Cargill had produced 1.25 million doses of LSD. Owsley now aimed, along with the chemist and former League member Nicholas Sand, Owsley's lab partner Tim Scully, and John Griggs's group of hippie drug dealers called the Brotherhood of Eternal Love, to make and distribute 750 million doses, enough to free the consciousness of every single American three times over.

IT SEEMS FATED THEN that Timothy and Rosemary would join Owsley and Sand's mission to turn on the masses by joining the Brotherhood of Eternal Love. Perhaps he felt it was his only viable move after the arrest, the end of Millbrook, and the advent of politicized youth revolution.

To the Brotherhood of Eternal Love, Timothy was a messianic figure. As opposed to the college-educated crowds of the New Left and renegade psychologists at Millbrook, most Brothers had barely graduated from high school. Instead, the media-shy group of outsiders acted as suppliers of the underground, offering up six-millimeter tabs of mind-bogglingly potent Orange Sunshine to "turn on everyone in the world," as the chemist Sands said, and to create "a new world of peace and love." The Brothers genuinely believed in this mission, not just for their bottom lines, but in their souls. They incorporated their own acid church in 1966, using Timothy's *Psychedelic Experience* and *Psychedelic Prayers* as biblical texts. The Brothers referred to Timothy as the godfather, or "the focal point," as Brother Michael Randall described him, a kind of honorary degree for all the work he had done in opening up the minds of humanity.

The Brotherhood never sloughed off their criminal pasts. In addition to running a church, the Brotherhood also oversaw a vast smuggling network through the South Asian leg of the hippie trail that ran from Western Europe through Afghanistan. The Afghans manufactured the cheapest and highest-quality hash in the world—twenty or more varieties—with insanely high THC content. During this era, Afghanistan grew into an international exchange station for hashish and opium, thanks in part to the Brotherhood, who'd transported their wares from Afghanistan in false-bottomed Volkswagens and hollowed-out surfboards.

Surfing wasn't just a cover. The Brothers established a home base in Laguna Beach, a halfway station between the wilds of the Haight in San Francisco and their additional drug sources in Mexico. The coastal city's main thoroughfare, the Pacific Coast Highway, housed shops and restaurants that catered to surfer dudes and freaks, a bastion of hippie lassitude in conservative Orange County, California. Shirtless men roamed the streets with guitars and flutes. A stucco Spanish Mission–style Taco Bell served as a meeting house of sorts, where small-time drug deals went down. After doing the Lord's work, they'd grab lunch and go find "God in the curl." Despite being awash in cash, most of the Brothers still lived like a "gang of dharma bums," as Timothy described them. They considered themselves more like Robin Hoods on surfboards than West Coast Mafia dons. "They were not bigshots at all. None of them ever drove anything better than a VW bus," Timothy said. "They were just kind of in it for the spiritual thrill."

Although a world away from serene Millbrook and Harvard Yard, Timothy and Rosemary developed a deep affinity for the Brotherhood's leader, John Griggs, which had begun during their Southern California "Celebrations" tour in 1967. When Griggs had offered to house, protect, and feed their minds with unending streams of drugs in Laguna Beach, Rosemary and Timothy jumped on board with both feet.

Timothy and Rosemary settled into a dreamy existence in Laguna that recalled the best times at Millbrook. The group called each other "family" and seemed to mean it. They supplied the couple with a house by the beach. The Brothers even did the Learys' laundry. Some Brothers gawked at the number of silk robes in Timothy's possession. John Griggs employed Susan and Jack at the Mystic Arts World, a metaphysical bookstore, handmade clothing store, art exhibition hall, community gathering space, and juice bar all wrapped up in one legitimate psychedelic, moneymaking emporium on Pacific Coast Highway.

The couple moved into the inland Brotherhood enclave that they called Dodge City, a rabbit warren of ramshackle A-frames nestled in a canyon between golden hills. The Brothers read the landscape like Braille, navigating the winding secret pathways overgrown with weeds in the pitch-dark. And since eucalyptus trees canopied the canyon, the Brothers could work and party out in the open, without being overtly observed, all the while monitoring who came in and out. Houses were allegedly color coded according to what products they sold. Chickens ran wild. Wild dogs roamed. A monkey climbed the trees and screeched into the early hours. An older neighbor, originally from New York, no taller than five feet, roamed the streets, like a witchy version of John the Baptist, yelling prophecies and frightening the young men with her inexplicable knowledge about their family secrets.

The chaos made good company for the Learys, who seemed to be mending under the California sun. Even Susan and Rosemary had started getting along. "Susan is great," Timothy wrote to his son. "She has lost 35 pounds and is very trim, graceful and beautiful." He didn't acknowledge that the men passed around Susan like many of the other women. These so-called "girls of the canyon" would arrive with dreams of Haight-inspired free love. Months would go by, and their eyes would go dead. They'd stop wearing clothes. When many inevitably wound up pregnant, their choices were to keep babies they couldn't care for, seek dangerous underground abortions, or return, hat in hand, to their families across the country and disappear. They were, one local Laguna resident observed, mere "pleasure units."

GRIGGS INVITED TIMOTHY, Rosemary, and thirty or so carefully chosen Brotherhood couples and families (he excluded most single people) to live out his communal ideal in a valley oasis called Fobes Ranch, an eighty-acre desert valley compound. The former cattle ranch (defunct now that they refused to raise animals for food) was nearly impossible to raid, with two locked cattle gates set up along the single five-mile dirt road. If the cops arrived, you'd see them coming for miles. Off the grid and self-sustainable, the compound was, according to Rosemary, as "close to heaven as you could get." Timothy added, "We have no electricity unless we go and feed the generator ourselves. No TV, no radio. We bring our water in; we grow our own food. . . . We feel we are doing what the affluent, bourgeois middle-class members will be doing in 20 years. But we're doing it now—sort of like time travelers."

Griggs gave Rosemary and Timothy the compound's one stand-alone house and an eighteen-foot-high teepee made of sailcloth. She threw away her nylon stockings (replacing them with several coats of baby lotion) and swapped out her East Coast wardrobe for cotton peasant dresses and fringed paisley shawls. Rosemary and Timothy gathered squash from the veggie garden, cooked on wood fires, killed rattlesnakes, and slept together in a double sleeping bag, blasting Jimi Hendrix as they named the stars from the constellations learned from one of Jack Leary's high school astronomy textbooks.

"My body is a hammock for my soul today," she told Timothy—a return to the dreamy way she felt in the early months at Millbrook before their first arrest. They rarely left the cloistered compound, other than once-a-week visits to the nearby town of Idyllwild to check on news of Timothy's Laredo appeal.

"The ranch had become my ancestral home," she wrote. "Millbrook my lost kingdom."

Rosemary and Timothy regularly took the sacrament together, or with a group, disappearing into the mountain range to drop acid and run around naked in the ancient geometric paradise where they claimed to see UFOs. She believed that "if I just got high enough, and if I were pure enough," then the aliens would take them.

Rosemary brought her pamphlet on a style of breath-work yoga called pranayama, counting her breaths and exhalations—*inhale 1, 2, 3, 4, hold, exhale, 1, 2, 3, 4*—as she contrasted the whiteness of her husband's nude body against the mountains, sagebrush, and gnarled trees. Inevitably, Timothy would say, "You were made to be a mother, beloved." Or, "What a beautiful child we'll have." An echo from their first month together.

"And what if I can't have children?" she asked him.

This was the crux of their marriage. If she embodied the fertility goddess then what would it mean for the public view of their relationship if she could not bear children? The essence, in both of their eyes, of the ancient feminine ideal.

"You can have children; I know you can if you really want to," he would say.

She could not ignore her desire for a baby on the compound. Women were fecund with life. Children roamed. Bellies grew. Griggs had even arranged for women to train as midwives to deal with the onslaught of pregnancies.

But Rosemary's baby hadn't materialized. She sought aid from various guides, using *The Moon Book*, ancient herbal remedies, the tarot, and the stars, trying to sync her cycle to celestial bodies for greater success. They traveled to a Navajo reservation in New Mexico to take part in a healing peyote ceremony to pray for a baby. She worked on quieting her ego, taming her perseveration on the negative, staying open, and above all else *believing*. Nothing worked.

Timothy quietly arranged for Rosemary to visit the San Francisco gynecologist Dr. Alan Margolis, a respected clinician known today as an abortion pioneer. Margolis suggested that Rosemary undergo a hysterosalpingogram, an X-ray of the uterus and the Fallopian tubes. This involved inserting a screwlike catheter into the cervix to make a watertight seal—a procedure painful enough to warrant general anesthesia. Radio-opaque dye material snaked its way through the cervical canal and revealed a whole world to the doctor: Rosemary's uterus was atypical. She had a congenital abnormality, a defect in that precious part of herself; instead of pear-shaped like a typical uterus, hers was separated in two, a condition called bicornuate uterus. A heart-shaped womb.

The condition was rare, but well documented. Outcomes ranged.

Some women conceived and birthed from one chamber successfully, but Rosemary also had obstructions in both of her Fallopian tubes. Add this to Rosemary's medical history, which included three miscarriages, one abortion, and at least one prior case of the clap, and a viable pregnancy would be nearly impossible.

The news devastated Rosemary to such a degree that she could not write about it. The only account of her suffering is filtered through Timothy's recollection and is limited in its emotional insight. The couple dropped acid to make sense of the news.

"Session at the waterfall," he wrote. "You freaked out about your uterus. I tried to cheer you up with 'our love.'"

"Not good enough," Rosemary said to him.

Rosemary took a trip into the San Jacinto Mountains, where she felt the most direct communion with God, with three Brotherhood women. She had never been alone in the copper-headed mountains without men before. Carol Griggs, with her striking blue eyes and a closet filled with bright embroidered clothes, louder than Rosemary's but just as stylish, joined them. She left behind a baby whom she was still breastfeeding. Women couldn't easily disconnect and disappear into the mountains. They were the spokes that kept the wheels of the Brotherhood going. This was a different kind of sisterhood from the one championed by the women's liberation movement with the motto "Sisterhood is powerful." This was powerful, too, in its own way. It was not lost on them that the women of the Soboba Band of Luiseño Indians had thrived on these mountains. Rosemary imagined herself as one of them, gathering acorns, drying them, and grinding them into meal while carrying a baby on her back.

The four women read aloud and meditated on the Four Immeasurables—the Buddhist virtues of loving kindness, compassion, sympathetic joy, and equanimity. Rosemary reached into her bag to find the matchbox that held the sacrament. When she slid it open, the box was empty. She had forgotten the key ingredient of the trip. Rosemary could sense the other women's relief. Carol's breasts leaked. Thoughts were with their babies back down the mountain. They had so much to do back home.

They cast coins to consult the *I Ching* and received hexagram 47 (Exhaustion): "There is no water in the lake."

They headed back down the mountain.

❧

AT 11:05 ON THE NIGHT after Christmas 1968, a year after their wedding and almost three years to the date after their Laredo arrest, the law caught up with the Learys again. The whole family was driving along Laguna Beach before heading back up to San Francisco with a stash of Brotherhood-provided gifts. Rosemary also had her handy supply of Ritalin, a "psychic energizer" that suppressed her appetite and helped her stay thin. Even with all that talk of natural beauty—no bras, no makeup, no shaving—the expectations remained, heightened in fact, to be naturally beautiful.

They dropped Susan off at a friend's house in Laguna and then stopped in Dodge City, where a twenty-eight-year-old rookie police officer named Neil Purcell approached the car. He noticed Jack on all fours, scrambling in the backseat with dilated pupils the size of washers. Busted again.

Purcell asked Timothy to step out of the car. Rosemary joined him. In an attempt to hide her stash—a thwarted reprise of her Wonder Woman reflex during the raid at Millbrook—she piled all the goods in her hat and then plopped it on her head. It was a stoned person's good idea. *Plunk!* The officer took the hat from her and found a pipe, a one-inch chunk of hashish, a coin purse with six more pieces of hash, a tinfoil package with ten white pills, and an aspirin bottle with seven blue-green pills, both of which were LSD. In the din of the chaos of the moment, Rosemary thought, *Thank God Susan isn't here.*

No marijuana was found on Leary, only residue and seed fragments on his shirt and pants. After the search was complete, officers confiscated around two hundred grams of marijuana, including two half-smoked roaches, and forty LSD capsules.

The timing couldn't have been worse. They were awaiting the outcome of Timothy's appeal to the Supreme Court for his 1966 Laredo conviction and couldn't bear the brunt of yet another hit to his reputation. And yet here they were, pulled back into the shitstorm.

ROSEMARY AND TIMOTHY traveled out of the country later in 1969, animated by irreverence, a thirst for experience, and a search for a remedy for Rosemary's infertility. It took a full day to reach the foothills of the Ahl Srif Mountains in Morocco to visit the famed Master Musicians of Joujouka, musical healers who mended broken people with their ancient songs.

The show began with a violin. Pennywhistles joined in. Rosemary placed a tab of LSD on Timothy's tongue and then one on her own. Men in hoods rose and lifted wooden pipes that sounded at first, before your ears adjusted, like a shrill scream. The men played these *rhaitas*, double-reed horns, so seamlessly that it was impossible to pick one out as the note stretched on into a drone. Drums joined them, adding an elaborate rhythm in clear celebration of new life, reminding Rosemary of Igor Stravinsky's *Rite of Spring*. The throbbing beat was irresistible. "My breath was caught by the horns; my pulse by the drums. . . . Was this music, or the thunder of mammoth hooves, screams of birds of prey? It seemed the very tempo of life in my body. Eardrums could be shattered. Hearts could burst from these sounds."

The Bou Jeloud, a man covered in goatskins and wearing a straw basket hat covered with leaves, jumped out into the center of the crowd. He began to pound his feet to the beat of the music. Rosemary, overwhelmed by the sight, jumped up. She felt embodied and emboldened and started to swish her hips. The goat man thrust his pelvis and lunged at her, lashing her with a handful of long branches used to beat the barrenness out of women.

The Bou Jeloud unleashed something fertile within Rosemary, though it did not lead to the kind of pregnancy that Rosemary had yearned for. The music and dancing fed a generative force—the fire, perhaps, that had smoldered inside her since she had danced at her father's bar as a child. All the men, including Timothy, saw it. "For just one perceptible second," Timothy wrote in *Jail Notes*, "she . . . showed them a laughing glimpse of her ancient, familiar, Aphrodite power, a single, simple, perfectly controlled body shot a block-buster flash of full woman power that blew the roof off the room."

That blockbuster flash lasted only a moment. All at once the magic left her, and she felt embarrassed to have been overtaken by it. But she would hold on to this moment for decades, returning to it at key moments during her life as proof of her own potency.

Twelve

Rosemary Wept

The second half of 1969 continued on like a death march, testing Rosemary's faith—in her religion, body, relationship, and country. She was, as she wrote, "lurching from one tragedy to the next." The country, still reeling from the losses of MLK and RFK, lurched along with her—from the actress Judy Garland's overdose to the exposure of the My Lai massacre, in which American soldiers murdered and maimed hundreds of Vietnamese women and children, to the Manson Family murder of the eight-months pregnant actress Sharon Tate, stabbed sixteen times on Los Angeles's Cielo Drive.

It had started so well. On May 19, 1969, the Supreme Court, in a unanimous decision, had ruled in favor of Timothy's appeal of his 1966 Laredo sentencing. Timothy's new lawyers had dropped his religious argument, focusing instead on the unfair double-jeopardy tax on marijuana. The Supreme Court agreed that the tax required self-incrimination and overturned Timothy's conviction. The Learys finally had something to celebrate.

The day of the ruling was delightful. The sun kissed the San Jacinto Mountains. Bees buzzed and apple blossom pollen scented the air as the Learys welcomed reporters cross-legged under a pear tree by their teepee in Fobes Ranch.

A TV reporter asked them how they felt. Timothy, without irony, called it "the happiest day since the Emancipation Proclamation."

What's next? the reporter asked.

Rosemary, dressed in a red tunic, like a psychedelic trophy wife, beamed her blissful smile as he spoke. "I'm going to run for the governorship for the state of California. I think we need a new party and by party, I mean party."

Rosemary's face betrayed nothing. Later she would admit that in that moment she was as distraught as John and Carol Griggs, who cried when they heard that their messiah had debased himself into a political candidate.

"You know, you could stir up a lot of people with these ideas," said one reporter.

"That's what I'm afraid of," said Rosemary.

The campaign started in earnest the next week outside the offices of the *Los Angeles Free Press*. When Timothy officially announced, it was not his but *their* run. "I'm going to run, with my no—we're going to fly—with my mate for the governorship of California in 1970," he said. How did it land with the straight press? Pure gold. What wasn't there to love about an acid freak and his wife running for office against Ronald Reagan, a fellow outsider, a former Hollywood actor turned politician running for a second term? The alt press ate it up, too; the *Berkeley Barb*, the *Los Angeles Free Press*, and *The Oracle* all endorsed him. But almost no one took his run seriously.

On the campaign trail now, Rosemary mirrored Timothy's new hippie look in a bright printed blouse, one strand of a white beaded necklace, and her long straight hair dyed a deep auburn with Kiehl's henna powder. The newspapers never missed an opportunity to run her picture alongside his.

"Have you thought about that—going into the marijuana business?" one reporter asked him.

"There's going to be high taxes," Timothy said.

"Your wife gives you all those adlibs, doesn't she?"

"My best lines come from Rosemary."

Timothy advocated growing your own marijuana since, as he saw it, the Supreme Court's renouncement of the marijuana tax called into question the federal government's stance on its illegality.

"Now there's no federal law against marijuana," Timothy said. "You can go to a National Park and smoke it."

"Plant it, darling," she said. "Plant it!"

Rosemary condensed Timothy's ramblings into coherent one-sentence quips. "I was a bit of a sloganeer in those days," she would later say, "and Tim would ask, 'What do I say?' And I would say something flip." One of those flip sayings would become their new campaign slogan—"Come together, join the party"—and the title of the future Beatles No. 1 hit "Come Together," which Lennon had originally written (with different words) for Leary's run.

Ten days after Timothy's announcement, Lennon invited the Learys to room 1742 at the Hotel La Reine Elizabeth in Montreal during the Bed-In for Peace—a protest against the Vietnam War.

The suite was packed with people; friends, fans, and cameramen filled the room to record a new song, "Give Peace a Chance." Timothy and Rosemary are name-checked in it. Listen closely and you can hear their voices.

The couples compared notes about their recent drug busts; Lennon and Yoko had been arrested in England in October 1968 for possession of hashish (a scandal in part because Yoko was pregnant). Yoko had subsequently lost her baby, six months into her pregnancy, a loss she blamed, in part, on the stress related to the arrest and resultant publicity. They buried the baby, named John Ono Lennon II, in a secret location. Later Yoko included a recording of his fetal heartbeat on her and Lennon's 1969 album *Unfinished Music No. 2: Life with the Lions*.

During their time together, Yoko gave Rosemary a mum flower, which Rosemary wrapped up and kept for months, even after it wilted and dried up.

ROSEMARY'S FIRST PUBLIC tragedy of 1969 happened that summer at Fobes Ranch. No one knew the girl well. She had arrived with Susan Leary. But Rosemary noticed her. "Long-legged, long-haired, graceful," Rosemary wrote, "a clear-eyed beauty. Gentle, she seemed a bit shy, but playful with the children." Her name was Charlene "Charlie" Renee Almeida. She was seventeen. Her close friends called her Dolcino, a sweet Italian wine.

Ten days later, Timothy and Rosemary heard distant cries and followed the sounds of distress until they could make out the words: "Charlie's gone." Rosemary ran to the lake through the orchards, and Timothy dove in the water.

"I've found her!" a woman yelled. "Help me!"

They carried the girl's nude body from the lake, her long legs dangling lifelessly, and set her down as Timothy, on his hands and knees, attempted mouth-to-mouth resuscitation. He was too late. From what they could gather, Charlie dove off a pontoon float in the middle of the thirty-foot-deep lake. Disoriented, she hit her head on the way back up and drowned before anyone noticed she hadn't surfaced. An autopsy report revealed that the girl hadn't eaten anything in the prior twenty-four hours and had a significant amount of LSD in her bloodstream.

When the authorities came to take her body away, Timothy stood by the water and told the detectives, "There's nothing wrong with the drugs. They do more good than harm."

Rosemary wrote about the aftershock of Charlie's death: "That night we gathered at the shore. The children said that now she is a star in heaven. No one knows why she died or cares to think we might have saved her." She would later refer to this as "our own Chappaquiddick," a reference to the death of Mary Jo Kopechne, the twenty-eight-year-old woman whom Senator Ted Kennedy left to die, submerged in a car off the coast of Martha's Vineyard.

Charlie's death made the papers and Timothy's involvement, as a candidate for governor, placed the news above the fold. Timothy and Rosemary called a press conference in front of a crowd of forty reporters in the parking lot of the *Los Angeles Free Press*. The police interrupted with a warrant to arrest Timothy for contributing to the delinquency of a minor. The charge alleged that Timothy had "by threat, command and persuasion" induced Charlene Almeida to "lead an idle, dissolute, and immoral life." The story appeared on page A-1 of the *Los Angeles Times* the next day with a picture of Timothy clutching Rosemary, who wore oversized glasses and her hair in pigtails, making her appear a decade younger than her age, right before the police cuffed him and led him back to the precinct. "This is a ghoulish thing," Rosemary told reporters. "They're trying to make political capital out of a young girl's death. We loved her very much." He was released on bail an hour later and the charges were dropped, but the damage was done.

A month separated the first ranch death from the second one. In that time, a man walked on the moon and glimpsed the infinite while Earth burned. Antiwar protesters moved from heightened rhetoric and violent protests to all-out homegrown terrorism. In the first ten months of 1969, there were eighty bombings and bomb threats at draft boards and ROTC centers. Hijackers took over fifty planes— more than any other year in American aviation history—often diverting them to Cuba. The FBI responded by adding thousands of new agents and hundreds of informants to take down the New Left, whom they viewed as an existential threat to American democracy.

The Brotherhood leader, John Griggs, had scored a crystal form of psilocybin from one of the underground chemists. As the drug took hold, Griggs ran from his teepee to warn the others not to take the stuff. Convinced he had been poisoned, he began to chug water to flush it out of his system. When he collapsed into unconsciousness, his friends decided to take him to a nearby hospital. The papers said he died from canned beans and peaches—and then rumors of his being poisoned with strychnine made the rounds—but physicians later determined that Griggs had overdosed on psilocybin, an exceedingly rare but apparently not impossible feat. John Griggs was twenty-five years old. His youngest son, Full Moon Buck Griggs, was only five days old.

Days later cops raided the Fobes Ranch but found only empty teepees. People had scattered, back to Laguna, off to Hawaii, or to other safe havens. The Brotherhood would never be the same. Nor would Rosemary and Timothy, who had lost their protector and advocate while realizing that no utopia existed for them. In the five years since she first met Timothy, Rosemary had been arrested three times; Timothy at least eight. Their legal bills ran into six figures. They faced three trials now—a retrial of the overturned Laredo smuggling case, an indictment pending in Dutchess County regarding Millbrook, and, of course, the Laguna bust.

The two deaths—especially that of a female minor—added a layer of nefariousness to the Leary enterprise. Timothy, no longer a benign mad professor, had blood on his hands. And, as was his habit, he threw lighter fluid on the controversy, penning an explosive op-ed in *The East Village Other* called "Deal for Real" in which he argued that dealing drugs is one of the noblest professions. The dealer is "pure," he wrote, "righteous and courageous." He urged people to take part in the great tradition themselves: "not for the money but simply to pay tribute to the most honorable profession."

Then the TV funnyman Art Linkletter, whose easy, fun-loving banter with children on the show *Kids Say the Darndest Things* made him a household name, blamed Timothy for the loss of his daughter.

On October 4, Diane Linkletter, just shy of her twenty-first birthday, jumped from the kitchen window of her sixth-floor apartment building in West Hollywood after allegedly taking LSD. When she hit the ground, she was still breathing. Paramedics were unable to revive her mangled body.

Linkletter's words to the press were the raging cries of a man filled with grief. "It wasn't suicide," he said. "She was murdered by the people who manufacture and sell LSD. . . . It was Tim Leary and his band of sick supporters. . . . If I ever get my hands on him, so help me God, I'll kill him," he said.

Linkletter left out key details of his daughter's story. He did not tell reporters that her brief marriage—which her father had not approved of—had recently ended in annulment. He did not say that she suffered from several career setbacks as an aspiring actress and struggled with living in the shadow of her famous father.

When a toxicology report came back clean, Linkletter doubled down, saying that his daughter jumped because she experienced acid flashbacks—a concept that had been described in the medical literature since 1954 but became colloquialized in 1969. Linkletter wasn't totally out of line. Buried in the hysteria was a kernel of truth. Flashbacks, though relatively rare, can happen. Some see perseverating shapes or visual snow. Some are walloped by the full emotional force of a bad trip years later. In the limited literature published on harm, one study found that around 10 percent of people experience a transient impairment—anxiety, derealization, or even suicidal thoughts.

A much smaller percentage of users take months if not years to recover. Around 4 percent of people experience persisting issues, called hallucinogen-persisting perception disorder. There's still no consensus as to who is at greater risk.

Nixon keenly identified Linkletter as an ally in what he would, in 1971, inaugurate as the war on drugs, inviting him to tell Diane's story to Congress. Like Timothy, Nixon understood that narratives are far more effective than cold statistics.

On January 28, 1970, the sixty-page Controlled Substances Act passed unanimously in the Senate, spurred on, at least in part, by stories like Diane's. The bill, which Nixon signed into law nine months later after it was broadened to address treatment and drug education, provided five highly unscientific categories, called Schedules, for substances according to their potential for abuse and possible medical use. Schedule I drugs—which included marijuana, heroin, and LSD—were deemed illegal and unsafe under almost all conditions. In other words, not only was it against the law to possess, sell, and consume them, but in most cases it was now also illegal to study them. Cocaine and methamphetamine were placed on Schedule II—meaning they were illegal on the black market but retained highly regulated acceptable medical use. Amphetamines, meanwhile, which had hit epidemic levels of consumption by the end of the 1960s, were placed on Schedule III, meaning that they received far less oversight, mainly refill limits and manufacturing quotas. The most substantial difference among the Schedules, however, involved criminal sentencing guidelines. Schedule I drugs now carried the harshest penalties. Mere possession of marijuana could get you decades in prison; trafficking could send you to prison for life.

In his State of the State address, Governor Ronald Reagan spoke of "the increasing problem of drug use," noting that drugs were being "touted by many who influence our youth." He pledged to "wage a war against the peddler and the pusher." Since he was vying against Timothy for the governorship of California, no one had to say his name to know whom Reagan was talking about.

Timothy Leary, President Nixon would later say in private recordings, "was the face of the enemy."

Back in Houston for the retrial of the Laredo arrest, Timothy waived his defense, because he planned to appeal to a higher court once the guilty verdict came down again. The jury took ten minutes to return the guilty verdict they had all been expecting. The judge delayed sentencing so that Timothy could travel back up north for his second trial in California with Rosemary and Jack.

⁓

MEANWHILE, an interlude—a silver lining, a message from the universe, a wink from the cosmos. Timothy received a phone call.

"Dr. Margolis said yes," Timothy told her. This was Dr. Alan Margolis, the gynecologist who had diagnosed Rosemary with bicornuate uterus. Today, he had an update: with suitable intervention involving surgery and fertility treatments, she had a chance—around 20 percent—that she could conceive.

Rosemary scheduled the experimental surgery that Margolis had suggested at the University of California, San Francisco, Medical School. The surgeon, a man named Edmund Overstreet, known as an abortion pioneer and advocate of sterilization, operated on her dual-chambered uterus and installed polyethylene plastic hoods into the Fallopian tubes to keep them open.

Rosemary expressed an uneasiness about Dr. Overstreet, whom she described (despite his stance on abortion) as "a Republican doctor." She disliked the intern who asked her "about my drugs and politics while he ineptly poked my arm for a blood sample."

The newspapers referred to the surgery as "a female complaint."

༄

AFTER A DELAY of nearly a year, Timothy's Laguna Beach drug trial opened on February 9, 1970, on the sixth floor of the Santa Ana courthouse. Timothy's defense centered on Officer Neil Purcell: Did he have probable cause to search their station wagon that night? Could he really tell that the burning marijuana bud he smelled came from Timothy's car? Did he plant the roaches as Timothy and Rosemary (but not Jack) alleged?

Rosemary suspected that their case had no chance, just as she had during her own grand jury hearing back in Poughkeepsie, but she sat beside Timothy for two weeks under the harsh lights on the hard-bottomed chairs that made her tremble with pain. Something was wrong in her body since the surgery, but she wouldn't find out how wrong for another year. The newspapers—mostly California-based outlets at first—noticed the change. "Mrs. Leary, still recovering from recent surgery, shows the effects of that ordeal, her cheeks and eyes appearing almost hollow," wrote the *Los Angeles Times*. Timothy was altered, too. "His lined face is beginning to turn a little fleshy, the bags under his eyes are more pronounced now and the jowls of his cheeks are starting to sag a bit," the *Times*'s reporter observed. Jack struggled, too. He chewed on Kleenex tissues and spit them on the carpet in a strange act of dissociative rebellion. At one point, Purcell watched Timothy smack his son in the face in the middle of the courtroom.

Timothy, cocksure as ever, invited a British documentary crew to film the trial. Even if he was convicted, he rationalized, he'd appeal and be out on bail, just as he had in his Laredo trial. In Timothy's prepared statement, he discussed Rosemary's astrological sign compared with his as a way of making sense of the ordeal. "My wife is a Tauran," he wrote, a line that sounds like an opening to a bad joke, "a sign notorious for its possessiveness, living with three Librans," as if the jury, which comprised housewives, an accountant, an aerospace engineer, and a riveter—all residents of a conservative catchment area of the Golden Coast—would be taken in by such logic.

Halfway through the trial, Rosemary and Jack, represented by different counsel from Timothy, conceded that the drugs in the car belonged to them. Timothy, on whom no drugs were found, portrayed himself as an innocent bystander. When the jury left to deliberate, people in the courtroom overheard Timothy bragging that Jack and Rosemary took the blame to save him. The jury deliberated for twelve hours before returning the verdict around midnight: guilty on three counts, marijuana possession for the mad professor, and two counts each for his wife and son, for marijuana and LSD possession, both illegal in California. Rosemary and Jack were released on bail, while Timothy's bail was denied. All three awaited sentencing.

The next day Rosemary wrote her first in a series of solo articles for the *Berkeley Barb*. Under the headline LAUGHING LEARY, she sought help to fund his appeal and implored the public to show their support by filling up the empty courtroom so that there would be witnesses to the government's war on its citizens. She also announced Timothy's plans to continue his run for governor. "It really isn't a marijuana case or a crime and punishment or a search and seizure or a crime in the streets. We're dealing with the pride and prejudice of the older generation," she wrote. "When they jail the revolutionaries, they must jail the prophets."

Rosemary then appeared at a rally at the Family Dog ballroom in San Francisco, where she and Ken Kesey threw the *I Ching* to name their Leary defense fund. They got "Holding Together," the eighth hexagram.

Holding Together brings good fortune.

It sounded great, if you ignored the sentences that followed: "But such holding together calls for a central figure around whom other persons may unite. . . . Therefore let him who wishes to gather others about him ask himself whether he is equal to the undertaking, for anyone attempting the task without a real calling for it only makes confusion worse than if no union at all had taken place."

For the time being a worthy person had emerged. An article by the *Berkeley Barb* summed up the underground's collective respect for Rosemary. "Those who have been with her recently are somewhat amazed at her strength. She appears tired, but the force of her own energies and those around her have been keeping her spirits up."

ON MARCH 2, 1970, in Houston, Judge Ben Connally sentenced a smiling Timothy to ten years in prison and a $10,000 fine. "He has preached the length and breadth of the land and I am inclined to the view that he would pose a danger to the community if released," Connally said.

Ten years.

The vastness of the number stunned Rosemary. Ten years meant no children. Ten years meant no house in the woods. Ten years was three times the length of their marriage, twice as long as they'd known each other. A lifetime, really. Her legs buckled.

An Associated Press reporter, one of the many national news outlets now covering the trial, documented how stricken Rosemary appeared.

Ten years.

Then another shock: no bail pending appeal. The court based the decision on Timothy's persistent advocacy of narcotics, recent arrest in Laguna, and the dual deaths of Charlene Almeida and John Griggs. "Whether or not Leary bears any liability at law for these deaths, these persons would, as a matter of simple, factual cause and effect, in all probability have been alive today had Timothy Leary not been at large during the latter part of the year 1969," the bail denial report read.

Outside the courtroom, Timothy's lawyer, Michael Standard, overseeing his forthcoming appeal, held hands with Rosemary in front of a mob of reporters. Standard had a folk hero reputation for representing Puerto Rican antiwar protesters who had been drafted to Vietnam.

Rosemary's black long-sleeved minidress hung off her body. She wore the League for Spiritual Discovery's beaded medallion necklace and rose-colored bug-eye sunglasses that highlighted the redness around her eyes. Her hands shook as she read aloud the statement Timothy had scrawled on a piece of ripped-out notebook paper. "These are the times," Timothy had written, paraphrasing Thomas Paine, a British philosopher who supported the American Revolution, "which test the depth of our faith, trust, and patience. Love cannot be imprisoned." The word "faith" was nearly unreadable, smeared by Rosemary's tears. Facsimiles of the note appeared the next day in the underground press with the parts where her tears had fallen highlighted for effect. The headline read, ROSEMARY WEPT.

"What do you plan to do?" a reporter asked her.

"I plan to use every means to free my husband and myself and our son and our brothers and sisters from the strictures of these laws, which deny our rights as guaranteed to us under the Constitution. I feel that Judge Connally is right: My husband *is* a menace. We are all menaces to the community which makes a mockery of the Constitution of this country."

❧

FOUR DAYS LATER, on March 6, a bomb exploded in Manhattan on West Eleventh Street just two blocks away from Rosemary's old apartment. Three people died. The perpetrators of the bombings were also its victims. The town house was a cell for the Weather Underground, a group of mostly middle-class students and academics who made up the militant Marxist arm of the more peaceful Students for a Democratic Society (SDS). The Weather Underground had seceded from the SDS in 1969 and announced plans earlier to bring the war home with a series of bombing campaigns. One of the survivors, Kathy Boudin, who emerged naked from the toppled town house, happened to be the daughter of the civil liberties attorney Leonard Boudin, a partner of Timothy's appeal lawyer Michael Standard.

Five days later, the judge sentenced Rosemary and Jack. Rosemary received six months with five years' probation, released on appeal bond. Jack would begin a compulsory ninety-day psychiatric evaluation in the California Institution for Men in Chino, a rough place known to be brutal to younger inmates. The sentences sound harsh to modern ears but were light compared with what would befall Timothy Leary.

Timothy's Laguna sentencing followed. Groups of hippies answered Rosemary's invitation and flocked to the courtroom. They adorned Timothy's defense table with pink and white carnations, red roses, and two orchids, led prayer and drum circles outside, and chanted inside the courtroom—an unintentionally similar spectacle to that of the Manson Family trial. At various points, the judge threatened to throw the crowd out for being too rowdy. At least one person declared how high he was on LSD.

The Orange County judge Byron K. McMillan stood before them all and laid down the hammer: Leary was "a pleasure-seeking irresponsible Madison Avenue advocate of the free use of LSD and marijuana." Judge McMillan denied Leary's bail request and sentenced him to the maximum: another ten years.

Thirteen

The Surrogate Monarch
of Psychedelia

Rosemary examined her face in miniature in the pools of Timothy's eyes. After denials of visits based on her own criminal record, an airline employee strike, and then, finally, a postal workers strike, which prevented written communication from reaching Timothy for days, she was finally able to visit him on March 19, 1970, for the first time in two interminable weeks at one of the country's roughest lockdowns, the California Institution for Men in Chino.

He had bragged in a letter that, thanks to handball and daily yoga practice, he felt twenty years younger. But to Rosemary, he looked more like a child in his oversized prison work shirt and oddly shorn hair buzzed in the back and sides—a baby, reaching out for his mother. Ginsberg nailed it when he said, "Jail honed him down to rib and soul."

Timothy, meanwhile, had sent Rosemary at least one letter every day. She responded nearly as often. "I fear I'm swamping you with words," he wrote. They were over-the-top romantic affairs, including "108 Memories of Our Current Incarnation," a list of the special moments in the five years they had spent together.

"Number 11: Seducing you—we kissed on the bridge by the lake that night. I told you the story of 'What Woman Wants.'"

"Number 42: Standing on stage at celebrations—reciting our poetry and hearing your soft voice echoing back—what beauty our love created for the world. Now that John and Yoko are in retirement we are the world's great lovers. May we be blessed with babies."

"I feel your presence everywhere," she responded. "In this house, in the sky, in the sun, particularly in the sun—its warmth and light are you, my heart."

She was his "perfect mate"; he was her "twin star." He sent her astrological readings, and she sent *I Ching* hexagrams.

In no conceivable version of the future did he end up behind bars. "I had beautiful specific detailed visions of our future. Our house, our serene routine, sunshine, babies, we'll get very healthy and brown," he wrote.

"How beautiful our children will be. I picture the boy—black hair, tall, athletic, proud, merry, deep. And the girl. Oh, the girl. Mixed of her mother's beauty and her father's love . . . Thy fruitful womb."

He signed his letters with the words "new life soon."

Now in the visiting room, the gray hue of the fluorescents gave his face a shadowy, forlorn quality. His eyes were red. She had never seen him cry before. Rosemary grabbed for the phone as they made fish faces at each other. Their phones hadn't yet connected.

A visiting toddler ran around behind her. The toddler held a balloon that floated above Timothy's head in the looking glass—a glimpse of the child they would not have. She recalled their second meeting at the art gallery opening in Manhattan, where she had held that trick mirror between their two faces to compare features. Five years later, in the prison visiting room, she could see her grief overlaid on his face. They placed their hands on the glass, fingertips to fingertips, palm to palm. "Here you are with me always," she wrote to him upon her return home. "I feel you inside myself, my very self."

When the phone finally cracked back to life, she heard his words: "You've got to free me. You've got to get me out of here."

Rosemary tried to tell him about the lawyers and the fundraising and the media, but he interrupted her. "Don't trust the lawyers. You've got to free me. You do it."

"How?" she asked.

"I don't care how."

"I will," she said. She was crying now, too. "I will free you, my love."

～

ROSEMARY'S EXISTENCE OSCILLATED between prison visits and a coordinated effort to raise awareness and funds and galvanize grass-roots support for Timothy's defense: interviews with television shows, local radio stations, and underground newspapers, inquiries into Timothy's literary estate and opportunities for more writing and movie deals, making sure she paid the water and electricity bills on time while also checking on Susan and visiting Jack. She opened piles of mail sent by strangers from around the world to Holding Together, Timothy's defense fund—envelopes that contained anywhere from one Mexican peso to a thousand Canadian dollars. As Leary's biographer John Bryan wrote, "Rosemary Leary hustled every dime she could lay her strong little hands on. . . . She was not about to quit, no matter what." The right side of her face flared red with acne thanks to the hours spent on the phone as she racked up $400 monthly telephone bills. Rosemary joked that she deserved a "Stand By Your Man Award."

Owing to the draconian length of Timothy's sentencing, and also to Rosemary's newfound mediagenic powers, the vast majority of outlets sympathized with the Learys. The papers ran full-page appeals for Timothy's defense fund signed by John and Yoko, Allen Ginsberg, and the *Magnificent Seven* actor James Coburn. "Energy wanted. $300,000 Ransom needed for the release of Timothy Leary." The youth revolution's heads and fists rallied behind them, forgoing any prior beef as they reclassified him from a washed-up, touchy-feely self-promoter to a tried-and-true political prisoner. Rosemary met with leaders of the Gay Liberation Front and posed for a publicity shot with the bound-and-gagged Yippie leaders Jerry Rubin and Abbie Hoffman, who had once disparaged Timothy for his mealymouthed politics.

She met reporters at the redbrick Victorian law office of Kennedy & Rhine, which was handling Timothy's Laredo appeal. The firm operated as a safe house of sorts for California's New Left, where Picasso prints and political art hung on the wall, while bookshelves featured works from writers like Eldridge Cleaver and Bertrand Russell. The location of her media interviews telegraphed her revolutionary state of mind.

Michael Kennedy, a sandy-haired and handsome thirty-three-year-old superstar of the political left, housed the Yippies Rubin and Hoffman, counseled Jane Fonda in the wake of the "Hanoi Jane" fiasco, and considered the leader of the Weather Underground, Bernardine Dohrn, a close confidante. Dohrn would land on the FBI's Most Wanted List as "the most dangerous woman in America"—a label similar to the one later attached to Timothy.

Kennedy, who shared Timothy's innate distrust of authority, prided himself on attracting clients who, as he put it, were "anyone who the government didn't like." *The New York Times* christened him the "patron lawyer of unpopular causes," and his philosophy seemed to be that if you weren't pissing off people in power, you weren't doing your job. At the same time, he could be ruthless and mercenary, earning his rent by representing the legally and morally encumbered Mitchell brothers, who relied on the First Amendment to keep their porn theater open. As Jerry Rubin said, Michael's goal was "to be part of the passions of his times."

Rosemary bonded with Kennedy's larger-than-life second wife, Eleanora, who was almost a decade younger than Rosemary, but acted as her fairy godmother, sprinkling money and sisterly advice. Eleanora was once a buyer for Saks Fifth Avenue department store so she knew how to ensure that Rosemary presented as gracefully as possible while hopscotching around the country to raise money. This was one of Eleanora's many roles: Not only did she accompany her husband to jury selection meetings, maintain his books, and help interview his clients, but she also dressed them. "As a team, I was all intuition and Michael was all intellect. . . . Together we didn't miss much, ever," she said. *New York* magazine named her the paragon of "radical chic," perfectly encapsulated by their purple Porsche 911T. "A Chanel suit took me places where no one else could tread," she quipped.

Decked out in Eleanora's designer garments, Rosemary traveled differently now—more self-assured, with the certitude of a woman on a mission. "It's been such a surprise to have found this measure of confidence. Certainty. Freedom in a way," she wrote.

The Kennedys counseled Rosemary on the far-out philosophy of the New Left beyond drugs and self-experimentation. Rosemary began then to speak of the U.S. government as a tyrannical oppressor— "Amerika," as many members of the New Left now spelled it. Before her husband's imprisonment, she wasn't interested in insurrection but "anyone who has had a loved one imprisoned unfairly understands that rage and the sense of helplessness," she wrote. Rosemary felt that the system was rigged. And her impotence in the face of oppression made her want to burn it all down.

Her rhetoric, delivered sweetly and even seductively, calcified: "As you must know, my husband has been kidnapped by the U.S. government officials. He has been moved secretly from jail to jail. He has been kept from his lawyers. He has been kept from his family."

Rosemary's soft voice delivered a strong message. "We are the majority. There are more dope smokers than any other religious groups," she told Bob O'Lear on the Bay Area radio station KQED. "You don't have to be a dope smoker. You can have a naked statue in your house. There are lots of things you're probably guilty of."

Moved by Rosemary's speech, O'Lear responded, "There are so many of us." But then backtracked. "I'm supposed to be objective."

While aboard a small twin-turboprop high-wing commuter plane heading from San Luis Obispo to San Francisco, the pilot searched for keys to the locked gate as the plane sat on the tarmac. When he got out to find someone to open the gate, Rosemary jumped off the plane, too, and hitched a ride on a baggage carrier. Rosemary didn't have time to wait for other people to save her. She lived, as she wrote, on "carrot juice and nerves," all the while "growing stronger and wiser with every moment away from him."

The *San Francisco Chronicle* christened her "the surrogate monarch of psychedelia." She educated *The New York Times* on the foundations of their religion: "The proper place to experiment with new substances is one's body. You shouldn't violate someone else's body, either a patient or a guinea pig. All Tim has done in the last few years is publish the results and findings of those experiments on himself."

The smitten male interviewers seemed content to let Rosemary frame her story. During one recorded interview, she told a *Berkeley Barb* reporter what the headline of the piece should be: NO TIME TO TURN ON or A SAINT IN CHAINS. (Newspaper editors chose the latter.)

Rolling Stone published two profiles of Rosemary, describing her as "the Public Figure." In one, she took the blame for Leary's inconsistency. "The thing to remember about Tim is that he didn't want all the notoriety—but there was no one else to do the things he thought should be done. He still considers himself a scientist. He is carrying out experiments with the human body and he wants to report his findings. *I* was the one who was always sort of pulling away from things. Tim has been consistent." Then she glanced at her watch. "Oh. We're running a little late. My probation officer is so understanding but I don't want to keep her waiting long." There is genius in inviting a charmed reporter to join you on a trip to the probation office. The piece would run under the front-page headline ROSEMARY LEARY IS MEETING HER PROBATION OFFICER.

She had learned from Timothy how to use her innate talent for quips to manipulate an audience and spin a media narrative. Timothy even called her "the media heroine, the grass widow."

When the *Rolling Stone* profiler asked about their run for governor, she laughed and leaned forward for emphasis. "Well, we were stuck with a public image, right? Drug doctor. Corruptor of Youth. We thought about it in two ways—if we were going to have an image, we might as well change it to 'political candidate' instead of 'drug doctor.' We thought we could go out with a flourish. The importance of what we were doing outweighed the immediate considerations, and we hoped Tim's candidacy could pave the way for something in the future." She had in one smooth talking point waved away the stink of that ill-fated campaign.

"She's so mellow, Rosemary Leary. You know how on acid things come to you in waves? Well, that's how Rosemary comes on. But the waves are gentle, more like ripples on a placid lake," the reporter Rick Heide wrote in the *Berkeley Barb*. "Rosemary was sitting on a big bed, rapping on the phone. As soon as we sat down with her I realized instant karma had hit us. Our whole mood was transformed to where Rosemary was at. We weren't coerced. It was gentle and natural. But it happened."

And she wielded Timothy's time-tested Marshall McLuhan route of communication: positivity. "We're rarely afraid," she told them, "and Tim never. Tim seems very serene and relaxed. He's been practicing a great deal of yoga these days."

As the philosopher Irwin Edman wrote, "It is myth, not mandate, a fable, not logic by which people are moved."

❧

IN TIMOTHY'S ABSENCE, Rosemary amassed a new army of followers—a team of Brotherhood protectors, pals from her old New York days, and a beautiful female chauffeur named Donna Motsinger, who didn't even have a license. She bridled the Brotherhood when they wanted to douse the steering wheels of the Laguna Beach Police Department with LSD and dimethyl sulfoxide (or DMSO), a combination that could, allegedly, speed up the skin's absorption of LSD. The Brothers loved the idea of turning on the whole police force, but Rosemary put a firm foot down. It went against their beliefs.

As Timothy would later write to his archivists, "It helps to have a network of loving fearless friends who will face death with you. Rosemary did." A favorite new friend, Oden Fong, was a charismatic musician with a hard-earned death wish and beautiful waist-length black hair that fluttered even when there seemed to be no wind. The Brotherhood tapped Oden, who moved drugs for the operation in Laguna Beach, to take care of Rosemary with a clear directive never to touch her. He accompanied her to interviews, acted as a confidant, and shuttled her around the state.

Fong had one of the few phones in Dodge City. When Rosemary visited, she would spend hours sitting on an overturned bucket in his kitchen talking to lawyers and the press. Oden was discreet and respectful; he had learned from his father how to keep powerful secrets. Oden's parents, Maylia and Benson Fong, were famous actors filling Hollywood's very short list of Asian roles. Oden was a rich kid who discovered early that even with all the glitz and glamour he would always be an outsider. So he embraced the role available to him, dropped out of the life handed to him, lived on the streets, picked up a guitar, and fell in with Rosemary, whom he identified as a fellow searcher. They spoke about spirituality and religion. "She was so serious about our concept of God," Oden said. "There are people that take [LSD] to try to get close to God. A lot of people think they are God. There are people who are self-realized when they take it. I think that Rosemary was one of those people. She was a true disciple of the cosmos, so to speak." She felt a similar fondness for Oden, whom she called her "mythic knight from Laguna."

On April 4, for Rosemary's forthcoming birthday, Oden accompanied her to a Moody Blues concert at the Long Beach Arena. They dropped LSD and danced to the dreamy music until, at one point, the band stopped playing and seemed to stare at Rosemary. A glance felt like five minutes.

A hiccup on the astral plane.

Stillness.

Hours (or seconds) later, Mike Pinder broke the spell, speaking from his perch at the keyboards: "For God's sake, let him out. Let him out! He's only talking."

"It's called 'Legend of the Mind.'"

The jangly guitar riff started first. Followed by the opening vocals: "Timothy Leary's dead."

The crowd of twenty thousand roared.

"No, no, no." The drums crashed. The violin soared. "He's outside looking in."

The hordes pressed up against them, moving closer to the stage, closer to the music, closer to her. They shouted his name. They pressed and reached, pressed and reached, singing and breathing and sighing as one united force. They existed together as one organism. Unity. Things like this just seemed to happen with Rosemary, Oden thought.

❧

A WEEK LATER, fifteen hundred people lined up outside the Family Dog, a sea-worn wooden rock ballroom on the coast along the Great Highway, bracing themselves against the brutal San Francisco breaker winds, waiting to attend Rosemary's Holding Together fundraiser that she had named the Om Orgy.

"Was it cold?" Rosemary asked a reporter on the scene. "I must have somehow acquired the secret of internal heat because I was warm." Rosemary in all her warmth and goodwill watched from the balcony as Allen Ginsberg chanted lines from William Blake's *Songs of Innocence and of Experience.* As the flickering of lit pipes passed through the audience, one of Kerouac's dharma bums, the writer Michael McClure, read from his *99 Theses,* and the poet Lawrence Ferlinghetti played an autoharp. The night netted the defense fund $2,500—a nice chunk of change and a bona fide success for Rosemary.

But the crucial connection of the night occurred behind the scenes, when two enthusiastic young book collectors and drug enthusiasts named Michael Horowitz and Bob Barker pitched their new drug library to Rosemary as an asylum for Timothy's growing archive. The two men had already pooled their personal libraries together into one, naming it after Fitz Hugh Ludlow, the nineteenth-century *Hasheesh Eater* writer, who, as lore would have it, introduced Mark Twain to the potent magic of smoking resin. Barker and Horowitz were curating chronicles of the drug experience—a part of the literary record long ignored and suppressed—with a focus on the emerging 1960s counterculture. Horowitz and Barker offered Rosemary a privately funded safe space for Timothy's archives to endure, overseen by curators who understood how important these documents were to humanity—worthy, they felt, of Talmudic reverence. They were instantly dedicated to safeguarding them.

Rosemary seemed intrigued, Horowitz would later say, but also cautious. "You could see she was under a lot of stress. We wanted to do anything we could to help her," he said. Something about these nerdy, earnest men made her feel comfortable enough to invite them to her home in Berkeley a few days later.

The three of them split a joint before Rosemary led them to the garage—the same garage where Timothy's first wife had taken her own life—and showed them four rusty four-drawer gray metal filing cabinets. Horowitz pulled out a folder at random marked "NOV. 1963-HUXLEY." Inside, a carbon copy of Laura Huxley's letter to friends describing her husband Aldous's final moments after she gave him LSD. "It was like the discovery of the Dead Sea Scrolls," Horowitz said. Bob Barker opened another drawer and came across the mimeographed reports of Timothy's early psilocybin study on recidivism, the Concord Prison Experiment, in 1961. "We were like kids in a candy store. Rosemary practically had to drag us away to continue talking about what to do with the archives," Horowitz said.

These files contained the names of anyone who had ever worked with Timothy or gotten high with him. In the wrong hands they could be manipulated, mistreated, or even destroyed. Rosemary had picked the right hands. In choosing these two new archivists to protect Timothy's files, she preserved an essential—but often misunderstood—piece of modern American history.

Fourteen

The Computer

Rosemary's efforts in front of the camera to drum up interest and raise money for Timothy's defense distracted from a second, secret strategy underway, which offered the most cinematic solution to Timothy's legal woes: a prison break.

The theater of the absurd that followed in the late spring and summer of 1970 blended melodrama with mythology—where the primary actors barely touched center stage, hiding in plain sight, while the understudies took on starring roles in Timothy's escape. There are reasons for this shadowiness: some wanted the credit in being associated with Timothy; others shrank from direct involvement because admitting so would end in disreputability and prison time.

The first step toward freedom occurred with Timothy's prison transfer from Chino to California Men's Colony (CMC), a minimum-security facility for elderly, nonviolent prisoners. After nearly two months of incarceration, prison psychiatrists had allegedly used Timothy's own Leary Circle personality test from his pre-psychedelic era as a research psychologist on its creator. Timothy knew what to say to make the psychiatrists view him as a nonthreat—a doddering, middle-aged hippie with no fight left in him. The results led them to approve a relocation to CMC's much cushier institution of golf courses and vegetable gardens. CMC also allowed for unsupervised visits, which meant that he and Rosemary could embrace and speak freely in private.

Rosemary didn't expect how painful it would be to touch him, to put skin to skin, walk hand in hand down the garden pathways in the open air while not actually being free.

The California courts had denied two bail appeals, and the couple now awaited the decision of Supreme Court Justice William O. Douglas, who oversaw appeals that reached the Ninth Circuit. Justice Douglas was one of the most progressive justices ever to sit on the bench. He had issued a stay of execution for the spies Julius and Ethel Rosenberg, supported Vietnam War protesters, advocated for the use of contraceptives, and even wrote about the virtues of folk music in the underground magazine *Avant Garde*. Reading Douglas's book *Points of Rebellion*, Rosemary nodded along with the justice's condemnation of "goose-stepping . . . conformity" and "the growing rightist tendencies in the nation that demand conformity—or else." She believed that the universe had gifted them the perfect person to free them. Timothy agreed, seeing Douglas as a kindred spirit whose respect for the youth generation would ensure his freedom.

Timothy sent Douglas a rambling missive called the "Eagle Brief," which read, in part, "Rosemary and I are American Eagles. Totem animals of this land. Wild. Free. High. Proud. Laughing."

"I'll be free in two, three weeks," Timothy wrote to Rosemary.

Somehow, they both believed this.

But their bad karma continued. After the success of the Om Orgy came the abject failure of the next fundraiser in New York at the Village Gate in May. Abbie Hoffman, stoned and angry, screamed about the massacre at Kent State, where the National Guard had gunned down four student protesters a week earlier. When Allen Ginsberg tried to save the day with rounds of "ohhhmmms," Hoffman exploded, stormed the stage, roughed Ginsberg up, and punched through a speaker. Most attendees had departed by the time Jimi Hendrix performed and before Rosemary could make her case for the big-ticket donations she had been counting on. In the end it took $8,000 to put the show on and they raised only $5,000. The New York debacle burned her out. "I wanted to be mousy in fact, hidden and not in the papers again," she wrote.

The stress took its toll. She developed a nervous tic, battling an unyielding urge to clear the pressure building inside her by yawning, pulling at her earlobes, and letting out emphatic sighs. She was sick, too. The pelvic pains from her surgery had never improved. Her holistic doctors ordered carrot juice cleanses and rest. "I've been concerned since Sunday about your health," Timothy wrote. "You have not been using good judgement, baby . . . getting overcommitted . . . moving around too much. . . . I long to be with you. . . . I'd cure you in a few minutes . . . center sweet girl . . . feel the solidarity of our love." He pressured her to "slow down" and "work on our book"—a book they were co-writing about their arrests and trial and his time in prison.

But she could not stop, not when he and the movement needed her most. The Brotherhood, which had reconfigured after Griggs's death under Michael Randall, who ran the Mystic Arts World head shop, secured her a house on the beach where she could hear the tides change from every room. Supporters at Esalen Institute, an incubator of the New Age movement in Big Sur, provided Rosemary with a second house, closer to CMC so she could visit Timothy more often. She had made a sleeping bag out of wolf fur and paisley, which, along with a Moroccan leather bag full of documents, she brought everywhere. She met with his editors—one of whom would publish Timothy's subsequent book *Jail Notes*—and an unending stream of interested newspaper and magazine editors. She still took every interview request and traveled from coast to coast to shore up grassroots support to free Timothy.

And then there was Susan, who had unraveled since her father's arrest and imprisonment—another suicide attempt, a pregnancy, an abortion, and a diagnosis of schizophrenia. Timothy's family doctor, Eugene Schoenfeld, who wrote a syndicated medical advice column in the underground papers under the name Dr. Hippocrates, had pulled some strings and found her a room at Herrick Hospital in Berkeley. In an institutional setting, she seemed to thrive, and even further softened to Rosemary, the "barren witch," as Susan once called her, who visited her and oversaw her care.

Then the most disappointing news yet: Justice Douglas decried Timothy's "messianic ideas" and upheld the bail denial, writing in his decision that there is "grave danger that he will advocate what to him is the fulfillment of his self-styled priesthood."

His lawyers would later say that this shock hardened Timothy's resolve to take matters into his own hands. "I think that was the first time he had begun to doubt seriously that the system was going to vindicate him and he was going to get out of jail," said Joe Rhine, who joined Michael Kennedy as Timothy's appellate co-counsel.

The morning of the denial, Rosemary hitchhiked to the prison wearing a simple crepe and silk shawl to comfort her husband, brushing aside fears about the Zodiac Killer operating in the area. Timothy immediately started whispering plans of escape in her ear.

THE LONGER TIMOTHY languished behind bars, the more erratic and demanding he grew. He asked Rosemary to hire a helicopter with a grappling hook to scoop him out of the prison yard. Or maybe she could somehow get her hands on a yacht waiting offshore to ferry him away? Or a submarine? Rosemary's dual role was to carry on his legacy on the outside and reconcile his fantasies with reality on the inside. She reminded him how many naval and army bases surrounded them. "I mean, I was a superwoman living on carrot juice in those days but even so I wasn't able to manage things like that," she said. She still held on to a shred of hope that they could do this legitimately—without breaking any more laws.

The ancient institutionalized men who had adapted to the daily routine—the three square meals and the endless rounds of golf—solidified Timothy's resolve to find a way out or else lose his mind. His world was bifurcated into outside versus in: those on the outside didn't know how it felt behind bars and couldn't be trusted. Rosemary's own prison time gave her further insider status. They began using code words in their correspondences. She called herself "the computer"—a secure vault for sensitive information. "There are few people that need to know everything," she wrote to him, "too much information is as hazardous as not enough. It is up to the two of us my dear, not three or four, just you and me."

Rosemary kept imagining her life was a darkly lit noir with villains. She fixated on the men who had arrived mysteriously to repair phone lines in the area, the twitchy affect of the deliverymen, and even began to suspect people she had once considered close confidants. "I feel I've created a great deal of uncertainty among my friends by my paranoid distrust of everyone. I want to resolve all this 'bridge over troubled waters,'" Rosemary wrote to Timothy.

Perhaps as a diversion, perhaps as a self-soothing technique, perhaps out of genuine love, Rosemary invited an old friend into her bed. Rosemary had a capacious sexual appetite, but John Schewel was more than just a mere lover. He was a warm and welcoming escape hatch.

John, the NYU student turned League member who had witnessed Rosemary and Timothy's spat at Nina Graboi's house, had traveled across the country in a ten-wheeler painted with a Technicolor antediluvian scene selling candles and playing music. They reunited by chance on the West Coast and reignited the spark they had shared during their chaste walks in the Millbrook forest. John, though a much younger man, was to Rosemary yet another magician.

The affair started in Los Angeles when he drove her to the producer Bert Schneider's ornate mansion in Beverly Hills, formerly owned by the Lithuanian actor Laurence Harvey, who played the brainwashed sergeant Raymond Shaw in *The Manchurian Candidate* (a movie that Rosemary's old friend the jazz legend David Amram had scored—synchronicity, yet again).

John had retired early and was awakened by Rosemary's naked body against him under the sheets. He could feel her breath on his back. "Her face was inches from me. Her eyes, liquid, drew me in. . . . I was enveloped by the Goddess," John would later write. John realized then that he had "loved her for all my lives."

Rosemary didn't love Timothy any less. John accepted the dynamic and, as a big believer in free love, harbored no hard feelings, even as he drove his lover to visit her husband in prison.

Rosemary wrote to Timothy upon her return from that trip: "By next year my belly will be full and each year after that and we will watch our children grow in love and beauty." She spoke openly to Timothy about her "new friend," as she called John. It's clear from Timothy's subsequent writing that the affair wounded him. He would later allege that jealousy motivated his decision to escape. Timothy needed to hold something against her while she sacrificed so much for him.

～～

MICHAEL AND ELEANORA KENNEDY would later insist that they had nothing to do with orchestrating or executing the escape. Kennedy's close friend and sometime co-counsel Michael Tigar wrote in his own biography that Timothy later pointed a finger at Kennedy, calling him the mastermind, in order to seek revenge after their future falling-out. Rosemary remained mum about the Kennedys' involvement, though there are references to secret meetings with them all over her letters.

Here are the facts: Michael Kennedy provided legal counsel for all three escape conspirators—the Learys, the Brotherhood, and the Weather Underground—and he is the one conceivable linchpin among them.

Bill Ayers, a key member of the Weather Underground, recalled that Kennedy acted as middleman between the Brotherhood of Eternal Love and the Weather. "Michael was our lawyer, and he was also their lawyer," Ayers said. "We met with Michael one day and he said, 'These folks are interested in getting Tim Leary out of prison, and they wondered if you all would be interested in helping if you had any capacity to do that?'" The Kennedys themselves even admitted to deploying less than aboveboard tactics for special clients. "We helped the Weathermen in any way we could," Eleanora said in a documentary later, "legal or illegal." "We do our best work in the dark," Michael added.

The Weather Underground agreed to take on Timothy's escape, even though their leader, Bernardine Dohrn, found Timothy lacking in depth. "Because he was, what, you know? I don't know, you know, a White man, self-centered, rich," she said. "But didn't deserve to be in prison for sure."

Motivations aligned, however unlikely, for the Weather Underground, who were enticed by the potential for unrest, the publicity, the training for other future prison breaks, and $25,000 in a paper bag supplied by the Brotherhood and exchanged on the Santa Monica Pier. But their reason for opting in ran deeper than the financial. As

Jeff Jones, another member of the Weather Underground, explained, they needed a radicalized Timothy to galvanize the disaffected drug youth. "Guns and grass are united in the youth underground. Freaks are revolutionaries and revolutionaries are freaks," read their "Declaration of a State of War" against the U.S. government. "Our intention is to disrupt the empire . . . to incapacitate it, to put pressure on the cracks . . . to attack from the inside." Freeing Timothy put "pressure on the cracks" by humiliating the men in power, namely President Nixon.

Rosemary didn't believe in violence, nor did Timothy, but now, out of necessity, she found herself a witness to heated debates about whether to use violence in Timothy's prison escape. She had even begun hedging on her League religion beliefs—especially the key commandment to never inflict harm on another person's reality. But Rosemary knew what it felt like to be imprisoned unfairly, and she was ready and willing now to do anything to save her husband from enduring the death of his mind behind bars. Whether she liked it or not, she was in bed with the revolution. And though Rosemary worried that the Weather Underground would use the Brotherhood's money to buy more dynamite, she still approved the handoff. (The Weather Underground would claim responsibility for twenty bombings around the country in the following five years, causing extensive property damage but no physical harm to any person.)

Poughkeepsie set his trial date for September 15, 1970. That case included eleven new counts against him, ranging from violation of drug laws to creating a public nuisance at Millbrook, and would undoubtedly add more prison time to his sentence. They were working against a tight deadline to get Timothy out before he was transferred.

Timothy's escape plan had coalesced into something more than a fantasy now: On a moonless night, Timothy would somehow scale the barbed-wire fence that surrounded the prison and find a Buddha statue by a tree outside the prison grounds, where a Weather Underground car would wait for him. From there, a Weather contact would usher him into a series of safe houses until they could find a permanent hideout overseas.

Rosemary knew that she had to go on the run with Timothy. If she stayed, the Feds would do everything in their power to turn her. She was the connective tissue that linked the whole plan together. Still, she hesitated, knowing that the act of disappearing would kick off a series of events she couldn't stop once started.

"Will this be the weekend he tells me what to do?" Rosemary wrote in her diary. "I pray not. I want to see my family once more. But if I do, I might break down."

To prepare herself and safeguard those who could be implicated, she began to push her friends away. She even shut out John. "You've done enough now," she said. "Go." Confused by the perceived rejection, John didn't realize yet that she was only trying to protect him.

❧

Now to say goodbye to her family.

On her way to her parents' house, she noticed the tract houses that she had laughed at with Timothy during his first visit to the suburban neighborhood only a few years earlier. Now she wondered about the happy existences of the people living inside. How had her life turned to this?

With her parents, she allowed herself to be vulnerable. "Strange to be here but safe and comfortable and full of love. Nice to be called 'baby' and hugged and kissed," she wrote in a letter to Timothy.

Next she arranged to meet her brother outside at a restaurant on Sunset Boulevard. Gary brought a friend, and the three chatted and ate under the hot Los Angeles sun. The last time Rosemary had seen Gary, he was still living with their parents, spending hours in his room under heavy headphones blasting Janis Joplin. He had been home from Vietnam for less than a year. Did they embrace? Share warm words? Gary doesn't remember. Rosemary noticed Gary's new-found obsessiveness. He repeated that he would never return to Vietnam as a soldier, only as a medic. "It was so sad to see him so. . . . Gary's eyes are like that now," she wrote. "Shadowed and scared. The family darkness," an allusion to some unspoken inheritance.

When the friend went for a bathroom break, Rosemary turned to Gary and her demeanor shifted.

"I'm not going to see you anymore, or the family," she said.

Gary looked at his sister quizzically.

"I can't talk about it. I'm not going to see you. I'll be in touch."

Gary examined her face, still trying to comprehend the hidden meaning of her words.

"Take care of Mom and Dad."

The friend returned and small talk resumed as both pretended nothing momentous had just transpired between them. When lunch concluded, the three walked out onto Sunset.

"Hey, we'll see you next month," she said.

Six years would pass before they'd see each other again.

Fifteen

Sylvia McGaffin

On September 1, ARIES—the astrological sign of the ram, the perfect code name for pugnacious Michael Kennedy—alerted Rosemary that a member of the Weather Underground would be in touch. In the meantime, she should pack and be ready to depart at a moment's notice and await a call to meet in person—no details shared over the phone they all knew was tapped. Rosemary endeared herself to the Underground contact with one demand: "I need two pounds of red henna hair dye from Kiehl's."

"Rosemary made a big impression on us," Jeff Jones said. When Jones changed his identity years later, he ran into other members of the Underground, also underground, shopping at Kiehl's. Give up your identity, sure, but not Kiehl's naturally scented soaps.

With that edict approved, Rosemary connected with Bernardine Dohrn, whom Rosemary called Pam, and visited a wig store in San Francisco. Rosemary tried on a feathery Keith Richards number that reminded her of a fancy bird plumage. *Too stylish*. Bernardine picked out a blond one, curled and short like June Cleaver, a typical Eisenhower-era housewife. When Rosemary put on the wig and looked in the mirror, she saw her midwestern cousins staring back at her.

Rosemary adjusted her new wire-rimmed glasses. Her scalp itched under the wig hair. "Oh lord must I look this way? Fresh from the beauty shop plastic lady. The longer I looked the less I liked her," she wrote. They bought a push-up bra and a smart short dress. She called herself Miss Priss.

Bernardine and Rosemary visited a department store where a clueless salesgirl helped Rosemary, in her new wig, apply makeup—orange-pink lipstick that worked in all the wrong ways, dark brown eye pencil, and false eyelashes. Rosemary hadn't worn this much makeup since her modeling days.

She made up a story about this new face in the mirror. Sylvia was a twenty-eight-year-old, good little Catholic girl who had only just moved out of her parents' house. She worked as a secretary at a law firm and was having an affair with an executive. This, Rosemary could work with. She couldn't believe how easy it was for her to slip into another person's life.

Rosemary then boarded a plane to Chicago to secure identification. The Weather Underground had already supplied Rosemary with a birth certificate from a child who had died in infancy named Sylvia E. McGaffin—a particularly ghoulish detail considering she was putting off the second phase of her fertility surgery to leave the country with Timothy. A new name mired in loss.

With a birth certificate, you could forge a new identity—a laminated student card, a library card, a driver's license, and then, ultimately, a passport.

The import of this moment—the finality of truly giving up herself—came to her here, in full disguise as Sylvia, in the passport office inside the coldly modern steel federal building in downtown Chicago. All the humor and excitement of the previous day gave way to a feeling of emptiness. *This was it.* She filled out the forms using national holidays for her parents' birthdays so that she could remember the answers if questioned.

Rosemary restrained herself from scratching at her wig. The other selves—the women that she might have been, the lives that she could have lived—suddenly passed through her mind's eye: finishing a shift at a bakery, loading books on the shelves of a local library, waiting for her professor husband to come home after a day of lectures, holding her babies, riding a bicycle to her house near the shore. *I want to go home*, she thought. But home didn't exist anywhere. Not anymore.

"I was now a fugitive," she wrote.

An officious woman talked on the phone and held her hand up as a sign for Rosemary to wait. The woman lowered the phone and lifted her eyes and said, "Name, please."

Rosemary felt her cheeks flush. Her mind faded to black. *Her name. Her name. What was her name!* She couldn't conjure any appropriate words. She felt the sweat form around her brow and found herself flailing, literally. She had thrown her bag into the air. A diversion. Not a graceful one, but it gave her a beat. As she collected her things, she bent down to pick up the contents on the floor, praying that her brain would start working again. *Think.*

As she stood up, the words found her: "I am Sylvia McGaffin."

ROSEMARY MADE AN APPOINTMENT to see a dentist, a luxury that would not be available on the run. She spent two hours under nitrous oxide and couldn't believe how high she got. "I can't begin to describe the experience," she wrote to Timothy. "It was more disorienting than any experience I've ever had and all the coordinates were gone. One thing left, breathe, breathe, moment to moment. If that ratio can be kept, perfect harmony. In touch with everything." The dentist expressed surprise. "It's a mystical experience!" he said.

She had already said her goodbye to Timothy in person. His final prison letter to Rosemary read, "Sunday . . . perfect . . . perfect . . .

perfect . . . what fun to see your mind in action . . . your metamorphosis."

She returned his letter with a coded message giving the green light to the escape by using her fertility surgery as shroud:

BELOVED,
OPERATION TOMORROW DOCTORS FEEL BEST NOT
TO WAIT TOTALLY OPTIMISTIC ABOUT SUCCESS AND
NEW LIFE DON'T WORRY I'LL BE BRAVE WON'T BE
DOWN TO VISIT SUNDAY BUT WE'LL BE TOGETHER
SOON I AWAIT YOU I LOVE YOU CONTACT ME AT THREE
TREE RECOVERY CENTER.
YOUR MATE

There was no going back now.

❧

ON SEPTEMBER 12, 1970, Timothy, rangy and supple from months of yoga and handball, somehow pulled himself up a telephone pole and then along a high wire over a twelve-foot chain-link fence wrapped in double strands of barbed wire. He followed railroad tracks to a small parking lot off Highway 1 surrounded by three trees. Twenty minutes later a car arrived and, as planned, put its right blinker on.

"Are you Nino?" the driver asked.

It was his new code name. Timothy got into a getaway car, driven by a Weather Underground contact. Along with his eyeglasses, his ID, and his meditation beads, he carried one possession: Rosemary's letters.

Timothy wrote the following message, released by the Underground to the straight and alternative presses: "I offer loving gratitude to my Sisters and Brothers in the Weatherman Underground who designed and executed my liberation. Rosemary and I are now with the

Underground and we'll continue to stay high and wage the revolutionary war. . . . I am armed and should be considered dangerous to anyone who threatens my life or freedom."

Meanwhile, halfway across the country, the FBI director, J. Edgar Hoover, launched a manhunt and an investigation into the breakout, telling a group of reporters, "We'll have him in ten days."

❧

FULL OF ANTICIPATION, Rosemary, with members of the Weather Underground, awaited Timothy's arrival in an abandoned farmhouse hideaway in Seattle. The barren safe house contained bare lightbulbs and political posters. No amenities of a homestead. "These college students, children of privilege, had no use for creature comforts," she wrote. Only the wealthy could choose to live this close to the bone.

Rosemary decided to feather her nest to provide Timothy with the softest landing possible for life back on the outside. She baked him bread and made soup and built a makeshift sweat lodge, gathering together loose branches and rocks to hold the heat. The queen of setting loaded up on his favorite foods—Portuguese wines, Danish cheeses, Tuborg beer, smoked oysters, artichoke hearts, plus Camel cigarettes—and bought orange Japanese paper lanterns, sheets from India, orange pillows and throws, incense and candles, and silk robes.

To signal that all was safe, Rosemary hung one of the orange throws in her window and waited. In that time, she became enmeshed in the Weather Underground operation, and despite her earlier hesitations she liked what she saw. Bernardine expressed a change of attitude about violence after the Manhattan town house explosion. "They now convincingly espoused peace and love and community service," Rosemary wrote. "I felt we were with people who shared a vision of the harmony of life and the dream of a world unified by freedom and justice for all. I liked them. And they had just risked their lives and their own freedom to help Tim." Bernardine in turn found an open and attuned audience in the Acid Queen, who absorbed each of the Weather leader's words about the state of women's liberation. As Rosemary would later write in a letter to the Weather, one aimed especially at Bernardine, expressing gratitude for her brief tutelage, "How very much you taught us, our dear wise family. . . . Your courage and laughter remain with us."

But it wasn't enough to learn how to be a revolutionary. She had to act like one, too. Bernardine and Rosemary discussed the Learys' possible next steps—how they would travel to Europe, find a hotel to stow away in for a few days, until they could, hopefully, persuade a country without an extradition treaty to take them in. They had suggested Algeria, where the Black Panthers had recently opened up an embassy.

Three days after his escape, Rosemary spied a figure in the distance. She recognized Timothy's walk and broke into a run. They embraced long and hard.

But their reverie lasted less than a day. Incarceration had changed Timothy. "In prison he became more consciously manipulative," she later said. Even his posture changed—less erect, more shadowy and insecure. He was 150 pounds soaking wet, angry, impatient, and ridiculous. He complained about missing newspapers and the Weather Underground's failure to secure his fake passports. Though verbose and charismatic as always, he had lost his confidence. His swagger was a facade. Their lovemaking, which he had waxed on about in his letters, disappointed her, especially when she compared it with the moans coming from Bernardine's room.

He continued to let her down in the days to follow. At the Sheraton Hotel and Motor Inn near O'Hare Airport in Chicago, while building his new passport around William McNellis, a dead four-year-old, Timothy, hair shorn bald and wearing a suit and a tie, was on edge. During check-in, he testily shouted, "Rosemary." Hearing her real name sent shivers down her spine. Once safely back in his room, she hissed at him, "Sylvia! Sylvia! Do you want to get us killed?"

On September 19, 1970, the day after Jimi Hendrix choked on his own vomit while high on barbiturates in a London apartment, the couple tested out their William McNellis/Sylvia McGaffin disguises at a local screening of the documentary *Woodstock*. They slid past the young cops, bought buttery popcorn and Hershey bars, and found seats in the first row, arriving in the middle of Richie Havens's opening performance. As the sugary confections hit their lips, they sang along with the chorus:

> *FREEDOM, FREEDOM*
> *SOMETIMES I FEEL LIKE A MOTHERLESS CHILD*

But what did it mean to her now, this freedom?

❧

THE GRIEF SHE FELT UPON leaving the Weather Underground to catch a flight to Paris surprised her. Rosemary, so quick to throw her heart into a community, something greater than herself, saw the Weather as a new family system. She seriously considered staying behind and working with them. Rosemary wrote an emphatic letter to Bernardine prior to her departure. "You freed me too from loneliness and silence, from rage that had no objective, from the solitude and loneliness and fear . . . of being an actress the rest of my life, from the bondage of probation," she wrote. "Oh, you saved me all right. I am yours, soul and heart."

Once they landed in Paris—a location chosen for aesthetic reasons rather than practical ones—the fabric holding husband and wife together continued to fray. Without a plan, once again.

Since every hotel they contacted was booked, Timothy decided to throw his fate into the hands of an acquaintance, a well-known French psychiatrist named Pierre Bensoussan who had written convincingly about marijuana legalization and with whom Timothy had traded amiable correspondence. But once again the specifics fell on Rosemary. While Timothy waited in a nearby café, Rosemary sussed out the doctor as friend or foe. When she walked into his office that smelled of incense and featured a poster of Jimi Hendrix on the wall, she decided to trust him.

Bensoussan invited them to stay at his apartment. "I was on the verge of a nervous breakdown and where better to break down than in a Parisian psychiatrist's more-than-luxurious apartment in the 16th arrondissement?" she wrote.

Now safely ensconced in Paris, outside a prison yard and without an audience, their rage unbridled, they fought out in the open about old lovers, lawyers, and unmet expectations. Rosemary wanted to relax and recover, while Timothy, always on the run, wanted to buy a Citroën and tool around Europe. He wanted parties and people and action. "Everything about him irritated me," she said. "I could not bear to be with him."

She took a bath when he left to board another plane to check out their possible next stop in Africa. Relief, along with the bathwater, washed over her. "Be free now," she told herself, "get out of this mess if you can." She continued to entertain joining the Weather Underground and had even called their contact number, but their warmth had cooled in her brief absence.

"Can you type?" an unnamed Weather member asked. The only role available was secretary, the kind of job she had run from when she left St. Louis nearly two decades earlier.

Once again, she was out of moves. She faced felony charges for aiding and abetting a prison escape, falsifying her passport, and whatever else they could tack on top of the six-month Laguna Beach sentence that she had fled.

When Timothy called two days later, she allowed herself to miss him.

"You've got to come right away. It's a perfect, perfect new life and I miss you," he said.

Once again she packed her bags—this time with tabs of Orange Sunshine sewn in the hem of her garments.

Sixteen

Maia Baraka

"Not knowing what to expect (an award? a decoration?) I crossed over to North Africa," wrote Rosemary, who now traveled under the name Maia Baraka. After getting bumped up by Air Algérie to first class, she drank champagne and imagined that Algeria would resemble Morocco—full of music, hashish, and spice markets. Armed with only a green leather-bound *English-Arabic Conversational Dictionary*, Rosemary admitted she was being naive. "I had no right to be there, no real right at all."

Algeria, now a free country, was still recovering from the seven-year war with the French after 132 years of occupation. Because Algeria had severed diplomatic ties with the United States in 1967 over its pro-Israel position in the Six-Day War, the countries didn't share an extradition agreement. Instead, Algeria embraced liberation movements from around the world—from Cubans to the Vietcong, to North Koreans, to the antifascists in Spain and Portugal. This open-door policy was a key reason that Algeria allowed Eldridge Cleaver, a fugitive, to install an international Black Panther headquarters in its capital a few weeks before Timothy's arrival. Unfortunately for the

Learys, the leaders of the Algerian revolution, fiercely nationalistic, believed that drugs like hashish were tools of colonialization.

When no one greeted Rosemary at the Maison Blanche Airport, she almost left with a steward who offered to take her home to his family. But before she departed with the stranger, Timothy arrived, dressed in a white turtleneck and a brown leather cap like a Soviet philosopher, and introduced himself as Nino.

"Did you bring some money?" Timothy asked. A familiar question.

"I have what I had before, except plane fare," she responded. She had stashed her portion of money given to them by the Brotherhood in the crotch of her panty hose and the wad dug against her thighs when she walked. "Why, don't you have any left?"

"I had to give it to Eldridge and he expects a lot more."

They hopped into a car parked outside the empty terminal. As he drove, Rosemary stared out the window at Algiers, a hill city surrounded by the aquamarine waters of the Mediterranean. The ancient part of the city, called the Casbah, a landscape of white stone mosques and buildings, featured narrow passageways leading to shadowy footpaths. Rosemary, peering out of the car window on empty streets, was disappointed by the absence of women, the abandoned facades, and the palm trees bent and stooped by rain.

Timothy spoke nonstop as they drove. He explained that Cleaver was friendly and waxed on with his typical forced enthusiasm about the serendipity of the Algerian government giving the Panthers an embassy at the same time that Timothy had escaped prison. He told her how the Yippie writer Stew Albert had arrived a few days prior on their behalf in order to persuade Cleaver to offer the Learys sanctuary. He shared what he'd learned about Cleaver's wife, Kathleen, who had briefly relocated to North Korea to give birth to her second child.

Beyond that, Rosemary had read Cleaver's blockbuster memoir,

Soul on Ice, which detailed the half of his life spent in reform schools and prisons, beginning with a felony marijuana possession as a teenager. In prison, he discovered Marx. "It was like taking medicine for me to find that, indeed, American capitalism deserved all the hatred and contempt that I felt for it in my heart," he wrote. He described his reinvention under incarceration as a Black Muslim and a follower of Malcolm X. "I had gone astray," he wrote, "astray not so much from the white man's law as from being human, civilized."

Rosemary was aware of his rise to power in the Black liberation movement. In 1966, after his release from prison, he took the role of minister of information of the newly founded Black Panthers. "You're either part of the problem or part of the solution," he famously intoned.

She had heard about his confrontations with the police. "The harassment and brutality extreme, their leaders imprisoned or slain, their numbers decimated by fusillades of police machine-gun fire," she wrote. By the time Cleaver had arrived in Algeria, police or FBI agents had killed twenty-eight Panthers. At the same time, an estimated 10 percent of Black Panther members acted as informants, part of the FBI's COINTELPRO program, which, in part, sought to implode Black nationalist movements from the inside by using undercover agents to stoke infighting. Cleaver received letters (often written by agents at COINTELPRO) accusing his closest confidants of flipping. He never knew whom to trust.

Rosemary believed that Timothy and Cleaver might be carved from similar archetypes. They were both tricksters with wild escape capers under their belts. While facing an attempted murder charge for shooting and injuring two police officers in Oakland, Cleaver fled the country by dressing up as an infirm old man in a wheelchair wearing a fake colostomy bag. He absconded to Cuba, until he was run out of the country by Fidel Castro's revolutionaries, after which he landed in Algeria. "The same pigs who wanted to ice me are after Leary," Cleaver said.

Cleaver, thirty-five, was a decade older than most of his fellow Panthers. Like Timothy, he had run for political office and made his living from public speaking fees and book advances. They shared co-medic, anarchic sensibilities that bordered on the absurd. "Ronald Reagan is a punk, a sissy and a coward, and I challenge him to a duel to the death or until he says Uncle Eldridge," he said. "I give him the choice of weapons—a gun, a knife, a baseball bat or marshmallow."

As Timothy quipped, "It was a new experience for me to be dependent on a strong, variable, sexually restless, charismatic leader who was insanely erratic. I usually played that role myself."

Despite lip service about her respect for him, Rosemary had read his book so she knew about Cleaver's crimes. He was a serial rapist. A self-professed one. In *Soul on Ice*, he called himself the "Ogre" who "started out by practicing on black girls," he wrote. "When I considered myself smooth enough, I crossed the tracks and sought out white prey. . . . Rape was an insurrectionary act."

Rosemary trusted that Cleaver had changed, as he had written he had—become a different man with age, experience, and religious conversion. Rosemary and Timothy truly believed that Cleaver would not only protect and house them but also "love us and agree with us," she wrote.

When Rosemary and Timothy arrived at the wrought-iron gated entrance of a three-story white embassy, the Black Panther headquarters, Eldridge Cleaver—nearly as tall as the gate itself, wearing a sand-colored military tunic, and holding an assault rifle—greeted them.

Rosemary reached out her hand to shake Cleaver's but grabbed his thumb instead. Cleaver ignored Rosemary and directed his commands to Timothy. "Put her bags in the hall," he said. "Go to the living room." Rosemary suddenly felt very tired. She wished she could have prepared—brushed her hair, taken a bath, smoked some hash, and napped in the arms of her husband before having to prove herself to this intimidating figure.

In the living room with walls decorated with photos of Chairman Mao and Che Guevara, and a portrait of the North Korean dictator, Kim Il Sung, Cleaver and several other Panthers sat around talking in hushed tones about fundraisers and politics. The only other female, an Algerian girl, refused to acknowledge them.

A man addressed Rosemary only after she inquired about Kathleen's whereabouts. She planned to return tomorrow, he said, and led Rosemary to Cleaver's bedroom. "You'd better change the bed, Malika's been staying here," he said, referring to the Algerian girl in the next room, the fifteen-year-old Malika Ziri.

Rosemary, fresh off talk of radical feminism with Bernardine, couldn't believe how her status had fallen. "Far out," she wrote, "here I am with the Panthers in Algeria and I'm changing the sheets and looking for stains on Cleaver's bed."

Then Cleaver demanded that Rosemary and Timothy sleep apart. Rosemary would stay in the embassy and Timothy would go to the hotel because their fake passports didn't have the same last name and unmarried men and women weren't allowed to share a room at the hotel.

"We go together," Rosemary insisted, holding Timothy's arm. Cleaver capitulated but seemed to enjoy the flash of her naked vulnerability. "Playful cruelty," she wrote. A taste of what was to come.

The Panthers installed them in a hotel room at Le Méditerranée Hotel in El Djamila, a resort town outside Algiers. "We are safe and well and happy. We are with good friends and have been warmly received in this beautiful country. I will telephone when we are settled," Rosemary wrote in a letter, sent through her lawyers, to her mother.

These letters show a measure of comfort in their exile—as if they were safe from the long arm of American law enforcement.

The early days in Algeria felt like a vacation in captivity: the sound of the lapping waves on the shore, Russian tourists playing volleyball, fresh croissants, sitting lotus-style on the balcony, listening to the morning prayers played over a scratchy record player, Rosemary's deep belly laughs as Timothy practiced his tortured French with the waiters. The food was a delight—shrimp, wine, oranges, olives, French desserts. They started working together again—*It's About Time*, a book about Timothy's daring escape and Rosemary's role in the lead-up, and a piece of collage art and poetry called *The He and She of It*, a title taken from James Joyce's *Finnegans Wake*. They argued in their serene little perch—mainly about Timothy's loose lips with names and details that could harm those who had helped them—but mostly they were happier than they'd been in years, safe and sequestered in their Cleaver-enforced love cocoon.

But Cleaver soon ordered them into political orientation classes, lending them five volumes of Kim Il Sung's biography—a primer on how to think like a revolutionary. Cleaver had tasked Stew Albert with monitoring and overseeing the reeducation of Timothy Leary.

Timothy had previously told reporters that "LSD blackens the white person." And, "blacks don't have to take LSD as much as whites to find brotherly unity." He wrote, "I have no sympathy with a civil rights movement which attempts to 'raise' the Negro to the level of the middle-class white American." And would later continue, "Psychedelic people inevitably became more and more like the artistic, the blacks, and the young—those three outgroups who live closer to a pagan life of natural fleshly pleasure."

In postwar Algeria at his hotel, Timothy called a Black male porter "boy."

"Algerians used to slit the throats of Frenchmen who called them 'boy.' He'd better watch out," Cleaver said.

When Timothy suggested that they host a Be-In in Algeria, Stew Albert threw up his arms in exasperation. Drugs were illegal. It was a Muslim-majority country.

Meanwhile, the papers reported on their arrival with the headline AFRO-AMERICAN PSYCHIATRIST AND WIFE GIVEN ASYLUM. The government would not be pleased to learn to whom they had really given asylum—a White man who peddled in sex, drugs, and mind expansion. When the Algerian minister of foreign affairs spoke at the United Nations about South Africa, he faced questions about drugs. Cleaver was put on notice.

∽

KATHLEEN RETURNED FROM North Korea and agreed to meet the Learys. Rosemary knew little about Kathleen, the Panthers' communication secretary, outside the popular images of her in stylish, thigh-high boots with her natural hair worn in an Afro, holding a semiautomatic rifle.

Unlike Rosemary and Timothy, Kathleen enjoyed a cosmopolitan upbringing thanks to her professor father, who joined the Foreign Service and moved the family with him around the world. Kathleen attended high school in America at a desegregated Quaker boarding school. When she read about how police turned fire hoses on nonviolent protesters in Birmingham, Alabama, she was inspired to join the Civil Rights Movement. She attended Oberlin College and then Barnard before dropping out to join the Student Nonviolent Coordinating Committee (SNCC), founded by a group of young Black activists. During a conference held by the SNCC over Easter weekend 1967, Kathleen, twenty-one, met Cleaver, who was ten years older. Cleaver said it was "love at first sight." Kathleen was more circumspect. "I saw this giant standing in a doorway, all the way to the top," she said. "And he had this very, sort of masklike expression, no expression." He pursued her. "I noticed that he was attracted to me and I was very impressed," she said. Her guard fell after they played a game of chess—and she won. "Then we fell in love."

But now in Algeria, an unfamiliar country under a military dictatorship, with two kids under two years old, Kathleen felt marooned. "You don't have to maintain your sanity, if you think any day you might get killed," she later told a *New York Times* reporter. Cleaver could be violent and irrational. He had allegedly murdered a fellow Panther who had been linked romantically to Kathleen.

At the embassy, waiting for Kathleen, Timothy suggested that Rosemary make herself useful. "There are a bunch of dirty dishes in the kitchen. It'd be a nice gesture if you'd washed them," he said.

By the time Kathleen arrived at the Panther embassy, Rosemary had cut her hand on a piece of broken glass. A bad omen. When Rosemary asked Kathleen for a bandage—a diaper even—Kathleen said that she couldn't spare one. Rosemary understood then that Kathleen would only ever view her as a burden. An interloper. An annoyance—which is, to be fair, what Rosemary was.

Longing for female connection, Rosemary visited a local hammam, a public bathhouse in the basement of a building in Algiers. Once she disrobed, the other women stopped staring at her. She started washing herself—the only solo bather—until another woman crossed the room and picked up Rosemary's shampoo bottle, thrusting her head under the flowing water. Rosemary's tensions eased under her expert hands that wrung her out like a washing rag. She cried as the woman worked. "I was a child at home again."

~

A MONTH INTO THEIR ASYLUM, more visitors arrived to celebrate Timothy's fiftieth birthday and cement their solidarity. Stew Albert, who had briefly left the country, chaperoned the new guests to Algeria: Anita Hoffman, who arrived in her husband Abbie's stead because he faced bail restrictions on travel; the Yippie journalist Jonah Raskin; and Bernardine Dohrn's sister Jennifer, who represented the interests of the Weather Underground. Together they made up three wings of the radical left—Panthers, Yippies, and flower children—supporting their complicated martyr, Timothy Leary.

Anita left first. When she witnessed Cleaver's outright misogyny, aimed especially at his wife, Kathleen, who was forbidden from spending time alone with any of the visiting American women, she wanted no part of his cause. "None of the other Americans ever considered for one moment standing up to Cleaver on any issue," Anita later wrote. "If anything united the counterculture it was a belief in the motivational possibilities of life rather than fear. But it was fear that operated in the exile community in Algeria, for whatever reasons, and I could not support it."

A few weeks later, locked in the embassy after being separated from the male members of her group, Anita climbed out of the bathroom window and hightailed it back to the airport to fly to Paris and reunite with her husband.

On November 17, Timothy and company arrived in Cairo, Egypt, for the first leg of their tour of the Middle East to declare the New Left's solidarity with the Palestinians against Israel. As Timothy rested on silk sheets and threw boisterous press conferences, Rosemary stayed behind with Cleaver and worked at the embassy collecting clippings from newspapers to catalog the atrocities according to type: APARTHEID, BANS, BOMBINGS, BUSINGS, CONTEMPT, DEATHS, EDUCATION, ENVIRONMENT, FRAGGING, GHETTOS, HARLEM, INSECTICIDES, JURIES, KU KLUX KLAN, LEAD POISONING, MURDER . . .

Cleaver taunted Rosemary about all the horrors that could befall Timothy on his tour—what if he was arrested, he asked, or killed?

"What would you do then?" Cleaver clearly wasn't her ally. She called him an "owl-eyed rapist."

Timothy's gallivanting drug circus couldn't have come at a worse time for the young country. Unbeknownst to the Panthers, the Algerians, warming to the United States, were securing two lucrative contracts to sell billions of cubic feet of natural gas to America. Nixon's secretary of state, William P. Rogers, admonished the American liaison in Algeria that harboring Timothy would have an "unfortunate impact" on U.S.-Algerian relations.

Once Jennifer Dohrn returned to America, she held a press conference confirming Timothy's political awakening. She played a fifteen-minute message from Timothy in which he lectured his audience, albeit without the dynamism of his acid talks, about "the violence in Babylon." He called it a "righteous act of self-defense" to "off a pig who threatens your life or freedom."

"In closing, Rosemary has a message for our friends in Babylon," he said. He handed the microphone to Rosemary.

"Smoke it," she said, her raspy voice retaining its sensuousness through the fuzziness of the recording. "Smoke it and blow it up."

Rosemary would later say that the rhetorical shift—which she admitted, in retrospect, sounded "shrill and self-serving"—emerged from a survival instinct, a quest to redeem themselves to the people who held their livelihoods in their hands. But Rosemary had changed after Tim's sentencing and during her time with the Kennedys and the Weather Underground. This was not merely a PR stunt or a strategic chess move—not for her.

"I want to go back to Amerika; I want to take revenge and blow things up," she told a reporter. "We used to quote from *I Ching* a lot, but now it's going to be Kim Il Sung and the thought of Chairman Mao."

The alternative press—once so behind Timothy when railroaded by the criminal justice system—felt perplexed by the couple's embrace of violence. Ken Kesey rolled his eyes and dismissed Timothy as "one more nut with a gun" in an open letter published in the November 1970 issue of *Rolling Stone*. Michael Standard, who handled Timothy's Laredo appeal, wrote, "Those who move to consciousness struggle harder at greater odds. You do none of those things." The Brotherhood, who continued to bankroll him, felt betrayed. "He forgot about God and his inner higher being," one Brother said.

Meanwhile, Timothy wilted without the watering of attention. His constant jocularity, his neediness, his attempts to fit in and impress these young, intensely serious men did not endear him to them. Even with healthy sips from the aftershave lotion bottle filled with Orange Sunshine and visits from Brotherhood adjacents who brought hash and goodwill, Timothy, the magician, mislaid his sleight of hand.

His attempts at frivolity infuriated the men, and his grasping of revolutionary language didn't land. Rosemary felt as if she were mothering her irksome toddler and felt a stifling combination of "embarrassment and protectiveness at what I imagined to be their offstage comments."

To Timothy, who was sitting cross-legged and shoeless on the couch of the embassy, one of the Panthers barked, "Sit right, this ain't a hippie pad."

Timothy neglected to bring his hearing aids to Algeria, so he relied on Rosemary to act as interpreter to the Panthers' hushed, conspiratorial conversations, just as he had during the early days at Millbrook, when she sat by his side, dutifully repeating everything he couldn't hear. They were more codependent than ever, and she pitied him. Yet she loved him best this way. It was part of what had attracted her to him in the first place. "This has been the best part of our life together. Very close, very centered," she wrote to her mother.

"Tim and I grow closer and closer—we dream the same dreams at night and telepathy between us increases."

Others noticed how bonded the duo appeared, acting like the only two people in the room, completely alone in their world. They showed off this reinforced solidarity during interviews with reporters, whom they viewed as antagonists—people whom they could no longer court or trust. The journalist and future biographer Robert Greenfield visited Algeria on assignment and remembers watching a mute Rosemary on the balcony of the hotel, sitting on tatami mats in lotus position and listening to Crosby, Stills, Nash & Young's *Déjà Vu*. "You were in the presence of someone who was far more evolved than you were. That's what she projected."

Timothy and Rosemary were closer than ever, but her light was dimming. She endured chronic pelvic and stomach pain. Dysentery was part of it, but mostly she suffered from the damaging aftereffects of her experimental fertility surgery, for which the second phase was now nearly a year overdue. Nearly skeletal, she looked as sickly as she felt and was racked by sudden coughing fits. She wasn't taking her typically meticulous care of her appearance. She went long periods without washing her hair because the hot water in their hotel never worked.

Cleaver's friend Elaine Mokhtefi, an American who also lived in Algeria, described her impression of the couple as "aging hipsters, passé stars from the silent film era. I don't know what I had expected: something visually crazier, flamboyant, exciting. Take away the LSD and they became ordinary."

⁓

TIMOTHY STILL SEEMED to truly believe that he could win over Cleaver if he would just "turn on." Cleaver brushed Timothy off, telling Stew Albert that he worried about mind control—that Timothy might use drugs to reprogram him. Then, out of the blue, a change of heart. Cleaver and Malika decided to give acid a try. Timothy dosed out the appropriate amount to get their neurons firing, and Rosemary gave Malika a hug and some candles, laying out the ingredients for a safe and comforting set and setting.

The trip didn't go well. Cleaver and Malika returned hours later bleary-eyed and agitated. Cleaver had spent the prior hours in a state of immobilization, obsessing about his inability to get to his gun. He had survived nearly a decade in some of the roughest lockdowns in America. No amount of candles or paisley throws could change that.

After Cleaver's bad trip, the Panthers confiscated thousands of hits of acid that friends sent in letters and packages. They even disassembled a speaker, finding Orange Sunshine tabs nestled inside. Border guards contacted Cleaver to tell them that Rosemary and Timothy had been apprehended in Bou Saada, "the Place of Happiness," for running around naked in the Saharan sand dunes. Upon their return, Cleaver confiscated their passports. The couple had become not only an embarrassment but a liability.

In December, Timothy and Rosemary finally moved out of the hotel into a two-bedroom apartment in central Algiers. The key exchange cost them $2,000. They were broke. Despite their destitution, when Christmas came, Rosemary realized that it was the most serene holiday of their relationship. "We're always broke on Xmas but at least this year we won't be getting busted," she wrote in a letter to her mom.

But another bust was on the way.

⌇

BACK IN THE UNITED STATES, Charles Manson was convicted of murder in the longest and most expensive trial in U.S. history, based in part on the argument that he had used LSD to train and incite murderers. Elvis Presley took a meeting with Nixon to show support for the new drug laws and his belief that communists deployed psychedelics to brainwash the youth.

In Algeria, the Learys were kidnapped.

On January 9, four months into their exile, as Rosemary sliced vegetables, the doorbell rang. Rosemary opened it to find four Panthers with guns. They carried Timothy out of the apartment first, hands over his mouth to muffle his cries for help and around his limbs to control his thrashing. Rosemary, resigned, didn't even try to fight. "Who would help us?" She maintained the presence of mind to turn off the stove and lock the door as she left with her captors.

The Panthers separated Rosemary from Timothy, put them in separate cars, and drove them to an abandoned house. Rosemary reunited with Timothy in a damp, empty room layered in French prerevolution-era illustrated magazines. She wasn't aware that the Algerian revolutionary party, the National Liberation Front, used to dispense with their enemies in this very house, or that this house was where, according to rumor, Cleaver held Kathleen's lover before dumping his body.

"I was full of dread; the hatred and the power of that hatred in the closed room were palpable, it hovered like cigarette haze above my head," Rosemary wrote.

Rosemary, increasingly desperate, tried to gauge the height of the drop from the open window. She wondered how she'd react if the Panthers aimed the rifles at her and fired. Would she jump in front of Leary? Or jump out of the window to try to save herself? She was filled with self-recrimination. How had she let this happen? How had she been so ignorant? "Unfamiliar culture, in a dangerous situation without anyone to come to my aid and totally alienated from my government," she wrote. "I had no one to be angry at, but myself and the laws of my country."

The next morning the Panthers took them to more comfortable surroundings in a furnished apartment with rugs and books, deco-

Rosemary Leary, bottom left, lived her life at the center of many of the counter-cultural shifts of the twentieth century. Here she sings along on the recording of "Give Peace a Chance" by John Lennon and Yoko Ono at the Bed-In for Peace in Montreal in 1969.

Photograph by Gerry Deiter. Copyright © 1969 by Joan E. Athey.
Used with permission.

Rosemary was a "brown-haired Shirley Temple," according to her beloved magician father, Verl. Rosemary, three years old, poses beside him outside their tract home in St. Louis, Missouri, in 1938.

Courtesy of Gary Woodruff

Rosemary was barely seventeen when she wed her air force officer boyfriend John Bradley in 1952. Despite her show of bravery in wearing of a pop of pink tulle under her virginal white dress, she was so nervous that she had to be propped up by her father as she walked down the aisle.

Courtesy of Gary Woodruff

Rosemary, still a teenager, left St. Louis for New York City as a divorcée without a high school diploma and jumped into the exploding beatnik movement. Ever the chameleon, Rosemary put her good looks to use as a model. She spent her nights in jazz clubs, where she learned how to get high properly, and spent her days reading literature and philosophy.

Courtesy of Gary Woodruff

Rosemary worked as a stewardess for various airlines in the early 1960s, when it was harder to land the job than to earn a seat at Harvard. Up in the air, she learned how to beautify, serve, and cater to men in tight spaces—early prep for her work as the queen of set and setting.

Courtesy of Gary Woodruff

Rosemary worked as an extra in the 1959 movie *Operation Petticoat*, where she managed to sneak a photograph with Tony Curtis, a star of the film. In one of the many synchronicities that characterized her life, Curtis's costar Cary Grant went public during the movie's press tour about his experiences with a life-changing new drug called LSD.

Courtesy of Gary Woodruff

The three lead researchers of the Harvard Psilocybin Project walk together in Laredo, Texas, during Timothy Leary's marijuana trial in 1966. From left to right: Richard Alpert, Timothy Leary, and Ralph Metzner.

Lawrence Schiller / Getty Images

When Timothy Leary invited Rosemary to join the magical wonderland of experimentation at the Hitchcock Estate in Millbrook, New York, Rosemary jumped in with both feet. Scenes like these—with Timothy on top of a majestic white horse—were daily occurrences around the "Big House," the estate's main building.

Photograph by Don Synder. Copyright © Don Snyder Estate. Used with permission.

Ralph Metzner was a renowned psychotherapist and psychedelic philosopher. Rosemary's brief but passionate fling almost ended her relationship with Timothy. The two bonded over their belief in the power of psychedelics—and the healing power of great sex.

Photograph by Don Synder.
Copyright © Don Snyder Estate.
Used with permission.

Ram Dass, formerly known as Richard Alpert, sits with a sitar at his father's estate after his return from India. His book *Be Here Now* would overtake *The Psychedelic Experience* as the era's Hippie Bible.

Photograph by Don Synder.
Copyright © Don Snyder Estate.
Used with permission.

Susan and Jack Leary pose in a tree on the Hitchcock Estate. Timothy's children were often neglected by the high priest. Though Jack and Rosemary had a loving friendship, Susan's relationship with Rosemary was rife with conflict.

Photograph by Don Synder. Copyright © Don Snyder Estate. Used with permission.

Rosemary went to prison in the spring of 1966 for being in contempt of court during the grand jury inquiry into Timothy and the Hitchcock Estate. Here she is photographed arm-in-arm with an unnamed inmate on their way to a bail hearing at the Dutchess County courthouse.

First printed in the Poughkeepsie Journal, *1966. Courtesy of Gary Woodruff.*

Taken in 1967 by a visiting photographer, this is a rare image documenting Rosemary's role in Timothy's work. Rosemary would often edit Timothy's books, articles, and speeches in bed.

Alvis Upitis / Getty Images

Rosemary poses in between two magicians—her father, Verl, and her husband, Timothy—during the western leg of their tour to hype the publication of Timothy's book of essays, *The Politics of Ecstasy*, in 1968.

Courtesy of Gary Woodruff. Used with permission.

Timothy and Rosemary were high and blissful during their third wedding ceremony at the bungalow in Millbrook in 1967. Newspapers across the country ran this image on their front pages.

Photograph by Don Synder. Copyright © Don Snyder Estate. Used with permission.

Rosemary and Timothy are photographed with John Griggs, the leader of the Brotherhood of Eternal Love, a group of ex-cons turned acid messiahs. Griggs embraced the Learys as family and invited them to live with him on the West Coast—opening up a new and complicated chapter in the Leary saga.

Photograph by Dion Wright. First printed in Laguna Magazine.
Courtesy of Gary Woodruff.

Rosemary appears in *The Berkeley Barb* in March 1969 as a media heroine, the Acid Queen, fighting for her husband's freedom as he languished behind bars. On the bottom portion of the page, *The Barb* ran a facsimile of Timothy's handwritten message—smeared by tears—that Rosemary read to the press after his sentencing. "Rosemary Wept," the note's title reads.

Rosemary poses with the ever-stylish Eleanora Kennedy and her lawyer husband, Michael—the epitome of radical chic. The couple helped Timothy with his appeal and with recruiting the Weather Underground to assist with Timothy's prison escape. They did, as Michael Kennedy once said, their "best work in the dark."

Photograph by John Schewel. Courtesy of Gary Woodruff. Used with permission.

Timothy and Rosemary are dressed as their alter egos—businessman William McNellis and secretary Sylvia McGaffin—that allowed them to flee the U.S. unnoticed. Rosemary would not return for six years.

Hashish Smuggling and Passport Fraud: "The Brotherhood of Eternal Love." *Hearing, 93rd Cong., first session, October 3, 1973.*

Rosemary and Timothy celebrated Christmas on the lam and under the care of the Black Panthers in their apartment in Algiers, Algeria. Trouble was waiting in the wings—a month later they would be kidnapped by the Panthers. Though they were closer than ever, Timothy and Rosemary were headed toward a crossroads.

Photograph by Louis Gimenez. Courtesy of Gary Woodruff.

Rosemary's lover and savior John Schewel arrived in Switzerland with cash and emotional support during her decision to leave Timothy. John and Rosemary lived underground together in the woods of Switzerland and the coast of Italy. In the shadow of the mythical Mt. Etna and under the Sicilian sun, Rosemary healed and fell in love with another man, Bubi, a count—until she got word from John that it was time to flee Europe.

Photograph by John Schewel.
Used with permission.

This is one of the few photos that exists of Rosemary and John during the three years they spent underground in South America, Central America, and the Caribbean. Here they pose for new passport photos in Nassau, Bahamas, in 1976.

Photograph by John Schewel. Used with permission.

Gary Woodruff visited his sister when she lived with John Schewel on Cape Cod in Eastham, Massachusetts, in the early 1980s. The two pose for a rare photo during a rare reunion.

Photograph by John Schewel. Used with permission.

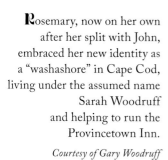

Rosemary, now on her own after her split with John, embraced her new identity as a "washashore" in Cape Cod, living under the assumed name Sarah Woodruff and helping to run the Provincetown Inn.

Courtesy of Gary Woodruff

David Phillips, pictured here, was one of the three most important men in Rosemary's later life. Their profound and platonic relationship, which started in Cape Cod, provided Rosemary with shelter, intellectual stimulation, good humor, and a path back to her home on the West Coast. David championed Rosemary's work as a writer and helped guide her decision to come aboveground.

Courtesy of Gary Woodruff

Rosemary returned to the West Coast in 1991 and reunited with Timothy Leary, who, along with David, helped her come aboveground. The two magicians rekindled their romance after two decades apart. Their great love affair nearly consumed Rosemary—but, as she said, "I was mated to him."

Copyright © Robert Forte. Used with permission.

Rosemary relocated to Aptos, California, to live with Denis Berry, photographed here in white. She joined a group of psychonauts in Santa Cruz and reluctantly reclaimed her aboveground persona. From left to right: Nina Graboi, who once oversaw the League of Discovery's outpost in Manhattan, Rosemary, and Denis Berry.

Courtesy of Gary Woodruff

Rosemary, who had reclaimed her throne as the Acid Queen in the reemerging psychedelic movement of the early 2000s, poses in all her regal glory for a final photoshoot before her death at age sixty-six in 2002.

Photograph by Robert Altman. Courtesy of Gary Woodruff.

rated in red and black. Rosemary palmed a half-smoked joint and lit up when the Panthers gave her a free moment to bathe. The Panthers offered leftovers—though most of it had long gone bad. Rosemary started making mental wish lists of foods: ice cream, apples, peanut butter, chocolate cookies. Later in the afternoon, baking tins filled with food arrived, sent by Kathleen. Rosemary scarfed down the pigs' feet and ribs. She wondered if this was her last meal.

It wasn't. Rosemary's old friend from her jazz days, the music journalist Michael Zwerin, arrived to conduct a profile of the Learys in exile for *The Village Voice*. Instead, Zwerin found the couple kidnapped by their supposed saviors. Cleaver, who shared Leary's love of the limelight, was always up for an interview and decided to hand Zwerin a scoop—"the revolutionary bust," as Cleaver called it.

"Do you know Leary?" Cleaver asked Zwerin when he arrived.

"No, Rosemary," he responded. "From another life."

After three days of confinement, Cleaver allowed Zwerin to visit the captive couple. "It was straight out of Kafka," Rosemary said. "Michael Zwerin berating us for letting this happen. We were looking at him like our great rescuer. Who would have thought? But in a way, he did rescue us. He was a reporter and he wrote the story."

Zwerin persuaded Cleaver to release the couple; in exchange, Cleaver demanded that Timothy condemn his drug advocacy in a recorded question-and-answer session between Timothy and Cleaver. The interview ran on February 4, 1971, in *The Village Voice*. In it, Timothy argued unconvincingly that his "Turn on, tune in, drop out" days were behind him. "I have no need or desire to talk about drugs," he said.

Cleaver also recorded an additional message for the press: "It has become very clear to me that there is something wrong with both Dr. Leary's and his wife's brain. I attribute this to the multiple, the uncountable number of acid trips they have taken. Your god is dead because his mind has been blown by acid."

On January 11, Rosemary and Timothy were freed after four days under Panther lock and key. The media gobbled up Zwerin's report. The mainstream press viewed the kidnapping as a ratings boosting farce— yet another example of the left eating its own tail. This outraged those who had hoped for a symbolic union. FREE TIM, AGAIN! the *Berkeley Barb*'s front-page headline read. The Yippies wrote, "Eldridge is a pig!"

⁓

CLEAVER SEEMS TO have orchestrated the kidnapping to scare the Learys into complying with Panther rules. And it worked. At least temporarily. Once released from bondage, Timothy kept his head down and worked as a janitor at the embassy. Rosemary babysat the Panther kids in the nursery. Malika spied on them relentlessly now, following them around the house and snooping without shame. Men trailed Rosemary as she shopped.

Two months after the bust, Timothy managed to persuade Cleaver to return their passports in order to deposit a check sent by the publisher of the escape book they were writing. Timothy promised Cleaver a cut of it, and so Cleaver acquiesced.

Armed with their travel documents—real and fake—they could finally escape their asylum and planned to board a flight to Copenhagen, where Timothy would give a paid lecture. They would pack enough to survive, but not enough to set off alarm bells with the Panthers.

Before her departure, Rosemary sent a letter to her friend Donna Motsinger, who had acted as her chauffeur back in California. "We are still fighting the same dreary battle, politics versus existing, control-freedom, and we seem to be alone, no mountain hide out, no family check in. Just these glaring lights, a microphone and a jeering audience," she wrote.

"We are tired, Donna, we long to change our names, our very selves, and disappear."

Seventeen

Marilyn Monroe

Out of Africa, Rosemary and Timothy closed their Black Panther chapter, only to head right into another trap. The U.S. government had allegedly tipped off the Danish authorities about Timothy's lecture in Copenhagen, and police planned to arrest him on sight. Fate intervened once again thanks to their French psychiatrist friend Pierre Bensoussan, who arrived at the Copenhagen airport early to pick up the couple and found the place buzzing with reporters.

Bensoussan got hold of Timothy during a layover at Geneva Airport. Over a pay phone, he warned Timothy not to come to Copenhagen, but to remain in Switzerland, a neutral country, with a lax stance on drug offenses. As they crafted a new plan, Bensoussan also arranged for the Learys to spend a few nights incognito in his Swiss banker friend's house.

While Timothy received the startling news, Rosemary encountered a silver-haired gentleman with bulging blue eyes and expensive clothing. She noted the thick knot of his silk tie and the sheen on his polished leather shoes. He noticed her, too, she could tell, but not in the way most men did. This man sniffed, literally raised his nose up in the air, and scoffed at her. She saw herself as he must have: bedraggled clothing, worn traveling boots, and dirty hair. She sensed the man's ability to assess wealth in a glance, and she felt economically naked before him, certain he could see the seven lone American cents in her pocket. She felt humiliated, "the little match girl dismissed by the rich man."

She also sensed that they would meet again.

Timothy, ever the optimist, interpreted the Copenhagen hiccup as a positive synchronicity. Switzerland was where his heroes James Joyce and Hermann Hesse lived and wrote, where Albert Hofmann had synthesized LSD and later, in 1943, accidentally ingested the chemical. Rosemary ignored her intuition and agreed. "It has been so miraculous," she wrote to her parents, "perhaps the beginning of a new life we've prayed for."

Days later, after they'd worn out their welcome at the banker's house, Bensoussan stepped in again by making an introduction to a person who, as he artfully explained, had more experience on the fringes of respectable society. Once again, Timothy stayed behind as Rosemary rode off with Bensoussan back to the airport. When the haughty man, who had dismissed her days earlier, greeted them, dressed down today in a Lacoste T-shirt and holding a German shepherd by a tight chain, Rosemary barely registered surprise. Madness and serendipity acted as her guides now.

Bensoussan introduced Rosemary to Michel-Gustave Hauchard. "This is Maia," he said, using Rosemary's Algerian pseudonym. "She might have need of your protection."

The next day Rosemary and Timothy moved into Hauchard's penthouse in Ouchy on Lake Geneva. To celebrate their new friendship, Hauchard invited the Learys to a nearby restaurant. They drove there in his convertible Rolls-Royce with the top down, the crisp Swiss air tousling their hair. Over champagne and hors d'oeuvres, Hauchard told them that he considered it his "obligation as a gentleman to protect philosophers" and shared snippets of his life, though he omitted most specifics. Hauchard's shadowy existence is barely documented outside his run-in with the Learys. Despite his over-the-top splashy lifestyle—he collected speedboats, fast cars, and faster women, drank Cristal champagne, and smoked Cuban cigars—Hauchard had managed to keep his name out of American newspapers until he met the Learys. The stories that trickled down involved a relationship with the French Resistance that soured and a turn to international arms dealing. One person alleged that he "enriched himself on the backs of the Biafrans" during their civil war with Nigeria in 1967. There were whispers of CIA involvement. Timothy nicknamed him Goldfinger. Only Rosemary wondered what this man gained from being so generous to them.

As the two men traded prison stories, Rosemary held herself back from adding her own, knowing women in this strata functioned only to be seen. "I had only to laugh in the right places and try not to feel miserable that I was so badly dressed in a restaurant full of fashionably attired people," she wrote. The other women in the restaurant all dressed exquisitely: gold bracelets, couture handbags, and diamond chains—expensive basics that screamed easy money—while Rosemary still wore the same soiled clothing that she had during her layover in Geneva.

Across the Atlantic Ocean, Nixon held a press conference at the White House, calling drug use "public enemy number one." He asked Congress for $350 million to devote to an "all-out offensive" that he christened "the war on drugs."

"I was a casualty of that war," Rosemary would later say, "and of my marriage."

❦

EXILE IN SWITZERLAND meant that Rosemary could undergo the long-delayed second phase of her operation, a cutting-edge ovarian

surgery unavailable in Algeria. Dr. Alan Margolis, who had originally diagnosed her condition back before the jail break, wrote to suggest that they contact Dr. Hubert de Watteville, one of the most
famous gynecologists in the world thanks to a successful fertility operation that he performed on the actress Sophia Loren. After one appointment with Dr. de Watteville in his Geneva office, Rosemary
consulted her astrological chart and the *I Ching* and booked the earliest surgery date available.

When Rosemary emerged from anesthesia, she found herself in a
hospital room fragrant with flowers. A sweet voice broke her out of
her dazed state.

"It's all right, beloved," Timothy said. "You are perfect. We'll have
babies."

As Rosemary recovered, Dr. de Watteville walked Rosemary through
his surgical discoveries, telling her, as she relayed in a letter to her
mother, that the "barbaric, unheard of operation" in California had
left loose plastic tubing banging around in her body for a year. Some
of the tubes had attached to her uterus, causing a severe infection. No
wonder she shivered with an almost constant aching pain. "The doctor who operated on me in '69 (Overstreet) is a well-known right wing
hippie hater, so he might have had his own politics in mind when he
inserted plastic tubes in me," Rosemary wrote to her mother. "They
had put me together all wrong."

Dr. de Watteville, inspecting his handiwork, told her that she'd
have a 20 percent chance of conceiving after twice-a-week treatments.
"Well, what equipment I have now is this—two newly repaired open
Fallopian tubes instead of a genetically deformed womb," she wrote to
her mother. "A nice roomy place for a soul to lodge comfortably."

"You're going to be a grandmother again," she wrote to her Nana.
Though not yet pregnant, she felt certain that she would be. "Yes, you
are in March or April of next year."

Under Hauchard's protection, Timothy emerged from his Algerian funk, relishing his enraptured audience, which included beautiful European socialites who crowded around him to share their own drug stories. "Hauchard was milking Tim's celebrity for all it was worth and we were dining out on it as well," Rosemary said.

To her embarrassment, Timothy made a farce out of the Panthers. He and Rosemary were, he wrote, "the first White Americans to live under Black political might." In leaving Algeria, they had "escape[d] slavery in less than 300 years." His willful ignorance and obvious pandering to his new audience disgusted her. "He had his racial joke in Algeria, we were the slaves this time, he said. I didn't agree, but there could be no argument. Now a different role but the same prisoners' posture: rump first and sly jokes."

The new context made it harder for Rosemary to ignore "the banality" of her husband's mind. "LSD was always the solution to the world's ills. Racial conflict? Free TV and LSD. Overpopulation? Tantra and LSD. Women's liberation? More LSD."

Timothy catered to a war profiteer who represented, to Rosemary, humanity at its least enlightened—a man who hungered for power and consumption with zero interest in mind expansion or unity or oneness. When Rosemary introduced Hauchard to weed, he grew so paranoid that he hallucinated snakes in his bathroom. He was not one of *their people*. But whenever Rosemary expressed doubts, Timothy brought up the operation, paid for by Hauchard, their new life, and their safety. "If I was depressed surely it was due to the painkillers. Perhaps I was jealous," she quoted him.

Rosemary examined her hands—she had picked up palm reading skills in her travels—for clues about their future and noted the spaces on her lifeline, which were believed to signify illness or incarceration. She dreamed of Poughkeepsie and the other women imprisoned behind steel bars, the clanging sound echoing in empty hallways, and the smell of acrid cleaning products. "Thoughts of prison plague me like flies, annoying," she wrote.

Fans of Timothy's visited them, including a psychologist couple who came bearing gifts of homemade baked bread and a novel psychological test based on tarot card readings. The woman made a spread for Rosemary, and the Ace of Pentacles, a card often representing children, came up reversed.

"That's your resistance to be a mother," Timothy interjected. "Your ambivalence."

 ༄

THE LONGER THEY remained in Switzerland, the more indebted they became. In addition to acting as host and benefactor, Hauchard took the role of manager, finding lawyers to oversee their bid for political asylum and working on selling a book about their escape, *It's About Time*, which continued from *Jail Notes* to include their time with the Panthers. Hauchard helped them set up an international corporation in Timothy's name so that they could collect the funds without the American government interfering. As a thank-you, Timothy handed the copyright of *It's About Time* to his savior, which explained why Hauchard was being so generous to them. Hauchard now owned Timothy's intellectual property.

All the while, the Nixon administration was pressuring the Swiss government to approve Timothy's extradition. To accomplish this, Nixon sent Attorney General John Mitchell to convince Swiss officials of Timothy's ongoing danger to society.

On June 13, 1971, *The New York Times* ran the first in a series of articles based on the work of the whistle-blowing military analyst Daniel Ellsberg. The Pentagon Papers detailed Washington's secret escalation of the war in Vietnam. Mitchell and Rosemary's old Millbrook nemesis G. Gordon Liddy would eventually face charges related to two infamous burglaries: the Fielding break-in of Ellsberg's psychiatrist's office on September 3, 1971, and, nine months later, the burglary of the Democratic National Committee headquarters at the Watergate Office Building. Mitchell's wife, Martha, famously leaked the story of the break-in to the press before she was forcibly sedated in a hotel room. The Fielding and Watergate scandals would later lead back to Nixon, initiating a slew of indictments and impeachment proceedings. But not yet—to those in charge, Timothy, halfway around the world, still represented a more serious threat to democracy than those who pursued him.

Hauchard rented Rosemary and Timothy an apartment in a chalet in the ski resort town of Villars-sur-Ollon, overlooking the Rhône valley at the east end of Lake Geneva, in the land of Europe's most expensive boarding schools. They would start family planning.

After weeks of painful fertility treatments, doctors pinpointed the weekend of the summer solstice on June 21, 1971, as the ideal time to try for a baby. She imagined conceiving in a meadow out in the sun on the longest day of the year. The most auspicious set and setting for their miracle baby.

Rosemary woke up early on the morning of their planned fertility rite to the sound of the door creaking open and the low timbre of a man's voice. With it came the familiar flash of fear—the Millbrook raid, Purcell at the car window, the Panthers with semiautomatic weapons.

She placed her palm over Timothy's mouth and whispered in his good ear: "Tim, someone's here." He put his clothes on and, as Rosemary hid their stash, walked into the living room, where three men in suits, unmistakably law enforcement, stood. They were honoring the American request for extradition, they said, and intended to apprehend Timothy and accompany him to prison in Lausanne. Rosemary pleaded their case, using Hauchard's name, but they stared back at her blankly. As Timothy drooped, resigned once again to his fate, she packed his shaving gear, cigarettes, matches, fresh shirts, and books.

On their way out, one of the policemen pointed to a vase of flowers that they had picked in the meadow. "It is forbidden to pick certain flowers, there are severe fines for such an offense. You must check the flower chart at the train station," he said, and then closed the door.

Rosemary caught the train back to Ouchy, crowded with holiday travelers trekking with walking sticks, woolen knee socks, and backpacks to celebrate the solstice. Watching the movie-set scenes of mountains and clear blue sky pass by her, she heard the chugging of the train: *No child, no child, no child.*

❧

OFFICIALS APPROVED ROSEMARY to visit Timothy in Lausanne's Prison du Bois-Mermet. The iron-studded door opened with a heavy creak. A shrill bell signaled the opening of a second smaller door where an old man greeted her and brought her into the near-silent prison, where one could hear the bristles of a twig broom brushing against the floor. As she waited in a visiting room, she studied the barred windows until the sound of squeaking shoes brought her back to the moment.

Even the short time in prison turned Timothy back into a prisoner—skinny, pale, and despondent—despite a constant stream of goodies sent by Hauchard to his cell: chocolates, fancy cigarettes, and aged meats and cheeses. Hauchard even gifted Timothy a typewriter so that he could finish his escape book. Still, no matter the accoutrements, a cell confined him.

With Timothy locked away in Lausanne, Rosemary relied on Hauchard now more than ever. Back in Ouchy, Hauchard embraced her, an attempt at comfort that felt like a stranglehold.

"How can I get him out?" she asked Hauchard.

"We must have money, lots of it. It is the only way to free him," he said.

He estimated that the legal cost of fighting extradition would be $150,000—curiously, the same price that had been quoted in the press during the Holding Together legal defense fundraiser. Meanwhile, Swiss officials required $20,000 for bail.

What else could she do but return to the roles she hadn't realized she'd been suited to—prison wife and media heroine. She did Timothy's laundry, burying her face in his shirts before she washed them, and brought him groceries. Rosemary worked every source that hadn't been sucked completely dry, raising capital and backing from around the world. She took a meeting with Yoko Ono's younger sister, Setsuko, who was studying business at the Graduate Institute in Geneva. Rosemary wanted Setsuko to tell Yoko so many things: "Take me away from Michel. Come to me and keep me safe. Cover me with your cloak of incorruptibility, put me in a bag in your closet and play songs to me through the door. Convince me that Michel means no harm. Free Tim and take us to the other side of the moon and then the four of us will be happy forever. Teach me to scream with rage and feel better."

Instead, she babbled incoherently. Setsuko promised that Yoko would be in touch.

She called on their U.S. contacts, praying that the monetary goodwill would continue to flow despite their political posturing in Algeria, which they already viewed as a misstep. She enlisted Allen Ginsberg, who secured the backing of dozens of San Francisco poets and luminaries to write a "Declaration of Independence for Dr. Timothy Leary," criticizing the government's "exasperating literary vendetta" against Timothy. Arthur Miller rallied the International PEN (Poets, Essayists, and Novelists) and even cabled the Lausanne police in support of Timothy. The religion scholar Walter Houston Clark, Timothy's friend from Harvard who worked with him on the Marsh Chapel Experiment, offered to mortgage his house as collateral.

The star-studded push for Leary's asylum, however, excluded his wife, who was doing the backbreaking work behind the scenes while facing the same threat to her freedom. Outraged by the oversight, Loni Hancock, Berkeley's lone councilwoman, released a statement that ran in the *Berkeley Barb* under the headline: BUT WHAT ABOUT ROSEMARY?

"Dr. Leary is not alone in Switzerland," Hancock said. "It is ironic and disturbing that a statement of support, especially here in Berkeley, should leave her unmentioned."

"Do the men in our community even know that Mrs. Leary faces the same jail sentence as her husband, in addition to any charges which might be levied against both of them in connection with his escape from prison? Do they consider her simply an appendage of her husband, so that any statement applies to him applies to her also?" Hancock asked. Hancock, a stranger with no direct relations, was one of the few who voiced the opinion that Rosemary was not a mere appendage but was as worthy of support as her husband.

The days passed. Rosemary could feel Timothy's bones through his shirt. He would not survive another month behind bars. She didn't have the heart to tell him that she believed Hauchard was yet another confidence trickster, worse perhaps—a thug. She didn't say that she suspected Hauchard had orchestrated the arrest, that he had used his connections to lock Timothy up and make sure he delivered the book so that he could monetize Timothy's infamy in a controlled environment.

During a visit, Timothy handed her a letter he wanted mailed to Hugh Hefner and published in *Playboy*. She opened it outside the prison. In it, Timothy placed the blame of his Swiss arrest squarely on

Rosemary's shoulders. "He was in a Swiss prison because I wanted a baby.... If we hadn't left Algeria ... If I hadn't needed an operation...," she recounted his words. It was a rank betrayal. And a lie.

Later that day at a lunch with Hauchard and Timothy's new legal counsel, her mind kept turning back to the letter. Though she knew she was not responsible for his arrest, she couldn't help but interpret something karmic about it happening on her most fertile day. She excused herself and sobbed in the bathroom before smoothing out her clothes and getting back to work.

Rosemary, mourning the loss of her chance at a child with Timothy—and perhaps with anyone, because the fertility treatments were costly and painful—had stopped eating and sleeping. She wept openly in the streets and on trains. She had endured a year of abdominal pain, two surgeries, and months of needles and jabs for a husband who so readily scapegoated her. To keep herself company, she played Janis Joplin, Jimi Hendrix, Otis Redding, and Jim Morrison on their language-learning tape player until she realized that the singers were all deceased.

In addition to raising funds, Rosemary now had to sing for her supper, providing entertainment to Hauchard's circle of friends—people who belittled their maids, fed their tiny dogs with silverware, and complained of the cost of shipping priceless art overseas. The people she enjoyed, the ones she felt she could actually hold a conversation with, tended to work with the CIA, Hauchard told her. Was he merely being provocative? Impossible to say. She existed now in a nest of the vapid and the viperous.

Despite the Hefner letter, Rosemary remained on task and appeared just as dedicated to freeing her husband as ever. Through her fundraising work, she raised $10,000. When she brought Timothy a check, he told her to hand it over to Hauchard. She managed "an obliging smile even though I'd just given $10,000 to a master conman who I was convinced had set us up, stage-managed the arrests, and convinced Tim he was the only one to save him," she wrote.

Her old friend John Schewel arrived, too. While in Algeria, Rosemary had sent an SOS message to the *East Village Other* editor Jaakov Kohn, asking him to share two words with John: "Help me." By the time the message reached John, Rosemary had relocated to Switzerland. It had taken him several months to find the funds, secure a safe house, and track them down. He arrived with Dennis Martino, whose twin brother, David, had married Susan Leary; Dennis's eight-months-pregnant wife, Robin, also associates of the Brotherhood; and a suitcase full of Rosemary's favorite Kiehl's products, drugs, and, most important, cash.

Every morning John emerged from Rosemary's bedroom, outraging Dennis, who could not conceive of a woman betraying the man he so admired.

Now flush with enough money for bail, Timothy faked a heart attack to convince officials that he needed medical help. The combination of money and health scare worked: the Swiss set him free.

Timothy walked out of prison with Rosemary toward a waiting group of reporters. All smiles and sound bites, he waved a Swiss franc and pointed to a woman wearing a crown on the note marked with the word "Libertas."

"The goddess of Switzerland!"

"Rosemary and I came to Switzerland for many reasons," he told reporters. "We hope to live here under the great symbolic aura of Hermann Hesse and Carl Jung. We're time travelers and hope to stay because of a tradition of freedom."

Rosemary added, "Perhaps we'll raise some children."

It was a full moon in Aquarius. A time of radical change. A time of letting go.

TIMOTHY LIVED UNDER HOUSE arrest as part of the bail agreement and surrendered his passports. Still, they were less isolated than they were in Algeria. They met with a revolving door of old friends, including Flo and Maynard Ferguson, who visited with their family, and Michael and Eleanora Kennedy.

John continued to live with them, even as the love triangle grew more complicated with all three under one roof. Though Rosemary wrote cheerful notes to her parents about Timothy's release and their reunion ("We are happier than we have ever been before!"), they were barreling toward a fork in the road. She had lost respect for Timothy, a man whose pathetic need to be loved by strangers trumped all else. How could she trust someone so gullible, so easily taken by champagne and money—and on top of it so heartless to her? Her faith had been wavering since Algeria. She had forgiven so much because she believed he was truly a great man. Now she wasn't so sure.

When Timothy took time away to undergo surgery on his bad ear—which would enable him to hear without his missing hearing aids—Rosemary learned that any future fertility treatments would be too risky. After years of longing to be a mother, she'd have to come to terms with life without children. "The death of that possibility for me was very hard to get over. For so long Tim had told me how 'perfectly suited I was to be a mother' and 'how beautiful I would look as a mother.' Now that that was not going to happen it was like I had to find myself another role to play."

After months of estrangement in prison and weeks of fights following his release, Rosemary—with the help of John, and his money, standing in the wings—decided to leave Timothy. In her mind, this wasn't a breakup—period, full stop—but a pause, more like a semicolon.

She would live nearby so that they could visit each other on a whim. She could return to him whenever she was ready, renewed, and in the meantime John would take care of her. Still, she and Timothy cried. "I just really needed to catch my breath," she said.

Rosemary packed her suitcase as Timothy, half-naked, watched her from the bed. She started to regret her decision and took more time packing, delicately matching her lingerie sets and painstakingly folding her dresses. She hoped he'd say something that would persuade her to stay.

Instead, he uttered two devastating words: "Marilyn Monroe."

Rosemary knew what he meant. She would fall apart in his absence. Bloated on barbiturates. Dead within a year of their separation. While he, the Arthur Miller of their marriage, would remarry, continue writing, and live into ripe old age.

She snapped her suitcase shut. "Take care of yourself."

❧

DESPITE WHAT HE HAD SAID and all that had happened, a few weeks later Rosemary returned to their house in Villars intending to initiate a reconciliation. Perhaps it would be better to be a dead Marilyn than no one at all. Plus, she missed him. She sincerely loved him. They had been through so much. And she had made a promise to herself to stand still, not to run, and she intended to keep it. They were mated.

But a teenage village girl named Emily had already taken her place. Emily slept in Rosemary's bed, wore Rosemary's clothes, lined her eyes with Rosemary's kohl, and sprayed herself with Rosemary's perfumes. During lulls in their conversation, Emily would pat her stomach maternally. Timothy's child. Timothy allowed Emily to perform this cruel pantomime. If Rosemary could take a younger lover, so could he.

Rosemary did not blame the girl. She flashed back to her own experience when Nena, Timothy's ex-wife, had returned to Millbrook and watched as Rosemary sat beside Timothy and whispered the snippets of conversation that he couldn't hear. "It was the concept of replaceable parts," she would later say, recognizing how easily she could be swapped out for a newer model.

"It was always his movie and I felt that I'd just slapped on some makeup to cover up the black eye and I didn't know my lines. I had a movie running in my head too—he wasn't the hero anymore," she wrote.

The curtain had fallen; the show had ended. Their story was finally, truly over.

John suggested that they all drop acid together to underscore the magnitude of this break. So the four of them spent a peaceful final night together tripping. John believed that Timothy didn't appreciate the gravity of the moment, nor did he understand how inadequate his life would be without his high priestess. "Her power of being was so strong that Tim didn't realize that a lot of his credibility was amplified and solidified by Rosemary being there," John said.

The next morning, John snapped a picture of Rosemary as she walked out of the apartment in Villars, eyes straight ahead, her Moroccan leather bag slung over her arm, filled with her diaries and writings, a manuscript in progress, into a new life.

Eighteen

Demeter

Rosemary and John lived, in another exile, in a farmhouse in Wintersingen, a northern district of Switzerland near Basel. John often photographed Rosemary during this time, before the paranoia hit and cameras became too dangerous. In his favorite photo, shot in the winter of 1972, Rosemary is dressed warmly in a camel suede winter coat lined in white fur. She stands sentry under the bare canopy of an oak tree holding a seven-foot-tall, Y-shaped tree branch, her hair held back by a thick band, the paisley printed hem of her jeans grazing the snow. Her face is in profile, her neck craning to the left, staring, not ahead at the future, nor behind at the past, but squarely in the face of the present.

"This is the wanderer," John thought as he snapped his picture. "The stance, the hat, the staff. Alone in the woods in the middle of winter." More alone than either of them knew.

In the months that followed her break from Timothy, Rosemary submerged herself in spiritual work. Cloistered in a primitive farmhouse and relieved of the many distractions that plagued her time with Timothy, other than daily rites of survival—carrying buckets of water from the nearby well and chopping wood for the stove—Rosemary and John were free to plunge into the mystical. They dropped acid, made love, and read esoteric books. They embraced the divine even in their boredom. Rosemary returned to the mystic Gurdjieff and reaffirmed her faith in astrology, particularly in the role of Neptune, the "drug planet," in her chart. They studied Aleister Crowley, learned to shape reality according to their will, and sought peak experiences, chasing ecstasy, "loosening the girders of the soul," as Crowley wrote. "Though he is ever so much younger, he is a wise soul and leads me into explorations that I have saved for my later years. We are deep into the hermetic mysteries and consider doing alchemy one day," she wrote to her mother.

John serenaded Rosemary with his guitar in the kitchen as she baked bread. They practiced yoga, worked on their French, and helped their landlord, an elderly farmer, who reminded Rosemary of her grandfather, labor in the fields, toasting a hard day's work with fermented apple cider as the farmer told dirty jokes in German. Few movies—*Deliverance* played at the movie theater nearby—pierced the dome of their ascetic solitude. They had, John said, "a complete alchemical partnership."

She lived by the mantra "Change yourself. Be silent." Different from her husband's "Turn on, tune in, drop out," Rosemary's maxim was quieter—harder, perhaps, to honor. "There are mysteries not to be revealed to the many but to the few who search diligently for them," she wrote.

The warm light of John's youth, his boyish exuberance, his beauty, and his uncomplicated sexuality soothed Rosemary's soul. John knew that he was not destined to have children—he didn't want them to get in the way of his work—so Rosemary was relieved of that aching pressure. Whereas Rosemary used to be the one to wake early and tend to her lovers, taking on the maternal role, John tended to his "magic lady," waking with the dawn to light the stove and make Rosemary coffee. He did not allow for wallowing. As a relentlessly positive man with his gaze aimed into the future, planning their next steps and adventures, he pushed Rosemary to stop brooding. "Optimism," he said, "is a circle shield against the darkness." He did not allow her to ruminate on past harms. She was the magician now.

While he might not have wanted to acknowledge his own disappointment, John mourned alongside Rosemary. John buried his League for Spiritual Discovery medallion under the oak tree where Rosemary had posed with her staff. "There is a shared feeling that we were betrayed by a man in whom we'd placed a lot of trust," Rosemary wrote to Flo Ferguson.

Rosemary exorcised her past through writing rather than burying it. John bought Rosemary her own Olivetti typewriter and urged her to write every day, as she once had done for her husband. She donned a work uniform of flowing cotton caftans, sitting in front of the open window that faced the wooded rolling hills around the farmhouse, and recorded, in the span of a few months, her year on the run with Timothy. To summon the muse, Rosemary cut out her typed sentences, placed them in a shoebox, and shook it. Then John removed the sentences at random and pasted them together—a writing embodiment of the divine synchronicity of the *I Ching*. Still, she often got stuck when trying to dig into her earlier days with Timothy and found herself reworking, creating dozens upon dozens of drafts. Rosemary stood at an impasse, John said, because "she was always editing her own life for the safety of others."

She sent one of these early edits to her mother, proud to show her work and all that she had accomplished, but in the chapters Ruth saw only the pain her daughter had endured, and she blamed herself for letting her daughter down in some essential way. "I'm sorry I wasn't a good mother to you," her mother wrote. "Perhaps I should have never had children. I look back over my life and I feel it was such a waste.

Guess I'm working out my karma." Rosemary was perplexed. "It shouldn't make you feel badly. It was meant in praise of you and Daddy," she wrote back. "Whatever I've experienced since is for my greater understanding of myself and life and is not YOUR KARMA! You have been and are a good and loving woman."

Her mother's negative reaction didn't stop her from pursuing publication. Rosalie Siegel, a young literary agent who made her name with the sale of the megahit *Papillon*, a French novel about a man who escapes a penal colony, which was made into a film starring Steve McQueen, took her on as a client. They worked together on shaping a draft to send to publishers, until the navy required Siegel's husband to serve in Guantánamo Bay. Siegel closed up shop and joined him. Rosemary's memoir remained untouched.

Meanwhile, the Swiss denied Nixon's push for extradition, a good sign, while also rejecting Timothy's bid for asylum, a bad one. No canton would take in Timothy as a permanent resident, requiring him to move to a new location every few months to avoid rearrest. The ultimate goal, as Nixon and his aides had devised it, was for Timothy to run out of unvisited cantons. At that point, where would they end up? What country would take them now?

Them. No longer. Rosemary and John soon learned that Timothy had removed Rosemary's name from his Swiss asylum appeal papers— a "spiteful act," John said. "He was going to make her and me pay for what we did to him," he said. Removing her name from official documents signaled to the world that "there was no more Rosemary Woodruff Leary."

⁓

LIKE TIMOTHY, John and Rosemary did not stay in one place for long. They secured a World Passport, a stateless travel document created by the peace activist Garry Davis that worked often enough to use somewhat reliably. Propped up by various travel documents, they left Europe and visited John's safe house in the snowy mountains of Montreal. Brigitte Mars, mere weeks away from giving birth, lived there with her partner, Sergai. Brigitte felt awed by the presence of the high priestess in their mountain oasis. She recalled that Rosemary wouldn't leave the house without sunglasses because she'd been in that Bed-In picture with John and Yoko and large segments of the population knew her face. Even with all the pomp and disguises, Rosemary was never haughty. "Her being such a queen, she was very kind and very humble," Brigitte said. "She really didn't seem to have a big ego." She thought of Rosemary as a teacher, especially vis-à-vis sessions using LSD. "We would spend a week getting ready," Brigitte said. "We would clean the house. We would make healthy snacks. We would even sew special dresses to wear to the sessions that would be easy to take on and off." The care of her dress, the sewing, the stage-managing—Rosemary was returning to herself.

Brigitte also recalls trading herbal remedies with Rosemary—cayenne to stanch bleeding and rosemary for memory. Thanks in part to Rosemary's guidance, Brigitte later devoted her life to plants and potions. She now works as an herbalist in Boulder, Colorado.

A few weeks into their visit, Rosemary, John, and Sergai Mars flew from Canada to Kabul, Afghanistan, on a moneymaking mission; they left Brigitte behind in the Canadian wilderness during the depth of winter with her newborn daughter, Sunflower, and $100. Brigitte survived by extracting nutrients from the few edible plants in the frozen landscape around the house—an example of the grit and ingenuity necessary to survive as a true hippie woman.

The three wanderers flew to Afghanistan to perform a "magical process," as John would later describe it. Rosemary used other words: They were there to make hash oil. "I won't be able to meet you for a while. I have to start traveling again, a small adventure to make some money," Rosemary wrote to her mother. In Afghanistan, Rosemary learned that a burqa was the perfect cover for concealing contraband. Despite her bravado, this was a brazen act. Though hash was startlingly easy to procure, a few years earlier, under pressure from then-U.S. allies Iran and Pakistan, Afghanistan had passed antismuggling laws. By 1973, when Timothy Leary placed a fateful foot there, drug seizures had increased eightfold.

Timothy sent word to Afghanistan through Dennis Martino that he wanted a reunion. Rosemary agreed to see him, despite John's hesitations, back in Switzerland. "It might be simpler to return to Tim, to once again be in the center of that maelstrom of activity and energy that he creates around him," she wrote. "Pulled to him by the lure of everything is perfect and if it isn't, why not take some more LSD? It might be easier to inhabit that world than it is to sit here now alone with my thoughts and self-reproach." Rosemary's perspective on the sacrament had changed. LSD was no longer solely about going within to find God. Now the pursuit of transcendence was wrapped up in escape, just as it had been for Charles Mills and Benzedrine and Allen Eager and heroin. Timothy and LSD were tools of avoidance—easy ways to avoid facing what was missing in herself.

Still, despite everything, Rosemary believed that Timothy would take care of her. He initially seemed worthy of her faith. He had bequeathed Rosemary all future royalties from the sales of *The Politics of Ecstasy*, which he had written under her care and support. He also affirmed her rights to their shared archive. But a letter from his publisher disabused her of any warm and fuzzy notions. There were no royalties. The government had placed a federal tax lien of $83,319.55 on Timothy's earnings.

"It has been so hard to wake up and be free of Timothy's influence," she wrote in a letter to her mother. "I have delayed over and over and over again a final separation, finding it difficult to believe that he's not the man he'd persuaded so many people that he was."

But when Rosemary met him at his new Swiss chalet on Lake Zug, she found him altered—physically, puffed up and tightened around the eyes thanks to a recent facelift, emotionally unmoored without a solid female relationship (no Emily, no baby, only "a succession of females, women, chicks, and girlfriends, but no real Acid Queen," according to a friend), and dependent on harder drugs. He lived with his daughter, Susan, her new baby, and a revolving cast of young socialites, musicians, and zany characters. Timothy bragged about the $250,000 advance that Bantam Books had paid for their escape book—now *his* escape book with the co-writer Brian Barritt titled *Confessions of a Hope Fiend*—though most of the money went to Hauchard. Rosemary, the original, unacknowledged co-writer, wouldn't receive a cent.

"I met him, expecting a change, a reconciliation. I found instead a man embittered and unreasonable with a desire to cause more pain and confusion, wanting me again under his control. . . . I saw a man who has never had any concern except for his own myth," Rosemary wrote.

She had been too overwhelmed, too high, really, to face the reality of her husband; only with distance did his limitations appear pathological. She traced back the moments that led her to relinquish her fantasy of who he was—the pathetic neediness in Algeria, the joker facade in Switzerland, the way he had shamed her for her inability to conceive, the subtle and overt betrayals over the years. She could not continue lying to herself. "He is convincing as long as there is not a moment's peace for reflection," she wrote to her mother. She had pitied him in the early part of their relationship and had yearned to assuage the loneliness at the core of his being. She realized now that she had reacted to his emptiness—not his loneliness. Where his heart chakra should be, there was, instead, a chasm.

She reinterpreted her time with Timothy as a kind of delusional state, a *folie imposée*, a delusion imposed onto other, more suggestible people. And she saw now how he had set the snares for her to take all the blame that should have landed on him—how he had so artfully attributed each piece of bad news to her karma, rather than taking any responsibility for his actions.

To the many ardent Leary admirers, Rosemary had abdicated her role as queen wife and got what she deserved. In interviews and writings to come, Rosemary was portrayed as the adulteress, and Timothy, the victim. She had left him (on his birthday, no less) with a younger man when he needed her most. The definitive social history of the psychedelic movement, *Acid Dreams*, published in 1985, for example, relied solely on Timothy's version of their breakup and solidified lore into fact: "While Tim was convalescing in a hospital after a minor operation, Rosemary had a love affair with an old friend. Leary was high on acid when he found out what had happened, and he told his wife to pack her bags and leave. It was a final break; he would almost never mention her name again."

With a sleight of hand, Timothy, ever the magician, could claim spousal abandonment, which meant he could also cut all ties to Rosemary without seeming like the villain. The people in Timothy's corner scorned her; those who despised or doubted Timothy dismissed her as his tool—an extension of him—and both groups stopped replying to her letters.

Timothy, however, could not actually stay away from Rosemary. Shortly after their meeting, he phoned with news of his "perfect love," the socialite Joanna Harcourt-Smith, whom Michel Hauchard had named one of his speedboats after.

Perhaps the new girlfriend "will not feel, as I do, that she was duped into supporting something that is less than human," Rosemary wrote.

※

ROSEMARY SEVERED DIRECT communication with Timothy, his friends, and his followers. She and John relocated to Cefalù, Sicily, the coastal town where Aleister Crowley established an occult "anti-monastery" called the Abbey of Thelema and wrote the scandalous auto-biographical novel *The Diary of a Drug Fiend*. Crowley's Cefalù period is among his darkest, when his heroin addiction escalated and a young follower died after a magic ritual—curious footsteps for the lovers to follow.

John and Rosemary kept a shared magic diary. They were searching, John said, for the point "where wisdom meets understanding"—the intersection of ancient and esoteric philosophies—from chakras to the tree of life to the Kabbalah. But the impending publication of Timothy's *Confessions of a Hope Fiend* (a take on Crowley's *The Diary of a Drug Fiend*) made it impossible for Rosemary to ignore the material world and fully immerse herself in their studies. With help from the lawyer Michael Tigar, a Kennedy associate, she secured an advance copy before its release in 1973.

In it, her name appeared only once, but Timothy didn't need to use her name in order to out her role in his crimes. He pilfered from her letters and stole from her writing, while referring to Rosemary throughout as the biblical She—the Eve to his Adam, on whom he laid blame the destruction of Eden. Rosemary populated almost every corner of the book. There She was in the peaceful stone house in Big Sur missing him. And, again, crying as She watched *Woodstock* in the dark movie theater after their escape. She bought wigs and secured fake identification with the Weather Underground and schemed with lawyers and the Brotherhood.

To top it off, Timothy's depictions of the Black Panthers mortified her. "The book lives up to my worst fears, escape, passports, connections, conspiracy and worst of all, the essentially racist point of view that is expressed throughout," she wrote to Tigar. She typed up pages of responses to the book as she read it, writing in the margins, "I wrote this" or "All of this portion I edited" or "I wrote parts of this and I AM NOT PROUD OF IT."

Tigar sent a strongly worded statement to Bantam Books, alleging plagiarism and libel. "Substantial portions of the book invade Mrs. Leary's privacy, at least by showing her in a false light and unjustifiably disclosing private facts about her," he wrote. The publisher responded tersely: If Rosemary wanted to stop publication, she had to show up in court and sue them. Would she like to do that?

The book nearly compelled her to try. But when her lawyers inquired about the charges she faced and the possible jail time, the minimum, three years, was a nonstarter. She couldn't do it. She called off the book inquiries and told her lawyers and mother never again to ask her about returning to America.

The book was an affront, a robbery, a gun pointed in her direction. "I believe that my survival is something he has difficulty tolerating as he had predicted my suicide or descent into heroined existence," she wrote to a friend. "I can no longer support either his public statements nor his style of life and I am ashamed that I have lent myself to perpetuating the myth of Timothy and Rosemary Leary."

Resigned but not broken, Rosemary mailed 51 francs and 75 centimes to post an ad in the *Herald Tribune*. The ad ran concurrently in the underground newspapers:

Rosemary wills it be known that for more than a year she has enjoyed a reality separately from Timothy Leary. She is not responsible for his debts karmic or financial. A wife is not property.

The book was not the only threat she faced. In August 1972, an international investigation of the Brotherhood resulted in the arrest of fifty-seven men and the seizure of two and a half tons of hashish, 1.5 million doses of Orange Sunshine, and "innumerable sets" of forged passports and IDs. Michael Kennedy, back in the mix, represented the Brotherhood's leader Michael Randall.

Billy Hitchcock, Millbrook's owner, who had funded the Brotherhood's drug manufacturing operation, surrendered to the federal attorney's office in New York City and was offered a deal in exchange for his cooperation. In a letter updating Rosemary about the trial, Eleanora Kennedy called Billy Hitchcock a "solid gold snitch."

Despite Timothy having nothing directly to do with the sting, the media characterized him as the Brotherhood's Mafia don. The *Los Angeles Times* reported that the drug smuggling operation was "founded by Dr. Leary." *The Washington Post* called it "the Tim Leary raid." The Orange County district attorney Cecil Hicks further blamed Timothy as "the brains" and the "god" behind the Brotherhood. Leary was "responsible for destroying more lives than any other living human being." He was, an official told the press, "the most dangerous man alive." (This label would stick, morph a bit, and eventually be attributed to Nixon.) The judge set bail for Timothy, who was still on the run, at $5 million. The arrow aimed at Timothy was also, by extension, trained on Rosemary, who knew all of Timothy's secrets and could corroborate his crimes.

After more than a year of media silence, Rosemary watched her name creep back into the press. *Rolling Stone* ran an exposé on the Brotherhood; the writer repeated rumors circulated by the police of wife swapping and orgies. "They all sat around in a circle, they slapped hands and everybody swapped partners. Then everybody held hands in a nude position, astraddle the male counterparts, and had at it. It was approximately at the time that one of the other members was shacking with Rosemary Leary and Leary was shacking with the man's wife. These orgies, sitting in a circle, were quite common."

In response, Rosemary wrote to *Rolling Stone*'s publisher, Jann Wenner, "It's somewhat disturbing to me to find myself reported as having illicit intercourse, in such an uncomfortable position too. You might have asked me to write for *Rolling Stone* rather than depend on police informers. . . . It is difficult enough being separated from my family and friends without having to read in *Rolling Stone* about all the fun I might have had." To rectify the magazine's mistake, she asked Wenner to print her karmic divorce statement, which he did in the following issue.

Nixon, meanwhile, called on the silent majority to secure an overwhelming forty-nine-state victory for a second term.

Rosemary still had no clue about how much danger she faced.

SHE MOVED TO another Sicilian city called Catania and seemed to heal under the warmth of the Sicilian sun. "It was summer and I was truly madly deeply in love." She lived with Adolfo Frenzi, or Bubi for short, a count, who looked like a Roman emperor crossed with Serge Gainsbourg, whom she met through Allen Ginsberg. Bubi soon became Rosemary's lover. His estate was eroding, just like his family money, but she didn't care. They made love in a secret grotto by a waterfall, drank grape brandy, and helped raise chickens, as she had imagined she would in her domestic life with Timothy. Meanwhile, John, who often reaped the benefits of being in an open relationship, watched her fall in love without resentment and, relieved by the feeling that Rosemary was in safe hands, felt comfortable enough to return to America.

"Sicily is full of magic and full of myth," she said. "I am so very happy here on this sun terrace, rise and sleep with the sun, draw cool water from the well to bathe, watch the grapes turn deep purple." She was surrounded by bounty—bread, eggs, wine, persimmons, pomegranates, and fig trees. "It's heaven really. Everyone smiles a lot. Families are large. And no baby cries for long. Pregnant women are queens. And beauty is loved."

She lived in the shadow of Mount Etna, where, the myths said, Persephone returns every spring after a long winter spent in the underworld. The ancient Greeks honored Persephone's mother, Demeter, the goddess of grain, whose grief over her daughter makes the fields infertile in winter. They called these secret rituals the Eleusinian Mysteries, initiations conducted by priestesses, involving the ingestion of psychedelic brews containing ergot, the grain fungus from which LSD is derived.

Rosemary read a feminist reinterpretation of Greek mythology by Edith Hamilton and felt the old gods in the landscape, especially Athena, the goddess of wisdom, who took the form of an owl. "That's what I felt I was in the most in need of, to find wisdom or to be a wise woman," she said.

Sitting on an empty beach, she wrote to Flo Ferguson, "Do I persist in dreams of children and gardens? Virgin, wife, mother, hag. What do you do if you can't have children, Flo?"

"Plant flowers and love God, I suppose," Flo wrote back.

Rosemary whiled away several months drinking with Bubi. She adored the glow of Bubi's face once cocktail hour started, how the edges softened as she tried to keep up with him. Drunk on endless glasses of Sangiovese wine, she willed herself to forget: forget the encroaching dangers; forget her husband in jail; forget about her parents back in California or her friends from the Brotherhood and the Weather Underground on the run. In a stupor, she fantasized that this dead end could be the rest of her life. But no matter how much she drank, she could not shake her anxiety.

Her mother sent her the newspaper clipping that changed everything: Timothy Leary had been arrested in Kabul with his "perfect love," Joanna. Rosemary had repeatedly warned Timothy and his friends that the Feds would nab him if he traveled by air. And here it was.

The front-page article featured a picture of Timothy in handcuffs, his hair and eyes wild, with a broad artificial smile, which disturbed her more than even the news of the arrest. "It was not the same smile I had known. It was inappropriate. It was a smile of resignation and I could see he had changed. . . . The smile of the ego," she later wrote.

In the aftermath of his arrest, Joanna Harcourt-Smith attempted to slip herself into Rosemary's shoes. Few newspapers referenced Rosemary outside short statements, like the *Los Angeles Times*: "No mention was made of the whereabouts of Leary's wife, Rosemary, who was reported with him earlier in his travels." Some didn't bother to differentiate between the two women: Joanna had helped him escape, had lived with him in Millbrook, had shepherded him through prior arrests. It must have been a relief, on some level, for Rosemary to relinquish her complicated identity to another woman. But for Joanna, the transition from one perfect love to another wasn't as seamless. Some called Joanna a CIA spook. Others believed she walked Timothy into his doom by persuading him to fly to Afghanistan. Allen Ginsberg, no fan of Joanna's, said that she was "not fit to be the next Acid Queen."

Rosemary, however, only pitied Joanna. Rosemary didn't know the half of it. Joanna's mother neglected her and was emotionally abusive. When she was sexually assaulted by her family's chauffeur as a child, her mother refused to dismiss him because, she told her daughter, "good chauffeurs were hard to find." She spent the rest of her life finding identity and meaning through sex. "Tim desires and attracts suicidal women," Rosemary wrote. She knew this because she had been one of these women—seeking escape through sublimation. "One woman paying with [her life] should have been enough for a lifetime. . . . It almost got me but I seem to have a guardian angel somewhere."

Then came another damning letter from her mother. Ruth wrote that Joanna Harcourt-Smith, who now went by Joanna Leary, had called offering $25,000 for Rosemary's whereabouts. When Ruth declined, Joanna offered $5,000 for a phone number. Ruth knew a setup when she saw one. She told her to take it up with Michael Kennedy. Joanna pushed back, saying that Timothy "didn't trust lawyers." She ended the phone call—to Ruth's bemusement—with "Timothy sends his love!"

The following day, a man from the State Department visited the Woodruffs and asked the family to identify photographs of Rosemary, explaining that their daughter faced charges related to passport fraud.

John returned to Sicily from the United States shortly after with an eight-page letter addressed to "Mr. and Mrs. Schewel" that had been sent to his parents' home in Miami. Timothy's scrawl was unmistakable, but the contents were startling, even for him. "It was a mistake in judgement for us to get involved with dope dealers and illegal revolutionaries," he wrote. He emphasized the line "Truth is the only hope."

"I believe that Rosemary should surface and cooperate with the government officials," he wrote. "Please do not fear the American Law or Law Enforcement Officials." The police were "honest, stronger, more dependable, and more humane than the other groups we have worked with." He included contact information for the FBI agent Roger "Frenchie" LaJeunesse, a top-level agent who had investigated Sirhan Sirhan after the assassination of RFK. And ended the letter with "Dearest Rosemary. I will always love you. Joanna (who is perfect) and I know that our destiny is linked to yours. We want you to be free."

Rosemary recognized that the letter was designed to entice her out of the underground to free him by sacrificing herself. Michael Tigar, who also defended the Brotherhood, knew about the Feds' behind-the-scenes arrangement with Timothy. Their goal wasn't just to beef up their case against the Brotherhood but to take down their true intended target: the lawyer Michael Kennedy. Timothy on his own wouldn't sway any jury, but Rosemary, "the computer," who held all the evidence, could help them make one of the all-time biggest cases against one of the most successful and mediagenic leftist defense lawyers of all time.

Now the Feds needed to track the queen down. "They went after Rosemary hard. Hard and heavy," Michael Kennedy said later—all with Timothy's help. In an interview with the FBI agent Jerry Utz, Timothy described Rosemary as "a queen. I was a martyr."

Joanna would later confirm this in *Timothy Leary* by Robert Greenfield. "That was part of the deal," she said. "Tim was going to find Rosemary."

A grand jury subpoenaed Michael Horowitz, the archivist whom Rosemary had tapped to safeguard Timothy's papers, demanding that he hand over "any documents concerning Rosemary Leary, who has disappeared from sight." This included more than a hundred love letters that the FBI sent to handwriting and cryptanalysis, employing Timothy himself to help break their code. In addition, the FBI sent agents to their Weather Underground safe house location in Seattle, the Sheraton Hotel in Chicago, and spots in New York where Rosemary had fundraised.

Timothy's betrayal of his wife bled out into the underground. "I knew Rosemary was on the lam and only she could corroborate it," meaning Timothy's case against the people who had helped him escape, said Paul Krassner, editor of *The Realist*. "I thought Tim was playing the game of his life."

In 1974, when a partial accounting of Timothy's cooperation with the Feds came to light, Timothy's former advocates held a press conference, called People Investigating Leary's Lies (PILL). Richard Alpert, now Ram Dass, denounced him as a scoundrel. Even Ginsberg decried him as "the false messiah." Jerry Rubin said that he felt "sick for the death of Tim Leary's soul." Abbie Hoffman used the harshest words: "I can't imagine anything close except children turning parents in under Nazi Germany."

But Timothy's son's critique hit the hardest. "Timothy has shown he would inform on anybody he can to get out of jail," Jack said, "and it would not surprise me if he would testify about my sister or myself if he could."

But long before PILL made headlines, Timothy's letter confirmed to John and Rosemary that their haven in Europe—and her romantic escape by the Mediterranean Sea—was no longer safe. Ruth sent one last letter, outlining the fears for her daughter. "If they give you complete immunity, you could come home," she wrote. "I just worry that if you do some of those involved might try to harm you. Please let us know. I hope you are trusting the right people."

Rosemary folded the letter, placed it in her suitcase, and bade farewell to her count. John called his contacts in South America and started making arrangements for another move.

"We are thrust into an insane life, with no opportunity of really surfacing anywhere," Rosemary wrote.

They were out of moves, goodwill, and people to trust. The stakes were too high, the road too treacherous, the downsides too steep. Their new motto, written in their shared magical diary, was "dissolve and coagulate"—meaning adapt and remain unnoticed.

It was time to go fully underground.

PART FOUR

The High Priestess of Innkeeping

It is a joy to be hidden, and a disaster not to be found.

—D. W. WINNICOTT, *The Maturational Processes and the Facilitating Environment*

Nineteen

Sarah Woodruff

The Provincetown Inn stands on the edge of the fist of land on Cape Cod that juts out into the Atlantic Ocean, at the site where the Pilgrims first landed in 1620 before moving onto their historic disembarkation farther west at Plymouth Rock. The hotel, considered luxurious when it opened its twenty-eight guest rooms in 1925, had lost its luster by the time Sarah Woodruff started working there in 1978. New owners had ballooned the hotel to a hundred rooms, earning it a reputation as the place to stay when you wanted to party on the cheap. Bellboys screamed at managers; waiters threw dishes when they weren't tipped out early to buy drugs; all kinds of debauched behavior took place in the Pilgrim-hat-shaped pool.

Sarah Woodruff started as assistant to the inn's owner, Brooke Evans, filling in at the front desk and for other jobs as needed until she climbed the rungs to corporate sales, selling blocks of rooms for conferences. Evans hired her because of her beauty but also discovered that Sarah was more than capable and, most important, reliable and sober. A woman like that was hard to find. The young staff were too busy stirring up as much shit as possible to do much in the way of hard work before they returned to their lives elsewhere—back to college, to stalled relationships, to their parents, or to lives in other countries. "Miscreants and malcontents," Brooke Evans's son Jeff, who worked at the inn, said. "But not Sarah. Never Sarah."

You wouldn't feel Sarah's presence in the hustle and bustle of the summer season, but rather in the muted, fogged-out New England winter, when the population settled to its core of around three thousand people who could somehow maintain their sanity amid the ever-present soundtrack of whistling wind and clanking shutters. Spirits emerged from their summer slumber, roaming the softly lit halls of the hotel, moving objects, flickering the lights of the imitation Tiffany lamps, inhabiting the eyes of a painted mermaid taken from the prow of a ship and then propped up on the bottom of a staircase.

There's beauty here, especially on the man-made jetty, a long finger pointing out to the end of the world. Sarah Woodruff walked this jetty, the wind whipping her hair, ocean salt sticking to her exposed skin, the seagulls dive-bombing around her as she imagined another life.

~

"WHAT'S THE DEAL with Sarah?"

It was a refrain thrown around town, offhandedly, by people watchers sitting on the benches outside town hall or in the cafés on Commercial Street whenever Sarah rode by on her bike.

"Funny, she doesn't look like a Sarah," one woman said.

Locals called people like her wash-ashores. No matter how long they'd lived there, they'd never truly be *from* there. These people tended to be searchers—tax evaders, draft dodgers, outsider artists—running from something or someone. They were people who had come to find themselves, their sexuality, their path, any option other than prison. Provincetown had provided a safe house for a rogues' gallery of thieves and radicals since the seventeenth century. Thanks to the preponderance of seamen and whores, locals called the fishing port Helltown.

"Every wash-ashore has a story behind them. I was just one of many," Sarah said. "There was a sense of endurance on Cape Cod of people who will always survive."

Before the true megabucks came to the region, you could live in this beach town, picking up odd jobs here and there: become a carpenter for a day and rip up flooring or clean a motel until the long, dark winter approached and you had to make do with what you had scrounged that summer.

Sarah Woodruff, who had arrived in the late 1970s without roots, took on various jobs that didn't require a Social Security number before she landed at the Provincetown Inn. She worked as a part-time office manager, sold jewelry and art glass to rich bankers and psychoanalysts on summer vacation, and volunteered as an underwriter at a local radio station. She was a gifted saleswoman. Her elegance, which could border on aloofness, freed customers to drop large sums of cash without feeling judged. Her slightly formal demeanor gave people the impression that she was, as one person said, a "person of some importance, a dignitary." She wore her hair shoulder length, a little wavy thanks to the ocean air, and styled herself primly in red lipsticks and pressed blouses, touches that made her stand out against a town full of peacocks, where assless chaps and nipple clamps would largely go unremarked upon, where you could stumble upon John Waters and his pencil-thin mustache buying candy at a soda fountain on Commercial Street or working on scripts at the Dairy Queen on Bradford and West Vine.

As Jeff Evans put it, "She stood out in a way because she was invisible."

But if you were truly paying attention, there were clues to an underlying incongruity—a mystery, perhaps.

People recalled specific outfits—a purple grosgrain coat came up repeatedly, an item too refined for Sarah's circumstances. Her car provided another clue. After three years of riding her bike in the rain and begging for rides from friends, she finally got a license when she could in good faith answer no to the question, "Have you been convicted of a felony in the past ten years?" She returned from a brief trip away with a hunter-green Mercedes-Benz convertible and a story about a dead aunt and an inheritance. People whispered. *How could she afford to keep a car like that?* They all knew what kind of money she made. But it wasn't just the Mercedes that got people talking. It was the wild serenity that they saw when she drove. She appeared to be so free, so easy with the top down, her bobbed hair flowing in the wind, smoking a cigarette and singing along to some indecipherable song, driving slowly, so slowly, but with obvious abandon.

Rumors clung to her like a shroud. People spoke in code. If you knew, you knew, and if you didn't, you best remain in the dark. At least one person spotted her picture in a bestselling history of the 1960s—sitting next to Ken Kesey as he read from the *I Ching*—and shared it among friends. Sarah had a different name, looked a bit younger and thinner, with "no hint of the dark cloud her face now carried," as one friend would later write. But it was Sarah, clear as day. When a man arrived calling himself a journalist, waving around a picture of Sarah from that same time, everyone remained mum.

Naomi Lake, a single mother who lived with her two young boys in Provincetown, recalled the blustery winter evening when she first met Sarah at a tarot card reading. A storm brewed in the distance, and Sarah had asked Naomi for a ride back to Provincetown.

They exchanged pleasantries as Naomi concentrated on driving.

"So where are you from?" Sarah had asked.

"Berkeley," said Naomi. The rain pounded on the windshield. There were few lights. They got on Route 6 and passed Pilgrim Lake.

"Oh, I lived in Berkeley, too, in the hills," Sarah said, offhandedly.

Something compelled Naomi to blurt out, "In Timothy Leary's house?" These words tumbled out of the blue; she had not heard any rumors, nor had she met Sarah before. They were still essentially strangers, even though they shared the experience of living there full time. But Naomi had the gift of intuition, which she would later capitalize on in her work as a psychic.

Sarah's face contorted. Naomi didn't press for more details. They never discussed it again.

Every night Sarah placed her shoes and a go bag by the door and her passport under her pillow. In the mornings when picking up her mail (the end of the world did not receive home delivery), she chatted with the mailwoman while scanning the back board for any wanted posters with her face on it.

There was a heaviness about her, some darkness people might have even recognized in themselves: the handsome woman with the hunted look.

~

ROSEMARY TOLD FRIENDS that after three years underground in Central and South America and the Caribbean she water-skied back to the country in 1976 in a bikini behind a boat that she and John had motored from the Bahamas—a story so wild as to be unbelievable. She also said she picked the name Sarah from Kabbalah numerology, but her archive includes copious references to John Fowles's 1969 book, *The French Lieutenant's Woman*, about a governess, also named Sarah Woodruff, who is publicly disgraced after confessing to an extramarital affair. The fictional Sarah made daily self-recriminating pilgrimages to a jetty to stare out at the ocean, waiting, or at least appearing to wait, for her long-lost French lieutenant lover to return to her. The act labeled her a whore in the Victorian era and made her attractive to a new suitor, a "moral" gentleman obsessed with collecting rare fossils. It's a novel of love, lust, morality, fate—and self-imposed exile.

Her copy of *The French Lieutenant's Woman* with underlining throughout had a star by one line: "I have forbidden myself to regret the impossible."

Back in 1973, before her return to the United States and following Timothy's arrest and after the jolt of receiving his shocking letter, John made arrangements for them to fly from Europe to Colombia via his contacts with another unnamed "family" in the drug trade. When they arrived, they lost their American passports and relied solely on their World Passports, essentially magical documents that conferred no real protection or authority. A connection back home advised John to avoid the U.S. embassy in Colombia because they would be arrested on the spot. They were fully stateless people.

They bought a farm above Tayrona Park in northern Colombia and spent two years where the jungle meets the sea, prepared to pack up and get out of town within twenty-four hours. She owned one dress and four pairs of underwear, enough clothes to stuff in a bag at a moment's notice, along with her *I Ching* and manuscript in progress, which she had not worked on since leaving Europe.

Rosemary devoted few pages in her archives to her time in Colombia—a few snippets of scenes written in a yellow legal notebook: short flashes of machetes and poisonous spiders, the framed photographs of SS men that she found in their first safe house, the waterfall on the farm in Tayrona Park that dried up during the drought, lying awake in a hammock listening to the night noises of frogs, the image of John cradling a mangled newborn colt in his arms. Tucked next to her entries, she placed a clipped-out article from *The Boston Globe*, an acknowledgment of the grave dangers she faced: US COUPLE MURDERED IN COLOMBIA. The couple, Martin and Barbara

Kaiper, were gunned down at their cattle farm in Bogotá. The paper described their "bullet-riddled bodies" and the speculation that the "murders were tied to drug smuggling from Colombia to the United States." In the margins of the article someone had written to Rosemary, "You have my deepest sympathy."

They lived in Colombia during the rise of the region's drug cartels. After two years, word went around that their cover had been blown. It became too hot, too dangerous, too filled with field agents for two Americans to remain unnoticed. They left their farm, boarded a plane, and never returned.

The couple began a yearlong hopscotch around the Caribbean, jumping from island to island. Along the way, they received safe passage from people with nicknames like "the peacemaker" and the "fugitive financier"—James Bond villains with scary caper stories of their own. According to John, they all wanted to meet Rosemary because they were eager to shake the hand of a woman who had successfully freed her husband from prison.

Rosemary and John almost died aboard a sea rescue vessel converted into a drug smuggling ship, sailing between Martinique and the Guadeloupe Islands. Waves hit the boat, which pitched so ferociously that speakers affixed to its walls flew out of glass windows and into the sea. John remembers riding the waves as if they were grasping onto an abandoned surfboard as it climbed and crashed down into the dark water.

Rosemary and John survived the Sturm und Drang, only to read, once they reached land, an article published in the *International Herald Tribune* that announced a California judge's dissolution of Timothy and Rosemary's nine-year marriage—a divorce granted because his wife was unreachable. Just in time for his release from prison, Timothy was a free man in all senses of the word.

State and federal authorities had rewarded Timothy's yearslong cooperation—in which he outed Michael Kennedy, several members of the Weather Underground, who were in hiding, and his Laguna Beach trial lawyer, George Chula—by granting him early parole from his two drug-related convictions. In the end, only one indictment came down for George Chula, who served forty-five days in Orange County jail for marijuana possession. By September 1975, the statute of limitations expired on the prison break and the federal grand jury still hadn't issued any indictments related to it. Timothy's eagerness to talk—and his public rejection of his former friends, including, bewilderingly, John Lennon—endeared him further to the authorities. Timothy served two years and eight months for his Laguna Beach conviction and then about a year out of his ten-year Laredo prison sentence. The newspapers reported that he left the lockup arm in arm with Joanna Leary, still not his legal wife, living in an undisclosed location as members of the Witness Protection Program. Rosemary, however, was not off the hook; there was still an outstanding bench warrant for her Laguna conviction, among other charges that could be tacked on if she refused to cooperate.

Timothy's release snapped Rosemary's resolve. She wanted to go home. From Bimini she and John posed as tourists out on a day trip and landed back in Coconut Grove, Florida. When they touched down on American soil for the first time in six years, no one gave them a second glance.

They traveled to John's parents' house in Miami and picked up a yellow Porsche with black flames down its side, the most outrageous getaway car imaginable. Old friends from their Canadian safe house days, Sergai and Brigitte Mars, joined them on their drive north to the Mars commune, where the group grew cannabis seeds sourced in Afghanistan on a two-hundred-acre farm in the backwoods of Missouri. The four of them briefly stayed in St. Louis, where Rosemary

grew up, at the storied Chase Hotel, a magnificent Art Deco building, where they gorged on room service and luxury bedding.

On their way back out of town, while refueling at a gas station,
Rosemary saw someone she used to know. Her face burned red hot,
and she slumped down in the backseat. Brigitte and John noticed.
Rosemary brushed off the encounter to John as a guy to whom she
lost her virginity but confessed to Brigitte that it was really her first
husband, John Bradley, the man whose rage had helped propel her on
a path that led her to that moment.

She had lived several lifetimes since she shakily leaned her body
against her father as she walked down the aisle toward her husband.
She had such naive trust that plunging forward into the great unknown would get her to the place where she was meant to be. Did she
still feel that way? Rosemary had traveled continents to return to the
site of her youth, and yet here she was, still shakily propped up by a
man who led her down an unsettled path.

They spent a few harried weeks in New York City until an old
friend found them a safe house in Eastham, Massachusetts, on Cape
Cod, settling down as outlaw expats in their own country.

In hiding, she had lost the pulse of the times. Cultural references
from the prior half decade sailed over her head in small-talk conversations. She interpreted every interested glance through worst-case sce-
narios. She was suspicious, hypervigilant, untrusting. She had lost her
goddess-like power to enrapture and set at ease almost anyone she met.
"There was a suspicion always that there was someone assigned to
watch me. It brought a crazy sense of self-importance to every public
gesture, a ritualistic method of self-examination." She worried about
how she presented—too ill or too tired—and she imagined that picture running in the paper, constantly thinking of herself as a heroine in
her own movie, an attainment she had once desired. "Being underground

is very schizophrenic. As a fugitive, you are so self-important to your-self, yet must appear anonymous to everyone else." The truth was that the Cape might have felt calmer, but it was also more precarious. All it took was one speeding ticket or one eagle-eyed passerby to recog-nize her for it all to go sideways.

She faced the mundane indignities of life underground without health insurance or extra money for doctor's appointments. She put off seeking treatment for a cough that had plagued her since Afghan-istan and hepatitis that she nearly died from in Colombia. Dentistry was a luxury. Years went by before she could afford the mouthful of fillings she had needed since she helped her ex-husband escape prison. The non-romantic realities of life underground.

She wrote to Bubi, her Italian lover, "I'm yet an exile, though in my native land. A recluse, secretive. Though there's no one to share in the secret—a stranger here—anywhere—no political party to adhere to, no clan to cling to . . . A kind of madness, perhaps, to be so alien-ated. Do you understand?"

But, of course, he didn't. Few could.

JOHN, MEANWHILE, devoted his energies to studying *The Book of the Sacred Magic of Abra-Melin the Mage*, a mysterious esoteric text suppos-edly written in the fifteenth century but first printed 250 years later, which described the magical process of meeting one's "Holy Guardian Angel." His prolonged studies required hours of ritualized contempla-tion in the house's attic, punctuated by trips out of town to pursue op-portunities to make money underground and outside the law—a career path that was becoming increasingly problematic for Rosemary. The two were heading toward an impasse that Rosemary had foreseen since they first got together. He was so much younger, and he had an unquenchable thirst for experience—whether that was with drugs, or other women, or mysticism. Rosemary wrote about their differences in desire in a parable about John buying live chickens in a market in Colombia. "John couldn't resist them. He saw all these little chicks pecking away, little gaping beaks, and he bought the whole box."

Rosemary felt that she needed a break from such passions. "I wanted to be quiet and knit my life back together and I was able to do that," she said. She had embraced what she called her "third stage in life," in which she was "no longer the virgin or the goddess. When the greatest strength is called for, the greatest wisdom is called for, and it's not the flowering Aphrodite rising from the seashell. It's something else."

Rosemary now lived her life almost completely sober. She confessed in a letter to a friend that after two hundred acid trips she hadn't "learned a thing." She couldn't stomach dipping a toe into another realm—or "awe—in that awful, be-mushroomed state of wonder"—when her footing in this one was so unsteady. "It was timidity. Fear, if you like, which imagined the LSD state as one of vulnerability," she added. "The idea of being high—and having to deal with the unexpected or the anticipated was intolerable."

Despite what she told her friend about her two hundred trips, Rosemary could not easily discard the insights she had gleaned from her time on the run, from her years of psychedelic use, from the dissolution of her identity. She was, perhaps, too open—someone who had laughed at the cosmic joke of existence, how small each of us is, yet how we are connected, all of us, to something greater. Once you see this, with or without the help of psychedelics, you have to make a choice: put the blinders on and return to the world as it is or throw the blinders away and live outside it. Timothy was someone who could put the blinders on at will. Rosemary could not.

She was haunted by an active dream life, captured in journals buried, poetically, in her ex-husband's archive. She dreamed of owls clawing out her eyes. She killed spiders with a sword and had nightmares of blood running from the faucet, making her call out for her daddy. In one complicated multipart dream documented but not directly commented upon, Rosemary observed a fetal ear develop in utero. She heard a voice say, "The little dears, listening for all their worth."

Rosemary reopened a direct line to her parents and discovered that her father had been seriously ill in her absence. They spoke on the phone a week before he underwent heart surgery. The news of his death came as a total shock: a blood clot had dislodged in the process and killed him on the table. John was out of the country when she learned that she would never see her father—the magician—again. Too dangerous for her to attend the funeral, she sat vigil across the country alone and wrote a poem: "To have such a father / I was blessed / I will be kinder / I'll even be better to myself / For his sake."

Soon after her father's death, Rosemary asked John to leave. Their mutual adoration emerged from the crucible of drama. Without it, in bucolic Cape Cod, their differences—in life stages, in temperament, in desires—were too hard to ignore. Looking back, John has a deeper understanding of the loss she experienced—how she still mourned the life she would never live. It took years; only after reading her private writings after her death did he understand how much she carried.

John took a final picture of Rosemary, in 1978, before their breakup. She looks a decade older than she did two years prior in a photo taken right before their return to the United States. Wrinkles had formed around her mouth, bags lined her eyes, her face was clouded by a miasma of disappointment. Was this the outcome of true ego death? Or reality landing after a life on the run?

"Ms. Everybody," she had written under the Polaroid. She was Sarah Woodruff, a Jane Doe, a woman just like anyone.

"She was really a ghost," John said. "A ghost in a fog."

Twenty

Flashbacks

Over the next decade, living as Sarah Woodruff on Cape Cod without a male anchor for the first time in her adult life, Rosemary expanded her world to include a small group of fellow searchers with whom she built a new version of the community she had sought at Millbrook and with the Brotherhood. She met Judy Givens first, an attractive fellow wash-ashore who shared a buried counterculture past as a member of the Family, a commune often compared to the Manson Family run by the folk musician Mel Lyman. Like Rosemary, Judy saw signs everywhere, seriously interpreted the symbolic messages of her dreams, and studied the tarot and the *I Ching*. Warm and open, Judy *believed*, too. She was one of the few people to whom Rosemary opened up about her past.

Judy's precocious daughter Olan remembers spending her seventeenth birthday with Rosemary because her mother, ten years into a diagnosis of Hodgkin's disease, was too ill to celebrate. Rosemary brought Olan to a Provincetown thrift store where the local drag queens bought their showstoppers. Olan, who knew aspects of Rosemary's real identity, picked through a bin of LPs as Rosemary narrated her connection to the famous names. When she stopped at Donovan, Rosemary pointed to his picture and said, "So flirty."

"She was just so lovely," Olan said of Rosemary. "We went out to lunch, and she made me feel really special, and not sad. It was a sad time, but she was able to make it a magical day."

The local poet Georgia Coxe, also a friend, recalled a similar sensation shopping with Rosemary in an unpublished poem: "It's that time of year again / when you and I go searching / searching through thrift shops / of other's castoffs hunting / hunting the magic object."

Through Judy, Rosemary met David Phillips, a hobbit-esque man with kind eyes who would become the third most important man in her life. Rosemary never had to hide from David, because he already knew who she was.

David, a child of Upper West Side privilege, was supremely persnickety about his preferences and routines but, as a lovable mass of contradictions, also habitually forced himself out of his comfort zone by traveling to developing countries around the world. He was generous and fundamentally *good*, despite not always being nice. (Just ask the servers at the restaurants he visited, whom he would berate because of the temperature or the noise level.) Naturally curious and "radically cerebral," as his brother Adam described him, he studied heraldry as a hobby while smoking cannabis nearly every day for more than three decades. At the same time, friends also noted a woundedness, a childish side—what close relations say resulted from his overbearing mother—that could be enthusiastic, petulant, and content to spend hours solitarily devoted to his varied obsessions.

In 1970, during his second year of law school at the University of Pennsylvania, David took a summer job clerking for Kennedy & Rhine while Michael Kennedy oversaw Timothy Leary's appeals. David met Rosemary outside the law firm's red Victorian building when she had offered him a sip from her cherry juice. Though Rosemary had long forgotten the exchange, David Phillips never did.

An acid trip persuaded David to take up taxi driving instead of the law, even after he passed the State Bar of California. He studied Buddhism and the Vedanta, and for months he carried a suitcase filled with copies of *Be Here Now*, written by Rosemary's old friend Richard Alpert, and passed them out to friends. The book, a countercultural bible, had overthrown *The Psychedelic Experience* as the seminal guide for the enlightened drug youth. The book emerged from Alpert's trip to India, where he studied under the Hindu guru Neem Karoli Baba, who renamed him Baba Ram Dass. "Somewhere inside everybody knows that there is a place which is totally fulfilling not a desperate flick of fulfillment," Ram Dass wrote in *Be Here Now*. "It is a state of fulfillment."

After his mother died in 1980, David and his siblings inherited the family vacation house, in Truro, a tiny village community outside Provincetown with only fifteen hundred full-timers and a downtown consisting of one convenience store, a gas station, a package store (Massachusetts parlance for a liquor store), a library, and a restaurant or two.

"Why not move to Truro?" David thought. "Plenty of nature there!"

Two years later, at age thirty-eight, with enough money socked away and very little interest in material goods, David entered into an early retirement, spending his days reading through the history books at the Wellfleet and Provincetown Public Libraries and hosting his own local television and radio shows.

He never married and felt relieved not to have been bogged down by children. "I am good at analysis but not so good at emotions," he wrote in his own 300,000-word unpublished memoir.

But when Judy introduced him to Sarah Woodruff, David identified a kindred spirit in Rosemary. Soon after, he offered her a room in his house rent-free. Rosemary accepted his generous offer, interpreting the village's name as "True Ro," a sign that she should settle here into her new self. She lived with him for five years, from 1983 to 1987, while she worked at the Provincetown Inn.

They reminisced openly about their surreal shared past lives. David had visited Timothy Leary in prison on behalf of Michael Kennedy to gather information to write his appeal; he had driven up to Millbrook with a friend on a lark (though Rosemary and Timothy were not present); and he had even crossed paths with Joanna Leary through a San Francisco journalist friend. David was so stalwart—so behind her, so safe. He offered her space to release the pressure of keeping silent. She felt lighter with him, more fully herself than she had, perhaps, with anyone else.

They developed a shorthand, spending hours hunched over a backgammon board talking about literature and history and playing a version of it that they invented. "Rosemary was extremely good company," David wrote. "She laughed at my jokes, and I laughed at her jokes, and we exchanged books (she was an insomniac and read through books at an amazing rate)." A shared history linked them initially, but a dedication to ethics bound them. David always defended the underdog, and he admired Rosemary's integrity in the face of some of the world's most intimidating opponents.

When Rosemary left the Cape in 1984 to sell used Pontiacs and live with her Millbrook friend Jean McCreedy in Tucson, Arizona, David persuaded Sarah—he refused to call her Rosemary, even in private—to return to the Cape. "A less suitable job for Rosemary would have been hard to imagine," he wrote. Plus, he was "kind of lonesome in that house in the woods by myself, and would be glad to have her company." He might never have said so, but it was clear as day to friends that David was in love with Rosemary.

With David Phillips's support, Rosemary returned to her memoir, working on a typewriter at a local library, this time heeding David's advice to make this "the Woodruff story." She reframed her intentions; now she wanted to use the book as a catalyst to "understand the process that had led me into exile" and to "reconcile the life I've lived to the life I'm going to live." She initially called the book *Holding Together*, but in the wake of her father's death she renamed it *The Magician's Daughter.*

"I've joined a weekly writing class," she wrote in her diary. The local psychic, Dy Jordan, another intimate, invited Rosemary to the writing group to read aloud from her work in progress (pure fiction, Rosemary insisted to the group) about the time she visited the hammam in Algiers. "I read last night, tremulously and tremendously nervous," she wrote in her diary. When she stopped reading, a hushed silence descended on the group, followed by an explosion of appreciation. "I felt so wonderful I could not believe the feeling. I've never read them aloud before. They work!" Over the coming years, Rosemary, emboldened, began to write more openly about her story. Jordan identified something special in Rosemary's work—and knew that not a word was fiction.

Through the book publishing network in Provincetown, Rosemary managed to land representation from one of the top literary agents in New York City, Frances Goldin, with the caveat that she would not come aboveground to promote the book. Goldin, who passed away in 2020 but whose agency still represents some of the brightest names in literature, famously declared, "I do not represent any material that is sexist, ageist or gratuitously violent." Rosemary's story fit squarely into Goldin's mission statement. The two worked together for several months whipping the manuscript into shape. Goldin even hired a lawyer to look it over to make sure that Rosemary did not plagiarize her own words—the ones that Timothy used in his book *Confessions of a Hope Fiend*. Goldin seemed confident that at least one of the major publishers would buy it. "Hang in there," Goldin wrote as she sent off her book to the industry's top editors.

The response, however, was a resounding no.

"I really don't care to hear again about Tim Leary and all of his friends and their LSD trips. Enough already!" one male editor from the now defunct Lippincott & Crowell wrote. Another editor said that he felt put off by "a too evident display of self-pity." A kinder response described it as "old news." This was the prevailing sentiment of the time. The war on drugs had successfully ended aboveground study of psychedelics. Even black-market sales of psychedelics had declined precipitously, according to the National Institute of Justice. Cocaine replaced consciousness expanders as the drug of choice for hippies turned yuppies in the Reagan era.

In the end, not one publisher thought that her story was worth telling.

She didn't document her disappointment, but once again put her writings back in her leather carrying case—her hope for publication never fully extinguished.

ROSEMARY SETTLED INTO her life as Sarah while the rest of America got a glimpse at the shadowy contours of its own government's invisible hand. The public's education began with the release, in 1978, of *The Search for the "Manchurian Candidate,"* written by the former State Department foreign service officer John Marks. The book pulled from sixteen thousand pages of the CIA's MK-ULTRA program, a mere fraction of the original documents, most of which were destroyed in 1972 at the close of the program by the CIA director, Richard Helms. The book detailed the concealed, decades-long, government-led experimentation in torture and mind control with drugs and behavior modification techniques.

"We weren't doing anything that dreadful; it was just herb for goodness sake it wasn't anything horrible. . . . All we wanted to do was stop the war, create our own religions, enjoy our family life and have a little fun. And in light of everything the government was doing in the 1950s, the MK-ULTRA stuff, the Nazi-like concept of how to treat patients and how to treat people . . . What we were doing seemed benign by comparison," Rosemary said.

After reading another eye-opening book, 1985's *Acid Dreams*, which illuminated the concerted effort of the CIA to fund academic research into psychedelics, including Timothy Leary's programs at Harvard, Rosemary began to doubt her own versions of events. She even admitted in one diary entry that she found it suspect how easily Timothy had escaped from prison. Timothy gave more fodder for her skepticism in various interviews, including one with the writer Walter Bowart, author of *Operation Mind Control* (who was also briefly married to Leary's ex-girlfriend Peggy Hitchcock). "I would say that eighty percent of my movements, eighty percent of the decisions I made were suggested to me by CIA people. I like the CIA! The game they're playing is better than the FBI." Did Timothy knowingly work with the CIA, or was he being provocative by embellishing the fact that a large portion of psychedelic research received trickle-down CIA funding in the 1950s and 1960s? Unclear. The point is that the more Rosemary learned about the government's role in the spread of psychedelics into the counterculture, the less safe she felt on the Cape. With a warrant for her arrest still open, she was convinced, even a decade after Timothy's release, that agents were still actively hunting her.

Meanwhile, many who benefited from Rosemary's silence were

coming aboveground. Bernardine Dohrn came out of hiding in 1980 with Michael Kennedy's help and, after most of the charges were dismissed due to the FBI's ill-gotten evidence, served seven months in prison for refusing to testify against an ex–Weather Underground member. Once released from prison, Dohrn worked as a law professor; her husband, Bill Ayers, who did not serve any time, became a professor of education. During his 2008 presidential run, Barack Obama's relationship with his Hyde Park neighbors Bill Ayers and Bernardine Dohrn became tabloid fodder as the Weather Underground's exploits reached yet another generation. Jeff Jones now lobbies for environmental issues in Albany, New York.

Michael Kennedy briefly went underground during the Brotherhood trial, but without Rosemary's cooperation he returned to the United States when no charges were filed against him. Kennedy continued to practice law for four more decades without the taint of aiding and abetting a drug convict's prison escape. Through Kennedy, Rosemary's silence reaches two U.S. presidents: Bill Clinton during his Whitewater case (Kennedy represented Susan McDougal, who refused to give testimony against Clinton) and Donald Trump (against whom Kennedy provided counsel to Ivana during their contentious divorce).

After seven years on the run, Eldridge Cleaver returned to the United States in 1975 and spent less than a year in jail awaiting trial for outstanding attempted murder charges related to the 1968 shootout that led to his exile. Cleaver eventually pleaded down to a lesser charge of assault and did twelve hundred hours of community service. Many accused him of cooperating with the Feds to get the reduced sentence, as Timothy did. Once released, he rebirthed himself as a born-again Christian minister and a virulent anticommunist and, eventually, became addicted to crack cocaine. Kathleen, meanwhile, divorced Cleaver in 1987, attended Yale Law School—"I wanted to learn how to get people out of prison," she said—and became a professor at Emory University, successfully campaigning on behalf of death-row inmates and members of the Black Panthers who had been incarcerated. Abbie Hoffman, dodging charges related to the intent to sell and distribute cocaine, disappeared in 1973, lived as Barry Freed in uppermost New York state, where the country touches Canada, resurfacing seven years later to serve a year in prison. In 1989, Abbie, who had been diagnosed with bipolar disorder, overdosed on phenobarbital at age fifty-two. The coroner determined that his death was a suicide. The Brotherhood leader Michael Randall went underground in 1973 but was busted at his home with his wife, Carol Randall (widow of the Brotherhood of Eternal Love founder, John Griggs), in 1983; he did five years in prison. Rosemary clipped out news of each arrest but did not maintain direct contact with any of them, other than Christmas cards sent by Carol, years after Randall's release, addressed to Sarah Woodruff.

※

ROSEMARY TOOK A LOVER, a married restaurant owner and legendary ladies' man whose restaurant centralized Provincetown's West End social world. The East and West Ends—the gay side of town and the domain of Portuguese fishermen, respectively—coexisted but rarely overlapped. Rosemary's lover probably couldn't have pointed out an LSD tab in a lineup, and that's the way she liked it. He bought her golf clubs and putted with her on the green, cooked her blood sausages, and clammed with her at Herring Cove Beach. Though prone to big emotions, crying and laughing easily, a "sucker for hard luck stories," as a local newspaper article described him, he had a wife and children. With him, Rosemary was insulated from too much love.

She lived this way, placid as the glacier lakes that dot the region, until she heard the familiar voice giving an interview promoting a new memoir titled *Flashbacks* on her local radio station, where she worked part time.

While Rosemary kept her head belowground, Timothy had secured a spot back in the sun. While in prison, he wrote about his new "PSY PHI" philosophy, as detailed in 1973's *Neurologic* and *Starseed* and 1974's *Terra II*, some co-written and all published by Joanna Leary, in which he described the "eight-circuit model" of the human nervous system, which could, if properly tuned, commune with alien life. Once released, however, he embraced the ethos of 1980s excess, embarking on a road tour as a philosopher/stand-up comedian, and even co-anchored a speaking tour with his onetime arch-nemesis G. Gordon Liddy. He remarried—though not Joanna Leary, whom he broke up with after his release from prison. His new wife was the glamorous Barbara Chase, a woman connected in Hollywood and almost always photographed in bug-eyed sunglasses. He adopted her five-year-old son, Zach. Once again, Susan was not pleased by the match. When she heard the news of their nuptials, she asked her father in front of Barbara, "Are you still married to Rosemary?"

With Barbara Chase by his side, Timothy was living the high life again—attending Andy Warhol's star-studded funeral, dining at Spago and Mr. Chow, posing for *Vanity Fair*. Still, he couldn't repress his trickster drive toward contrarianism. He often took his new wife's name when writing combative letters to the editors in newspapers across the country, protesting everything from traffic tickets to "literary dingbats" like Norman Mailer. Several brushes with the law followed—smoking a cigarette in an airport, for example, or a domestic disturbance call due to a bad trip with Barbara on ketamine at his Laurel Canyon home. In many ways, Timothy embodied the clown that he had envisioned himself to be during his shattering first acid trip taken from Hollingshead's mayonnaise jar.

But *Flashbacks*, published in 1983, represented a push toward legitimacy. This book, well written and engaging, captured a far wider market than work on alien life. *Flashbacks* was an attempt to reframe his legacy in a new era as a wise fool who had anticipated the future but never lost his sense of humor. Despite outright fabrications and over-the-top embellishments (such as an impossible sex scene with Marilyn Monroe), he was largely successful in reminding people of who he once was. The book became a comeback of sorts.

Flashbacks features Rosemary's name throughout. He included the story of their first encounter and the ardency of their love—the Wittgenstein and the sex by the waterfall and her influence on his writing and philosophy. He excluded the many hiccups and casual cruelties along the way, ascribing a mythological inevitability to their union—until she left him, depressed and desolate and briefly hooked on heroin.

Before the book, Rosemary believed that Timothy had no specific knowledge of her whereabouts. The few times that money had changed hands in an unwritten alimony agreement, her brother, Gary, acted as intermediary, gathering a few thousand here or there from Timothy and depositing it into a bank account, which Rosemary could draw from without direct contact and without his knowing her location.

But *Flashbacks* revealed that he knew more than he let on. Timothy described Rosemary's life on the run: "Rosemary, twelve years after our flight into exile, remains underground, the enigmatic figure of our dreams. Does she stand radiant, wrapped in a black cape on an Atlantic jetty, waiting for the sign to break her silence? Will her adventure ever be told?"

Timothy was clearly referencing *The French Lieutenant's Woman*—the name, the adultery, the jetty, the shawl, the silence. He knew that she lived at the end of the world.

Twenty-One

The Story of My Punishment

After five years together in Cape Cod, David decided to leave behind the dreary winters to return to the site of his initial awakening, where his life had once overlapped so cosmically with Rosemary's—back to San Francisco. He invited Rosemary to join him, but she declined. Unlike David, she was not yet prepared to face her past full time. Plus, where would she work? Who would hire the mysterious Sarah Woodruff? Instead, Rosemary stayed put on the Cape, relocating to the outermost part of it to a rental apartment in Provincetown with the cartoonist Eleanor Dalton.

Three years went by before Rosemary finally accepted David's invitation to house-sit while he traveled in Southeast Asia. She kept a diary of her trip, addressing her entries to David, as a chronicle of a life on the cusp of transition.

Each morning, she awoke to the familiar sounds of the sea in David's bedroom at the back of his 1930s center patio home in Outer Parkside. The view from his bay windows spanned across the Pacific Ocean to the Marin Headlands. She read John McPhee's book on Alaska, *Coming into the Country*, saw David Lynch's *Wild at Heart* in the theater, ate liver and onions at the Butler and the Chef restaurant, and smoked cigarettes during long soaks in his bathtub. Perusing the classifieds in the morning newspapers, she allowed herself to imagine a new life here. She met with old friends, including Carol Randall, who took her to a vegan restaurant—the food of their youth—but now she pined for more liver and onions.

Rosemary did not visit San Francisco as a mere tourist; she was a woman on a mission. Prior to her visit, Michael Kennedy had consulted on her bid for clemency and, after some digging, found that the Feds would agree to drop their charges if California would do the same. But when he made efforts with state officials, including former Governor Jerry Brown, they could not assure Kennedy that Rosemary would walk free without some jail time. It was too risky. "I've been thinking about having to be in prison," she wrote. "I don't think I could do it again willingly. The terrible fear in never knowing when you'll get out. Time can be tacked on for minor infractions of the rules. Once you are inside prison you are completely within the power of the system."

Rosemary also provided a second, less obvious reason for staying underground: resurfacing would open her back up to Timothy. As Sarah, she could live under the radar, but a trial would drag her name into the papers—providing Timothy with a new opportunity to usurp the narrative. "I think what she was concerned with was that he would smear her in some way with the Brotherhood. Smear her with Weather. Smear her with drugs. Smear her in some fashion. She was terrified. . . . She knew the treachery he was capable of," Michael Kennedy said.

"Whenever I weighed getting my name cleared and being able to see my mother and family freely, I had to weigh it against the real freedom I was feeling for the first time in a long time, which Cape Cod gave me," Rosemary said. It is clear that Rosemary was not hiding from the law alone or even Timothy—but from the person she had been with him. Cape Cod allowed her to slough off the past and grasp hold of a kind of liberation she had imagined for herself since boarding the train out of St. Louis in her teens. Each phase of Rosemary's path took its pound of flesh—compromises, sometimes impossible ones—but headed toward the attainment of freedoms: freedom of movement, freedom of love, freedom of the body, freedom of the mind, freedom from the ego, and finally, an elusive kind that seemed the most hard won and confusing, the freedom to remain anonymous. But was *this* what she had imagined? Or was it yet another incomplete state of yearning—of limbo? She clung to some desire to redeem herself—yet another type of freedom. This is why Rosemary had traveled across the country—to get a second opinion.

Unfortunately, the San Francisco lawyer, unnamed in her records, agreed with Kennedy's assessment of the situation and explained why her case was thornier than it appeared. Not only did she face six months in prison, but she had left the country with an outstanding arrest warrant, had violated her probation, and had abandoned her appeal. The result was a "nightmare of legal problems," he told her, according to her diaries. The only way to get a judge to drop the probation violation was to argue that Rosemary was a victim. "An argument could be made that I was essentially being manipulated—Tim's influence."

The news sickened her. "I am feeling like shit—looking at the past several decades as a total waste. No occupation, no skills other than minimal survival and still focusing on the possibility of prison. I want to be back on the Cape with the covers pulled over my head," she wrote. Rosemary continued to browbeat herself. "David are you as good as I remember you to be? Able to listen to swill such as this and not condemn me? I feel like such a fucking fool! I had such expectations for a life here and now I feel as though I'm condemned to the East and California is some bitch goddess forbidding entrance." Later that day, Rosemary crossed paths with a homeless man downtown holding a sign that read HARD TIMES. She imagined that hers would read PAST LIVES.

Still, she spent the rest of her time in San Francisco reconnecting with people from her Millbrook era: Peggy Hitchcock, Ram Dass, Billy Hitchcock, among others. She had no choice. An unexpected name had crept back into her life—a visitation from a ghost. Underneath the numbers and names of old friends was one line: "Of Susan I cannot speak just yet."

On September 9, 1990—two weeks into Rosemary's stay at David's house—Susan Leary's name appeared in the regional California newspapers under the headline DAUGHTER OF LSD'S LEARY DEAD FROM JAIL HANGING.

> LOS ANGELES: The jailed daughter of 1960s LSD guru Timothy Leary died of an apparent suicide two days after she was found hanging by a shoelace from the bars in her cell, authorities said Thursday.

Complicated and troubled, Susan had passed from this earth after a spiral so hideous that even Rosemary, who knew of the turmoil Susan faced from childhood, could never have anticipated how tragically her story would end. Timothy had described his daughter in a letter to a friend as "a little lost seven-year-old girl," but Susan was no longer the young woman who looked like a child, who loved modern dance enough to study it, who read J. D. Salinger, and who adored her father. In the years since, Susan had married David Martino, who shared many overlapping mental health issues, and had three children. All the while, as letters to her father over this period show, she grew unhinged, her notes taking on a lurid, fantastical, and childlike quality as she aged. Susan, too sick for the responsibility of motherhood and living on welfare and $300 monthly payments from her father, took her rage out on her children, especially on her oldest daughter, who had to be hospitalized in 1978 after Susan beat her with a mini baseball bat that Timothy had given her as a gift. Eventually, all of her children would enter the foster care system.

Susan had tried to get her life back on track by taking the most improbable route for a child of the high priest; in 1980, she enlisted in an army medic training program at Fort Sam Houston's Academy of Health Sciences in Texas. Routine seemed to work for her, with a few hiccups along the way, including angry witch spells sent to her father and arrests for a public nuisance crime. She appeared to pull her life together to some degree. By 1988 she was living with her boyfriend, the security guard Joel Ruben Chavira.

On the evening of December 18, 1988, Chavira woke up to a deafening explosion and Susan ranting that Chavira had given her AIDS. He realized when he felt the wetness at the back of his head that Susan had shot him, point-blank, as he slept. Chavira somehow survived, and Susan was arrested for attempted murder. Her six-year-old daughter was home when it happened. Found to be too mentally incompetent to stand trial, Susan spent the following year at the Los Angeles County women's corrections facility, the Sybil Brand Institute. There, she wrote an eleven-page document called "The Story of My Punishment." The pages were meant to be a recording of her life in prison—the intake, the forced showers, the texture of the prison uniform, the boredom, the soda machine, many impressions similar to the ones found in her father's *Jail Notes*. She hoped that it would make her family proud, raise her profile, and help her secure freedom. At the end of her book she had written, "To be continued."

Susan had waited for the perfect time to hang herself, the moment when the guards were farthest from her cell on rounds. She was still alive when the guards found her hanging by her shoelaces, just as her mother had been when she was found by Timothy in the garage.

Rosemary blamed herself for "not being a good enough mother to her." She called Ram Dass—the perfect voice from her past to absolve her from these unfair self-recriminations. "The die was cast for Susan regardless of what we did for Tim," Ram Dass said, according to her diary. "Let her go."

But the spigots that she had kept tightly closed had suddenly loosened. Seventeen years had passed since she'd seen Timothy's face up close. "Half of my life had revolved around his orbit," Rosemary wrote. "Despite countless name changes and various disguises and isolation in far-flung places in the world, all prompted by my life as a fugitive and a convicted felon, I had never been able to forget that we had been partners, lovers, mated."

"Finally, I forgave him," she wrote.

This forgiveness was not inevitable; she made the decision to invite him back into her orbit on her terms this time.

She called Timothy's number, supplied to her by Ram Dass. His wife, Barbara, picked up and wrote her name on a paper filled with the many other famous names who had called with condolences.

Timothy didn't return her call.

WHATEVER THE REASON or combination of reasons, six months later, in 1991, Rosemary moved to California. After her trip, Rosemary returned to the Cape briefly to her apartment in Provincetown to make an inventory of her belongings. She would consign a black coral bracelet from Timothy, melt down any gold, and give away most of her belongings—a few boxes of costume jewelry to Judy's daughter Olan, her lover's golf clubs to her psychic friend Naomi Lake, and a child's chest of drawers to her roommate, Eleanor Dalton. She'd sell the rest in a yard sale—though, she wrote, "perhaps a bonfire would be best." At the sale, people thumbed through handwoven shawls, her sheepskin jacket from Afghanistan that reeked of patchouli, esoteric books, cheap vintage furniture that looked impressively expensive, and bins of jazz records. A local psychiatrist bought most of her clothing, including a fabulous beaded fringe vest. Carolyn Miller, another town psychic, walked away with a full-length mirror that still hangs in her one-room house in Truro and was later involved in a supernatural event too strange to recount here. Bits and pieces of Rosemary scattered around the Cape.

Before she packed what remained, she brought an old photograph from her media heroine days to her stylist and asked him to cut her hair the same way—perhaps hoping to recapture the shine she had lost. And then she disappeared, up and left, leaving some friends and acquaintances wondering for years what had happened to the handsome woman with the hunted look. She would never live on the Cape again.

She first stayed with her mother in her retirement village in Southern California, the longest time they had spent together since Rosemary was a teenager. Rosemary regressed. Mother and daughter fought over minor things, like the smell of Rosemary's strange herbal teas and the way she hung her stockings to dry over the shower curtain. Neither of them seemed willing to discuss what really bothered them: the years of loss and resentment that stemmed from Rosemary's wanderings and Ruth's belief that she had failed as a mother. "I feel ashamed that I did nothing for her and she did everything for me. Well, now I have to make it up to her—as always," Rosemary wrote. The reunion didn't last long but did give her time to connect with her precocious niece, Gary's daughter, Kate, who loved reading as much as her mysterious aunt did. Rosemary gave her several books that would take on an almost fabled influence: the illustrated book *The Reason for a Flower*, about the processes of pollination, and later, when Kate was beginning to mature, the classic sex-ed guide *Our Bodies,*

Ourselves, which featured frank discussions of anatomy, birth control, masturbation, and abortion.

From her mother's house, Rosemary moved back in with David in San Francisco in the apartment on the ground floor, once again rent-free. Over countless cigarettes, they resumed their backgammon nights. David introduced her as "Sarah from Cape Cod" to his closest friends, Makiko and Les Wisner, who owned a café in San Francisco. The Wisners were charmed by her without knowing anything about her past, proving that she hadn't lost as much power as she had feared. Her range of literary references, especially her deep knowledge of the Beat writers, dazzled them. "She was really an impressive woman," Les said.

But being able to quote Beat poetry didn't necessarily lead to a viable career or life path. She made a list of what she wanted, this time around: an apartment with a garden, a job that would utilize her talents, affordable health care, to finish and publish her book in progress, and, finally, "the time and freedom to contribute to the wellbeing of others"—that sense of community that had always been at the core of her search for meaning.

Her dreams of finding meaningful work, however, faded away when facing the reality of the classified section. She begged her contacts for work, and even sent Ram Dass her résumé in the hopes that he could arrange something for her, but nothing materialized. Despite swearing never to work in hospitality again, she applied for a job as an innkeeper at a bed-and-breakfast south of San Francisco at Pillar Point, where the land spirals into itself in Half Moon Bay, a smaller, mirror image of her inn on the other side of the country. The inn itself was relatively new but also quaint, a New England–style bed-and-breakfast for weekenders honeymooning away from the stress of city life in San Francisco. When old friends heard of her new position, they started addressing letters to "Sarah Woodruff, the High Priestess of Innkeeping."

Nina Graboi—the grande dame of the League, who had recorded the first encounter between John Schewel and Rosemary at her party in Manhattan and had maintained sporadic contact with Rosemary since 1980—was one of the few people from *the before* invited to Pillar Point. The two women, bound by the past, would take walks or play Scrabble. In one letter written after a visit, Nina had asked, "Have you been able to keep your faith in a divine guidance through the times when all seemed dark?"

Nina had. She had relocated from Woodstock, New York, to Santa Cruz, California, drawn by the promise of working with a new generation of psychonauts engaged, as she wrote, "in educating the young to the possibilities and the pitfalls of the psychedelics that brought me here." Santa Cruz was the incubation site of the quiet re-birth of psychedelic studies. The Multidisciplinary Association for Psychedelic Studies (MAPS), a nonprofit research organization, had opened there in 1986. And the University of California, Santa Cruz, known for housing many psychedelic enthusiastic professors, made the surf city a destination for hippies run out of town elsewhere.

Rosemary had also reconnected with Jack Leary through letters after her return to California. One of the most moving statements she'd heard in her life was learning that Jack told a mutual friend that he considered her "as close to a mother as anyone he'd ever known." And the more she learned about the life Jack had created for himself since he was released from prison, the more she admired him. After his rift from his father, Jack relocated to the Pacific Northwest and trained to be a boilermaker, making refinery cooling towers for Bechtel, one of the largest construction companies in the world. He married and appeared by all accounts to be a devoted father, who provided his children with a safe and caring environment, removed from the lure of fame and alternate realities.

Rosemary, meanwhile, was still living a lie; her employer had no idea of her past or her real name, and, as she wrote to a friend, "if they did would probably fire me on the spot." Nothing about her time there was easy. Fourteen-hour days. Breakfast for the guests before they awoke. Planning guest services and handling reservations. She hired and fired the small staff, which meant that when someone didn't work out or show up, she'd have to clean up the mess, literally scrubbing the toilets. She had moved out of David's house to live in a small room on the property barely bigger than a utility closet with one day off a week. According to her tax filings, which she filed under her real Social Security number but with her fake name, she made $24,000 in gross wages. Once, when Rosemary was complaining about her finances to David's friend Makiko, she threw the obvious out there: "Why don't you just marry David?"

It would have made sense. They had so much in common; they made each other laugh; and he truly admired her—even saw the goddess within her. For her, though, David would not be a suitable romantic partner. She gave a typical Rosemary response: "That would be really easy, wouldn't it?"

The long days allowed few hours to write. Still, she cut out advice from authors and gathered materials to attend workshops and applied for grants, divulging her identity to nameless, faceless committees, begging them for money and a room of her own where she could finally finish her book. "To write has always been my wish—I hope the foundation can find some mechanism to enable me to quietly leave the position I am currently at which barely supports my rusting car," she wrote in an application. A few wrote back expressing their unfortunate inability to fund her writing. Most didn't reply. She put her work back in the drawer, again.

And then Timothy Leary called.

Twenty-Two

Her Story

At the bottom right corner on a stray page in Timothy Leary's archive in bubble letters filled in with pink highlighter is one word:

ROSEMARY

Timothy doodled his thoughts during a conversation with Ram Dass, who told him about Rosemary's return to the West Coast, how she worked as an innkeeper and wrote in her off-hours. Right above her name, in exaggerated scrawl highlighted in neon blue, Timothy wrote, "She has not gotten over me!!!"

Around the same time, Peggy Hitchcock, the great connector, who remained in contact with Timothy over the years, reunited with Rosemary. During an exchange, Rosemary had given her a photograph of Jack Leary and asked her to share it with Timothy. In the picture, Jack wears a washed-out red polo shirt and stands beside his wife and two sun-kissed children, Timothy's grandchildren, whom he had never met. They were estranged and had barely spoken since Jack's public denouncement of his father in 1974.

In light of Peggy's reveal, Timothy wrote to Rosemary in June 1992, the first time they communicated directly since the letter he sent to John's parents in Miami in 1973 urging her to cooperate with the FBI. The letter showed that despite time passing, not much had changed. He still had no concept of boundaries. He didn't apologize; there was no evidence of deference; instead, he dove deep into his own disappointment over the estrangement of his son and asked Rosemary—of whom he'd already demanded so much—to make an effort to reconcile them. His tone shifted into flirtation once he moved past the subject of his son. "I'd very much like to see you," he wrote, offering her an invitation to a dinner party at his house. "You are very dear and radiant in my memory banks. If you would like to have a reunion, I hope you will write or phone me."

It took her four months to respond. But recovering from the deaths of her Cape Cod friend Judy Givens, who had succumbed to cancer, and her former lover the Portuguese restaurateur, Rosemary, in a vulnerable, lonely state, felt receptive to reconciliation. She was also aware, through mutual friends, that Timothy faced his own health crucible and that Barbara had left him. She wrote him back succinctly and unemotionally: "Yes, let's meet, but not at a dinner party. Sunday, the 18th after 6pm is best. I'll call you to suggest a place."

On an overcast but temperate December evening, Rosemary waited for Timothy to show at the entrance of the Asian Art Museum in Golden Gate Park, the site where Leary had once announced his new slogan to the world without Rosemary. It was a serene location that was public enough to disappear into a crowd if she changed her mind. "I guess I still did not really trust him not to turn me in. I was still a fugitive," she said. She was ever the artful dodger.

She spotted him first by his jaunty walk, the same walk that had transfixed her at another gallery, in Manhattan, three decades earlier.

But up close Timothy was so physically altered as to be unrecognizable—gray, stooped, and frail. Rosemary realized how different she looked, too—heavier and older in her shapeless Eileen Fisher clothing—a woman who lost her breath when walking uphill and had to bring cookies to the car mechanic for him to pay any attention to her, as she joked to a friend. "Ms. Everybody," she called herself, "with age and weight as a costume." Aging was harder for Rosemary, the truly beautiful.

They embraced.

The park metamorphosized into a movie set. "Vista Vision. Technicolor. Widescreen," she wrote. They laughed and held hands. Eons transpired. No time had passed at all. With him, holding him, she remembered his humor and joy; how he filled the space with a great balloon of his enthusiasm. Timothy was "the brightest and funniest. . . . He's the most exciting game in town," she said. This was his power—their power together—the force of *them*. Without him, her life meandered into the humdrum. But with him, the excitement of possibility came rushing back like the force of the waterfall where they used to make love at Millbrook. Though she still resented the way he had used and endangered her, she loved him. And he needed her. She had been mated to him. These weren't mere words to Rosemary.

He asked her to marry him.

"No," she said.

"Well then," he said, laughing. "I'll have to cross you off my list."

She had stepped back into his vortex.

⁓

IN THE MONTHS after their first encounter, Timothy called Rosemary almost every day, sometimes multiple times a day, inundating her with daily letters and faxes, sending articles addressed to her alias about their varied escapades with love notes in the margins.

> Dear Sarah,
> Renewing our friendship in the last few months has been a precious experience. You are a truly magical, poetic, elegant spirit. What luck to have shared 7 years with you. I'm throbbing with admiration and affection for you.
> Signed Nino.

The juvenile eagerness of his passions had not coarsened. Next to an article he faxed her about his 1970 escape, he had written, "Darling Ro . . . When we end our phone calls I think 'Rosemary is the funniest—most elegant woman of the 20–21 century.' Much love, T." He sent over a blown-up image of them in the courtroom in Orange County, Rosemary in a printed peasant dress and Timothy, dapper and handsome in a suit. "Good morning," it read. "I love you." He tried to persuade her to give up her job and join him in Laurel Canyon, where he had lived with his ex-wife. "Everyone here loves you," he said, adding the following day that he wanted her to "join the family."

"Come down here and be my mate," he said, according to her transcription of their phone call. She had started taking notes again, as if her life mattered enough now to document it. She also revisited her memoir, sharing parts with him, opening herself up to his criticism. He urged her to tamp down her negativity about the past (a self-serving edit). He reconnected Rosemary with their old friend Anita Hoffman, who had escaped from the bathroom window in Algeria and with whom Timothy had rekindled a close friendship following Abbie Hoffman's suicide in 1989. Timothy suggested that Rosemary and Anita co-write a book together. Anita loved the idea, and the two began to work on a proposal, tentatively titled *Her Story*.

Few friends in their orbit held a grudge on Rosemary's behalf. In-stead, they sent adoring and supportive notes about their reunion. "Can't tell you how delighted I am by your good news! I'm so happy that you and Tim spent some time together and that some old wounds can heal," Nina Graboi wrote. Her Provincetown roommate, Eleanor Dalton, wrote, "I don't know why I'm so delighted at you and T. being in touch again and the proposal. Just seems something is right in the world again . . . and that is so wonderful." Even her mother wrote positively about the reconciliation, her handwriting tremulous in her advanced age: "I am happy for you and Tim and hope you both have much happiness and love for a long while."

At night, alone in her closet-sized room, Rosemary contemplated taking the leap back into Timothy's life full time and relocating to Los Angeles to live with him. The thought of giving up the grueling job—the needy, sometimes rude patrons, the early morning break-fasts, the constant revolving door of housecleaners and staff—and finishing her book was too attractive to ignore. She raised the subject with her brother, Gary.

"Well, Tim wants me to marry him," she told him.

Gary tried to hide his disapproval. "What's in it for you?" he asked.

He told her that he worried she would inherit all his debt when he died. That he needed a caretaker, not a wife. Gary's take must have lined up with her own fears, so she continued to turn down Timothy's marriage proposals. Just to make sure, she dusted off her tarot deck and recorded a reading of their possible union. "The devil crossed by virtue, covered by change. Disappointment. Indolence, leading to pleasure and [debauchery], prompted by the cruel Magus." If the tarot offered a Rorschach window into her psyche, then she was making the right decision.

Timothy needed the grounding force of a woman, but he also seemed to want to right a wrong; he urged Rosemary to seek legal counsel to clear her name and come back aboveground. He teamed up with David Phillips, who, like Gary, saw through the "naked opportunism of Tim's looking to Rosemary again wife-wise" but still supported her decision to reconcile. David considered Timothy one of his guides from his *Be Here Now* days and, despite knowing about his personal failings, maintained an enduring fondness for the man who had helped open his eyes to another way of living. Plus, Timothy could aid Rosemary's bid for clemency—at the very least help her raise money to get her case off the ground. In a satisfying role reversal, Timothy took this on as his mission, reaching out to a few interested parties on Rosemary's behalf while insisting he remain in the shadows. "I am a 'high profile,' controversial person. A Maverick, you know," he wrote to Nina Graboi, who joined the campaign to raise funds for Rosemary. Together they came up with $5,000—the bulk of the sum provided by an artist heiress and mutual friend, who preferred to remain anonymous.

David then suggested to Timothy that Rosemary should appeal directly to the authorities, something Rosemary had rejected summarily in previous discussions. Now with the two loudest male voices in her life directing her, one of whom was once the principal reason for not moving forward, Rosemary finally relented and placed her fate in the hands of the courts.

Timothy and David secured Rosemary new representation, a criminal defense attorney located in Santa Ana named Roger Hanson, who barely registered the name Timothy Leary when he was contacted—and doesn't remember the case, nor the client, today. They purposefully chose not a fancy, pedigreed lawyer who might make the DA feel territorial but a local, workmanlike one who could do the deal quickly and quietly without pissing anyone off in the process. Hanson agreed to do it for a bargain, taking home whatever was left of the $5,000 after paying her penalties.

Coached by Timothy and David, Hanson reached out directly to the Orange County Superior Court judge Michael Brenner, who had a reputation for fairness, and presented the argument for freeing Rosemary: Rosemary was a victim. Her crimes occurred when she was under the undue influence of a charismatic guru. She had lived a peaceful and law-abiding life since. Twenty years after a mistake in her youth. Wasn't it time to let the past go? Rosemary winced; she felt she was selling herself out as a brainless follower—it was the same role she had been forced to play during her first trial back in Poughkeepsie—but she understood now how necessary it was to make the argument stick. "Indeed," David wrote, concerning Timothy's influence, "there may have been some truth in it."

Hanson also contacted the U.S. Attorney to make an informal inquiry about federal charges for her interstate flight and passport violation; those too were forgotten.

The response came back from the Orange County DA: "All parties concur in finally terminating this case." The deputy district attorney Carl Armbrust believed that there was no point in sending her to jail. "So far as I could determine, she hasn't been in any trouble," he said. "I think she was led astray by Mr. Leary." The hearing was brief. "She desires to help her mother in Orange County, who is critically ill," the judge said. "With that in mind, I'm writing to grant that request."

Roger Hanson produced Rosemary's penalty check, while Rosemary stayed home, still too frightened to show up in court just in case the ruling went crosswise; plus, she refused to be photographed because her employers knew nothing about her criminal background. The check, which included a fine plus penalty assessments, totaled

$1,080, an auspicious, sacred number. In the dharmic religions the number 108 is a blessing—the number of questions that the Bodhisattva Mahamati asks the Buddha, the number of beads on a Tibetan rosary, the number of volumes in *The Word of the Buddha*, the number of temples of Vishnu. It was also the number of reasons for loving her that Timothy had outlined from his jail cell in "108 Memories of Our Current Incarnation."

And with that omen, "any bench warrants now outstanding for Ms. Leary are recalled and criminal proceedings against her herewith terminate."

Several national and local newspapers, including *The New York Times* and *The Orange County Register*, covered the trial; it wasn't front-page coverage, but she had joined the ranks of her many friends whose clippings she used to hide by her bed in her go bag in Cape Cod. Rosemary told the *Times*, "It is really difficult to describe how freedom has changed my life. I have the joy of being myself again, of not having a dual personality, not concealing myself and my past from my friends and the people I've met along the way." Rosemary sent a copy of this article to her old friends at the Cape Cod radio station and signed it "With love from Rosemary Woodruff."

Friends from all phases of her life reached out with notes of congratulations, as if celebrating the birth of a child. "You are incredible," read a note from the woman who had lent her house in Eastham to Rosemary and John when they first arrived on the Cape. "But we already knew that." Eleanor Dalton commented on her "quiet endurance and survival. . . . Hats off and I can't stop beaming. . . . How you did it so calmly and endlessly inventing a self is a mystery and a marvel and a tip to your vast resources." Her Millbrook friend and fellow League member Jean McCreedy, with whom she had lived in Tucson, wrote, "Now you can be Rosemary again."

David's friends Makiko and Les Wisner recalled that the moment they learned of the hearing was when they were out for lunch with Rosemary. Sitting across from each other, Rosemary reached into her purse and placed the *New York Times* newspaper clipping on the table.

"Makiko, this is me," she said.

Makiko read the headline: ONE OF TIMOTHY LEARY'S FORMER WIVES COMES IN FROM THE COLD.

Makiko was shocked. "You're a famous person!"

After twenty-four years on the run, Rosemary, fifty-eight years old, was finally free.

SEVEN MONTHS LATER, Rosemary attended an auction.

The competition was fierce, the auction house would later say. Most people came to bid on the correspondence of the American West outlaw Emmett Dalton, who had robbed two banks in one day in Kansas, or for the various first editions also on the block, including *Huckleberry Finn* and *The Federalist*.

The Pacific Book Auction Gallery, located in downtown San Francisco near the water, specialized in rare books, with the motto "The staff understands and appreciates not only rare books, but rare people." A young house in a world that valued the old, the company had held its first auction two years prior in 1992, and after $2 million in sales earned a reputation for being one of the most successful auction houses on the West Coast.

Rosemary stood by Lot 400. It consisted of seventy-four letters written, per the auction's internal newsletter, "by the wife of Timothy Leary to the LSD guru while he was in jail during 1970." She had reread the accompanying $10 catalog several times before her visit. The envelopes were addressed to Inmate No. 26358 and written on yellow paper in red scrawl.

"May I see this one?" Rosemary asked, pointing to a magenta paper covered in her own faint black scrawl. She didn't have to lean in to know what the words said. "I looked in the mirror and thought about you and I laughed and laughed and loved you so."

Another one: "We will have a beautiful life, my heart. By next year my belly will be full and each year after that and we will watch our children grow in love and beauty."

Seventy-four of her handwritten letters up for sale to the highest bidder. "This page is dedicated to the memories of Morocco." The smell of pungent burning rosewood and the warmth of the flickering flames in a room crowded with musicians playing thousand-year-old trance music floated up from the page. "I believe loving you, when you let me, is as natural as breathing." These images linked to others: the itch of a blond wig against her scalp, the sudden dissociation of not recognizing herself in the airplane's bathroom mirror, while $100 bills shoved in her underwear chafed against her inner thighs. These came with other sense memories: the smell of institutional cleaning supplies in Poughkeepsie and the sound of a swishing broom against concrete prison floors in Switzerland, the swaying of rain-battered palm trees in northern Africa, the feel of cool cotton against her skin in Afghanistan.

No one would dare connect this invisibly middle-aged woman with the countercultural goddess who had written those letters thirty years earlier.

Somehow (some have speculated that Timothy had left Rosemary's letters behind in an attic during a move), the lot had fallen into the hands of an unknown third party, who had approached the Pacific Auction House to profit off this intimate part of her history. Rosemary understood from battles over other estates that though the intellectual copyright still belonged to her, as the sender, the physical letters belonged to the person who possessed them. And she could not afford to buy her own letters.

By the end of the day the letters sold to Stanford University for $1,900, a few hundred dollars higher than the pre-auction estimate. Rosemary later told the same reporter for *The New York Times* who had covered her trial that the experience was "more emotionally upsetting than I could imagine."

"One reason is because I've been so encapsulated all these years," she said. "I've suppressed so many memories, they all came back fresh. Had I lived a normal life these 24 years, I would have had time to process my feelings about the past."

A normal life. As if she ever really wanted that.

Twenty-Three

Why Not

Rosemary was asleep when she heard the phone ring. Even in a half-awake stupor she knew that it was Timothy with bad news. He gave her the update as she jolted herself awake: his prostate cancer had spread. He followed up the phone call by faxing over the pages of his medical report to her inn. The first two and a half pages are barely legible, the rest are dark and splotchy, some are stark blank white, but there's one page clear enough to decipher these words: "Life expectancy between 3–5 years."

Timothy was dying.

He told her, as he would tell the international media who swarmed around him like vultures after his announcement, that he felt liberated by the prognosis. Death was inevitable for everyone, and Timothy was lucky enough to know his expiration date. But Rosemary recognized the familiar insincerity in his optimism.

"What do you want me to do?" she asked.

He said that he wanted her to quit her job and move in with him. She allowed herself to imagine this scenario, to fully let go of the grief of the lost time, as the words fell out of *her* mouth this time.

"Will you marry me?" she asked.

"Of course," he said.

Timothy altered his will to include Rosemary and designated her to be the principal trustee of his estate, the Futique Trust (opposite of antique), responsible for taking over the management of his archives from Michael Horowitz and maintaining his legacy. Later Rosemary would say that this role was more of a curse than a gift. "If you truly love someone and you have a complicated estate, don't make them your executor. I don't know if it was his last joke on me," she said.

Rosemary took a weekend off from innkeeping to visit him in Los Angeles—to hold him, comfort him, act as a wife would. Still carrying the long-held fear of getting pulled over, she drove well under the speed limit until she arrived at a classic mid-century ranch in the Hollywood Hills to find banners and balloons, a documentary crew, and Timothy in a silver spaceman suit welcoming her.

Rosemary's return to Timothy's world coincided with his third act, several years in the making, but set to hit another zenith during his "death tour." Timothy posed for a Gap ad—when that truly meant something to the culture—his face taped on the walls of teenagers' bedrooms around the country, the philosopher selling a chambray shirt for $34. He showed up to introduce Tool at Lollapalooza, partied at the Viper Room, and designed a video game. Generation X discovered their anarchic grandfather on their parents' bookshelves. They embraced Timothy's philosophy of individualism and contrarianism expressed in his bumper sticker slogan (one that characterized thirty-plus years of his writing): "Think for yourself and question authority." Disaffected teens and twentysomethings—cyberpunks and ravers, mostly—found illumination in his cyberdelic embracement of computers as the new enlightenment tool and followed his new motto, "Turn on, boot up, jack in."

Though many of Timothy's post-psychedelic musings seemed impossibly cartoonish, even unhinged, at the time, in retrospect some are uncomfortably prescient. Timothy predicted many cultural and technological realities today: the goal of separating mind from body through cyberspace, achieving immortality through DNA modification and nanotechnology, the rise of transhumanism, the merging of humans and machines. "In the near future, what is now taken for granted as the perishable human creature will be a mere historical curiosity," he wrote in his 1994 book *Chaos & Cyber Culture*. Few would outright scoff at that statement now. There is an argument to be made that the unwieldy path from Timothy's mind leads to Steve Jobs, who famously considered his encounter with psychedelics among the most meaningful experiences of his life.

Rosemary showed little interest in technology and this new phase in Timothy's philosophy. She had visited to test out a possible reunion with a man she considered a tragic hero. As Timothy poured Rosemary a glass of Cristal champagne, she took in the cluttered chaos of his home with its mishmash of psychedelic art and memorabilia: blown-up front covers of his own books, pictures of Johnny Depp, David Bowie, and Perry Farrell, a platinum record from the band Ministry, a drawing of Timothy's goddaughter Winona Ryder (the archivist Michael Horowitz's daughter), a *Glamour* magazine cover story featuring his second wife Nena von Schlebrügge's daughter, the actress Uma Thurman, and a rare and valuable Keith Haring painting. A reporter who visited the house noticed the revealing absence of the personal: "I didn't see any photos of his own family, or parents, or his children, Susan and Jack."

Timothy played Rosemary's favorite jazz recordings and plied her with attention, hanging on her every word. When she said something flippant about David Phillips's comment about her receiving "the double oak cluster"—a military decoration for those who have received multiple awards for service—for "standing by her man," Timothy ran off to write it down. They drank more wine and planned their wedding announcement, timing it to Valentine's Day (ever the relentless marketers). She found it harder to keep up with the pitter-patter of his mind, which had lost its focus and often disappeared down rabbit holes. "I'm too serious. I have to learn to be playful again," she wrote in her journal.

She slept in the guest room. Rather, she tried to sleep. Her body was unused to the alcohol, and the cat dander sprinkled around the house made her persistent cough worse. The next morning Timothy asked her to read a draft of his profile on Who's Who, a database of important people, and she saw that he listed their marriage date as 1955. She noted his compromised memory, moments of confusion, his frequent digressions, followed, as they were, by flashes of brilliance and clarity that could outdo people a quarter his age.

That night, awake again in the guest room, missing him, she padded down to the study to read. There he was, up too, reading his own memoir, *Flashbacks*. He told her that he was reading about her. It was sweet but heartbreaking. Was he doing this to remember what he'd forgotten?

These moments of intimacy—just like at Millbrook—didn't last long. Hangers-on always waited in the wings. If he had any choice in the matter, the bright lights of a camera were going to be the last lights he'd see. Beautiful young creatures now helped him manage his archives, launched his website on the World Wide Web, and handled requests for interviews from the press. As the novelty of her return wore off, Rosemary found it harder to keep his focus. "I had to shout to make myself heard and my jokes were never funny anymore. I didn't like LA and I didn't like the scene at the house and I couldn't see what would be in it for me," she said. "He couldn't change. He was stuck in his persona. He was caught, trapped being Timothy Leary, and he'd never be able to escape from it." As John Updike said,

"Celebrity is a mask that eats into the face." Timothy had chosen this mask, and now there was no taking it off.

By the end of her short trip, Timothy pulled her aside and turned down the marriage proposal that she made to him. They should be "best friends, not husband and wife," he said. "Move in as a permanent member, quit your job, move down here and be best friends." Her journal entry ends here, recalling his statement without any reaction to it. Did she feel relief? Affronted? Perhaps she felt a resigned sense of security in being able to warm her hands by the bonfire without getting burned up in it.

❧

AFTER TIMOTHY ANNOUNCED his cancer diagnosis and shared the news that he would not be pursuing treatment, the media interest went supernova. The interviews didn't stop. Timothy left the front door wide open, and the celebrities rolled in: Trent Reznor, Yoko Ono, *Penthouse* publisher Bob Guccione Jr., Ken Kesey, Oliver Stone, Michelle Phillips, the dolphin and LSD researcher John Lilly, the Dodgers catcher Johnny Roseboro, and Susan Sarandon and Tim Robbins, who dropped off a copy of their movie *Dead Man Walking*.

Timothy enchanted and exasperated the reporters who cycled in and out of his house. From his wheelchair, he told them, "When I found out I was terminally ill—and I know this can be misinterpreted— I was thrilled." He said that "death is the last taboo." He spoke sincerely about getting his head cryogenically frozen and about his mind being uploaded to a web page. He expressed an almost clinical interest in his pain, which had increased by several levels of magnitude as the cancer spread to his spine and which he managed with regular inhalations from nitrous-oxide-filled balloons—as enamored with laughing gas as Rosemary was during her dentist trip before Timothy's prison escape. Timothy documented his intake in a drug journal that he gleefully shared with the media. "He smoked 50 cigarettes and consumed two Dilaudid [an opioid], two lines of coke, .45 cc of ketamine, an unspecified amount of DMT, a fentanyl patch, 12 balloons of nitrous oxide, and two Leary biscuits, made by adding a lump of butter or cheese to a Ritz cracker, topping it with fresh marijuana bud and heating it up until the cheese or butter melts the THC." The list was intended to shock and titillate—"Why can't there be pleasure?" he asked—and it got ink.

Thousands of people pilgrimaged to his bedroom, where he feted his followers atop space-themed bedsheets that belonged in a toddler's room, next to a Macintosh LC III. People around Timothy, aware that they were witnessing history, found solemnity in every word. The kids listened; the cameras rolled. Everyone wanted a moment with the gaunt genius, a philosopher on his deathbed throwing out nuggets of wisdom. "You get the Timothy Leary you deserve," he told several visitors, aware of how his words were being appreciated now that he neared death. But being this close to the end didn't sharpen his emotional intelligence or ability to empathize. Timothy even had the audacity to call Michael Kennedy, his ex-lawyer whom he had turned on to free himself from prison, to say, "Michael, I'm dying, and I just want you to know . . . I forgive you."

"Once he announced that he was dying, what he said was that it is 'the best publicity move I've ever made,'" said Denis Berry, who lived with Timothy. "Everyone wanting to interview him. CNN, *60 Minutes*. It was like a constant parade of people." But the reality was—at least according to Berry—that "Leary was terrified. He was terrified and trying to put on a happy face because it was so public."

Denis had met Timothy through her employer, the *Top Gun* director Tony Scott. Denis worked for Scott as a "Dial-a-Wife" (her tongue-in-cheek business name), which involved taking care of the mundane realities of life that the rich and fabulous of Los Angeles didn't want to burden themselves with. That involved bringing Tony's watches to Cartier to get fixed or arranging the limo to come pick up his dog and take him to the groomer. She delivered a case of Cristal champagne sent by Tony to Timothy for a Christmas gift. After that, Tony would sometimes ask Denis to run some minor chores and errands for Timothy. Timothy, who wanted to be lionized by the culture but hated being idolized by the individual, loved Denis's ignorance of his fame and lack of artifice. Raised in a tight-knit Mormon community in Utah where she rebelled by becoming a Fundamentalist Christian in early adolescence, Denis had barely heard of the high priest. To school her on the subject of himself, Timothy suggested that she read his *Flashbacks*. He befriended the single mother of two, and when she hit a snafu regarding housing, Timothy offered his home to her. Denis, unlike Timothy's typical employees (also often his roommates), was a middle-aged mother who hadn't yet tried acid.

In this swirl of iniquity and death, Denis appreciated Rosemary's grounding force. Rosemary visited on her days off and supported Timothy from the background, reading a book with "an amused look as the media whirred around Leary yet again," as one reporter wrote. "She was one of the few people who could laugh at him when he started acting like he was something," Denis recalled. "She would be like, 'Oh my God,' kind of bring him back down." This was the special sauce of their relationship. Rosemary could laugh in the face of her ex-husband's hubris. She reminded him that he was human—that he was a joke, that they all were jokes. And, the best parts of Timothy loved her for this reminder of his own humanity while still publicly upholding his status as the great Timothy Leary.

But Rosemary's primary goal upon her return was to reunite Timothy with his estranged son. Rosemary even drafted a letter—perfect and heartfelt and true—from Timothy to Jack to get the ball rolling. It read,

Dearest Jack, dearest son my beautiful boy.

    *I have been sad about our separation and lack of
communication. I've hesitated to contact you because I've feared
your anger and, what I've felt to be, your contempt.*

    *Now, I ask you to forgive me for whatever wrongs you feel
I've done to you. I am aware there have been many times I've
failed you as father and a friend. My deepest sorrow has been
that Susan's tragic death did not allow us to grieve together.*

    *Then end your letter and tell him that you are proud of
him for being a wonderful father. Be brave!*

Timothy kept nearly all of Rosemary's words, adding a line about the photograph Peggy shared with him ("I have studied daily this photo wondering about you and missing you," he wrote), though it's unclear if this version was ever sent, and if it was, if Jack ever responded to it.

Through various mutual friends and back channels, perhaps also thanks to the letter itself, Jack agreed to see Timothy. "He was just terribly scared," Rosemary wrote of Timothy's reaction to the reunion. The date they settled on landed, intentionally or not, on a reunion of the Harvard Psilocybin Project. Jack arrived; Timothy ignored him to drink in the sweet draft of nostalgia. The past he shared with Jack was far less palatable, so he avoided it. "Think what it must have been like for Jack," Rosemary would later say. "All of those people, just as at Millbrook, telling Jack how lucky he was to have Tim for a father and how they wished he was their dad." Jack stayed for a few hours before leaving in a cab to head back to the airport. Jack never saw his father alive again. To this day, he does not want to be associated with Timothy in any way.

At a dinner party decades later with a few of his father's friends, Jack had asked them, "Why didn't anybody help us? It was like there weren't any adults there, and we were just kids."

Two months later, on May 31, 1996, word leaked to the media: Timothy Leary was dead.

"Just after midnight, in his favorite bed among loving friends, Timothy Leary peacefully passed on. His last words were 'Why not,'" the *San Francisco Chronicle* reported. He repeated that phrase dozens of times that last day—in a near-death daze perhaps, or more likely well aware that these words would be the last ones recorded for posterity. Rosemary sat vigil at his bedside with his adopted son, Zach, and a handful of close friends.

Two memorials celebrated his life. A larger one was set in an airplane hangar in Los Angeles, where Winona Ryder gave a eulogy about her godfather. Rosemary spoke at a slightly smaller gathering in San Francisco, at the Unitarian church where Timothy, when he still considered himself a psychologist, had lectured on how to change minds using LSD.

Under gray skies, 250 people entered the granite First Unitarian Church, shuffling to their seats, passing stained-glass windows while listening to "Over the Rainbow," as a projector beamed out pictures of Timothy. With so many psychedelic luminaries present—Diane di Prima, Ralph Metzner, Ram Dass, the Grateful Dead writer John Perry Barlow, among others—anticipation ran high.

Rosemary was the third to speak. She walked up to the lectern after Ralph Metzner finished his heartfelt ode to "smiling men with bad reputations." Her hair was shorter than she usually wore it and blown out. She wore round glasses, pearls, and a black blazer. The hollows of her cheeks resulted from a combination of drastic dieting and stress. Many people didn't recognize her. She was exhausted, felled by pneumonia, which hit her every few years as a souvenir of her life underground. Still, her voice purred as it did when she was young.

"I'm Rosemary Woodruff Leary and I've had the great good fortune to be reconciled to and loved a man that has occupied thirty years of my life."

She told the audience about the night she moved into Millbrook, when Timothy hosted a paid Castalia Foundation seminar weekend. Rosemary didn't mention her discomfort at having to cover up her black eye.

"He proposed that we were all alone on a spaceship, traveling into space," Rosemary said. "And we had but just a few moments of oxygen left and what could be our message home?"

The screen behind flashed a photo of Timothy in profile. For a few seconds as she spoke, his image projected over her face, blurring together like a 3D image.

"People spoke of family, some people spoke of guilt over things undone," she paused, taking the time to find the right words. "Everyone was perhaps a little self-conscious but trying very hard to live up to Tim's expectation. And then it was time for Captain Tim because he was obviously the captain of this enterprise and at that moment the fuses blew."

She paused. The room erupted in laughter.

Pleased by the reaction, she repeated herself. "The lights went out and the microphone was dead and he got a little testy."

More laughs.

"Because he was the philosopher and humorist that he is, he left a message that made us laugh at him, with him, in joy and appreciation. I'm sure some of you have heard the message, but I repeat it here." She paused. "It was with every inflection he's ever given anything he said, with every lift of eyebrow and curl of mouth," she said.

She was shaping the mythology, molding his legacy, blending his final words with her interpretation of them.

"'Why not?'" she asked. Then, "'Why not.'"

Twenty-Four

My Work

Time meandered after Timothy's death. Rosemary's health, which had long been in a fragile state, declined rapidly. Hacking coughs and heart issues plagued her, consequences of decades of smoking and the years spent underground without access to medical care. Unable to keep up with the demands at her inn, she quit her job and moved in with Denis Berry, Timothy's "Dial-a-Wife" in the beach town Aptos a few miles south of Santa Cruz. Their house, nestled on the edge of a ravine, overlooked a canopy of redwood trees, and though mired in darkness and mold, it was Rosemary's own—not Sarah's, not the inn's, not Timothy's. She told Denis that she received "so much pleasure just from walking out to the mailbox every day."

Timothy left little in the way of financial assistance beyond a life insurance policy—divided up among his heirs—and unpaid tax bills. In its place, Rosemary was propped up by $10,000 annual payments from the same artist/heiress who had supplied the bulk of the funds so that Rosemary could reemerge safely aboveground, along with a part-time salary from a local thrift store.

Rosemary cocooned herself for the first year. She preferred watching TV or playing solitaire on her computer to socializing. But she could hide for only so long with her cover blown. Invitations rolled in. She was now Timothy's number one ex-wife, and with the designation came new demands on her time. Timothy's third act had rolled into a postmortem fourth one. The Berkeley book publisher Ronin bought the rights to *The Politics of Ecstasy* and *High Priest* and republished them as part of the 1990s psychedelic revival. Tower Records displayed a new edition of the book of poetry *Psychedelic Prayers*—with edits and a new foreword written by Rosemary—by its register. Several documentaries got green-lighted, along with the publication of his posthumous book 1997's *Design for Dying*. Apple even approached Rosemary about featuring Timothy Leary as a face of its new Mac, but she declined, because the price wasn't right—a decision she would later regret.

Since their reunion in 1992 there had been rumblings of revolution in regard to psychedelic research. A 1992 *San Francisco Examiner* article written in that same year trumpeted (preemptively, as it turns out), U.S. MAY LIFT "BAN" ON LSD TESTING. In the article, the reporter had written that Timothy was "responsible for the death of research into [psychedelic] drugs." (In response, Timothy had written in the margins, "I'm proud to have 'killed' government authorized research on psychedelics.")

After a quarter century—the length of time Rosemary had been underground—the FDA opened a preliminary review of psychedelic research protocols. In the mid-1990s, the psychiatrist Rick Strassman published a series of long-term studies of DMT on humans, the first government-funded research approved by the Drug Enforcement Administration in two decades. Meanwhile, scientists in Germany studied mescaline and its ability to induce a kind of pseudo-psychosis (a clear nod to early–pre-Timothy Leary 1950s psychotomimetic research, which posited that acid created schizophrenic-like behaviors).

At the same time, the drug of choice for the growing rave culture was ecstasy, also known as MDMA, a well-established psychoactive empathogen, categorized as a Schedule I drug in 1985.

Rosemary's neighbor in Santa Cruz, the Multidisciplinary Association for Psychedelic Studies (MAPS), which has since relocated to San Jose, California, was growing into the world's leading nonprofit in the psychedelic space. Its former executive director Rick Doblin, who founded MAPS in 1984, became the movement's primary proselytizer of legalization and medicalization, prompting some to compare his PR prowess with Timothy's. In 1996, the same year as Leary's death, the professor of clinical psychiatry Charles Grob published the first FDA-approved safety study of MDMA using placebo controls with MAPS backing. Since then, MAPS has homed in on the use of MDMA as a treatment for post-traumatic stress disorder as the clearest path toward decriminalization. In subsequent years, thanks in large part to MAPS, veterans' hospitals have embraced psychedelics as a tool to heal soldiers and several Republican politicians have gotten behind the push—which almost no one would have seen coming in the 1960s.

The question of what to do with the Leary archive loomed—a valuable asset but nearly impossible to make liquid since no major institution wanted it. Michael Horowitz had maintained the files since the Feds returned them after seizing them in 1975. During Timothy's escape trial, Horowitz had established a legal precedent for the neutrality of archivists when he risked being held in contempt of court for refusing to answer the court's questions. Since then he had taken meticulous care of the more than three hundred boxes in Timothy's archive. Now the Futique Trust needed to find a home that appreciated their worth not only financially but historically. Trouble was, Timothy was still considered a pariah in most academic circles. As the trust waited for the tide to turn regarding Timothy's legacy, the archives lived in a rented house in the Valley with its own hired caretaker until the trust ran out of money, at which point they were moved to an un-ventilated attic near Santa Cruz.

Meanwhile, Rosemary still hunted for magic objects from their shared history to complete Timothy's archive. Denis recalls the time a man with a van arrived with boxes from the Millbrook era. Rose-mary, excited about the possibilities inside, bought the files without opening them, only to be disappointed when the boxes contained no sentimental or monetary value. "I think she was looking for—it's like when we go through our parents' scrapbooks from our childhood," Denis said. "This was her life, too."

Over time, Rosemary opened up to the psychonaut scene, the "Santa Cruz circle," who embraced her as a returning hero. The circle revolved around the psychedelic grandmother Nina Graboi and the 1970s counterculture literary icon and futurist writer/psychologist Robert Anton Wilson. One of Nina's friends, Valerie Corral, a death doula and advocate for the use of medical marijuana, remembers that Rosemary was an icon, esteemed within the group. "Everyone had known who [Rosemary] was and what she did in breaking her hus-band out of prison," Valerie said. "She was a hero, a goddess." Sherri Paris, feminist writer and professor, who advocated for medical mari-juana use as a member of the Wo/Men's Alliance for Medical Mari-juana with Valerie, held a similar reverence. "Rosemary was just treasured. Everybody loved her," she said. "The jailbreak blew me away." The writer David Jay Brown concurred: "She was just a power-ful symbol of integrity, and of just not backing down, and standing up to the federal government."

Around the same time, in 1998, a documentary called *Beyond Life: Timothy Leary Lives*, which featured a series of deathbed inter-views with Timothy, devoted a fleeting reference to Rosemary's underappreciated courage under fire. Rosemary, interviewed for the movie, spoke for the first time about her role in Timothy's escape and his cooperation with the FBI, though she waved away the subsequent betrayal, mitigated the harsh realities of life underground, and reduced her simmering rage to a quiet murmur. "I think he told the truth as he saw it and as he knew it to be with a great deal of hyperbole," she said and smiled.

The progressive lawyer and Brooklyn judge Gustin Reichbach, however, put her humility into necessary context. "There are few of us who want to speak ill of the dead; but nevertheless, when the dead deserve to be spoken ill of, I'm not so hesitant," he said. "It wasn't through any action of his that these people avoided indictment and perhaps incarceration. It was only because Rosemary refused to participate in Leary's cooperation that there was no indictment returned." (The full extent of Timothy's cooperation emerged a year later, in 1999, when the Smoking Gun released FOIA-ed FBI documents in an article titled "Turn On, Tune In, Rat Out." In a file that reads like a movie script, Timothy monologues about the various steps of the escape, identifying by name one of the Weather Underground members who drove the camper out of prison. Rosemary's name was redacted but present throughout.)

This was more attention than Rosemary had received since word of Timothy's cooperation hit the underground press in the mid-1970s. But she seemed to merely tolerate the admiration. The spotlight didn't seem to animate or enliven her. Rosemary, Denis explained, did not feel comfortable with the new set of friends who were aware of the Rosemary Leary of the past—the woman whose footsteps she had tentatively stepped back into, but whose legacy she had long since outgrown. When Denis and Rosemary threw yearly memorial parties for Timothy—where a punch bowl full of Timothy's ashes were left for visitors to take home in small baggies—Rosemary grew anxious, ornery even, in the lead-up to the event and always threatened to cancel.

During "death circles," as Rosemary and Denis called them, when a group, led by Valerie, would pray and offer support to a dying member of the community, Rosemary and Denis would leave. "We didn't know these people; we weren't invested emotionally," Denis said. She wasn't the psychedelic feminine goddess of their collective imaginations, not anymore, and people did not seek her out or prop her up as a spiritual guide in the way that Oden Fong, Brigitte Mars, and so many others had viewed her before. She had discarded that identity when she left South America. There was a cost to having all of that "god energy" projected onto her.

Some read her diffidence as haughtiness and assumed that she expected to be treated with white gloves because of her royal status. But David Jay Brown sensed that her reserve emerged after years of receptivity following the regular use of LSD. Once the world had turned on her—held her as a prisoner, chased her through the world, betrayed her, and then forgot she existed—she had built armor that she wasn't born with to protect herself from that openness.

Despite, or maybe because of, this anxiety about being pigeon-holed as the woman who broke Timothy Leary out of prison, Rosemary continued to labor over her work in progress. The memoir, nearly thirty years in the making, was now buried under edits from ex-lovers, her ex-husband, various friends, editors, and agents. Her brother, Gary, lugged her pages to his job at Union Bank and fed them into a gigantic, state-of-the-art photocopier, which sputtered and broke, chomping up the disintegrating pages. She spent days putting it all back together again as a bound copy, which her brother would one day refer to, reverentially, as "the blue binder." She dreamed of this binder, waking up in the middle of the night to write down snippets of conversation or a detail she remembered. One morning, she even found a line that she had written in a dreamscape: "Use Tim's quote about me from his book for my book." She laughed. There was Timothy again inserting himself in her narrative, even from the beyond. "Last laugh, Tim, you rascal," she wrote.

At the same time, she and Anita Hoffman put their finishing touches on *Her Story*, their dual memoir, spurred on by Timothy before his death. The proposal summarized the book as the story of two women "raised to become wives and mothers, who became wives all right—to the most notorious rebels of the sixties counterculture. . . . And being rebels themselves, they helped create the history, myths and legends we remember as the sixties."

An agent was shopping the proposal when Anita learned that her breast cancer, which had been in remission, had recurred. Anita did not plan to undergo any Western treatment (much to the chagrin of her son, America) and had accepted that this may well be the end of her story. As a parting gift, she asked Rosemary to arrange a ceremony on her behalf— one more trip before she passed on. Rosemary gathered together three of their closest female friends—Denis Berry, Nina Graboi, and Cynthia Palmer, writer, editor, and wife of the archivist Michael Horowitz.

Forty years after trying peyote for the first time, Rosemary brewed a ceremonial tea for her dying friend on the fall equinox, when the sun moves from north to south over the equator, ushering in autumn. This time she would right the wrongs of her first experience by engaging with the cactus in the purest way: by acting in service to another. With acquired wisdom from witnessing a peyote ritual at a Navajo reservation in New Mexico, where she had prayed for a baby with Timothy, combined with her own well-honed techniques, sharpened in perspective by abstention, she prepared the setting. She placed vibrant pillows on the floor, gathered wood and built a fire, fanning the smoke with an eagle feather, and lit sage and cedar. She cooked nourishing and grounding foods—salads and mac and cheese—to provide a warming foundation. They made sure to dose appropriately and, most important, gave "the focus of our attention on the one who needed us," Rosemary wrote.

The serious-mindedness of the ceremony was broken up mid-meditation by Anita's New York accent, which pierced through the weighty silence: "All right! All right! Enough already!" All four women convulsed with laughter—a fitting moment in a Rosemary-assisted psychedelic experience: passion punctuated by humor and a touch of the absurd.

Anita passed away a few months later, on December 27, 1998, at Winona Ryder's house in San Francisco. Rosemary moved in to tend to her ailing friend, and even crushed Anita's final dose of morphine pills into a cup of vanilla yogurt—intended to hasten Anita's death. When Anita spotted the yogurt packaging, she offered one more quip: "Even now it has to be low fat?" Denis remembers the lift she felt once Anita's soul left her body—a sense of relief of an ending on her own terms after a life fully lived. Anita might not have accomplished all that she had intended to, but there was an acceptance that her time had come and, with that, the full joy of letting go.

That same year, Rosemary's mother died, leaving a complicated trail of grief behind in her passing. Ruth had protected her daughter—hidden information from law enforcement, sent her money, and worked in the background with lawyers—all the while never outright complaining, not in letters at least. Rosemary had not, in the eyes of her mother, returned the favor. Ruth had never forgiven her daughter for remaining at large as long as she had, and, more pointedly, for not attending her beloved father's funeral. Rosemary hadn't forgiven herself for that, either.

∼

PROFESSOR SHERRI PARIS feared she had imposed on Rosemary when she had asked her to guest lecture for a class on the history of the 1960s at the University of California, Santa Cruz. But the truth was Rosemary was thrilled by the endorsement from the hallowed halls of academia—especially as a high school dropout. But she did not share this satisfaction with her friend.

Before the start of the class, Rosemary told Sherri her intentions for the college-age audience. She wanted these young people, especially the women, to appreciate the power of the drugs to make people more receptive and, in turn, more vulnerable. "The drugs really open up your head, and that everything that happened while you were on them was going to imprint in a serious way," Sherri recalled Rosemary telling her. "If you were going to do them at all, they should be very, very careful with them."

Thirty or so students watched Rosemary, who was the same age as many of their grandmothers, collect herself in front of the classroom, her voice wavering, before she launched into a lecture on her life story, titled "From Magician's Daughter to Wizard's Wife." She read aloud from her favorite parts of the book no one wanted: Algeria and the Black Panthers, LSD trips with the Brotherhood of Eternal Love, and the raid on Millbrook. The students, likely unfamiliar with many of the names she mentioned, expressed sincere fascination not only with the circumstances of her life but with this timid woman who had once lived so dangerously. When her voice broke into whispers under the strain of emotion, the students implored her to speak up. One of the more empathetic students wanted to embrace Rosemary and "make all the terrible things you've seen disappear."

One student's essay reaction, written later, summed up the class's perspective on the lecture: "This was the highlight of my school career so far." Rosemary kept this and all the other essay responses in a special folder tucked away in her archives, alongside her prison letters and book drafts, an indication of how meaningful this day was to her.

Sherri hoped that Rosemary's lecture would become an annual

tradition and invited her back during the spring semester of 2002. Rosemary would not return.

By that time, Rosemary's health had further deteriorated. She had survived at least one heart attack, though the extent of her health issues was unknown to most friends. Denis knew about the hospital visits and the recurrent breathing issues only because they lived together.

In the late winter of 2001, Rosemary complained that she feared her heart would give out. She told Denis that she could actually feel her heart lurching in its struggle to pump blood through her body. One evening, she spent an entire night staring at a hostile red void. She could see her own battered heart, in a way similar to the first time she had taken acid with Susan Firestone back in Manhattan, when she had sprawled out on the floor, watching the skylight, waiting for Kali to appear, as she envisioned the organ sending hot red blood through her veins. This time the vision felt more like the end than the beginning.

Rosemary waited until morning to ask Denis to take her to the hospital, where an attending physician examined her and sent her home, despite her agony. She returned to the hospital again the next day, where another doctor confirmed what Rosemary had suspected: her heart was failing. He gave her three months, max, to live.

Denis arrived at the hospital shortly after the news but found Rosemary calm and centered—a dramatic shift from the worn woman with whom she had shared a house for half a decade. With an intensity she had never seen before, Rosemary turned to Denis and said, "You're really my idol. You have such an easy way of being with people. I wish I could do that."

Denis realized then the toll of those years underground—how Rosemary had isolated herself from humanity and how counter this ran to her authentic need for connection. Denis felt a gust as a window cracked open in Rosemary's psyche. This was not who Rosemary was meant to be.

"Please bring me my tarot cards," Rosemary said then, referring to the Aleister Crowley Thoth deck that had accompanied her underground after leaving Timothy in Switzerland and had, like the *I Ching*, counseled her in almost every fateful life decision that followed. "I have neglected my work for too long."

Denis felt the flash of Rosemary's youth—the woman who relied on synchronicity and signs, who threw herself headfirst into the unknown, the woman who *believed* that something greater guided her.

Now, on her deathbed, at age sixty-six, Rosemary called out for that woman.

But by the time Denis returned with her cards, Rosemary was already unconscious.

Her brother, Gary, arrived, determined to release her from the hospital so that she could die at home as she had intended. Somehow, with the help of his wife, who worked as a nurse, he was able to get her transferred back to Aptos, where she received hospice care.

During the transfer, Rosemary grabbed her brother's hand and said, "I understand now."

These were her final words.

Twenty-Five

Ghosts and Minor Characters

On the morning of February 7, 2002, the calls went around to Rosemary's circle of friends: Rosemary would not make it through another day. A hospice nurse allowed her friends to administer the morphine. Valerie Corral, the death doula, whom Rosemary once nicknamed the "doyenne of death," anointed Rosemary with oils and dressed her in a linen caftan from Afghanistan, her favorite dress. She positioned Rosemary in the center of the living room under a skylight, surrounded by candles and flowers, staging befitting the queen of set and setting—a soft place to land. Her body remained there after death for two days for witnesses to pay their respects.

Her brother, Gary, was the one who held Rosemary's hand as she passed, and as the house lights flickered, he noticed a bird flying overhead in the skylight. Denis, who had also accompanied Anita Hoffman as she died and felt the full release of her spirit, did not feel a similar letting go with Rosemary. There was still unfinished business. Having never seen a dead body before, David Phillips fixated on her slack jaw, vacant open eyes, and sallow skin. He hated that Rosemary's was the first corpse he'd seen up close.

Two months after Rosemary's death, on her birthday, Denis hosted a memorial service for Rosemary at their Aptos home. The vibe was festive. Various luminaries from psychedelic history—Ralph Metzner, Ram Dass, and Peggy Hitchcock—paid their respects. Friends from Cape Cod arrived and still, despite themselves, called her Sarah. John Schewel led the room in a prayer initiated by the resounding boom of a Tibetan gong.

At Denis's insistence, Gary left Rosemary's closet intact instead of donating her clothing to a local charity. Rosemary's essence lingered in her wardrobe, which had protected, shielded, amplified, and obscured her across space and time. Denis let the items sit untouched for several months until she decided to give them away, piece by piece.

"Come over," Denis would tell their friends. "Get something of Rosemary's to keep."

Valerie and Sherri picked cashmere sweaters; two young women who had never met Rosemary chose business suits for job interviews; someone ended up with a black full-length cloak with a cigarette burn hole in its sleeve. "Whoever came and tried something on, it fit them," Denis said. "It was a magical thing with those clothes."

Meanwhile, Gary packed up drafts of her memoir, dropping photographs, news clippings, letters, receipts, diaries, and old calendars into several boxes and shipping them back to his home in Southern California, where they spent the next decade in his garage. A life in eleven boxes. Sometimes when the mood struck, Gary would thumb through the artifacts of his sister's existence, getting lost in Rosemary's world. He almost always found something uncanny, as if Rosemary were speaking to him from the other side. On a stray note card, included among the nighttime notes about her memoir in progress, she had written, "The history of a life does not always end with the final passing of that life."

A Post-it note atop a grouping of fifty-eight letters written by Timothy to Rosemary while he was in prison read, in Rosemary's tidy, unassuming scrawl, "Most precious treasure. Please preserve." They were letters that contained deep love; she was protecting them even after death. No one had ever seen these prison letters before, and despite years of financial hardship she had never sold them.

What would become of these artifacts now? Rosemary spent so much of her life as a shadow—the woman in the background, behind the great man, the woman on the run, erased from the record. Was there anywhere her unexplored legacy could endure or even be celebrated?

If the saga that followed Timothy's archive allocation was any indication, Rosemary's posthumous prospects looked doubtful. For years, Denis, who had been named as an alternate trustee of the Futique Trust after Rosemary's death, couldn't find a home for Timothy's scholarship. A Texas college made an offer, but Denis declined because she believed they were worth triple. The better offer came nearly two decades after his death, from one of the most prestigious institutions in the world. In 2011, the New York Public Library paid $900,000 for 465 boxes—money well spent considering that the Timothy Leary Papers continues to be one of the most requested archives in the library's vast collection.

Denis and the Futique Trust set aside funds to throw a party at the New York Public Library to celebrate. On the night of the party, Denis walked past the marble lions—Patience and Fortitude—standing sentry at the front entrance at Forty-Second Street and Fifth Avenue. She climbed the grand internal staircase to the second floor into the Sue and Edgar Wachenheim III Trustees Room, where twenty feet of glass displayed items from the archive: letters from Allen Ginsberg, notes about meeting the Beatles, mimeographed recordings of a DMT trip, and an invitation to the Castalia Foundation's weekend "meditation sessions." The dimmed lights cast an otherworldly glow, amplifying the old-moneyed walnut paneling and silk tapestries, making you feel as if you had taken a party dose and time traveled back to Billy Hitchcock's bungalow at the Millbrook estate. Denis felt validated by the impressive surroundings, not just for her own belief in Timothy Leary and the value of the archive, but for psychedelics and the people who use and study them. She considered the library party among the most meaningful days of her life, second only to giving birth. "I felt so, like I had completed"—Denis paused, her voice catching in her throat—"like I had taken my job seriously."

Denis acknowledged, even in the midst of the celebration, the debt owed to Rosemary, who had not only protected the secrets that had kept the underground from splintering and turning on itself but sacrificed her security to preserve her ex-husband's body of work. Denis felt Rosemary's presence everywhere—in the letters, in the background of the photos, in her editing touches on some of Timothy's key texts.

At the party, Denis embraced her friend Maria Mangini, a fellow psychonaut who had acted as a psychedelic midwife in the underground for the prior half century. Maria supported various male luminaries from the sidelines, working as an assistant for the consciousness researcher Stanislav Grof, the medical cannabis pioneer Dr. Frank Lucido, and the psychologist Leo Zeff, the "secret chief" of the continued research into psychedelic practice.

In her aboveground work, Maria worked as a real midwife. She deployed the skills she learned catching babies and applied them to her underground work: facilitating transitions; using intentionality to step into another realm; and blending science and inherited wisdom to provide a safe set and setting without inflicting one's own beliefs or expectations. Similar routes to consciousness expansion that Rosemary had once reverentially followed.

Four decades earlier, as a student at Vassar, Maria often hitchhiked to Millbrook and observed Rosemary in action. To Maria,

Rosemary wasn't a mere figurehead—just an acid queen—she also provided inspiration for how someone with soft power should wield it. "She was kind, and she took notice of people who were minor characters, which, if you're a minor character, was very cool," Maria said. That impression stuck.

In 2000, Maria received her PhD in community health nursing with a focus on psychedelics—a feat that would have been dismissed as a pipe dream while Rosemary was underground. Seven years later, Maria helped found the Women's Visionary Council, a group that seeks to address the gross gender imbalance in psychedelic research and academic conferences. She now works with two California universities offering training programs in legal psychedelic-assisted research. Rosemary, and the other silent women in the underground, are never far from her mind. "Rosemary made some personal decisions that had very far-ranging impact on the lives of a lot of other people," Maria said. "A lot of the people who were the beneficiaries of her self-sacrifice have gotten to tell their stories."

FIVE YEARS AFTER the Leary acquisition, Denis and David Phillips contacted the New York Public Library to inquire about placing Rosemary's papers there, too. David argued that Rosemary's archive should not be "subsumed into" Leary's papers, but should exist as an allied collection. "She was a separate person with a separate voice and viewpoint and identity," he wrote in a 2016 email. The library agreed. As Thomas Lannon, assistant curator of the NYPL, said, "It would be a bad thing to hide this in Timothy's archive, because again she'd disappear. These are her papers. She's the author. She's the creator."

Before they made the donation, Gary had the archive appraised. He was shocked by how high the appraisal was—$80,000. Gary kept the Timothy Leary prison letters that Rosemary had set aside as her "most precious treasure," but he and his daughter, Kate, donated the rest to the library, where they live on—in twenty-three neatly organized bankers boxes—as the Rosemary Woodruff Leary Papers in the Manuscripts and Archives Division of the New York Public Library.

While Rosemary lived underground, and no publisher found any worth in her story, psychedelic research had nearly been extinguished. The straight world wanted to stay as far away from people like Rosemary as they could. Now studies have been conducted on psychedelics at the world's most prestigious universities—Johns Hopkins, New York University, UCLA, and Imperial College London, to name a few—and some universities have dedicated entire departments to their study. The nexus of research is on treatment for PTSD, addiction, and end-of-life distress. But that's just the beginning. They are also being studied as treatments for depression, anxiety, brain injury, and personality disorders. Some researchers believe they are the key to address more wide-ranging issues, like healing the effects of racism and easing climate change distress. The goal of the brave new world of psychedelics, as communicated by its figurehead Rick Doblin at the biggest ever psychedelic conference hosted by MAPS in June 2023, is "net-zero trauma." The market is wide; the expectations enormous.

A broad public acceptance of psychedelics has followed the science, spurred on by popular works like Michael Pollan's 2018 bestseller, *How to Change Your Mind.* LSD use increased 50 percent between 2015 and 2018, and more than 5.5 million Americans reported using psychedelics in 2019—with the biggest increases in LSD use seen in college-educated people aged thirty-five to forty-nine. The possible cause of the rise? "Chemical escapism," *Scientific American* wrote—a way to cope with an increasingly bleak world.

Psychedelics have rightfully sloughed off their reputation as a tool used by the fringes. Now Goop-inspired suburban mothers micro-dose to ease the stress of modern parenting; straitlaced neuroscientists vie for positions as psychedelic researchers at a host of new biotech companies; and a new army of psychedelic facilitators, once called guides, spend upward of $10,000 to learn how to help people through a still not federally legal endeavor. If Rosemary were alive today, she could find a conference to attend or a panel to appear on almost every day of the week. Perhaps because there is much financial incentive to sell a magic bullet, the field is plagued by hype and over-enthusiasm, as thousands of studies explore psychedelics' potentials, while far fewer, at least as of this writing, are dedicated to studying the potential harms and pitfalls. Psychedelics have become too big *not* to fail. The twin issues that helped curtail the study of these substances in the 1960s are back: evangelism and hubris. And in 2024 they were cited as two of the key reasons why the FDA rejected MDMA as a treatment for PTSD, delivering a massive blow to the psychedelic industry.

Despite what you might have heard, these drugs aren't for everyone. People with histories of serious mental illness are taking a risk when trying these substances. For others, a risk, however small, still remains, and it mostly involves less tangible changes involving the self. Psychedelics do make many people softer, kinder, and more open; others are amplified in the opposite direction. Ego inflation—that messianic phase of Timothy and Rosemary's early days—runs rampant. Myopic narcissism and grandiosity are often by-products of the early stages of psychedelic enthusiasm. Sexual abuse happens. People are malleable, easily influenced and coerced, especially when faced with a hierarchical imbalance between healer and healed, physician and patient, shaman and believer. You have to ask yourself, *Do I want my life to change*, and if so, *Am I comfortable with it changing in a way I can't anticipate?*

Rosemary went on the record repeatedly to warn against the dangers of psychedelic evangelism—"the responsibility!" she once said, likening the power of the guide to the one who holds the ring in *The Lord of the Rings*. This is what she warned her students about during her lecture in Santa Cruz: If you are to engage with these substances, you must respect them enough to prepare yourself for both the light and the shadow. Rosemary's perspective is far less tangible and commodifiable than the prevailing narrative surrounding psychedelics sold in Instagram ads, and it doesn't have a place in American medicine as it stands today. Note the hedging and the humility—"the responsibility!"—the hesitation. This is not a sales pitch but an authentic discussion of the risks and benefits of lifting the veil. You can't sell this kind of perspective on the S&P 500; nor will insurance companies shell out thousands of dollars for such double-edged realizations. Nonetheless, this insight—that psychedelic use comes with trade-offs—is key to making sure that the past does not repeat itself.

A few years before her death, Rosemary talked about what she felt was the legacy of her prolonged use of psychedelics—or what it means to live a *psychedelic life*: "I can't say that I believe in anything specific but I can believe in a certain feeling of joy that overcomes me from time to time. And I do believe that joy or that sense of grace, if you will, has something to do with my experience with psychedelic substances. It made me aware of another reality than this reality that we experience in our daily lives. The fact that we have blinders on and don't pay attention to it. So, I'm more inclined to pay attention to beauty had I not done these things.

"I believe everything," Rosemary said, "and at the same time almost nothing, but it leaves me in a very comfortable place."

The Magician's Assistant

The effect of her being on those around her was incalculably diffusive: for the growing good of the world is partly dependent on unhistoric acts; and that things are not so ill with you and me as they might have been, is half owing to the number who lived faithfully a hidden life, and rest in unvisited tombs.

—GEORGE ELIOT, *Middlemarch*

The triumphant placement of Rosemary's personal effects in one of the most storied institutions in America might seem like a fitting final tribute, but David Phillips, Rosemary's longtime confidant, knew that his friend dreamed of something more concrete: authorship. In the two decades after her death, David went to work. He photocopied the dozens of drafts of her memoir in progress and collated them, examining the words with such care that he could spot slight differences in comma placement among the drafts. He endeavored to remove the veneer shellacked over the narrative by ex-lovers and agents as one would strip a one-of-a-kind vintage mahogany table that had been hidden under layers of paint. As the container ships inched their way across the shoreline and the seagulls scoured the shore for food, David sat at his office desk poring over her words in an attempt, he would write, "to preserve Rosemary's story and her voice and her memory."

"He empathized with her so profoundly," said David's brother Adam, who had lived with them on Cape Cod. "He felt the sadness and the incompleteness of all this material being out there without any organizing principle, but he was very, very careful not to overlay a lot of what he put in her words, and he tried to keep her voice in there."

David propped a framed picture of Rosemary on the bookshelf behind his desk with a black mourning ribbon from her memorial. In the image, Rosemary rests her head in her hand, smiling at the camera, a model's pose, but older, wiser, more elegant—the high priestess in all of her regal glory.

"I let myself be guided by the sound of her voice," he wrote.

He worked on this project through several health setbacks, including a cancer diagnosis and too-long-delayed kidney dialysis, until his health failed.

In March 2020, David underwent surgery; he kept the details secret from most of his close friends and family. A few weeks later, on March 26, 2020, during the height of the pandemic, alone at the hospital, he died.

A year later, in 2021, a Vermont-based publisher released Rosemary's book, edited by David, under the title *Psychedelic Refugee*. Though Rosemary was not present to express her gratitude and David was not there to receive it, a note written after her first draft, while under David's guidance in his house on Cape Cod, gives us a sense of what she might have felt: "The book, which seemed never finished, neverending, began when I was in exile. Now it is being completed when I am finally home again with the hope of leaving my past in good order for those who care to know it—for history, for lessons learned, for journeys taken."

In the foreword of *Psychedelic Refugee*, David left a small note embedded that would help persuade me to take on Rosemary's story: A biography "is needed," he wrote. "It should be done while witnesses to Rosemary's life still remain and remember."

~⌖~

I RECEIVED A PREPRINT of *Psychedelic Refugee* from Gary Woodruff in late 2020. I had learned about Rosemary a few months earlier from an unlikely but appropriate source: a clothing store. While I was perusing a whimsical and expensive boutique in Park Slope, Brooklyn, my eye caught on a graphic black-and-white caftan covered in poppies and made by the Swedish clothing company Rodebjer, inspired, the label's website said, by "the free intellect and relaxed style of psychedelic pioneer Rosemary Woodruff Leary."

Psychedelic Refugee emerged at exactly the time I needed it—when I was settling into my life as a mother in suburbia, ghostwriting a book, and giving up other groundless paths for something more solid. I was a year removed from my own recent consciousness expansion, without having ingested any psychedelics, following the birth of my twins. The cosmic feeling hit me on the FDR Drive, hurtling home through space after a difficult hospital birth in the middle of winter, with two pink vulnerable souls in the back of my car. I gazed out of the passenger seat window at the various bodies trudging through the chill with zipped-up winter coats, upturned collars, under layers of scarves, and thought to myself, in full befuddled awe, *Everyone has been born.* The realization, as obvious as it may seem, made my heart swell and my stomach turn. *Everyone has been born.*

I recognized this feeling from when I was sixteen. In the afterglow of consuming musty mushrooms in my friend's garage, I experienced a similar interconnectedness. From a distance of two decades, I reach for words that are as clichéd as they come, but I felt as if I'd unlocked some door to a new room in my house that was always there. The same Door, I believe, that Rosemary and Timothy walked through.

I was drawn back to this experience once my twins were weaned and there was space again to come back to myself, just as I started to research Rosemary. Drawn by the lure of peak experiences and the stories of rebirth shared by friends, or perhaps desiring a taste of the transgressive openness of my youth, I began asking the question: Could I take this kind of a leap again as a mother? Could I step into another realm after suffering from a brain illness—that brought with it a prolonged and painful experience with altered states—in my twenties, just as I was coming into my own as a woman?

I got mixed responses from experts given my health history (the brain encephalitis would likely exclude me from most clinical trials). But the wise psychonaut midwife Maria Mangini reframed my tentative wanderings with one sentence.

Embarking on a psychedelic experience is much like leaning in for a kiss, she told me: "If you have to ask, you shouldn't do it."

Rosemary never felt she had to ask. But I knew too much about the literal "Not-I"—about the horror of true ego loss—to jump without a sturdy tether. I still had some questions.

Two years later, deep into my study of Rosemary, pregnant again, I attended a party in the East Village, a few blocks away from the apartment where Rosemary had lived with the accordionist Mat Mathews. I spoke of my new subject like an old friend, sharing her stories about the Black Panthers and the Brotherhood of Eternal Love as enthusiastically as if they were my own. But when the host suggested we take the party to the rooftop, which required scaling a perpendicular wrought-iron ladder with an increasingly cumbersome belly, I balked. Just as I was about to refuse, however, a new friend to whom I'd been babbling turned to me and said, "What would Rosemary do?"

Those four words provided all the prompting I needed: Rosemary would climb that ladder. I decided my one self-conceived action would be to head to the rooftop, and there I sat for the rest of the party, giddy with my own small triumph.

While writing about Rosemary, I opened myself up to the synchronicities that animated her life while trying hard not to become too consumed by them. This became a vocation. I practiced her style of hatha yoga; mimicked her breath work; listened to the music of her era, made possible by the psychedelics she championed. Once I tuned in to her way of seeing, the signs emerged. A chance throw of the *I Ching*—the same version of the book she used—helped me decide to turn down another writing project that would have gotten in the way of telling Rosemary's story. I ordered a used copy of the book *Birth of a Psychedelic Culture* and found a small note of encouragement signed by the deceased Ralph Metzner on its title page. During a walk around Brooklyn in the earliest stages of the writing, I came across a blank card featuring an owl—which I would later discover is the symbol of Athena, the goddess with whom Rosemary identified after leaving Timothy—with multicolored mushrooms growing out of its head. I met for lunch with a friend at a restaurant in the East Village that just happened to be four houses away from where I would learn that Rosemary had lived. While driving around Cape Cod with two sleeping toddlers in the backseat, I took a turn toward Nauset Light Beach as a way to extend their nap, only later to discover that I had driven past Rosemary's first house on the Cape.

I followed Rosemary's voice—just as David Phillips had—allowing myself to be thrown off course in ways big and small, little swerves that sometimes made life feel less certain, more destabilized, more interesting.

I often returned to the first chapter of Rosemary's book, which describes her father, Verl Woodruff, entrancing a crowd as a traveling magician. "My father plucked pennies from my ears, dealt cards to choose and remember, placed back in the deck they'd appear next in my hair, four kings in a row beside them. His finger was a wand to be watched carefully, it created invisibility. He is slender, elegant in tails with slick black hair, smiling at the costumed girl beside him. He stands with a rifle, there's a hole in the Ace of Spades. The photograph calls him Victor the Magician."

The perfect origin story for the future wife of a magician on a grander scale.

But later, as I dove deeper into Rosemary's archives and unearthed some of her buried secrets, I tracked that passage down to its original source: a letter to her mother, to whom she had sent the paragraph for her feedback while she lived underground with John Schewel, working on her book by candlelight in Switzerland.

Her mother loved the passage—which was less polished but largely the same—and shared it with her father, who offered an important correction in 1972. "Daddy laughed when he read your letter," she wrote. "He says that you are giving him too much importance. He was just an assistant, not the magician."

Just an assistant. Her father had not entranced audiences. He had helped another man accomplish this task, just as she had. And yet, even though Rosemary knew the truth for more than three decades, the opening passage appeared unchanged in *Psychedelic Refugee.* Later, Gary Woodruff shared the picture that inspired that paragraph, and there it was in black and white: her father was the assistant.

Rosemary was shaping a story—imposing her own version of history for posterity, erecting a mythology around Rosemary Woodruff Leary, the character she had created. She had conceived of a new legend—the story of the muse on her own terms.

Long before she had tried psychedelics, ever since she was eight years old, the year she had her first mystical experience, when time stopped and the earth around her glowed, Rosemary saw herself in mythic terms. Psychedelics helped her unlock this potential within— to connect to something larger—by offering her a tool, much as writing, the *I Ching*, and the tarot did, to alchemize herself as a main character in her own story. Rosemary told herself stories not just to live, as Joan Didion wrote, but to *live more heroically*.

A few weeks after I learned of Rosemary's intentional misdirection, I also discovered this handwritten note in her archives: "The eyes of the audience must be on the assistant when the magician's hands are distorting reality."

With the sleight of her own hand, Rosemary revealed the multilayered nature of magic at work in her own story. There is the typical tale of the magician who draws the eyes of the world and commands an audience, and that of the assistant, who aids the magician behind the scenes, doing the unacknowledged work. But then there are more complicated stories—rarer ones, too—of those who harbor both abilities, whose hands distort our realities by making others believe that they hold the power.

That's the mark of a true magician—the imbuing of others with the remarkable, the ability to locate the meaningful in the mundane and find magic in something that we had never noticed before— making us feel, whether we deserve it or not, that the magic is within us.

Acknowledgments

This book was possible only because of the generosity showed to me by Rosemary's inner circle. Getting to know you all was a highlight of the past four years. I owe a special and heartfelt thanks to Gary Woodruff, who was my key point person, and his wonderful daughter Kate. Gary spent hours with me on the phone and in person. He also—miraculously—got me back in shape after my pregnancy and introduced me to Total Immersion swimming. I promised him that we would do a triathlon together and now that I've put it down on the page, I better start working. Before she died, Rosemary told Gary to always trust John Schewel—and so to get John's support meant the world to me. John has acted as a guide and a teacher, spending hundreds of hours with me on Skype and in person. Thank you also to John's wife, Cindia Beckering, for her genial warmth and loveliness. And, finally, thank you to Denis Berry, who was kind enough to spend time with me when she had more than enough on her plate. Your laugh is my happy place. Thank you all for everything that you have done for Rosemary—and for me.

And then there's Andrea Schulz, my extraordinary editor. Andrea's insights are on every page. She just *got* this story from day one. She was there at the earliest planning stages and took my second and third and fourth (and so on) drafts and elevated them beyond my wildest dreams. I am so lucky. Thank you to Elizabeth Pham Janowski, who worked tirelessly to get this book shored up and ready for release. The Viking team is spectacular: Colin Webber and Amanda Dewey blew me away with the cover and interior designs; Mike Brown made sure the production process went so smoothly; and Ingrid Sterner is hands down the best copy editor I've ever worked with. I'm so grateful to Brian Tart for seeing the value in Rosemary's story and putting your faith in me to tell it. Thank you also to the team at Canongate UK—Jamie Byng, Simon Thorogood, Francis Bickmore, and Jenny Fry—for their continual support of my work. I'm so excited to be publishing *The Acid Queen* with you.

Kim Witherspoon does not mince words, so I won't: Kim, you're the best agent in the business. Thank you also to Maria Whelan for your tireless work at every stage of the process and to Alexis Hurley for the work to come.

The Acid Queen is an ode to libraries—and it was my pleasure to spend blissful research days in the New York Public Library. Not only did the NYPL house and safeguard Rosemary's work, but it also stayed open during the height of the pandemic. Thank you especially to the wonderful team in the Brooke Russell Astor Reading Room for Rare Books and Manuscripts headed by reference archivist Tal Nadan.

There are so many remarkable humans who helped me—too many to name here. But I'll try. Special thanks to Adam and Christopher Phillips, who invited me to David Phillips's memorial service in San Francisco. Poet Kathy Shorr not only trespassed with me but wrote the article about Rosemary in *The Provincetown Independent* that inspired me to write this book. Maria Mangini was a mentor to me while writing this book. Her wisdom has touched every corner of my life. Oden Fong gave me a tour of Laguna Beach; Noel Tepper drove with me around Poughkeepsie; David Amram walked me down his musical history with Rosemary; Cathy Coleman not only gave me great details but also provided the most on-point astrological reading I've yet had; Bob Greenfield, whose book became a touchstone, met and spoke with me on several occasions; Donna Motsinger gave me so much trust; writer Dana Peleg threw a wonderful Rosemary remembrance party for me in Santa Cruz with Valerie Corral, Suzanne Wouk, Sherri Paris, and Angela Welty; Robert Forte gave me his only copy of Nina Graboi's book after he lost nearly everything in a fire; Brigitte Mars shared her memoir-in-progress with me and stayed in touch after surviving a near-death experience; I had a blast with the lovely Makiko and Les Wisner; and I'm so grateful to have interviewed the truly remarkable Peggy Hitchcock before her death. Thank you to Jack Leary, who responded to my interview requests with kindness.

Many other people contributed and are thanked in the notes, but I would like to highlight a few names in particular: Matthew Baggott, Dr. Anthony Bossis, Dr. Corine de Boer, David Jay Brown, Carol D'Amico, Rick Doblin, Zayd Dohrn, James Drice, Erika Dyck, Ross Ellenhorn, Jeffrey Evans, Dr. Gabriella Gobbi, Roger Hanson, Martina Hoffman, Jeff Jones, Naomi Lake, Devin Lander, Thomas Lannon, Pantelis Leptourgos, Glenn McCreedy, Dr. Hannah McLane, Hal Mermelstein, Carolyn Miller, Dr. Michael and Annie Mithoefer, Dimitri Mugianis, David Nickles, Michael O'Dowd, David Padwa, Jonah Raskin, Judge Albert Rosenblatt, Lily Kay Ross, Robert Ross, Angela Ruiz, Julie Salinger, Eugene Schoenfeld, Rosalie Siegel, Elinore Standard, Robert Tierney, Michael Tigar, Alvis Upitis, Dr. Rosalind Watts, and Drs. David and Bit Yaden. Thank you also to Mikki Maher and Joan Athey for all your work on photo permissions.

My friends know that I feel passionately about fact-checking books. It's so important! Rachel Stone, who fact-checked this book over nearly six months, is an especially brilliant and curious fact-checker. Thank you also to Julie Carlsen who did research assistance for me in the Berg Collection. Thank you to Casey Scieszka and Steven Weinberg at Spruceton Inn for housing me in the ideal setting. And a great big thank-you to Jeffrey Robinson, who helped me with my FOIA and FOIPA requests (much below market rate).

I have the best friends / first readers in the world. Thank you to Bob Kolker who gave me the title. David Gutherz is an intuitive genius who helped crystalize the best moments in this book. I can't wait for our next project! Bighearted Ada Calhoun gave me the support I needed in the book's earliest drafts; Abbott Kahler pushed me to provide the next level of detail in the second draft stage; Florence Keller and LaDoris Cordell provided wisdom and saved me from all manners of mistakes—breaking a wrist in the process; Mary Jane and Steve Gunn provided crucial Laredo specifics; Shannon Taggart kept me weird and changed my life; Dominic Sisti made essential changes at zero hour; Jae Connor sat through a reading of the entire book and gifted me with his enthusiasm and knowledge of the subject; Amy Jones added layers of emotional depth (and nods to psychedelic narcissism); and finally Maureen Callahan, a powerhouse, urged me to be strong and clear—and made this book so much better.

And there there's Stephen, who heard this book read aloud five times or so and sat through my yammering about it for years. Thank you for letting me close my office door while you took on the lion's share at home. Sammy, Genevieve, and Caleb are so lucky—as am I.

Bibliography

I've broken up the bibliography into sections to make it easier for the reader to track down information. I've listed each citation only once even if it informed multiple parts. The following are just books; articles, podcasts, documentaries, and so on cited directly are in the notes.

Relevant Timothy Leary Writing

Leary, Timothy. *Changing My Mind, Among Others: Lifetime Writings.* Englewood Cliffs, N.J.: Prentice-Hall, 1982.

——. *Chaos & Cyber Culture.* Berkeley, Calif.: Ronin, 2014.

——. *Confessions of a Hope Fiend.* New York: Bantam Books, 1973.

——. *Flashbacks: An Autobiography.* New York: G. P. Putnam's Sons, 1990.

——. *High Priest.* Berkeley, Calif.: Ronin, 1995.

——. *Interpersonal Diagnosis of Personality: A Functional Theory and Methodology for Personality Evaluation.* New York: Ronald Press, 1957.

——. *Jail Notes.* New York: Grove Press, 1970.

——. *The Politics of Ecstasy.* Oakland: Ronin, 1998.

——. *Psychedelic Prayers.* Oakland: Ronin, 1997.

——. *Start Your Own Religion.* Millbrook, N.Y.: Kriya Press, 1967.

——. *Terra II.* Internet Archive.

——. *Timothy Leary, the Harvard Years: Early Writings on LSD and Psilocybin with Richard Alpert, Huston Smith, Ralph Metzner, and Others.* Edited by James Penner. Rochester, Vt.: Park Street Press, 2014.

———. *What Does Woman Want?* Phoenix: Falcon Press, 1988.

Leary, Timothy, Ralph Metzner, and Richard Alpert. *The Psychedelic Experience.* 1964. New York: Citadel Press, 2007.

Biographies and Memoirs Related to Rosemary Woodruff Leary and Timothy Leary

Albert, Stew. *Who the Hell Is Stew Albert?* Los Angeles: Red Hen Press, 2003.

Anolik, Lili. *Hollywood's Eve: Eve Babitz and the Secret History of L.A.* New York: Simon & Schuster, 2019.

Ayers, Bill. *Fugitive Days.* Boston: Beacon Press, 2001.

Barritt, Brian. *The Road of Excess.* London: PSI Publishing, 1998.

Boucher, Sandy. *Dancing in the Dharma: The Life and Teachings of Ruth Denison.* Boston: Beacon Press, 2005.

Bryan, John. *Whatever Happened to Timothy Leary?* San Francisco: Renaissance Press, 1980.

Davis, Tom. *39 Years of Short-Term Memory Loss.* New York: Grove Atlantic, 2010.

Druch, Theodore P. *Timothy Leary and the Mad Men of Millbrook.* Puerto Vallarta, Mexico: PVWG, 2012.

Graboi, Nina. *One Foot in the Future: A Woman's Spiritual Journey.* Santa Cruz, Calif.: Aerial Press, 2000.

Greenfield, Robert. *Timothy Leary: A Biography.* New York: James H. Silberman Books, 2006.

Harcourt-Smith, Joanna. *Tripping on the Bardo with Timothy Leary: My Psychedelic Love Story.* North Charleston, S.C.: Create Space, 2013.

Higgs, John. *I Have America Surrounded.* Fort Lee, N.J.: Barricade Books, 2006.

Hollingshead, Michael. *The Man Who Turned on the World.* London: Blond & Briggs, 1973.

Kleps, Art. *Millbrook: A Narrative of the Early Years of American Psychedelianism.* Original Kleptonian Neo-American Church, 2005.

Lattin, Don. *The Harvard Psychedelic Club: How Timothy Leary, Ram Dass, Huston Smith, and Andrew Weill Killed the Fifties and Ushered in a New Age for America.* New York: HarperOne, 2010.

Leary, Rosemary Woodruff. *Psychedelic Refugee: The League for Spiritual Discovery, the 1960s Cultural Revolution, and 23 Years on the Run.* Edited by David F. Phillips. Rochester, Vt.: Park Street Press, 2021.

Liddy, G. Gordon. *Will: The Autobiography of G. Gordon Liddy.* New York: St. Martin's Press, 1996.

Minutaglio, Bill, and Steven L. Davis. *The Most Dangerous Man in America: Timothy Leary, Richard Nixon, and the Hunt for the Fugitive King of LSD.* New York: Twelve, 2018.

Phillips, David. *What I Remember About My Life.* www.radbash.com/autobiography/.

Ram Dass. *Be Here Now.* San Cristobal, N.M.: Hanuman Foundation, 1978.

———. *Being Ram Dass.* Boulder, Colo.: Sounds True, 2021.

BIBLIOGRAPHY

Ram Dass and Ralph Metzner. *Birth of a Psychedelic Culture: Conversations About Leary, the Harvard Experiments, Millbrook, and the Sixties.* With Gary Bravo. Santa Fe, N.M.: Synergetic Press, 2010.

Schou, Nicholas. *Orange Sunshine: The Brotherhood of Eternal Love and Its Quest to Spread Peace, Love, and Acid to the World.* New York: Thomas Dunne Books, 2010.

Sirius, R. U. *Timothy Leary's Trip Through Time.* Futique Trust, 2013.

Slack, Charles. *Timothy Leary, the Madness of the Sixties, and Me.* New York: Peter H. Wyden, 1974.

Tendler, Stewart, and David May. *The Brotherhood of Eternal Love.* London: Panther Books, 1984.

Tigar, Michael. *Sensing Injustice.* New York: Monthly Review Press, 2021.

Ulrich, Jennifer. *The Timothy Leary Project: Inside the Great Counterculture Experiment.* New York: Abrams Press, 2018.

Whitmer, Peter O. *Aquarius Revisited: Seven Who Created the Sixties Counterculture That Made America.* New York: Macmillan, 1987.

Books Rosemary Woodruff Leary Cited in Her Writing

Bradley, Marion Zimmer. *The Mists of Avalon.* New York: Ballantine Books, 1982.

Bullfinch, Thomas. *Bullfinch's Mythology.* New York: Avenel Books, 1979.

Dick, Philip K. *The Three Stigmata of Palmer Eldritch.* New York: First Mariner Books, 2011.

Fowles, John. *The French Lieutenant's Woman.* New York: Back Bay Books, 1969.

———. *The Magus.* New York: Picador, 1988.

Hamilton, Edith. *Mythology: Timeless Tales of Gods and Heroes.* New York: Grand Central, 1999.

Heinlein, Robert A. *I Will Fear No Evil.* New York: Ace, 2021.

Hesse, Hermann. *The Glass Bead Game.* New York: Henry Holt, 1990.

———. *Steppenwolf.* Translated by Thomas Wayne. New York: Algora, 2010.

Huxley, Aldous. *The Genius and the Goddess.* New York: Harper Perennial, 2009.

Jung, Emma. *Animus and Anima.* Putnam, Conn.: Spring Publications, 2004.

Kazan, Elia. *The Arrangement.* New York: Avon Books, 1967.

le Carré, John. *The Night Manager.* New York: Ballantine Books, 1993.

Leo, Alan. *Key to Your Own Nativity.* London: L. N. Fowler, 1970.

Neumann, Erich. *The Origins and History of Consciousness.* Princeton, N.J.: Princeton University Press, 2014.

Piercy, Marge. *Vida.* 1979. Oakland: PM Press, 2012.

Tiptree, James, Jr. *Her Smoke Rose Up Forever.* San Francisco: Tachyon Publications, 2004.

Wilhelm, Richard, and Cary F. Baynes, trans. *The I Ching; or, Book of Changes.* Princeton, N.J.: Princeton University Press, 1977.

Winsor, Kathleen. *Forever Amber.* Chicago: Chicago Review Press, 2000.

BIBLIOGRAPHY

Books about Psychedelics

Aaronson, Bernard, and Humphrey Osmond, eds. *Psychedelics: The Uses and Implications of Hallucinogenic Drugs*. New York: Doubleday, 1970.

Artaud, Antonin. *The Peyote Dance*. Translated by Helen Weaver. New York: Farrar, Straus and Giroux, 1976.

Breen, Benjamin. *Tripping on Utopia*. New York: Grand Central, 2024.

Brown, David Jay, and Rebecca McClen Novick. *Mavericks of the Mind: Conversations for the New Millennium*. Freedom, Calif.: Crossing Press, 1993.

Cashman, John. *LSD Story*. Greenwich, Conn.: Fawcett, 1966.

Devereux, Paul. *The Long Trip: A Prehistory of Psychedelia*. Brisbane, Australia: Daily Grail, 1997.

Dunlap, Jane. *Exploring Inner Space: Personal Experience Under LSD-25*. New York: Harcourt, Brace & World, 1961.

Dyck, Erika. *Psychedelic Psychiatry: LSD from Clinic to Campus*. Baltimore: Johns Hopkins University Press, 2008.

Farber, David, ed. *The War on Drugs: A History*. New York: New York University Press, 2022.

Friedman, B. H. *Tripping: A Memoir*. Provincetown, Mass.: Provincetown Arts Press, 2006.

Giffort, Danielle. *Acid Revival: The Psychedelic Renaissance and the Quest for Medical Legitimacy*. Minneapolis: University of Minnesota Press, 2020.

Gips, Elizabeth. *Scrapbook of a Haight Ashbury Pilgrim: Spirit, Sacraments, and Sex in 1967/1968*. Santa Cruz, Calif.: Changes Press, 1991.

Grof, Stanislav. *Realms of the Human Unconscious: Observations from LSD Research*. London: Souvenir Press, 2019.

Harris, Rachel. *Swimming in the Sacred: Wisdom from the Psychedelic Underground*. Novato, Calif.: New World Library, 2023.

Hofmann, Albert. *LSD: My Problem Child: Reflections on Sacred Drugs, Mysticism, and Science*. San Jose, Calif.: Multidisciplinary Association for Psychedelic Studies, 2017.

Holland, Julie. *Good Chemistry: The Science of Connection, from Soul to Psychedelics*. New York: Harper Wave, 2020.

Huxley, Aldous. *The Doors of Perception*. New York: Harper Perennial, 2009.

Huxley, Laura Archera. *This Timeless Moment: A Personal View of Aldous Huxley*. San Francisco: Mercury House, 1991.

Jarnow, Jesse. *Heads: A Biography of Psychedelic America*. New York: Da Capo Press, 2016.

Jay, Mike. *Psychonauts: Drugs and the Making of the Modern Mind*. New Haven, Conn.: Yale University Press, 2023.

Kempner, Joanna. *Psychedelic Outlaws*. New York: Hachette, 2024.

Kinzer, Stephen. *Poisoner in Chief*. New York: Henry Holt, 2019.

Lee, Martin A., and Bruce Shlain. *Acid Dreams: The Complete Social History of LSD: The CIA, the Sixties, and Beyond*. New York: Grove Press, 1985.

BIBLIOGRAPHY

Marks, John. *The Search for the "Manchurian Candidate."* New York: Times Books, 1979.

Moore, Robert. *Facing the Dragon: Confronting Personal and Spiritual Grandiosity.* Asheville, N.C.: Chiron Publications, 2013.

Newland, Constance A. *Myself and I.* New York: Coward-McCann, 1962.

Palmer, Cynthia, and Michael Horowitz, eds. *Sisters of the Extreme: Women Writing on the Drug Experience.* Rochester, Vt.: Park Street Press, 2000.

Papaspyrou, Maria, Chiara Baldini, and David Luke, eds. *Psychedelic Mysteries of the Feminine.* Rochester, Vt.: Park Street Press, 2019.

Pollan, Michael. *How to Change Your Mind.* New York: Penguin Books, 2018.

Richards, William A. *Sacred Knowledge: Psychedelics and Religious Experience.* New York: Columbia University Press, 2018.

Solomon, David. *The LSD Game.* New York: Putnam, 1965.

Strassman, Rick. *DMT: The Spirit Molecule.* Rochester, Vt.: Park Street Press, 2000.

Tafur, Joseph. *The Fellowship of the River: A Medical Doctor's Exploration into Traditional Amazonian Plant Medicine.* Phoenix: Espiritu Books, 2017.

Watts, Alan W. *The Joyous Cosmology: Adventures in the Chemistry of Consciousness.* Novato, Calif.: New World Library, 1962.

Texts That Provided General Historical Context

Adler, Margot. *Drawing Down the Moon: Witches, Druids, Goddess-Worshippers, and Other Pagans in America.* New York: Penguin Books, 1986.

Amram, David. *Offbeat: Collaborating with Kerouac.* Boulder, Colo.: Paradigm, 2008.

———. *Upbeat: Nine Lives of a Musical Cat.* London: Routledge, 2016.

———. *Vibrations: A Memoir.* New York: Thunder's Mouth Press, 2001.

Babitz, Eve. *Eve's Hollywood.* New York: New York Review Books, 2015.

Bebergal, Peter. *Season of the Witch: How the Occult Saved Rock and Roll.* New York: Jeremy P. Tarcher/Penguin, 2014.

Bingham, Clara. *Witness to the Revolution: Radicals, Resisters, Vets, Hippies, and the Year America Lost Its Mind and Found Its Soul.* New York: Random House, 2016.

Boyle, Kevin. *The Shattering: America in the 1960s.* New York: W. W. Norton, 2021.

Broyard, Anatole. *Kafka Was the Rage.* New York: Vintage, 1993.

Castaneda, Carlos. *The Teachings of Don Juan.* Berkeley: University of California Press, 1998.

Charters, Ann, ed. *The Portable Sixties Reader.* New York: Penguin Books, 2003.

Cleaver, Eldridge. *Soul on Ice.* New York: Delta Books, 1999.

Conners, Peter. *The White Hand Society: The Psychedelic Partnership of Timothy Leary and Allen Ginsberg.* San Francisco: City Lights Books, 2010.

Cunningham, Michael. *Land's End: A Walk in Provincetown.* New York: Picador, 2002.

BIBLIOGRAPHY

Davis, Erik. *High Weirdness: Drugs, Esoterica, and Visionary Experience in the Seventies.* Cambridge, Mass.: MIT Press, 2019.

Dickstein, Morris. *Gates of Eden: American Culture in the Sixties.* New York: Liveright, 2015.

Didion, Joan. *Slouching Towards Bethlehem.* New York: Farrar, Straus and Giroux, 1961.

———. *The White Album.* New York: Farrar, Straus and Giroux, 2009.

di Prima, Diane. *Memoirs of a Beatnik.* New York: Penguin Books, 1998.

Eig, Jonathan. *The Birth of the Pill: How Four Crusaders Reinvented Sex and Launched a Revolution.* New York: W. W. Norton, 2014.

Emerson, Rick. *Unmask Alice: LSD, Satanic Panic, and the Imposter Behind the World's Most Notorious Diaries.* Dallas: BenBella, 2022.

Estés, Clarissa Pinkola. *Women Who Run with the Wolves: Myths and Stories of the Wild Woman Archetype.* New York: Ballantine Books, 1992.

Evans, Sara M. *Born for Liberty: A History of Women in America.* New York: Free Press, 1997.

Fanon, Frantz. *A Dying Colonialism.* New York: Grove Press, 1965.

Farrell, John A. *Richard Nixon: The Life.* New York: Doubleday, 2017.

Finch, Robert. *Common Ground: A Naturalist's Cape Cod.* New York: W. W. Norton, 1981.

Ford, Phil. *Dig: Sound and Music in Hip Culture.* London: Oxford University Press: 2013.

Frum, David. *How We Got Here: The 70's.* New York: Basic Books, 2000.

Gage, Beverly. *G-Man: J. Edgar Hoover and the Making of the American Century.* New York: Viking, 2022.

Gifford, Justin. *Revolution or Death: The Life of Eldridge Cleaver.* Chicago: Lawrence Hill Books, 2020.

Guinn, Jeff. *Manson: The Life and Times of Charles Manson.* New York: Simon & Schuster, 2013.

Gumbo, Judy. *Yippie Girl: Exploits in Protest and Defeating the FBI.* New York: Three Rooms Press, 2022.

Gysin, Brion. *The Process.* London: Quartet Books, 1969.

Hillen, Andreas. *1973: Nervous Breakdown.* New York: Bloomsbury, 2008.

Hodgdon, Timothy. *Manhood in the Age of Aquarius: Masculinity in Two Countercultural Communities.* New York: Columbia University Press, 2008.

Hoffman, Abbie. *Soon to Be a Major Motion Picture.* New York: Perigree, 1980.

Hoffman, Abbie, and Anita Hoffman. *To America with Love: Letters from the Underground.* New York: Stonehill, 1976.

Horgan, John. *Rational Mysticism: Spirituality Meets Science in the Search for Enlightenment.* Boston: Mariner Books, 2004.

Hyde, Lewis. *Trickster Makes the World: Mischief, Myth, and Art.* New York: North Point Press, 1998.

James, William. *The Varieties of Religious Experience: A Study in Human Nature.* New York: Modern Library, 1994.

BIBLIOGRAPHY

Jezer, Marty. *Abbie Hoffman: American Rebel*. New Brunswick, N.J.: Rutgers University Press, 1993.

Johnson, Joyce. *Minor Characters: A Young Woman's Coming-of-Age in the Beat Orbit of Jack Kerouac*. New York: Doubleday, 1994.

Johnson, Robert A. *Owning Your Shadow: Understanding the Dark Side of the Psyche*. New York: Harper Collins, 1991.

Jones, Hettie. *How I Became Hettie Jones*. New York: Grove Press, 1990.

Jones, Thai. *A Radical Line: From the Movement to the Weather Underground, One Family's Century of Conscience*. New York: Free Press, 2004.

Kirkpatrick, Rob. *1969: The Year Everything Changed*. New York: Skyhorse Publishing, 2011.

Koerner, Brendan. *The Skies Belong to Us: Love and Terror in the Golden Age of Hijacking*. New York: Crown, 2013.

Kramer, Jane. *Paterfamilias: Allen Ginsberg in America*. London: Gollancz, 1970.

Lachman, Gary. *Turn Off Your Mind: The Dedalus Book of the 1960s*. Sawtry, U.K.: Dedalus, 2009.

Leadabrand, Russ. *Guidebook to the San Jacinto Mountains of Southern California*. Los Angeles: Ward Ritchie Press, 1971.

Lemke-Santangelo, Gretchen. *Daughters of the Aquarius: Women of the Sixties Counterculture*. Lawrence: University Press of Kansas, 2009.

Linkletter, Art. *Drugs at My Door Step*. Waco, Tex.: Word Books, 1973.

Mailer, Norman. *Tough Guys Don't Dance*. New York: Ballantine Books, 1984.

McShane Wulfhart, Nell. *The Great Stewardess Rebellion*. New York: Anchor, 2022.

Menand, Louis. *The Free World: Art and Thought in the Cold War*. New York: Farrar, Straus and Giroux, 2021.

Miles, Rosalind. *The Women's History of the Modern World: How Radicals, Rebels, and the Everywomen Revolutionized the Last 200 Years*. New York: William Morrow, 2021.

Mokhtefi, Elaine. *Algiers, Third World Capital*. London: Verso, 2018.

Muraresku, Brian C. *The Immortality Key: The Secret History of the Religion with No Name*. New York: St. Martin's Press, 2020.

Partridge, Christopher. *High Culture: Drugs, Mysticism, and the Pursuit of Transcendence in the Modern World*. New York: Oxford University Press, 2018.

Perlstein, Rick. *The Invisible Bridge: The Fall of Nixon and the Rise of Reagan*. New York: Simon & Schuster, 2014.

Raskin, Jonah. *Out of the Whale: Growing Up in the American Left*. New York: Links Books, 1974.

Rosen, Ruth. *The World Split Open: How the Modern Women's Movement Changed America*. New York: Penguin Books, 2006.

Roszak, Theodore. *The Making of a Counterculture*. Berkeley: University of California Press, 1995.

Rozzo, Mark, *Everybody Thought We Were Crazy*. New York: Ecco, 2022.

Schulman, Bruce J. *The Seventies: The Great Shift in American Culture, Society, and Politics*. New York: Da Capo Press, 2001.

Sheldrake, Merlin. *Entangled Life: How Fungi Make Our Worlds, Change Our Minds, and Shape Our Futures*. New York: Random House, 2020.

Shorr, Kathy. *Provincetown: Stories from Land's End*. Beverly, Mass.: Commonwealth Editions, 2002.

Smith, Huston. *The World's Religions*. New York: Harper One, 1991.

Smith, Richard J. *The I Ching: A Biography*. Princeton, N.J.: Princeton University Press, 2012.

Snyder, Don. *Aquarian Odyssey: A Photographic Trip into the Sixties*. New York: Liveright, 1979.

Spalding, Phebe Estelle. *The Tahquitch Maiden: A Tale of the San Jacintos*. San Francisco: Paul Elder, 1911.

Stanley, Rhoney Gissen. *Owsley and Me: My LSD Family*. Rhinebeck, N.Y.: Monkfish, 2012.

Starhawk. *Dreaming the Dark: Magic, Sex, and Politics*. Boston: Beacon Press, 1997.

Storr, Anthony. *Feet of Clay: Saints, Sinners, and Madmen: A Study of Gurus*. New York: Free Press, 1996.

Trilling, Diana. *We Must March, My Darlings: A Critical Decade*. New York: Harcourt Brace Jovanovich, 1964.

Turner, Fred. *From Counterculture to Cyberculture: Stewart Brand, the Whole Earth Network, and the Rise of Digital Utopianism*. Chicago: University of Chicago Press, 2006.

Wakefield, Dan. *New York in the Fifties*. New York: Greenpoint Press, 1992.

Walsh, Pilar. *How I Survived the 60's*. Pilar Walsh, 2013.

Washington, Peter. *Madame Blavatsky's Baboon*. New York: Schocken Books, 1996.

Wilson, Colin. *The Occult*. London: Watkins, 2015.

Wolfe, Tom. *The Electric Kool-Aid Acid Test*. New York: Bantam, 1967.

———. *The Purple Decades*. New York: Farrar, Straus and Giroux, 1982.

———. *Radical Chic and Mau-Mauing the Flak Catchers*. New York: Bantam Books, 1970.

Zwerin, Michael. *Close Enough for Jazz*. London: Quartet Books, 1983.

———. *The Silent Sound of Needles: The Nightmare World of the Junkie and His Heroic Struggle to Be Reborn*. Englewood Cliffs, N.J.: Prentice-Hall, 1969.

Notes

I relied most heavily on the Rosemary Woodruff Leary Papers in the Manuscripts and Archives Division of the New York Public Library; Rosemary's personal files, which include diaries and many drafts of her memoir, in Gary Woodruff's possession; and the Timothy Leary Papers also in the New York Public Library. Unless otherwise noted, dialogue and Rosemary's thoughts come from these sources. I quote from Rosemary's published memoir, *Psychedelic Refugee*, throughout and have cited it extensively in my notes. I also included quotations from Rosemary's letters in Stanford's Special Collections. Some archival documentation also came from the Ludlow–Santo Domingo Library collection at Harvard. Noel Tepper, Eleanor Standard, and John Schewel also shared their personal archives, which include letters, newspaper articles, photographs, and a magic diary. I am indebted to the biographies that have come before—particularly Robert Greenfield's *Timothy Leary*, which is quoted throughout. I also included a great deal of information from a wide variety of secondary sources on the history of psychedelics, the counterculture, and the drug wars, which are in my bibliography.

NOTES

Preface

xiii THE BRIEF was: Letters from Gary Woodruff's personal archive. Discussion of the code found in Timothy Leary's FBI files, in the Timothy Leary Papers, New York Public Library.

xiii "I can be free": Exchange recorded in Rosemary's diary found in Rosemary Woodruff Leary Papers, New York Public Library. Also found (with key differences) in Rosemary Leary, *Psychedelic Refugee*, 150, and Timothy Leary, *Confessions of a Hope Fiend*, 87.

xiv Her new name, Sylvia E. McGaffin: In both Rosemary's and Timothy's personal writing they use the pseudonym Margaret Ann McCreedy, but this was a fake alias created by Timothy for *Hope Fiend*. The real name can be found in the Senate hearing "Hashish Smuggling and Passport Fraud," Oct. 3, 1973. Thank you to Minutaglio and Davis's *Most Dangerous Man in America* for clearing this confusion up for me.

xiv dubbed her "the Woodruff woman": "Woodruff Avoids Appearing," *Poughkeepsie Journal*, June 1966.

xiv "the former administrative assistant": Murray Illson, "Dr. Leary Weds His Former Aide," *New York Times*, Nov. 29, 1967.

xv "hadn't worn a bra in years": Minutaglio and Davis, *Most Dangerous Man in America*, 55.

xv "the broad in [Leary's] bed": Kleps, *Millbrook*, 147.

xv "As beautiful as she was": Druch, *Timothy Leary and the Mad Men of Millbrook*, 333.

Part One: The Stewardess
Chapter One: The Genius and the Goddess

5 It's common for children: For more on mystical experiences in childhood see Tobin Hart, *The Secret Spiritual World of Children* (Novato, Calif.: New World Library, 2010).

5 But like many seers: Harris, *Swimming in the Sacred* has great details on the overlap between female shamans and early childhood mystical experience.

6 "Protective of my budding self": Rosemary Leary, *Psychedelic Refugee*, 14.

7 "laughter, the silliness": di Prima, *Memoirs of a Beatnik*, 72.

8 harder to get into than Harvard: This and details to follow come from McShane Wulfhart, *Great Stewardess Rebellion*.

9 "We didn't simply read": Broyard, *Kafka Was the Rage*, 30.

9 "the new consciousness": A phrase attributed to Allen Ginsberg, Jack Kerouac, William Burroughs, and later Tom Wolfe.

10 "I am condemned": *Being and Nothingness* (New York: Washington Square Press, 1992), 439.

10 "Don't lies eventually lead": *The Fall* (London: Amish Hamilton, 1917), 92.

10 "say nothing and wear black": Jack Kerouac, "The Origins of the Beat Generation," *Playboy*, June 1959.

11 "Rosemary was a truly special": Amram, interview by author, April 22, 2022.

11 Alice B. Toklas's famous 1954 cookbook: *The Alice B. Toklas Cook Book* (New York: Harper Perennial, 2021) contained an entry for "Haschich Fudge," a recipe sent to her by the painter, writer, and Moroccan expat Brion Gysin. The "food of paradise" contained spices, nuts, figs, and cannabis, prompting "laughter floods of thought."

13 Charles was a prodigy: "Charles Mills," Broadcast Music, Inc., http://acacomposers.s3.amazonaws.com/documents/millscharles-brochures.pdf.

14 "enough," as one priest told him: Artaud, *Peyote Dance*, 35.

14 inspiring works like Allen Ginsberg's: Joanna Pawlik, "Artaud in Performance: Dissident Surrealism and the Postwar American Literary Avant-Garde," *Papers of Surrealism*, no. 8 (2010): 10.

14 extolled mescaline's ability to induce: Huxley, *The Doors of Perception*, 19, 17.

14 "The man who comes back": Huxley, *The Doors of Perception*, 79.

15 "'the genius and the goddess'": Kate Coleman, "Rosemary's Journey," *7x7 San Francisco*, Oct. 2001, 78.

Chapter Two: *The Book of Changes*

17 "I have trouble relating": Bryan, *Whatever Happened to Timothy Leary?*, 114.

18 *That's how he does it!*: Gary Woodruff, interview by author, Jan. 21, 2021.

18 "but one special type of consciousness": James, *Varieties of Religious Experience*, 388.

18 Madame Helena Petrovna Blavatsky: There's a great variety of sources on Blavatsky. I found the following particularly helpful: Matthew Wills, "Spiritualism, Science, and the Mysterious Madame Blavatsky," *JSTOR Daily*, Oct. 25, 2016; Washington, *Madame Blavatsky's Baboon*.

19 "Ever since I was five": Alexandra David-Neel, *My Journey to Lhasa* (London: William Heineman, 1927), ix.

19 an English translation of the *I Ching*: Throughout I will be referencing the Wilhelm and Baynes *I Ching*. Special thanks to "Episode 82: On the *I Ching*," *Weird Studies*, podcast, Sept. 16, 2020, for crystallizing the text's importance in Rosemary's life.

20 He told a reporter: The interview, resultant publicity, and eventual drama between the interviewer and Grant is chronicled beautifully in Stephen Siff, *Acid Hype* (Champaign: University of Illinois Press, 2015).

20 "Kaleidoscopic, fantastic images": Hofmann, *LSD*, 14.

20 American psychiatrists had embraced LSD: See bibliography for a list of early American psychedelic history sources, but special acknowledgment goes to Dyck, *Psychedelic Psychiatry*. I also had the pleasure of interviewing Dyck on several occasions.

NOTES

20 **Sandoz sent supplies of LSD:** Kempner, *Psychedelic Outlaws*, 102.

21 **"castrating and unfeeling":** Harold Greenwald, preface to *My Self and I*, by Newland, a fascinating account of an anonymous woman's LSD therapy.

21 **CIA's clandestine MK-ULTRA experiments:** There is so much more to say about this. But brevity is the soul of wit, especially with something so nefarious and diffuse. *Acid Dreams* is a great place to start.

21 **"destroy integrity and make indiscreet":** Kinzer, *Poisoner in Chief*.

21 **the CIA also provided funding:** Al Larkin Jr., "LSD Tests on Humans Is Denied: Harvard Outlines Its CIA Work," *Boston Globe*, Sept. 27, 1977. Also see Jonathan D. Moreno, *Mind Wars* (New York: Bellevue Literary Press, 2012).

21 **upward of $5,000:** Jules Evans, "The Trials of Psychedelic Therapy," *Ecstatic Integration*, Sept. 3, 2022, www.ecstaticintegration.org/p/the-trials-of-psychedelic-therapy.

22 **"Eyes upturned, crescent moons":** Rosemary Leary, *Psychedelic Refugee*, 23.

23 **"Before my first psychedelic experience":** Rosemary Woodruff Leary, interview by Joyce Johnson, *The Sands of Time*, WOMR, 1991. Thank you to John Braden for finding this audio.

23 **"It was part of my journey":** From an undated interview with Dana Peleg.

23 **six stewardesses had killed themselves:** McShane Wulfhart, *Great Stewardess Rebellion*, 80.

25 **"What we cannot speak":** Ludwig Wittgenstein, translation by D. F. Pears and B. F. McGuinness, *Tractatus Logico-Philosophicus* (New York: Humanities Press, 1961), T.7.

25 **"You are the kindest man":** Timothy Leary, *Flashbacks*, 229.

Chapter Three: A Real Visionary

26 **"the death-rebirth experience":** Timothy Leary, *High Priest*, 9.

28 **"a middle-aged man involved":** Timothy Leary, *High Priest*, 41.

28 **"My darling, I cannot live":** Lattin, *Harvard Psychedelic Club*, 14.

29 **Rose of Leary, would be used by employers:** Astrid Pratidina et al., "Leary's Rose to Improve Negotiation Skills Among Health Professionals," *Education for Health* 26, no. 1 (2013): 54–56.

30 **"was above all and without question":** Timothy Leary, "The Religious Experience: Its Production and Interpretation," *Psychedelic Review* 1, no. 3 (1964): 324.

30 **"I learned more about psychology":** Tom Koch, "How to Go Out of Your Mind—the LSD Crisis," CBC, www.youtube.com/watch?v=sIkot1DYC8Q.

30 **"You are never the same":** Timothy Leary, *High Priest*, 34.

30 **With full support of the department:** This support included the father of personality theory Henry Murray, who worked for the Office of Strategic Services, a precursor to the CIA. If you want to go down a rabbit hole, Murray also designed the humiliation tests that the Unabomber, Ted Kaczynski, underwent as an undergrad at Harvard.

31 **"Now here is a man":** Greenfield, *Timothy Leary*, 109.

31 **"I cannot believe":** Babitz, *Eve's Hollywood*, 178.

31 **"deadly mechanical spider's web":** Ram Dass and Metzner, *Birth of a Psychedelic Culture*, 29.

31 **"barrel through the house":** Ram Dass and Metzner, *Birth of a Psychedelic Culture*, 33.

31 **"If you encountered Hollingshead's":** Andy Roberts, *Divine Rascal: On the Trail of LSD's Cosmic Courier, Michael Hollingshead* (Strange Attractor Press, London, 2019), 11.

31 **"pathetic clown":** Timothy Leary, *High Priest*, 257.

32 **return imprisonment rates reportedly cut:** Important to note that these figures would later be successfully debunked by Rick Doblin in a thirty-four-year follow-up study. Instead of dropping from a 56 percent recidivism rate to a 32 percent rate, Doblin found that the control number was closer to 34 percent—a mere 2 percent drop.

32 **"relaxed and natural atmosphere":** The descriptions of sessions come from Timothy Leary, George H. Litwin, and Ralph Metzner, "On Set and Setting Theory," in Timothy Leary, *Timothy Leary, the Harvard Years*, 73–98.

33 **"The nervous system, stripped":** Timothy Leary, "Languages: Energy Systems Sent and Received," *ETC: A Review of General Semantics* 22, no. 4 (Dec. 1965): 441.

33 **"A frown. A gesture":** Timothy Leary, *High Priest*, 159.

34 **"She doesn't want you there":** Timothy Leary, *High Priest*, 100.

34 **"I was afraid I would get high":** Greenfield, *Timothy Leary*, 188.

34 **"I took care of the kitchen":** Bryan, *Whatever Happened to Timothy Leary?*, 112.

35 **"the right, right now":** Timothy Leary, *Politics of Ecstasy*, 84.

35 **"the long telephone wire":** Koch, "How to Go Out of Your Mind."

36 **for $1 a year:** Ram Dass, *Being Ram Dass*, 112.

36 **"The history of our research":** Timothy Leary, *High Priest*, 171.

37 **"a cult turned inward":** Ram Dass and Metzner, *Birth of a Psychedelic Culture*, 81.

37 **"road maps for new interior territories":** Leary, Metzner, and Alpert, *Psychedelic Experience*, 3.

37 **"Whenever in doubt":** Leary, Metzner, and Alpert, *Psychedelic Experience*, 6.

37 **"LSD is a strange drug":** Ram Dass, *Being Ram Dass*, 14.

38 **"Of course for every hundred men":** "Tim Leary Interview, Part One," n.d., www.dailymotion.com/video/x7ktzn.

NOTES

38 **"the first draft of pure oxygen"**: This and dialogue to come found in Rosemary Leary, *Psychedelic Refugee*, 28.

39 **"An entire mythology"**: Ludwig Wittgenstein, *The Mythology in Our Language* (Chicago: Hau Books, 2018), 198. He uses "deposited" instead of "stored," which is more often used as translation.

Chapter Four: The Match

40 **"We have this friend"**: Thank you to Peggy Hitchcock for speaking to me. This scene comes from our conversation on June 22, 2022.

41 **"swinging door relationship"**: Interview with Hitchcock found in Ram Dass and Metzner, *Birth of a Psychedelic Culture*, 58.

41 **"Why didn't you come"**: Exchange comes from Rosemary Leary, *Psychedelic Refugee*, 41, and Timothy Leary, *Flashbacks*, 231.

43 **"precedent for illumination"**: Timothy Leary, *Flashbacks*, 189.

43 **Dieterich named the sprawling estate**: Details of the estate come from Carrie Hojnicki, "Timothy Leary's Hitchcock Estate in Millbrook, New York, May Be the State's Strangest Home," *Architectural Digest*, July 28, 2017, www.architecturaldigest.com/story/timothy-leary-hitchcock-estate-millbrook.

44 **"designed for soft landings"**: Timothy Leary, *Flashbacks*, 189.

44 **"kindly check your esteemed ego"**: Graboi, *One Foot in the Future*, 164.

45 **As was his relationship with Richard Alpert**: Bryan, *Whatever Happened to Timothy Leary?*, 112.

45 **Timothy's friends, Flo and Maynard Ferguson**: There's so much more to say about Flo Ferguson. A wonderful resource is her daughter, who is interviewed here: "Interview with Lisa Ferguson," Timothy Leary Archives, www.timothylearyarchives.org/interview-with-lisa-ferguson-millbrook-kid-and-director-of-children -of-the-revolution/.

45 **"I'll tell you a story"**: Timothy Leary, *Psychedelic Prayers*, 44.

46 **"I looked at you"**: Timothy Leary to Rosemary, April 12, 1970.

46 **culled the number of authorized research projects**: Kempner, *Psychedelic Outlaws*, 145.

46 **Sandoz would deliver, in an armored car**: Katherine R. Bonson, "Regulation of Human Research with LSD in the United States (1949–1987)," *Psychopharmacology* 235 (2018): 597.

47 **summer weekend at Millbrook**: Details of seminar weekends found in archives.

47 **"One of the oldest methods"**: Quotation found in Hollingshead, *Man Who Turned on the World*.

48 **"A modern man lives in sleep"**: P. D. Ouspensky, *In Search of the Miraculous* (New York: Harcourt, 1950), 66. Thank you to Anthony Storr's *Feet of Clay* for its brilliant summary of Gurdjieff's work.

48 **"We live as sleeping robots"**: Timothy Leary, "Languages: Energy Systems Sent and Received," 442.

48 **The footage opens**: Koch, "How to Go Out of Your Mind."

49 **"You have to lose your mind"**: Rosemary Leary, *Psychedelic Refugee*, 30.

Chapter Five: The Apprentice

51 **"There was always the possibility"**: David Jay Brown, "The Magician's Daughter," interview with Rosemary Woodruff Leary, Mavericks of the Mind, Nov. 16, 2011, www.davidjaybrown.com/rosemary-woodruff -leary/.

52 **"I didn't think he was crazy"**: Larry Hughes, "Leary Lived Here," *Poughkeepsie Journal*, June 2, 1996, 1D.

53 **"She was about the sanest and kindest"**: Jack Leary, email with author, Oct. 22, 2022.

53 **"thought more of her as my mother"**: Bryan, *Whatever Happened to Timothy Leary?*, 165.

53 **"She was the best-read person"**: Timothy Leary, *Flashbacks*, 235.

54 **"I dare say that we shall"**: Sigmund Freud and C. G. Jung, *The Freud/Jung Letters* (Princeton, N.J.: Princeton University Press, 1974), 186. First came across this lovely quotation in Storr's *Feet of Clay*.

54 **A "polyphase orgasm"**: More on this found in Davis, *High Weirdness*, 228.

55 **"Can you, murmuring"**: Timothy Leary, *Psychedelic Prayers*, 92.

55 **"He had that glorious thing"**: Bryan, *Whatever Happened to Timothy Leary?*, 52.

56 **"integration or union"**: Description comes from Leary's fellow Harvard Psilocybin Project researcher and friend Huston Smith, *World's Religions*, 27.

57 **Nganasan female shamans**: For more on this, see Anastasiia Fedorova, "Capturing the Treasured Wisdom of Female Shamans in Russia," Vice.com, Jan. 29, 2016, www.vice.com/en/article/jpy7ad/capturing-the -treasured-wisdom-of-female-shamans-in-russia.

57 **famous *curandera*, María Sabina**: For more on Sabina, see Osiris Sinuhé González Romero, "María Sabina, Mushrooms, and Colonial Extractivism," Chacruna, May 27, 2021, chacruna.net/maria-sabina -mushrooms-and-colonial-extractivism.

58 **"release from the finitude"**: Smith, *World's Religions*, 21.

58 **"Rosemary—sophisticated, worldly"**: Timothy Leary, *Flashbacks*, 233.

59 **"Through Rosemary I learned"**: Timothy Leary, *Flashbacks*, 233.

60 **"I don't really count it"**: Interview with Susan Homer, in Ram Dass and Metzner, *Birth of a Psychedelic Culture*, 148.

60 **"The Millbrook community flowered"**: Metzner, introduction to *Psychedelic Prayers*, by Rosemary Leary, 20.

NOTES

Part Two: The Assistant
Chapter Six: Morning Glory Seeds

66 **"Who does Rosemary remind you of?":** Rosemary Leary, *Psychedelic Refugee*, 38–39.

67 **Timothy was *"prohibido"*:** Timothy Leary, *Flashbacks*, 235.

67 **shoring up its anti-drug presence:** Details about the border found in Farber, *War on Drugs*.

68 **"Have you ever been":** Interview with Rosemary, in Greenfield, *Timothy Leary*, 242.

68 **"Jackie, shake this out":** Rosemary Leary, *Psychedelic Refugee*, 53.

68 **"All the grass out":** Timothy Leary, *Flashbacks*, 239.

69 **"You can't study consciousness":** Seymour Krim, "Dr. Leary's Defense," *New York Herald Tribune*, April 6, 1966, 1. Originally found in Greenfield, *Timothy Leary*, 246.

70 **they called her his "assistant":** "'Not the Homecoming We Planned,' Says Leary on Greeting Assistant," *Poughkeepsie Journal*, June 3, 1966, 11.

70 **Timothy's response:** "Rose Mary Woodruff": Greenfield, *Timothy Leary*, 250.

71 **"I no longer regretted":** Timothy Leary, *Flashbacks*, 252.

71 **"In my panties":** Marya Mannes, "Young People and LSD: A Talk with Susan Leary," *McCall's*, July 1966, 115.

71 **She even resorted to eating food:** Bryan, *Whatever Happened to Timothy Leary?*, 89.

71 **"slow to realize how much":** Timothy Leary, *Flashbacks*, 242.

72 **"Tim wanted to make this":** Ram Dass and Metzner, *Birth of a Psychedelic Culture*, 195.

72 **"Things don't matter, really":** Mannes, "Young People and LSD," 115.

73 **"It was like society was coming apart":** Hughes, "Leary Lived Here," 1D.

73 **On Saturday, April 16:** There have been dozens of accounts of the raid. I relied on Rosemary's and Timothy's of course, but also Eve Babitz's account in *Eve's Hollywood*, 178–79, and Marya Mannes, "The Raid on Castalia," *Reporter*, May 19, 1966.

73 **"You'll never guess what":** Liddy, *Will*, 110.

74 **"the nuclear bomb of the psychedelic family":** Timothy Leary, "Programmed Communication During Experiences with DMT (DIMETHYLTRYPTAMINE)," *Psychedelic Review* 8 (1966): 83–95.

74 **"There are a bunch of hunters":** This and the rest of the raid scene described in Rosemary Leary, *Psychedelic Refugee*, 49–51.

74 **"Wonder Woman reflex":** This line and the rest of the raid described in Timothy Leary, *Flashbacks*, 243–44.

75 **Sometimes you see what you hope:** For the record, Jack Leary also doesn't remember Rosemary wearing a revealing gown the night of the raid as he wrote in an email to the author dated Oct. 14, 2022.

Chapter Seven: The Woodruff Woman

77 **The Poughkeepsie lawyer Noel Tepper:** Interviews conducted with Tepper over the phone and in person throughout 2021. He also shared his archives with me, including several undated *Poughkeepsie Journal* pieces that were essential to the trial. These included "Miss Woodruff Avoids Appearing," June 30, 1966; "'Not the Homecoming We Planned,' Says Leary on Greeting Assistant"; and "Miss Woodruff Called by Jury After US Plea Fails." Wonderful photographs in Rosemary's archive also brought this lost grand jury hearing to life for me.

79 **"epidemic of acid heads":** "Psychiatry: An Epidemic of Acid Heads," *Time*, March 11, 1966, content.time .com/time/subscriber/article/0,33009,899088,00.html.

80 **"Don't you realize":** Rosemary Leary, *Psychedelic Refugee*, 59.

80 **"I didn't like my role":** Rosemary Leary, *Psychedelic Refugee*, 59.

81 **Judge Raymond Baratta:** From *Poughkeepsie Journal* files and obituary: "Raymond C. Baratta," *Poughkeepsie Journal*, Oct. 20, 1990, 4a.

81 **"What is the name of this religion":** This exchange and more about the grand jury hearing found in Rosemary Leary, *Psychedelic Refugee*, 54–58.

82 **The jail was in frequent violation:** Mary Knox, "Women Behind Bars at the Dutchess County Jail," *Vassar Chronicle*, April 14, 1977, https://newspaperarchives.vassar.edu/?a=d&d=vcchro19770414-01.2.16&e= -------en-20--1--txt-txIN-------.

84 **bulldozed by Senator Ted Kennedy:** U.S. Congress, "The Narcotics Rehabilitation Act of 1966: Hearings Before a Special Subcommittee, Eighty-Ninth Congress, Second Session," Washington, D.C., Library of Congress, 1966.

84 **"A pioneer experimenter . . . acknowledged":** "Drug out of Control," *Daily Standard*, May 13, 1966, 1.

84 **She licked every page:** Sal Coxe, interview by author, Dec. 13, 2021.

85 **"I've lost twenty-five days":** "Rosenblatt Searches in Vain: Miss Woodruff Walks Out of Scheduled Jury Hearing," *Poughkeepsie Journal*, n.d. Found in Rosemary's archives.

86 **"it looks like I can go home":** Rosemary Leary, *Psychedelic Refugee*, 72.

86 **"Miss Rosemary Woodruff?":** "A Hurried Exit," *Poughkeepsie Journal*, n.d.

86 **"I tried to talk of jail":** Rosemary Leary, *Psychedelic Refugee*, 72.

87 **lessons learned from 311 trips:** Bernard Gavzer, "The *Playboy* Interview with Timothy Leary," *Playboy*, Sept. 1966, www.playboy.com/read/the-playboy-interview-with-timothy-leary.

NOTES

88 **"pure gifts of the Gods'":** C. G. Jung, *Letters of C. G. Jung: Volume 2, 1951–1961* (Florence: Taylor & Francis, 2015). Thank you to Jules Evans, "Five Reservations About Psychedelic Therapy," *Ecstatic Integration*, March 15, 2024, for confirming the importance of this quotation.

89 **"the Woodruff appeal":** "Mrs. Leary's Conviction to Go to Supreme Court," *Poughkeepsie Journal*, Feb. 23, 1968, 1.

Chapter Eight: Death of the Mind

90 **"Like every great religion":** "Doctor Forms Religion Based on Use of Drugs," *San Francisco Chronicle*, Sept. 1966. Found in archive, no page number, no date.

90 **"alter the consciousness of thy fellow man":** Timothy Leary, *Politics of Ecstasy*, 95.

91 **"peddled LSD as a chemically synthesized":** Stew Albert, "Death of a Salesman: Remembering Tim Leary," *Tikkun*, Sept. 1996, www.yippiegirl.com/stew/leary.htm.

91 **the Commodore, a five-story redbrick vaudeville:** A great description comes from Allison B. Siegel, "History of the Fillmore East in the East Village as the Allman Brothers Say Farewell," Untapped New York, untapped cities.com/2014/02/05/history-of-the-fillmore-east-in-the-east-village-as-the-allman-brothers-say-farewell/.

92 **As the master of ceremonies:** Descriptions come from *Psychedelic Refugee*, Leary's writing, surviving show pamphlets, and, especially, Diane Trilling, "Celebration #1," *New Yorker*, Oct. 1, 1966, 40–41.

92 **"Entrance for madmen only":** Hesse, *Steppenwolf*, 130, rb.gy/kjyv9.

93 **"a mind-loss experience":** Timothy Leary and Ralph Metzner, "Hermann Hesse: Poet of the Interior Journey," *Psychedelic Review* 1, no. 2 (Fall 1963): 172, maps.org/research-archive/psychedelicreview/v1n2/012167lea.pdf.

93 **"the biggest off-Broadway event":** Eleanore Lester, "'Taking a Trip' with Leary," *New York Times*, Dec. 4, 1966, D5. Found thanks to Greenfield, *Timothy Leary*, 287.

93 **"could not hold the two of us":** Rosemary Leary, *Psychedelic Refugee*, 77.

94 **"He's the devil":** Rosemary Leary, *Psychedelic Refugee*, 80.

96 **"it was truly beautiful":** Greenfield, *Timothy Leary*, 325.

96 **In 1967, the year Timothy entertained:** Menand, *Free World*, 456.

97 **"People should not be allowed":** Bryan, *Whatever Happened to Timothy Leary?*, 96

97 **"You are only as young":** David Colker, "The Terminal Man," *Los Angeles Times*, Aug. 28, 1995, www.la times.com/archives/la-xpm-1995-08-28-ls-39657-story.html.

98 **"No romance had ever had":** Slack, *Timothy Leary, the Madness of the Sixties, and Me*, 222.

98 **he lived on Grape Nuts:** Greenfield, *Timothy Leary*, 295.

98 **"totally inept at being a father":** Interview with Jack Leary, in Greenfield, *Timothy Leary*, 295.

99 **a form of psychedelic "spiritual narcissism":** Roos Vonk and Anouk Visser, "An Exploration of Spiritual Superiority," *European Journal of Social Psychology* 51, no. 1 (2020): 152–65.

99 **Chögyam Trungpa:** Another complicated figure, plagued with controversy, especially in relation with women, who died of cirrhosis of the liver at age forty-eight.

99 **"infinitely superior to anything":** Aleister Crowley, *Diary of a Drug Fiend* (London: W. Collins & Sons, 1922), 89.

99 **The goal was "ego death":** A special thanks to Adam Aronovich's work, especially Dr. Lynn Marie Morski, "Psychedelic Narcissism with Adam Aronovich," *Plant Medicine Podcast*, 2021, www.plantmedicine.org/podcast/psychedelic-narcissism-adam-aronovich.

99 **"unearthly" and "radiant":** Graboi, *One Foot in the Future*, 207–8.

100 **Nina was more than just an admiring visitor:** Information on Graboi comes from *One Foot in the Future* and conversations with her friends in Santa Cruz.

100 **"I cannot now remember":** Graboi, *One Foot in the Future*, 170.

100 **"He smells of glue":** Graboi, *One Foot in the Future*, 242.

101 **familiar reality had cracked":** Graboi, *One Foot in the Future*, 244.

101 **As Timothy held court, Nina observed:** Scene from Graboi, *One Foot in the Future*, 266–69. Additional details found in an unpublished draft of the chapter found in the NYPL's Rosemary Woodruff Leary Papers.

101 **Susan called Rosemary an "evil woman":** Kleps, *Millbrook*, 189.

102 **"More than attraction at the central level":** Schewel, interview by author, July 8, 2021.

103 **And John saw it, too:** Schewel, interview by author, Sept. 15, 2021.

104 **"a star whose essence":** Rosemary Leary, *Psychedelic Refugee*, 103.

Chapter Nine: The Robot

105 **"gathering of the tribes":** This and other descriptions of the Be-In were found in the Berg Collection at the New York Public Library.

105 **Dennis Hopper stood in the crowd:** Helpful depiction of the Be-In and Hopper's role in it found in Rozzo, *Everybody Thought We Were Crazy*.

105 **Timothy, dressed in white:** Tony Bove, "Timothy Leary—Turn On," YouTube video, 2:16, 2013, www .youtube.com/watch?v=IPSzTBP5PAU.

106 **a trend called the "dropout effect":** Discussed in detail in Giffort, "Turn On, Tune In, Go to the Bake Sale," in *Acid Revival*.

106 *The Saturday Evening Post* **warned:** Bill Davidson, "The Hidden Evils of LSD," *The Saturday Evening Post*, Aug. 12, 1967, bibliography.maps.org/resources/download/11416.

106 **a soon-to-be-retracted article:** G. J. Alexander, "LSD Injection Early in Pregnancy Produces Abnormality in Offspring of Rats," *Science* 157, no. 459 (1967).

107 **"Are you sure you guys get high?":** Rosemary Leary, *Psychedelic Refugee*, 86.

107 **the chemist Melissa Cargill:** Cargill is a shadowy figure. Thanks to Emily Dufton, "Hidden Figures of Drug History: Melissa Cargill," *Points History*, June 11, 2019, pointshistory.com/2019/06/11/hidden-figures-of-drug-history-melissa-cargill/.

108 **they called the Brotherhood of Eternal Love:** Many details about the Brotherhood come from Schou, *Orange Sunshine*.

108 **"Although unschooled and unlettered":** Tendler and May, *Brotherhood of Eternal Love*, 36.

108 **He ran home, high as hell:** William Kirkley, director, *Orange Sunshine*, Go Digital, 2016.

109 **"I could see what he meant":** Rosemary Leary, *Psychedelic Refugee*, 92.

110 **"We were saddled with enormous":** Brown, "Magician's Daughter."

110 **"a barroom brawler's face":** Rosemary Leary, *Psychedelic Refugee*, 112.

110 **"Their sessions became a battle":** Ram Dass and Metzner, *Birth of a Psychedelic Culture*, 200.

110 **When the photographer Alvis Upitis:** Upitis, interview by author, June 17, 2022.

113 **"Every night he loved me":** Rosemary Leary, *Psychedelic Refugee*, 105.

113 **"wanted to be fucked":** Robert Greenfield, interview by author, March 8, 2022.

113 **"the broad in his bed":** Kleps, *Millbrook*, 144.

113 **"a virtually celestial being":** Kleps, *Millbrook*, 120.

113 **"Rosemary, beautiful as she was":** Druch, *Timothy Leary and the Mad Men of Millbrook*, 333.

114 **"It was a paradise to some":** Graboi, *One Foot in the Future*, 164.

114 **Peggy Hitchcock remembers this:** Peggy Hitchcock, interview by author, June 10, 2022.

114 **"I was always the kind of homemaker":** Boucher, *Dancing in the Dharma*, 113.

115 **"The light came in":** Diane di Prima, "The Holidays at Millbrook—1966," *The Portable Sixties Reader*, 345.

115 **Nina Graboi documented a scene:** The altercation is described in Graboi, *One Foot in the Future*, 205–6.

115 **acid mixed with apple cider:** Found in a fascinating article from Poughkeepsie's underground newspaper, run by a group of local kids. "Chez Jim: Ovum Visits Castalia," *Ovum*, 1967, www.chezjim.com/ovum/castalia2.html. Confirmed in interviews with Leary at the time and in Greenfield's *Timothy Leary* that acid was given to children.

115 **"lances and they were piercing":** Interview with Jeanne di Prima appeared in Greenfield, *Timothy Leary*, 295.

116 **"living in a church":** Coleman, "Rosemary's Journey," 78.

116 **One former resident of Millbrook:** Druch, *Timothy Leary and the Mad Men of Millbrook*, 224.

118 **So destabilized she could no longer:** Thank you to the work of Jules Evans and his Challenging Psychedelic Experiences Project, which was helpful in framing this "acid overdose." His Substack was integral to this book. For more on depersonalization see Jules Evans, "I Don't Feel Like I'm Fully Here," *Ecstatic Integration*, Nov. 17, 2023, www.ecstaticintegration.org/p/i-dont-feel-like-im-fully-here?utm_source=post-email-title&publication_id=1072242&post_id=138947877&utm_campaign=email-post-title&isFreemail=false&r=1r9q5.

Chapter Ten: The Seagulls

121 **"tantric love goddess":** Metzner, introduction to *Psychedelic Prayers*, by Rosemary Leary, 20.

122 **Metzner used MDMA to great effect:** Sophia Adamson and Ralph Metzner, "The Nature of the MDMA Experience and Its Role in Healing, Psychotherapy, and Spiritual Practice," *ReVision: The Journal of Consciousness and Change* 10, no. 4 (1988), maps.org/research-archive/mdma/revision.html.

122 **he called drugs like MDA:** Ralph Metzner, "Letter from Ralph Metzner," *Multidisciplinary Association for Psychedelic Studies* 4, no. 1 (1993): 44, maps.org/news/bulletin/remembrance-and-renewal/.

125 **Her hexagram: number 45:** The hexagram was found in her contemporary diary, and the text comes from Wilhelm and Baynes, *I Ching*, 615. But Rosemary has changed the hexagram several times. In *Psychedelic Refugee* she says that the throw yielded hexagram 32, "Duration," which reads, "The way of a husband and wife should be long lasting." Robert Greenfield interviewed Rosemary, who told him that the throw was hexagram 37, "The Family," which reads, "The perseverance of the woman furthers . . ." I've gone with her diary, but whichever way you read it, a similar message is being communicated.

125 **"The wedding march was a symphony":** Rosemary Leary, *Psychedelic Refugee*, 121.

125 **"He directed Tim to place":** Rosemary Leary, *Psychedelic Refugee*, 123.

126 **Timothy wished the cops:** Cay Parker Jones, "Hitchcock Due to Appear," *Poughkeepsie Journal*, Dec. 11, 1967, A-1, www.newspapers.com/image/114761711/?terms=%22timothy%20leary%22%20%22marriage%22&match=1.

128 **read one headline in the *Poughkeepsie Journal*:** "Leary Retirement Thrills Millbrook," *Poughkeepsie Journal*, Nov. 29, 1967.

128 **"I still count those sixty-four rooms":** Greenfield, *Timothy Leary*, 324.

129 **The reporters directed questions:** "Leary Going Underground," AP News Wire, Feb. 16, 1968.

129 **Timothy repeated his promise:** Ralph Dighton, "Leary Seeks 'Wise Man of Century' Title," *Long Beach Post-Telegram*, Feb. 15, 1968, 15.

129 **"Marriage hadn't changed anything"**: Rosemary Leary, *Psychedelic Refugee*, 111.

129 **"sneeze and make headlines"**: Albert, "Death of a Salesman."

130 **"I think you're full of crap"**: Interview with Timothy Leary, *The Dick Cavett Show*, April 1968.

130 **"He must have been nervous"**: Dorothy Manners, "Timothy 'LSD' Leary Visits 'Alice' Set," *Indianapolis Star*, Feb. 6, 1968, 12.

130 **"He kept looking at Rosemary"**: Ram Dass and Metzner, *Birth of a Psychedelic Culture*, 213.

131 **"strong influence on her lover"**: Bryan, *Whatever Happened to Timothy Leary?*, 165.

131 **"Tim and Rosemary as a dyad"**: Slack, *Timothy Leary, the Madness of the Sixties, and Me*, 20.

Part Three: The Acid Queen
Chapter Eleven: Blinded by the Sun

135 **There were at least four deaths:** These included the Berkeley teen Vernon Cox, fifteen-year-old Michael Barnhardt, a twenty-nine-year-old woman in London, and a "young man" in New York City who leaped out of a fourth-floor window in Manhattan, according to several sources. Many more are unnamed with only vague descriptions and are impossible to verify.

135 **"One should never take LSD":** "Ex–Harvard Prof Says LSD Should Be Under Control," *Gettysburg Times*, Sept. 15, 1966, www.newspapers.com/image/46272843/.

135 **J. Anthony Lukas wrote:** J. Anthony Lukas, "The Two Worlds of Linda Fitzpatrick," *New York Times*, Oct. 16, 1967, archive.nytimes.com/www.nytimes.com/books/97/10/26/home/luckas-fitzpatrick.html.

135 **A former medical student stabbed:** Warren Hall, "Atomic LSD Will Be Tough to Stop," *Daily News*, May 1, 1966, www.newspapers.com/image/463235555/.

135 **college student fell into a viaduct:** "Took LSD Trip from Viaduct," *Montreal Star*, April 29, 1967, 4.

136 **"produce a psychosis of the population":** Solomon, *LSD Game.*

136 **the kind of psychedelic bioweapon:** "Project Mk-Ultra-Intellipedia," CIA.gov, December 28, 2022, https://www.cia.gov/readingroom/document/06760269.

136 **"was first set in motion":** Stew Albert, "Free Tim!," *Quicksilver Times*, April 3–13, 1970, washington spark.files.wordpress.com/2020/04/1970-04-03-quicksilver-vol-2-no-9-rotate-center.pdf.

136 **with three hundred U.S. soldiers dying:** "24 Americans Killed in Week, Lowest Toll in War Since '65," *New York Times*, Nov. 6, 1970, 4.

136 **Gary essentially shrugged:** Gary Woodruff, interview by author, July 5, 2022.

137 **"Don't vote," Timothy would say:** Greenfield, *Timothy Leary*, 303.

137 **"Your peace-and-love bullshit":** Timothy Leary, *Flashbacks*, 269.

138 **"well-fed Brahmin prince":** Bryan, *Whatever Happened to Timothy Leary?*, 96.

138 **In his State of the Union:** Lyndon B. Johnson, "Annual Message to the Congress on the State of the Union," Jan. 17, 1968, American Presidency Project, www.presidency.ucsb.edu/node/237325.

138 **Drugs destroyed families:** Great details on Nixon's philosophy, as guided by J. Edgar Hoover, found in Gage, *G-Man.*

138 **"besotted, applauded with the rest":** Rosemary Leary, *Psychedelic Refugee*, 105.

139 **"I was with him now":** Rosemary Leary, *Psychedelic Refugee*, 104.

139 **"the wisest man of the twentieth century":** Dighton, "Leary Seeks 'Wise Man of Century' Title."

139 **Owsley Stanley later estimated:** Pierre Perone, "Owsley Stanley," *Independent*, March 15, 2011, www.in dependent.co.uk/news/obituaries/owsley-stanley-sound-engineer-and-muse-to-the-grateful-dead-whose -lsd-laboratory-helped-shape-sixties-counterculture-2241794.html.

139 **to make and distribute 750 million doses:** William Grimes, "Nicholas Sand, Chemist Who Sought to Bring LSD to the World, Dies at 75," *New York Times*, March 12, 2017, www.nytimes.com/2017/05/12/us /nicholas-sand-chemist-who-sought-to-bring-lsd-to-the-world-dies-at-75.html. See also the documentary *The Sunshine Makers.*

140 **"turn on everyone in the world":** Grimes, "Nicholas Sand."

140 **The Brothers genuinely believed in this mission:** Great sources for Brotherhood details came via interviews, the documentary *Orange Sunshine*, and Schou's *Orange Sunshine.*

140 **They incorporated their own acid church:** Benjamin Ramm, "The LSD Cult That Transformed America," BBC, Jan. 12, 2017, www.bbc.com/culture/article/20170112-the-lsd-cult-that-terrified-america.

140 **"the focal point":** Interview with Michael Randall, *Orange Sunshine*, directed by William Kirkley.

140 **Afghanistan grew into an international:** Great history of drug trafficking in Afghanistan found in Farber, *War on Drugs.*

140 **A stucco Spanish Mission–style Taco Bell:** Special thank-you to Oden Fong for the tour and sharing so much insight.

141 **"They were not bigshots":** C. D. Stelzer,"Dredged from the Hard Drive: A 1992 Interview with the LSD Guru," *Riverfront Times*, Nov. 8, 1992, stlreporter.com/2020/11/08/timothy-learys-dead/.

142 **"We have no electricity":** Bryan, *Whatever Happened to Timothy Leary?*, 181.

143 **"My body is a hammock":** Rosemary Leary, *Psychedelic Refugee*, 127.

143 **"if I just got high enough":** Rosemary Leary, *Psychedelic Refugee*, 134.

144 **"And what if I can't have children?":** Rosemary Leary, *Psychedelic Refugee*, 119.

144 **hysterosalpingogram, an X-ray of the uterus:** Information about this procedure found in Timothy Leary's FBI files. Thank you to Drs. James Drife, Maria Mangini, and Michael O'Dowd for their above-and-beyond help in making sense of this condition.

145 **Rosemary took a trip:** Scene described in private writings and Rosemary Leary, *Psychedelic Refugee*, 131.

145 **the women of the Soboba Band:** "The Luiseño of California," Native Talk, 2005, nativetalk.org/the-luiseno-of-california/.

146 **"There is no water":** Wilhelm and Baynes, *I Ching*, 182.

146 **a "psychic energizer":** Greenfield, *Timothy Leary*, 346.

146 **They dropped Susan off:** Arrest details come from Greenfield, *Timothy Leary*, 346, court documents in archive, and various interviews with Neil Purcell.

146 **found a pipe, a one-inch chunk of hashish:** Despite all the newspaper coverage and books written about this, it was surprisingly difficult to find concrete numbers of what was confiscated. I got this information from Rosemary's probation report.

147 *Thank God Susan isn't here:* Greenfield, *Timothy Leary*, 343.

147 **Rosemary and Timothy traveled:** Scene described at various points in Rosemary's writings, including in *Psychedelic Refugee*, and in Timothy Leary, *Jail Notes*.

147 **"My breath was caught by the horns":** Rosemary Leary, *Psychedelic Refugee*, 146.

148 **"For just one perceptible second":** Timothy Leary, *Jail Notes*, 144–45.

Chapter Twelve: Rosemary Wept

150 **"the happiest day":** "Leary's Next Vision: Governor," *Dayton Daily News*, May 20, 1969.

150 **"I'm going to run for the governorship":** "Leary to Run for Governor," *Statesville Record and Landmark*, May 22, 1969.

150 **"You know, you could stir up":** Timothy Leary, *Flashbacks*, 279.

150 **"I'm going to run, with my":** "Leary tosses head into the ring," *Los Angeles Free Press*, May 23, 1969. The following interview quotations with Rosemary come from this article.

151 **"Now there's no federal law":** "Leary Planning Party, to Run for Governor," United Press International, May 21, 1969.

151 **"I was a bit of a sloganeer":** Greenfield, *Timothy Leary*, 355.

152 **Later Yoko included:** "Unfinished Music No. 2: Life with the Lions," Beatles Bible, Sept. 7, 2010, www.beatlesbible.com/people/john-lennon/albums/unfinished-music-no-2-life-with-the-lions/.

152 **Her close friends called her Dolcino:** Joe Eszterhas, "The Strange Case of the Hippie Mafia," *Rolling Stone*, Dec. 7, 1972, 30. Details from this death come from Rosemary's writing, this article, and several other contemporaneous articles in the archive.

153 **"by threat, command":** "New Leary LSD Death Counts Due," United Press International, Aug. 1969.

153 **"This is a ghoulish thing":** "Leary Arrested in L.A., Then Released as Bail Is Posted," *Los Angeles Times*, July 26, 1969, A1.

153 **there were eighty bombings:** Kirkpatrick, *1969*, 15.

153 **Hijackers took over fifty planes:** For more details on this, see Koerner, *Skies Belong to Us*.

153 **The FBI responded by adding thousands:** Micah Uetricht, interview with Aaron J. Leonard, "Infiltrating the Left," *Jacobin*, Aug. 22, 2018, jacobin.com/2018/08/fbi-infiltration-new-left-aoki-sds.

154 **John Griggs, had scored a crystal form:** Details of John Griggs's passing come from Schou, *Orange Sunshine*, 189–91.

154 **The dealer is "pure":** Timothy Leary, "Deal for Real," *East Village Other*, Sept. 1969, 43.

155 **"It wasn't suicide":** Robert H. Schuller, *Turning Hurts into Halos, and Scars into Stars* (Nashville: Thomas Nelson, 1999), www.google.com/books/edition/Turning_Hurts_Into_Halos/CfTUC87NOqoC?hl=en&gbpv=1&bsq=if%20i%20get%20my%20hands.

155 **acid flashbacks—a concept:** Laura Orsolini et al., "The 'Endless Trip' Among the NPS Users: Psychopathology and Psychopharmacology in the Hallucinogen-Persisting Perception Disorder," *Frontiers of Psychiatry* 8 (2017): 240.

155 **Some see perseverating shapes:** This and the other examples come from the work of Jules Evans and his Challenging Psychedelic Experiences Project. See also Shaunacy Ferro, "Are Acid Flashbacks a Myth?," *Popular Science*, Sept. 23, 2013, www.popsci.com/science/article/2013-08/fyi-can-acid-trip-really-give-you-flashbacks/.

155 **one study found that around 10 percent:** Otto Simonsson et al., "Prevalence and Association of Challenging, Difficult, or Distressing Experiences Using Classical Psychedelics," *Journal of Affective Disorders* 326 (April 2023): 105–10, www.sciencedirect.com/science/article/pii/S0165032723000915.

156 **the sixty-page Controlled Substances Act:** "Public Law 91-51-Oct. 27, 1970," govinfo.gov, www.govinfo.gov/content/pkg/STATUTE-84/pdf/STATUTE-84-Pg1236.pdf. For a great summary, see chapter 10 in Farber, *War on Drugs*.

156 **Nixon signed into law:** "Comprehensive Drug Control Bill Cleared by Congress," CQ Almanac 1970, https://library.cqpress.com/cqalmanac/document.php?id=cqal70-1293935#:~:text=S%203246%20(which%20the%20Senate,modifying%20the%20original%20Administration%20proposal.

NOTES

156 **Amphetamines, meanwhile, which had hit:** "Drug Wars," *Frontline*, www.pbs.org/wgbh/pages/frontline/shows/drugs/buyers/socialhistory.html#fn.
156 **"the increasing problem of drug use":** Ronald Reagan, "State of the State," Jan. 6, 1970.
157 **"was the face of the enemy":** Minutaglio and Davis, *Most Dangerous Man in America*, 14.
157 **"a female complaint":** "Wife's Absence Postpones Dr. Leary Drug Case Again," clip of an article in archive, dated Sept. 26, 1967.
158 **"Mrs. Leary, still recovering":** Don Smith, "Timothy Leary Playing His Role as High Priest to Hilt," *Los Angeles Times*, Oct. 27, 1969, B3.
158 **Purcell watched Timothy smack:** Greenfield, *Timothy Leary*, 368.
159 **people in the courtroom overheard Timothy:** Greenfield, *Timothy Leary*, 368.
159 **"It really isn't a marijuana case":** Rosemary Leary, "Laughing Leary," *Berkeley Barb*, Feb. 27, 1970, 3.
159 *Holding Together brings good fortune:* Wilhelm and Baynes, *I Ching*, 36.
160 **"Those who have been with her":** Rob Hayes, "Leary Hassle: Law on Bum Trip," *Berkeley Barb*, March 6–12, 1970, 8.
160 **"He has preached the length":** "Judge in Texas Sentences Leary," *Rochester Democrat and Chronicle*, March 3, 1970, 5A.
161 **Her hands shook as she read:** "Rosemary Wept," *Berkeley Barb*, March 6, 1970, 7.
162 **Leary was "a pleasure-seeking":** "Leary Requests Bail," *Ithaca Journal*, April 8, 1970, 2.

Chapter Thirteen: The Surrogate Monarch of Psychedelia
163 **"Jail honed him down":** Bryan, *Whatever Happened to Timothy Leary?*, 195.
163 **Timothy, meanwhile, had sent:** The bulk of these letters and the details in this chapter come from letters in Gary Woodruff's possession that have never been seen before.
165 **"You've got to free me":** Rosemary Leary, *Psychedelic Refugee*, 150.
165 **"Rosemary Leary hustled every dime":** Bryan, *Whatever Happened to Timothy Leary?*, 198.
166 **"anyone who the government didn't like":** Interview with Kennedy in Kirkley, *Orange Sunshine*, 2016.
166 **"patron lawyer of unpopular causes":** Sam Roberts, "Michael J. Kennedy, Lawyer for Underdogs and Pariahs, Dies at 78," *New York Times*, Jan. 28, 2016, www.nytimes.com/2016/01/27/us/michael-j-kennedy-lawyer-for-underdogs-and-pariahs-dies-at-78.html.
167 **"to be part of the passions":** This and many details came from Michael Gross, "Ivana's Avenger," *New York*, Feb. 18, 1991, 33–41.
167 **"As a team, I was all intuition":** Interview with Eleanora Kennedy, *Radical Love*, directed by William Kirkley, 2020. This short documentary provided a treasure trove of information.
167 **"anyone who has had a loved one":** Rosemary Leary, *Psychedelic Refugee*, 134.
168 **my husband has been kidnapped:** "Statement by Rosemary," *East Village Other*, April 1, 1970, 20.
168 **Rosemary's soft voice delivered:** Found in Holding Together records, audio files, New York Public Library.
168 **christened her "the surrogate monarch of psychedelia":** Carolyn Anspacher, "Mrs. Leary Holding Together," *San Francisco Chronicle*, March 21, 1970.
168 **"The proper place to experiment":** Steven V. Roberts, "Leary Goes to Prison on Coast to Start Term of 1 to 10 Years," *New York Times*, March 22, 1970.
168 **During one recorded interview:** Found in the Holding Together records.
169 **"The thing to remember about Tim":** John Lombardi, "Mrs. Leary Is Meeting Her Probation Officer," *Rolling Stone*, October 1, 1970, 18.
169 **"the media heroine, the grass widow":** Timothy Leary, *Flashbacks*, 291.
169 **"Well, we were stuck":** Lombardi, "Mrs. Leary Is Meeting Her Probation Officer," 18.
169 **"She's so mellow, Rosemary":** Rick Heide, "Holding Together," *Berkeley Barb*, March 20, 1970.
170 **"We're rarely afraid":** "Bad Trip for Learys," *Harvard Crimson*, March 17, 1970, www.thecrimson.com/article/1970/3/17/bad-trip-for-learys-ptimothy-leary/.
170 **"It is myth, not mandate":** Irwin Edman, *The World, the Arts, and the Artist* (New York: W. W. Norton, 1928), 39.
170 **A favorite new friend, Oden Fong:** Fong, interviews with author, April 2022.
171 **Mike Pinder broke the spell:** "Moody Blues/Poco/Turley Richards/Steve Miller Band," Concert Archives, recorded April 4, 1970, www.concertarchives.org/concerts/the-moody-blues-poco-steve-miller-turley-richards-steve-miller-band.
172 **"Was it cold?":** Richard Ogar, "Uncle Tim's Om Orgy," *Berkeley Barb*, May 1, 1970, 7.
172 **the crucial connection of the night:** This meeting was described in *Psychedelic Refugee* and Rosemary's personal writings, as well as by Michael Horowitz in "Acid Bodhisattva," Timothy Leary Files, www.timothylearyarchives.org/acid-bodhisattva/, and Lisa Rein, "Interview with Timothy Leary Archivist Michael Horowitz," *Boing Boing*, Aug. 30, 2017, boingboing.net/2017/08/30/interview-with-timothy-leary-a.html/.
173 **"You could see she was under":** Interview with Horowitz, in "Acid Bodhisattva."

Chapter Fourteen: The Computer
175 **"goose-stepping conformity":** William O. Douglas, *Points of Rebellion* (New York: Random House, 1969), constitution.org/2-Authors/wod/wod_por.htm.

NOTES

175 "Rosemary and I are American Eagles": Timothy Leary Memorandum to the Supreme Court and related documents, Manuscripts and Archives Division, New York Public Library.

177 Dr. Hippocrates, had pulled some strings: Schoenfeld, interview by author, Nov. 15, 2021.

177 Justice Douglas decried Timothy's: "Leary Loses Bid for Bail," *Shreveport Times*, May 20, 1970, 4.

177 "I think that was the first time": Interview with Joe Rhine in "Second Bardo: The Period of External Game Reality," *Psychedelic Review*, no. 11 (Winter 1970/71): 28, maps.org/wp-content/uploads/2007/11/n110 28rhi.pdf.

178 "I mean, I was a superwoman": Greenfield, *Timothy Leary*, 383.

179 "Her face was inches from me": John shared this excerpt of his work in progress: Schewel, interview by author, Aug. 11, 2022.

180 Tigar wrote in his own biography: Tigar, *Sensing Injustice*, 391–92.

180 "Michael was our lawyer": Interview with Bill Ayers, "New Morning," *Mother Country Radicals*, podcast, June 23, 2022, crooked.com/podcast/chapter-5-new-morning/.

180 "We helped the Weathermen": Interview with Eleanora Kennedy, *Radical Love*.

180 "Because he was, what": Interview with Bernardine Dohrn, "New Morning," *Mother Country Radicals*.

180 $25,000 in a paper bag: I've seen different figures, but $25,000 is repeated most often and by the people closest to the money.

181 they needed a radicalized Timothy: Jones, interview by author, July 13, 2022.

181 "Guns and grass are united": "Communique #1 from the Weather Underground," May 21, 1970, www .socialhistoryportal.org/sites/default/files/raf/0419700521.pdf.

181 "Our intention is to disrupt": Weather Underground, *Prairie Fire: The Politics of Revolutionary Anti-imperialism* (San Francisco: Communications Co., 1974), 13, https://www.sds-1960s.org/PrairieFire-re print.pdf.

182 Gary brought a friend: Gary Woodruff, interview by author, June 2, 2021.

Chapter Fifteen: Sylvia McGaffin

184 "I need two pounds": Jeff Jones, interview by author, July 13, 2022.

184 whom Rosemary called Pam: Thank you to David Phillips, who revealed Pam's identity in the footnotes of *Psychedelic Refugee* on page 152.

185 "Oh lord must I look this way?": Timothy Leary, *Confessions of a Hope Fiend*, 96–98. A good deal of the escape comes from parts of *Hope Fiend* written by Rosemary (and published without her consent). Corresponding notes in her personal archive support the *Hope Fiend* version.

185 Rosemary then boarded a plane: There are some discrepancies about timeline and location. Leary has written that Rosemary got her passport in New York; Greenfield wrote that they all got their passports at the same time in Chicago. Rosemary's version (that she and Pam went to Chicago first) lines up with supporting documents in the archive and the FBI version of events.

187 On September 12, 1970: Details of Leary's escape come from *Confessions of a Hope Fiend*, 388–90, and Minutaglio and Davis, *Most Dangerous Man in America*, 7–9.

187 "I offer loving gratitude": Timothy Leary, "The P.O.W. Communiqué," found in Rosemary's New York Public Library archives.

188 "We'll have him in ten days": Peter Ainslie, "Focus: How Tim Leary Fled Jail for Greener Grass: Extradition Remote," *Women's Wear Daily*, Oct. 8, 1971, via Minutaglio and Davis, *Most Dangerous Man in America*.

188 "These college students": Rosemary Leary, *Psychedelic Refugee*, 151.

188 "They now convincingly espoused": Rosemary Leary, *Psychedelic Refugee*, 153.

189 "In prison he became": Rosemary Woodruff Leary, interview by BBC, unaired, found in Timothy Leary Papers.

191 "I was on the verge": Rosemary Leary, *Psychedelic Refugee*, 158.

191 "Everything about him irritated me": Greenfield, *Timothy Leary*, 395.

192 "You've got to come right away": Rosemary Leary, *Psychedelic Refugee*, 165.

Chapter Sixteen: Maia Baraka

193 "Not knowing what to expect": Rosemary Leary, *Psychedelic Refugee*, 165.

194 "Did you bring some money?": Rosemary Leary, *Psychedelic Refugee*, 166.

195 "It was like taking medicine": Cleaver, *Soul on Ice*, 12.

195 "You're either part": "Cleaver's Message, Complex, Revealing," *Daily Tar Heel*, Oct. 19, 1968, 2. A good deal of the information about Cleaver comes from Gifford, *Revolution or Death*.

195 "The harassment and brutality": Rosemary Leary, *Psychedelic Refugee*, 167.

195 10 percent of Black Panther members: Gage, *G-Man*, 692.

196 "The same pigs": Bryan, *Whatever Happened to Timothy Leary?*, 205.

196 "Ronald Reagan is a punk": Gifford, *Revolution or Death*, 170.

196 "It was a new experience for me": Bryan, *Whatever Happened to Timothy Leary?*, 205.

196 he called himself the "Ogre": Cleaver, *Soul on Ice*, 33.

197 "You'd better change the bed": Rosemary Leary, *Psychedelic Refugee*, 168.

197 "Far out," she wrote: Rosemary Leary, *Psychedelic Refugee*, 168.

198 **"LSD blackens the white person"**: Bryan, *Whatever Happened to Timothy Leary?*, 174.

198 **"I have no sympathy with a civil rights"**: Timothy Leary, *Politics of Ecstasy*, 216.

198 **"Psychedelic people inevitably became"**: Timothy Leary, *Flashbacks*, 154.

198 **Timothy called a Black male**: Jonah Raskin, interview by author, July 22, 2022. Also in Raskin, *Out of the Whale*, chap. 9.

199 **Kathleen enjoyed a cosmopolitan upbringing**: Information about Kathleen Cleaver's history comes from Kathleen Cleaver, interview by Joseph Monier, Sept. 16, 2011, Civil Rights History Project, Southern Oral History Program under contract to the Smithsonian Institution's National Museum of African American History & Culture and the Library of Congress, www.loc.gov/resource/afc2010039text.afc2010039_crhp 0051_cleaver_transcript/?st=pdf.

200 **"You don't have to maintain"**: Somini Sengupta, "Memories of a Proper Girl Who Was a Panther," *New York Times*, June 17, 2000, 9.

200 **"I was a child at home again"**: Rosemary Leary, *Psychedelic Refugee*, 180.

201 **Anita left first**: Information about Anita found in her unpublished book proposal "Her Story" (written with Rosemary) and Jezer, *Abbie Hoffman*. Confirmed via America Hoffman, interview by author, June 19, 2023.

201 **"None of the other Americans"**: Anita Hoffman quoted in Jezer, *Abbie Hoffman*, 219.

202 **"owl-eyed rapist"**: Rosemary Leary, *Psychedelic Refugee*, 178.

202 **would have an "unfortunate impact"**: Minutaglio and Davis, *Most Dangerous Man in America*, 137.

202 **a fifteen-minute message from Timothy**: "Eldridge Cleaver from Algiers," KPFA, Feb. 1, 1971, www .pacificaradioarchives.org/recording/bb5482.

202 **"shrill and self-serving"**: Rosemary Leary, *Psychedelic Refugee*, 180.

202 **"I want to go back to Amerika"**: Stew Albert, "Tim Leary and Wife in Algeria," *San Diego Street Journal* 2, no. 68 (1970), www.jstor.org/stable/community.28045378.

203 **"one more nut with a gun"**: Ken Kesey, "An Open Letter to Timothy Leary from Ken Kesey," *Rolling Stone*, Nov. 1970, 31, 70.

203 **"He forgot about God"**: Greenfield, *Timothy Leary*, 392.

203 **"embarrassment and protectiveness"**: Rosemary Leary, *Psychedelic Refugee*, 175.

204 **Robert Greenfield visited Algeria**: Greenfield, interview by author, March 8, 2022.

204 **"aging hipsters, passé stars"**: Mokhtefi, *Algiers, Third World Capital*.

206 **Rosemary, resigned, didn't even try to fight**: Rosemary Leary, *Psychedelic Refugee*, 190.

206 **"I was full of dread"**: Rosemary Leary, *Psychedelic Refugee*, 189.

207 **"Do you know Leary?"**: Minutaglio and Davis, *Most Dangerous Man in America*, 177.

207 **"It was straight out of Kafka"**: Greenfield, *Timothy Leary*, 418.

207 **"I have no need or desire"**: Michael Zwerin, "Revolutionary Bust," *Village Voice*, Feb. 4, 1971, 19.

207 **"It has become very clear"**: Susan Almazol, "Eldridge Cleaver Denounces Acid, Leary, Yippies," *San Francisco Examiner*, Feb. 2, 1971, 39.

208 **"Eldridge is a pig!"**: Minutaglio and Davis, *Most Dangerous Man in America*, 187.

Chapter Seventeen: Marilyn Monroe

210 **"the little match girl"**: Greenfield, *Timothy Leary*, 422.

210 **Michel-Gustave Hauchard**: Rosemary uses various pseudonyms for Hauchard in her writing and letters, including Miguel (no last name) and Michael.

211 **"enriched himself on the backs"**: Éric Gerdan, *Dossier A comme arms* (Paris: A. Moreau, 1975), 261.

211 **"all-out offensive"**: "Nixon Declares Narcotics War," *Albany Democrat-Herald*, June 17, 1971, 1.

212 **Dr. Hubert de Watteville**: Rosemary Leary also used the pseudonym Dr. Lucien Mattern for Dr. de Watteville in her letters.

212 **"It's all right, beloved"**: Rosemary Leary, *Psychedelic Refugee*, 213.

213 **"Hauchard was milking Tim's celebrity"**: Greenfield, *Timothy Leary*, 423.

213 **"the first White Americans"**: Timothy Leary, *Flashbacks*, 305.

213 **"He had his racial joke"**: Rosemary Leary, *Psychedelic Refugee*, 216.

213 **"LSD was always the solution"**: Rosemary Leary, *Psychedelic Refugee*, 216.

213 **When Rosemary introduced Hauchard**: Barritt, *Road of Excess*, 214.

213 **"If I was depressed"**: Rosemary Leary, *Psychedelic Refugee*, 214.

217 **She did Timothy's laundry**: "Latest on Leary," *Los Angeles Free Press*, Aug. 1971, 8.

217 **"exasperating literary vendetta"**: Allen Ginsberg and San Francisco Bay Area Prose Poets' Phalanx, "Declaration of Independence for Dr. Timothy Leary: Model Statement in Defense of the Philosophers Personal Freedom," July 4, 1971.

218 **headline: BUT WHAT ABOUT ROSEMARY?**: "But What About Rosemary," *Berkeley Barb*, July 16–22, 1971, 5.

219 **"He was in a Swiss prison"**: Rosemary Leary, *Psychedelic Refugee*, 224.

220 **"The goddess of Switzerland!"**: Minutaglio and Davis, *Most Dangerous Man in America*, 241.

221 **"The death of that possibility"**: Rosemary Woodruff Leary, interview by Robert Greenfield, New York Public Library archives.

222 **Rosemary packed her suitcase:** Rosemary Leary, *Psychedelic Refugee*, 233.

223 **"Her power of being was so strong":** Schewel, interview by author, June 21, 2021.

Chapter Eighteen: Demeter

224 **"This is the wanderer":** Schewel, interview by author, March 28, 2023. Many of the details in this chapter come from dozens of interviews with John over three years.

225 **"loosening the girders of the soul":** Aleister Crowley, *The Confessions of Aleister Crowley* (New York: Penguin Books, 1989), 124.

225 **"a complete alchemical partnership":** Schewel, interview with author, July 1, 2024.

227 **Rosalie Siegel, a young literary agent:** Siegel, interview by author, June 9, 2021.

228 **"Her being such a queen":** Brigitte Mars, interview by author, May 2021. Follow-up interviews and sections Mars shared with me from her unpublished book provided key details for this chapter.

228 **"I won't be able to meet you":** Rosemary Leary, *Psychedelic Refugee*, 236.

229 **Rosemary learned that a burqa:** David Phillips, *The Learyiad*, 489, www.radbash.com/.

229 **drug seizures had increased eightfold:** Farber, *War on Drugs*, 255.

230 **"a succession of females":** Barritt, *Road of Excess*, 259.

230 **"I met him, expecting a change":** Rosemary Leary, *Psychedelic Refugee*, 248.

231 **"While Tim was convalescing":** Lee and Shlain, *Acid Dreams*, 270.

233 **"Rosemary wills it be known":** Rosemary Leary, "A Wife Is Not Property," *Berkeley Barb*, Dec. 15, 1972, 9.

234 **the arrest of fifty-seven men:** "Interpol: An Undramatic Band of Super Sleuths," *Newark Advocate*, Sept. 20, 1972, 16.

234 **the seizure of two and a half tons:** Farber, *War on Drugs*, 42.

234 **"innumerable sets" of forged passports:** Dana Adams Schmidt, "Joint Force Raids Coast Drug Cult," *New York Times*, Aug. 6, 1972, 19.

234 **"founded by Dr. Leary":** Bill Hazlett, "Key Suspect in Smuggling Network," *Los Angeles Times*, Aug. 11, 1972, 1.

234 **"the Tim Leary raid":** William Claiborne, "Agents Nab Cash, Hash, 42 Persons in Tim Leary Raid," *Washington Post*, Aug. 6, 1972, 11.

234 **"the brains" and the "god":** Joe Eszterhas, "The Strange Case of the Hippie Mafia," *Rolling Stone*, Dec. 7, 1972, 49.

234 **"responsible for destroying more lives":** "Leary Charged in Narcotics Ring," *Morning Herald*, Aug. 7, 1972, 13.

234 **the press, "the most dangerous man alive":** The original source of this is incredibly difficult to track down, though it's clear that Nixon is not the source. Author John Bryan attributed the quote to Cecil Hicks but did not supply a source. The earliest attribution I could find is to an unnamed official in Evan Maxwell, "Dream of Universal Love Shattered by Drugs," *Los Angeles Times*, Feb. 20, 1973, 8. Interestingly, "the most dangerous man alive" was also used in ad campaigns for the movie *Serpico*, which premiered the same year, 1973.

234 **"They all sat around in a circle":** Eszterhas, "The Strange Case of the Hippie Mafia," 30.

235 **"Sicily is full of magic":** Rosemary Woodruff Leary, interview by Adam Phillips, recorded and shared with the author.

236 **The ancient Greeks honored:** Particular thanks to Muraresku, *Immortality Key*, and Elizabeth Vandiver, "The Eleusinian Mysteries and Afterlife," *Classical Mythology*, audio, Great Courses, 2000, www.thegreatcourses.com/sets/set-great-mythologies-of-the-world-classical-mythology.

237 **Rosemary had repeatedly warned:** Barritt, *Road to Excess*, 265.

237 **"It was not the same smile":** Rosemary Leary, *Psychedelic Refugee*, 265.

237 **"No mention was made":** Evan Maxwell and Al Martinez, "Leary Saga Ends in L.A. . . . in Handcuffs and a Driving Rain," *Los Angeles Times*, Jan. 19, 1973, www.newspapers.com/image/386316791/.

237 **"not fit to be the next":** *My Psychedelic Love Story*, directed by Errol Morris, 2020.

237 **Joanna's mother neglected her:** Information via Harcourt-Smith, *Tripping on the Bardo with Timothy Leary*; and Morris, *My Psychedelic Love Story*.

237 **"good chauffeurs were hard to find":** Harcourt-Smith, interview by Morris, *My Psychedelic Love Story*.

238 **"It was a mistake":** Rosemary Woodruff Leary Papers, New York Public Library. Also quoted at length in Greenfield, *Timothy Leary*, 488–90.

239 **Michael Tigar, who also defended:** Tigar, *Sensing Injustice*, 391–92.

239 **"They went after Rosemary":** Greenfield, *Timothy Leary*, 490.

239 **"That was part of the deal":** Greenfield, *Timothy Leary*, 487.

239 **"any documents concerning Rosemary":** Steve Long, "Timothy Leary and the San Francisco Grand Jury," *Los Angeles Free Press*, Sept. 5, 1975, 6.

239 **"I knew Rosemary was on the lam":** Greenfield, *Timothy Leary*, 505.

240 **"the false messiah":** Greenfield, *Timothy Leary*, 506.

240 **"sick for the death":** Greenfield, *Timothy Leary*, 505.

240 **"I can't imagine anything close":** Greenfield, *Timothy Leary*, 508.

240 **"Timothy has shown he would":** "Tim Leary, State's Witness?," *Ann Arbor Sun*, October 25, 1974.

Part Four: The High Priestess of Innkeeping
Chapter Nineteen: Sarah Woodruff

243 The Provincetown Inn stands on the edge: Along with Rosemary's and David Phillips's writing, several Provincetown locals contributed to this chapter. Special thanks to Kathy Shorr, Jeff Evans, and the manager of the Provincetown Inn who provided a tour of the property.

243 its twenty-eight guest rooms: Elias Duncan, "A Weekend at the Provincetown Inn," *Provincetown Independent*, Sept. 20, 2023, provincetownindependent.org/news/2023/09/20/a-weekend-at-the-provincetown-inn/.

244 "Miscreants and malcontents": Jeff Evans, interview by author, Oct. 4, 2021.

244 its core of around three thousand people: Katharine Seelye, "Welcome to Provincetown. Winter Population: Dwindling," *New York Times*, Dec. 20, 2015, www.nytimes.com/2015/12/21/us/welcome-to-provincetown-winter-population-dwindling.html.

244 Provincetown had provided a safe house: Cape Cod history comes from Shorr, *Provincetown*, 9.

245 "Every wash-ashore has a story": Judy Johnson, "A Fugitive and 60's Survivor Reveals Her Cape Cod Chapter," *Cape Codder*, Jan. 5, 1999, 1.

245 John Waters and his pencil-thin mustache: James Egan, ed., *John Waters Interviews* (Jackson: University Press of Mississippi, 2011), 69.

245 working on scripts at the Dairy Queen: Shorr, *Provincetown*, 103.

246 "no hint of the dark cloud": Kathy Shorr, "A Public Secret, Finally Revealed," *Provincetown Banner*, Sept. 18, 1997, 9.

246 "So where are you from?": Lake, interview by author, Nov. 2021.

248 "I have forbidden myself to regret": Fowles, *French Lieutenant's Woman*, 350.

248 acknowledgment of the grave dangers: "US Couple Murdered in Colombia," *Boston Globe*, Nov. 6, 1977.

249 a California judge's dissolution: "Notes on People," *International Herald Tribune*, July 10, 1976.

249 State and federal authorities had rewarded: "3 Subpoenaed over a Movie on Radicals," *New York Times*, June 5, 1975.

250 one indictment came down: "Longtime Defense Attorney in County Faces Drug Charges," *Los Angeles Times*, Sept. 6, 1974, 5.

250 the statute of limitations expired: Greenfield, *Timothy Leary*, 516.

250 public rejection of his former friends: Greenfield, *Timothy Leary*, 520.

250 The newspapers reported that he left: "Drug Culture Apostle Fearful of Vengeance," *Naples Daily News*, April 22, 1976, 2.

250 members of the Witness Protection Program: Greenfield, *Timothy Leary*, 516.

250 the group grew cannabis seeds: Mars, unpublished book shared with author. Rosemary's road trip confirmed in conversations with Mars and Schewel.

253 "I wanted to be quiet": Rosemary Woodruff Leary, interview by Joyce Johnson, WOMR.

253 "third stage in life": Rosemary Woodruff Leary, interview by Adam Phillips, recorded but never aired, 1988. Thank you to Adam for sharing with me.

254 "She was really a ghost": Schewel, interview by author, April 20, 2023.

Chapter Twenty: Flashbacks

255 She met Judy Givens: Thank you to Olan Givens for sharing information about her mother.

256 "She was just so lovely": Givens, interview by author, Nov. 3, 2021.

256 David, a child of Upper West Side privilege: Thank you to David's friends and family for sharing so much. Special thanks to Adam and Christopher Phillips, who not only spoke to me but invited me to David's memorial service. Many of these anecdotes come from David's own memoir, which can be found here: www.radbash.com.

257 "Somewhere inside everybody knows": Ram Dass, *Be Here Now*, 10.

257 "I am good at analysis": Phillips, Radbash.com, 867.

258 interpreting the village's name as "True Ro": Givens, interview by author, Nov. 3, 2021.

258 "Rosemary was extremely good company": Phillips, Radbash.com, 490.

258 "A less suitable job": Phillips, Radbash.com, 490.

259 "I do not represent any material": Sam Roberts, "Frances Goldin, a Crusader for the Lower East Side, Dies at 95," *New York Times*, May 18, 2020, www.nytimes.com/2020/05/18/nyregion/frances-goldin-dead.html.

261 "We weren't doing anything": Rosemary Woodruff Leary, interview by Joyce Johnson, *The Sands of Time*, WOMR, 1997. Thank you to John Braden at WOMR for tracking this audio down.

261 Timothy Leary's programs at Harvard: Walter H. Bowart, "How the CIA Planned the Drugging of America," excerpt of *Operation Mind Control*, found in FBI documents, Sept. 1979.

261 "I would say that eighty percent": Walter Bowart, "Lords of the Revolution: Timothy Leary and the CIA," whale.to/b/bowart8.html.

262 Bernardine Dohrn came out of hiding: Nathaniel Sheppard Jr., "Bernardine Dohrn Gives Up to Authorities in Chicago," *New York Times*, Dec. 4, 1980.

262 FBI's ill-gotten evidence: Anthony Lewis, "Dohrn Got Probation, but What of the Others?," *New York Times*, Jan. 18, 1981, www.nytimes.com/1981/01/18/weekinreview/dohrn-got-probation-but-what-of-the-others.html.

262 served seven months in prison: Susan Chira, "At Home With: Bernardine Dohrn; Same Passion, New Tactics," *New York Times*, Nov. 18, 1993, www.nytimes.com/1993/11/18/garden/at-home-with-bernadine-dohrn -same-passion-new-tactics.html.

262 Barack Obama's relationship: Justin Sink, "Report: Obama and Bill Ayers Attended Same 2014 Wedding," *The Hill*, Feb. 12, 2015, thehill.com/homenews/administration/232674-report-obama-and-bill-ayers-attended -2014-wedding/.

262 Kennedy continued to practice law: Roberts, "Michael J. Kennedy, Lawyer for Underdogs and Pariahs, Dies at 78," *New York Times*.

262 Kennedy represented Susan McDougal: Susan Schmidt, "McDougal Seeks Release from Prison," *Washington Post*, May 20, 1997, www.washingtonpost.com/archive/politics/1997/05/20/mcdougal-seeks-release -from-prison/39f9bb21-0fc1-4cbb-9420-faaeda47ff40/.

262 Kennedy provided counsel to Ivana: Gross, "Ivana's Avenger," 32.

262 Eldridge Cleaver returned to the United States: T. D. Allman, "The 'Rebirth' of Eldridge Cleaver," *New York Times*, June 16, 1977, www.nytimes.com/1977/01/16/archives/the-rebirth-of-eldridge-cleaver-the-old -cleaver-wanted-to-overthrow.html.

263 divorced Cleaver in 1987: Sengupta, "Memories of a Proper Girl Who Was a Panther."

263 "I wanted to learn": "How Kathleen Cleaver Conquered War with Love," *AFRO*, April 13, 2018, afro.com /kathleen-cleaver-conquered-war-love.

263 Abbie Hoffman, dodging charges: Linda Greenhouse, "Abbie Hoffman Among 4 Held on Charges of Selling Cocaine," *New York Times*, Aug. 29, 1973, www.nytimes.com/1973/08/29/archives/abbie-hoffman -among-4-held-on-charges-of-selling-cocaine.html.

263 lived as Barry Freed: "Abbott (Abbie) Hoffman," *The Sixties: The Years That Shaped a Nation*, PBS, www .pbs.org/opb/thesixties/topics/revolution/newsmakers_2.html.

263 The coroner determined: Wayne King, "Abbie Hoffman Committed Suicide Using Barbiturates, Autopsy Shows," *New York Times*, April 19, 1989.

263 Michael Randall went underground: Bobby Black, "Radical Law," World of Cannabis Museum, Sept. 23, 2022, www.worldofcannabis.museum/post/radical-law.

263 busted at his home: Interview with Michael and Carol Randall, *Orange Sunshine*, directed by Kirkley.

263 he did five years in prison: Johnny Dodd, "Memories from the Summer of Love," *People*, Sept. 4, 2017, people.com/human-interest/michael-carol-randall-lsd-orange-sunshine-documentary.

263 "sucker for hard luck stories": Mary-Jo Avellar, "My Friend Joe," *Advocate*, Oct. 21, 1993, 16.

264 "eight-circuit model": Timothy Leary, *Terra II*, 20.

264 "Are you still married to Rosemary?": Higgs, *I Have America Surrounded*, 238.

264 smoking a cigarette in an airport: "Timothy Leary Arrested for Smoking in Austin Airport," *Fort-Worth Telegram*, May 12, 1994, 26.

264 a domestic disturbance call: Greenfield, *Timothy Leary*, 538.

265 "Rosemary, twelve years after": Timothy Leary, *Flashbacks*, 374.

Chapter Twenty-One: The Story of My Punishment

267 "I think what she was concerned": Greenfield, *Timothy Leary*, 491.

267 "Whenever I weighed": Johnson, "Fugitive and 60's Survivor Reveals Her Cape Cod Chapter."

269 "LOS ANGELES: The jailed daughter": AP, "Daughter of LSD's Leary Dead from Jail Hanging," *Orlando Sentinel*, Sept. 7, 1990, www.orlandosentinel.com/1990/09/07/daughter-of-lsds-leary-dies-after-jail -hanging/.

269 Timothy had described his daughter: A good deal of information about Susan was found in the Timothy Leary Papers. Greenfield's *Timothy Leary* also filled in some knowledge about her life after Rosemary left Timothy.

270 took her rage out on her children: Greenfield, *Timothy Leary*, 557.

270 who had to be hospitalized in 1978: Information about Susan's children can be found in the Timothy Leary Papers.

270 she enlisted in an army medic: Found in a letter from Susan to Jack Leary in the Timothy Leary Papers.

270 On the evening of December 18, 1988: Details of the crime come from various articles in the Timothy Leary Papers: Brad Anderson, "Leary Considers Visit to Daughter in Jail," *The Glendale Star*, Jan. 13, 1989, 8; Brad Anderson, "Leary Kin Placed in Foster Care System," *The Glendale Star*, Jan. 16, 1989; Christopher Tyner, "AIDS Given as Possible Reason for Shooting by Leary Daughter," *Burbank Leader*, Jan. 25, 1989; "Timothy Leary Kin to Stand Trial in Shooting," *Los Angeles Times*, Jan. 26, 1989, 3.

270 Susan had waited: Greenfield, *Timothy Leary*, 562.

272 a supernatural event: Carolyn told me the story of how the mirror seemed almost embodied and fell off the wall onto her during a time when her house was haunted by a malignant entity. She has since cleared her house of that dark energy.

272 she brought an old photograph: Story via Kathy Shorr and confirmed with the stylist Donald Sheardown.

273 "She was really an impressive woman": Les and Makiko Wisner, interview by author, June 22, 2021.

274 "in educating the young": Graboi, *One Foot in the Future*, 414.

274 **"as close to a mother":** Rosemary Woodruff Leary, interview by Bob Greenfield, unpublished but found in the New York Public Library.

Chapter Twenty-Two: Her Story
277 **"I guess I still did not really trust":** Rosemary Leary, *Psychedelic Refugee*, 269.
278 **"Vista Vision. Technicolor":** Rosemary Leary, *Psychedelic Refugee*, 269.
278 **"the brightest and funniest":** Interview with Rosemary in "Designer Dying," *San Jose Mercury News*, Feb. 27, 1996.
280 **"Well, Tim wants me":** Gary Woodruff, interview by author, March 11, 2021.
281 **"naked opportunism of Tim's looking":** Phillips, Radbash.com, 491.
281 **who preferred to remain anonymous:** Her name is Carolyn Kleefeld, as confirmed by Gary Woodruff and Denis Berry. Kleefeld declined to be interviewed.
281 **Roger Hanson, who barely registered:** Hanson, interview by author, July 19, 2021. Thank you to Roger for tracking down legal documents.
282 **"Indeed," David wrote, concerning Timothy's influence:** Phillips, Radbash.com, 494.
282 **"All parties concur in finally terminating":** *People v. Rosemary Leary*, C-21237, Superior Court of the State of California for the County of Orange, March 22, 1994.
282 **"So far as I could determine":** "23 Years as a Fugitive Ends as Sentence Is Dismissed," *Orange County Register*, March 22, 1994.
283 **"It is really difficult to describe":** Nadine Brozan, "Chronicle," *New York Times*, March 30, 1994, 26.
284 **"Makiko, this is me":** Wisner, interview by author, June 22, 2021.
284 **"The staff understands and appreciates":** *Pacific Currents*: *Pacific Book Auction Galleries Quarterly* 3, no. 2 (1994).
284 **per the auction's internal newsletter:** *Pacific Currents* 3, no. 5 (1994): 1.
285 **"I looked in the mirror":** Rosemary Leary to Timothy Leary, April–Sept. 3, 1970, Special Collections, Manuscript Collection, Stanford Libraries, searchworks.stanford.edu/view/4084136.
286 **sold to Stanford University for $1,900:** Nadine Brozan, "Chronicle," *New York Times*, Oct. 26, 1994.
286 **"more emotionally upsetting":** Brozan, "Chronicle," *New York Times*, Oct. 26, 1994.

Chapter Twenty-Three: Why Not
288 **"If you truly love someone":** Rosemary Woodruff Leary, interview by Joyce Johnson, WOMR, 1997.
288 **"Turn on, boot up":** Greg Miller, "Turn On, Boot Up, Jack In," *Wired*, Oct. 1, 2013.
289 **"In the near future":** Timothy Leary, *Chaos & Cyber Culture*, 220.
289 **"I didn't see any photos":** Lewis MacAdams, "Tune In, Turn On, Drop Dead," *L.A. Weekly*, May 17, 1996.
291 **"Celebrity is a mask":** John Updike, *Self-Consciousness: Memoirs* (New York: Random House, 1989), 252.
291 **After Timothy announced his cancer:** This is perhaps the most documented time of Leary's highly documented life. I relied on dozens of articles, several documentaries, and interviews with people present. An especially helpful documentary was *Timothy Leary's Dead*, directed by Paul Davids, 1996.
291 **"When I found out":** David Colker, "Timothy Leary, Knocking on Death's Door," *Washington Post*, Aug. 28, 1995, www.washingtonpost.com/archive/lifestyle/1995/08/29/timothy-leary-knocking-on-deaths-door /b606d323-8d05-4751-b508-0424acaf36c5/.
291 **"death is the last taboo":** "Leary's Ultimate Trip," *Chicago Tribune*, Dec. 12, 1995.
292 **"He smoked 50 cigarettes":** "Tim Leary: Tune In, Turn On, Drop Dead," AlterNet, April 26, 2000, www .alternet.org/2000/04/tim_leary_tune_in_turn_on_drop_dead.
292 **"Michael, I'm dying":** Interview with Eleanora Kennedy, "Cannthropology with Eleanora Kennedy," Haze Radio Network, www.facebook.com/hazeradionetwork/videos/209910784387524/.
292 **"Once he announced that he was dying":** Berry, interview by author, Sept. 20, 2021.
293 **"an amused look as the media":** MacAdams, "Tune In, Turn On, Drop Dead."
293 **"She was one of the few people":** Berry, interview by author, March 26, 2022.
294 **"He was just terribly scared":** Rosemary Leary, *Psychedelic Refugee*, 271.
294 **"Think what it must have been like":** Greenfield, *Timothy Leary*, 586.
294 **he does not want to be associated:** Jack Leary, email with author, Oct. 14, 2022.
294 **"Why didn't anybody help us?":** Berry, interview by author, April 27, 2022.
295 **"Just after midnight":** Edward Epstein, "'60's Icon Timothy Leary Dies," *San Francisco Chronicle*, June 1, 1996, 1.
295 **250 people entered:** "San Francisco / Hundreds Gather to Mourn Leary," *CT Insider*, June 13, 1996, www .ctinsider.com/news/article/SAN-FRANCISCO-Hundreds-Gather-To-Mourn-Leary-2978527.php.
296 **"I'm Rosemary Woodruff Leary":** "Memorial for Leary in San Francisco, June 12, 1996," Timothy Leary Archives, archive.org/details/Timothy_Leary_Archives_89-a.dv.

Chapter Twenty-Four: My Work
297 **"so much pleasure just from walking":** Berry, interview by author, Sept. 30, 2021.
298 **"responsible for the death":** Sarah Pekkanen, "U.S. May Lift 'Ban' on LSD Testing," *San Francisco Examiner*, July 27, 1992.

NOTES

298 "I'm proud to have 'killed'": Found in Timothy Leary Papers. Originally read this in Giffort, *Acid Revival*, 101–34.

298 Rick Strassman published a series: Described in detail in the classic Strassman, *DMT*.

298 scientists in Germany studied mescaline: Leo Hermle et al., "Mescaline-Induced Psychopathological, Neuropsychological, and Neurometabolic Effects in Normal Subjects: Experimental Psychosis as a Tool for Psychiatric Research," *Biological Psychiatry* 32, no. 11 (1992): 976–91.

299 the world's leading nonprofit: Amy Emerson et al., "History and Future of the Multidisciplinary Association for Psychedelic Studies (MAPS)," *Journal of Psychoactive Drugs* 46, no. 1 (2014): 27–36. Rick Doblin, interview by author, May 3, 2021, and Corine de Boer, interview by author, May 12, 2021.

299 the first FDA-approved safety study: Emily Williams, "Towards Breakthrough Healing," *MAPS Bulletin* 27, no. 1 (Spring 2017), maps.org/news/bulletin/towards-breakthrough-healing-a-history-and-overview-of-clinical-mdma-research-3/.

299 veterans' hospitals have embraced psychedelics: Ernesto Londoño, "After Six-Decade Hiatus, Experimental Psychedelic Therapy Returns to the VA," *New York Times*, June 24, 2022, www.nytimes.com/2022/06/24/us/politics/psychedelic-therapy-veterans.html.

299 Horowitz had established a legal precedent: "Jennifer Ulrich Interviews Michael Horowitz Re: The Archival Catastrophe of 1975 and the Birth of ARCANA," Timothy Leary Archives, Aug. 13, 2012, www.timothylearyarchives.org/jennifer-ulrich-interviews-michael-horowitz-re-the-archival-catastrophe-of-1975-and-the-birth-of-arcana/.

300 "I think she was looking for": Berry, interview by author, March 27, 2022.

300 The circle revolved: A special thanks to a wonderful evening in Santa Cruz in March 2022 with women of this circle: Valerie Corral, Dana Peleg, Suzanne Wouk, Sherri Paris, and Angela Welty.

300 "Everyone had known who [Rosemary] was": Corral, interview by author, March 27, 2022.

300 "Rosemary was just treasured": Paris, interview by author, March 8, 2022.

300 "She was just a powerful symbol": Brown, interview by author, Oct. 24, 2022.

301 "I think he told the truth": *Beyond Life: Timothy Leary Lives*, directed by Danny Schechter, 1998.

301 "There are few of us": *Beyond Life*, Schechter, 1998.

301 the Smoking Gun released FOIA-ed FBI documents: "Turn On, Tune In, Rat Out," Smoking Gun, July 3, 1999, www.thesmokinggun.com/documents/investigation/turn-tune-rat-out.

302 "We didn't know these people": Berry, interview by author, Sept. 20, 2021.

302 "god energy": For more on this kind of projection see Robert Moore, *Facing the Dragon* (Asheville, N.C.: Chiron Publications, 2013).

303 Forty years after trying peyote: Rosemary wrote repeatedly about this experience. I'm drawing mostly from Palmer and Horowitz, *Sisters of the Extreme*, 226.

304 "the focus of our attention": Rosemary Leary, *Psychedelic Refugee*, 140.

304 "All right! All right!": Berry, interview by author, April 27, 2022.

304 "Even now it has to be low fat?": Makiko Wisner, interview by author, June 22, 2021.

305 "The drugs really open up": Paris, interview by author, March 8, 2022.

306 Denis arrived at the hospital: Scene at the hospital from many interviews with Denis, but mainly on Sept. 20, 2021.

307 "I understand now": Gary Woodruff, interview by author, June 2, 2021.

Chapter Twenty-Five: Ghosts and Minor Characters

308 the morning of February 7, 2002: Thank you to Denis Berry, Gary Woodruff, Katie Woodruff, Valerie Corral, Sherri Paris, Suzanne Wouk, David Jay Brown, Robert Forte, and Makiko and Les Wisner for providing information about Rosemary's final moments.

309 "Come over," Denis would tell: Berry, interview by author, March 26, 2022.

310 the New York Public Library paid $900,000: Patricia Cohen, "New York Public Library Buys Timothy Leary's Papers," *New York Times*, June 15, 2011, www.nytimes.com/2011/06/16/books/new-york-public-library-buys-timothy-learys-papers.html.

310 twenty feet of glass displayed items: Special thanks to Maria Mangini for sharing her unpublished writing about this party.

311 "I felt so, like I had completed": Berry, interview by author, March 26, 2022.

312 "She was kind": Mangini, interview by author, June 19, 2023.

312 "Rosemary made some personal": Mangini, interview by author, April 7, 2021.

312 should not be "subsumed into": Phillips, email to Thomas Lannon, March 11, 2016.

312 "It would be a bad thing": Lannon, interview by author, Jan. 23, 2023.

313 treatments for depression, anxiety: Scott Huler, "Could Psychedelics Solve Anxiety, Depression and Addiction?" *Duke Magazine*, Sept. 5, 2023, https://dukemag.duke.edu/stories/could-psychedelics-solve-anxiety-depression-and-addiction.

313 brain injury: Jonathan Moore, "Can Psychedelics Heal Severe Brain Injury?," *National Geographic*, April 2, 2024, www.nationalgeographic.com/premium/article/severe-brain-injury-unprecedented-therapy-psychedelic.

313 personality disorders: Ann M. Inouye, Aaron S. Wolfgang, and Lianne T. Philhower, "MDMA-Assisted Therapy for Borderline Personality Disorder," *Journal of Psychedelic Studies*, 7, no. 3 (December 2023): 227–37.

313 effects of racism: Joseph Williams, "Are Psychedelics a Fix for Racial PTSD?," *Dallas Weekly*, Sept. 17, 2023, dallasweekly.com/2023/09/are-psychedelics-a-fix-for-racial-ptsd/.

313 easing climate change distress: "Psychedelic Therapy May Help with Climate Change Anxiety," *Washington Post*, Nov. 3, 2023, www.washingtonpost.com/wellness/2023/11/03/psychedelics-therapy-climate-change-eco-anxiety/.

313 LSD use increased 50 percent: R. Andrew Yockey, "Trends in LSD Use Among US Adults: 2015–2018," *Drug and Alcohol Dependence*, 201 (May 2020), www.sciencedirect.com/science/article/abs/pii/S0376871620302362.

313 more than 5.5 million Americans: Ofir Livne et al., "Adolescent and Adult Time Trends in US Hallucinogen Use," *Addiction* 117, no. 12 (Dec. 2022): 3099–109.

313 the biggest increases in LSD use: Yockey, Vidourek, and King, "Trends in LSD Use Among US Adults: 2015–2018."

313 "Chemical escapism," *Scientific American* wrote: Rachel Nuwer, "Americans Increase LSD Use—and a Bleak Outlook for the World May Be to Blame," *Scientific American*, July 10, 2020, www.scientificamerican.com/article/americans-increase-lsd-use-and-a-bleak-outlook-for-the-world-may-be-to-blame1/.

314 suburban mothers microdose: Allison Sherry, "Thousands of Mothers Are Microdosing with Mushrooms to Ease Stress of Parenting," NPR, Sept. 13, 2022, www.npr.org/2022/09/13/1121599369/thousands-of-moms-are-microdosing-with-mushrooms-to-ease-the-stress-of-parenting.

315 "I can't say that I believe": Rosemary Woodruff Leary, interview by Joyce Johnson, WOMR, 1997.

Epilogue: The Magician's Assistant

318 "to preserve Rosemary's story": David F. Phillips, "Rescuing Rosemary's Memoir," prologue to *Psychedelic Refugee*, by Rosemary Leary, xxii.

318 "He empathized with her": Adam Phillips, interview by author, June 17, 2021.

318 "The book, which seemed never finished": Rosemary Leary, *Psychedelic Refugee*, 8.

319 A biography "is needed": Phillips, "Rescuing Rosemary's Memoir," xxi.

319 "the free intellect and relaxed style": "Pre Spring 2020," Rodebjer, www.rodebjer.com/us/pre-spring-2020.html.

321 "My father plucked pennies": Rosemary Leary, *Psychedelic Refugee*, 10.

Index

INDEX

INDEX

INDEX

INDEX

INDEX

100 YEARS of PUBLISHING

— ◇ —

Harold K. Guinzburg and George S. Oppenheimer founded Viking in 1925 with the intention of publishing books "with some claim to permanent importance rather than ephemeral popular interest." After merging with B. W. Huebsch, a small publisher with a distinguished catalog, Viking enjoyed almost fifty years of literary and commercial success before merging with Penguin Books in 1975.

Now an imprint of Penguin Random House, Viking specializes in bringing extraordinary works of fiction and nonfiction to a vast readership. In 2025, we celebrate one hundred years of excellence in publishing. Our centennial colophon features the original logo for Viking, created by the renowned American illustrator Rockwell Kent: a Viking ship that evokes enterprise, adventure, and exploration, ideas that inspired the imprint's name at its founding and continue to inspire us.

— ◇ —

For more information on Viking's history, authors, and books, please visit penguin.com/viking.